DYNAMIC GLOBAL MANAGEMENT

Prof. M.N. Rudrabasavaraj
Chairman and Chief Executive Officer,
MNR Associates.

First Edition: 2013

Himalaya Publishing House

MUMBAI • NEW DELHI • NAGPUR • BENGALURU • HYDERABAD • CHENNAI • PUNE • LUCKNOW • AHMEDABAD • ERNAKULAM • BHUBANESWAR • INDORE • KOLKATA • GUWAHATI

First Edition : 2013

Published by : Mrs. Meena Pandey for Himalaya Publishing House Pvt. Ltd., "Ramdoot", Dr. Bhalerao Marg, Girgaon, Mumbai - 400 004. Phone: 022-23860170/23863863, Fax: 022-23877178 E-mail: himpub@vsnl.com; Website: www.himpub.com

Branch Offices :

New Delhi : "Pooja Apartments", 4-B, Murari Lal Street, Ansari Road, Darya Ganj, New Delhi - 110 002. Phone: 011-23270392, 23278631; Fax: 011-23256286

Nagpur : Kundanlal Chandak Industrial Estate, Ghat Road, Nagpur - 440 018. Phone: 0712-2738731, 3296733; Telefax: 0712-2721215

Bengaluru : No. 16/1 (Old 12/1), 1st Floor, Next to Hotel Highlands, Madhava Nagar, Race Course Road, Bengaluru - 560 001. Phone: 080-32919385; Telefax: 080-22286611

Hyderabad : No. 3-4-184, Lingampally, Besides Raghavendra Swamy Matham, Kachiguda, Hyderabad - 500 027. Phone: 040-27560041, 27550139; Mobile: 09390905282

Chennai : No. 8/2, 2nd Madley Street, Ground Floor, T. Nagar, Chennai - 600 017. Mobile: 09345345055

Pune : First Floor, "Laksha" Apartment, No. 527, Mehunpura, Shaniwarpeth (Near Prabhat Theatre), Pune - 411 030. Phone: 020-24496323/24496333; Mobile: 09370579333

Lucknow : House No 731, Shekhupura Colony, Near B.D. Convent School, Aliganj, Lucknow - 226 022. Mobile: 09307501549

Ahmedabad : 114, "SHAIL", 1st Floor, Opp. Madhu Sudan House, C.G. Road, Navrang Pura, Ahmedabad - 380 009. Phone: 079-26560126; Mobile: 09377088847

Ernakulam : 39/176 (New No: 60/251) 1st Floor, Karikkamuri Road, Ernakulam, Kochi - 682011, Phone: 0484-2378012, 2378016; Mobile: 09344199799

Bhubaneswar : 5 Station Square, Bhubaneswar - 751 001 (Odisha). Phone: 0674-2532129, Mobile: 09338746007

Indore : Kesardeep Avenue Extension, 73, Narayan Bagh, Flat No. 302, IIIrd Floor, Near Humpty Dumpty School, Indore - 452 007 (M.P.). Mobile: 09301386468

Kolkata : 108/4, Beliaghata Main Road, Near ID Hospital, Opp. SBI Bank, Kolkata - 700 010, Phone: 033-32449649, Mobile: 09883055590, 07439040301

Guwahati : House No. 15, Behind Pragjyotish College, Near Sharma Printing Press, P.O. Bharalumukh, Guwahati - 781009, (Assam). Mobile: 09883055590, 09883055536

DTP by : HPH, Editorial Office, Bhandup

Printed at : M/s. Aditya Offset Process (I) Pvt. Ltd., Hyderabad. On behalf of HPH

Dedicated with all my love and affection to my beloved Son,

SRI M.R. SATSHESHATEJASVI

(Who was born after 18 years of my marriage, that too, with the help of Divine Intervention!)

Who has given us so much Love, Joy and Happiness.

Preface

We are living in desperate times facing a global recession triggered by the all-consuming greed of bankers, financial and investment executives and realtors of USA, building financial castles in the air that collapsed like a worthless pack of cards wiping out trillions of dollars, jobs, well-known companies and economies of renowned countries. We are facing a situation worse than the Depression of 1929. A great institution like General Motors, No. l on Fortune 500 for so many years and known for its sound management is facing bankruptcy. Iceland has gone bankrupt. America has lost face and management has lost face. Industry has gone bankrupt. Out here in Bengaluru in India, once booming real estate and construction industries have come to a halt. The hotel industry, once prosperous, charging highest rates for their rooms, higher than New York, London, Stockholm, Geneva, is facing the heat. Companies have told their executives, no parties, no training, no conferences, no lunch and dinner in hotels. Companies have proscribed air travel. Air India, Jet Airways, Kingfisher have to cancel their flights, lay-off the pilots and staff. The latter two had just started international operations and the recession has hit them very badly. Jet Airways carried, the story goes, one passenger to London and brought 20 back. How can you keep up the international operations? Bad timing, unfortunately for them.

The resulting consequence is that people have lost confidence in Management and are livid that greed had overtaken good sense and sound management. The humanity is at the cross-roads, as we face the 21st Century and the second millennium. The people of the world and the leaders in global business and management face the daunting challenge ahead of them in improving human condition, rebuilding collapsed confidence in global business, economies and management and creating jobs and wealth and growth for the society as quickly as possible.

In order to achieve this, we need a new concept of global management, a new approach and philosophy of management and new model of management to promote global economic growth, global human growth and global business growth with a mission of service to the community, nation and the world. In short, building a new world order of prosperity, happiness, peace and compassion.

Hence, the birth of our new book. We call it **'Dynamic Global Management'.** Dynamic because the management must be extremely fast in not only reacting to overcome the desperate and changing times, but also be creative and innovative be proactive in creating desirable and successful outcomes fast in the future; global because we are in a globalised world, where the impact is global and everybody is going global; management, with a new mission of service, creation for wealth for society, utilise the new philosophy, systems and techniques of management to build a better world of peace, prosperity, happiness and compassion and to get out of the global recession in a year or two at the most.

We have designed and structured our book in four parts, each dealing with certain core areas of Dynamic Global Management.

A. Core Areas: The first part deals with core area of fundamentals — (1) What is the purpose of business? The mission of business is to provide goods and services in abundance, thus creating jobs and wealth for the nation and world. (2) Glimpses of global business and management, best practices of global management through such leaders as Wal-Mart, GE, Matsushita, Shell, IBM, Tatas, etc., as well as managing global business, which are so large in size, sophistication and complexity, sharing global fortune top 10 companies in sales, assets, employment, etc., (3) Global management philosophies and strategies and the traits of global business.

B. Philosophy of Global Management: Dealing with theory of philosophy of global management and practice of philosophy of global companies like General Motors, Exxon Mobil, Matsushita and Shell.

C. Strategy of Global Management: This chapter deals with theory and definition of strategy, strategic management, good business strategy, seven– S Model, Vigin case of strategy implementation and everyday low prices at Wal-Mart.

D. Leadership of Global Management: The chapter deals with theory and essentials of management leadership, managerial leadership styles, and the models of leadership in global management like Shell, Samuel Walton, Jack Welch and Matsushita.

The Second Part deals with the theory and practice of the processes of global management such as Planning (Chapter 5), Organising (Chapter 6), Staffing (Chapter 7), Directing (Chapter 8) and Controlling and Evaluating (Chapter 9) with the case studies drawn from global companies to illustrate how for instance, GE or Shell or Matsushita, etc., plan, organise, staff, direct and control and evaluate the achievement of predetermined objectives.

The Third Part deals with three core chapters— (1) Motivating, (2) Developing future managers and (3) Managing diverse people and cultures — a great challenge in global management.

The Fourth Part tackles the futuristic chapters where the global management has a great opportunity changing the world for the better through Chapter 13 dealing with Global Human Growth Model, the implementation of which is through 3 pillars of growth, (1) Education, (2) Employment and (3) Energising all to realise their maximum potential will usher in an era of unheard of prosperity, gross global product happiness, peace and compassion; and through Chapter 14 dealing with dynamics of global management under the topics of (1) Managing growth and expansion, (2) Creating wealth for society, (3) Nurturing executive talent, (4) Building a new world order, and (5) Life-long learning to create the desirable future.

We shall discuss the theory and practice of the Dynamic Global Management in 14 chapters spread over 450 pages, tables and graphics as well as the high drama of management of leaders, who have shaped modern business of trillions of dollars around the world.

The grand vision and mission of Dynamic Global Management is the utilisation of the new philosophy, strategy and leadership to build dynamic global business and companies to serve the people, communities, nations of the world by using sound dynamic management processes of planning, organising, staffing, motivating, controlling, evaluating and marketing executive talent with a view to building a new world order of prosperity, happiness, peace and compassion, eradicating illiteracy, unemployment, poverty and human insecurity from the face of the earth.

The present volume is the result of several years of continuous research, experiments and experiences and in writing this volume, I have drawn rather freely upon the writing and research, done by the outstanding scholars and great institutions, Conference Board, American Management Association, British Institute of Management, International Association of Japanese Management, All India Management Association, Australian Institute of Management, etc., and upon the experiences and experiments of great global corporations and the pioneering entrepreneurs and leading exponents of modern management thought. Many leading global corporations and their Chairmen and CEOs have co-operated in giving valuable information including their management philosophies, systems techniques and manuals and speeches, The author is grateful to all of them. Perhaps, this is the appropriate place to remember my dear wife and to express special thanks to her for compiling all the materials, graphics and tables. She has typed all the 22 books and proofread all of them with great patience. In writing a book such as this, I am indebted to so many persons that it is impossible to give all due credits. But to all I extend my sincere thanks while bearing responsibility for any sins of omission and commission. Finally, my publishers Himalaya Publishing House Pvt. Ltd., who have published all my 22 books. I am deeply grateful to them for a great job of publication.

My global executive friends, I invite you and all the people around the world to join me in this great voyage of discovery of human spirit in changing global business and management scene in order to build a better world for ourselves, our family, nation and world.

We are always at your service, ready, willing and able to assist you and your dynamic global management in building a new world order hitherto undreamt of through the sound art and science of dynamic global management.

Bengaluru,
Singapore

M.N. RUDRABASAVARAJ

Contents

PART - I

PART - II

PART - III

PART - I

In Part, I we shall turn to a discussion of processes of Global Management such as Glimpses of Global Management, Philosophy of Global Management, Strategy of Global Management, Leadership of Global Management in the four chapters.

Let us start with the most important process of Global Management.

They are:

1. Glimpses of Global Management
2. Philosophy of Global Management
3. Strategy of Global Management
4. Leadership of Global Management

1 Glimpses of Global Management

The chapter is discussed under the following headings :
• Introduction • Glimpses of Global Business Management • Evolution of Global Business Management • Global Management Philosophies & Strategies • Global Business Traits

I. INTRODUCTION

Four decades ago, I returned to India from USA, after completing my Masters in Business Administration and working for Conference Board (then known as National Industrial Conference Board) in New York, full of vim and vigour and ideas. I wanted to change India now and not later and wrote a lot of articles. One of them was "Industrialisation by invitation" in the Economic Times. I suggested in that piece that the challenge of developing India was too big for India alone and it must change its policy of a closed economy to that of open economy and invite the top companies of the world to operate from India. They would bring the much needed capital, management, science and technology and would provide employment, improve productivity and export their products which are highly competitive in cost, pricing, quality and thus, promote the economic development of India. Many people were opposed to what they called this a new type of economic imperialism, displacing recent political colonialism.

However, Singapore adopted this policy of industrialisation by invitation and became a developed economy with full employment and per capita of nearly $ 42,000. If India had followed the open economic policy by inviting the world's top companies, India would have become a developed economy by now, removing illiteracy, unemployment, poverty and human insecurity.

Konosuke Matsushita

I have worked closely with PHP Institute, founded by Konosuke Matshushita in 1946, to promote peace and happiness through prosperity by organising conferences on Matshushita Autonomous Management and Philosophy of Human Resources Management in Indonesia, Singapore, Malaysia and Thailand and organising Business Observation-cum-Study (BOS) visit to Japan. When we met Matsushita, he was 88 years old and stood and spoke for 45 minutes on "How business should contribute to raising the standards of living of people around the world" in the OECD conference in Tokyo.

Once a customer takes Matsushita to visit his sect's temple and he is impressed by the grand and dignified buildings, the huge scale of everything, industrious activity of workers, the piety of worshippers, the comprehensive way everything was managed and so on. While returning home in the train, he thinks what he had seen was a model of superior management. He discovers a close correlationship between the Management of the temple and his own business management. He observes, "Religion is a holy pursuit aimed at guiding people out of suffering and towards happiness and peace of mind. My business, too, is sacred, I thought, in the sense that industry provides necessities that sustain and improve man's existence." The visit to the temple awakens in him a new spirit of management and the true mission of business.

What is the mission of business? In the words of Matsushita: "The mission of a manufacturer is to overcome poverty, to relieve society as a whole from misery of poverty and bring it wealth. Business and production are not meant to enrich only the shops or the factories of the enterprise concerned, but all the rest of the society as well. And society needs the dynamism and vitality of business and industry to generate its wealth. Only under such conditions will business and factories truly prosper, but their prosperity is secondary. Our primary concern is to eliminate poverty and increase wealth. How? By producing goods in abundant supply. No matter what the condition of society is, a manufacturer must sustain his efforts in making available large volumes of goods. This is his true mission."

"Water, that is, tap water, is a resource that is processed and priced. Anyone who partakes of a valuable product without permission is liable for punishment, but a traveller, thirsty from a long journey, who turns on a roadside water tap and drinks his fill will not be accused of wrongdoing or punished for drinking the water itself. Why? Because the price of water is so very low. And the tap water is cheap because it is produced in plentiful supply. This is what the entrepreneur and manufacturer aims at: To make all products as inexhaustible and as cheap as tap water. When this is realised poverty will vanish from the earth".

"Only after there is limitless supply of material goods as well as spiritual peace of mind will man achieve happiness. I believe that here is the manufacturers' true mission and mission of Matsushita Electric. I would like you all to keep in mind the true mission of Matsushita Electric is to ensure inexhaustible supply of goods, thus, creating peace and prosperity throughout the land". (Konosuke Matsushita, **Quest for Prosperity — The life of a Japanese Industrialist**). This idea and ideal became a cornerstone of Japanese Industrial Philosophy and Japan has emerged the second most prosperous country in the World, after USA.

IBM Corporation

Delivering the McKinsey Foundation Lectures at Columbia University, Thomas J. Watson Jr, Chairman of IBM, very forcefully expresses the faith of his Corporation and certain basic beliefs of IBM!

"This, then, is my thesis, I firmly believe that any organisation in order to survive and achieve success must have a sound set of beliefs on which it premises all its policies and actions".

"Next I believe that the most important single factor in corporate success is faithful adherence to those beliefs".

"And finally, I believe that if an organisation is to meet the challenges of a changing world, it must be prepared to change everything about itself, except those beliefs as it moves through corporate life".

"In other words, the basic philosophy, spirit and drive of an organisation have far more to do with its relative achievements than to technological or economic resources, organisation structure, innovation and timing. All these things weigh heavily in success.

But they are, I think, transcended by how strongly the people in the organisation believe in its basic concepts and how faithfully they carry them out".

"IBM's philosophy is largely contained in those beliefs:

1. "I want to begin with what I think is the most important: **Our respect for the individual.** This is a simple concept, but in IBM it occupies a major portion of management time. We devote more effort to it than anything else".
2. "IBM means service". It is a succinct expression of our second basic belief. We want to give the best customer service of any company in the world.
3. The third IBM belief is really the force that makes the other two effective. We believe that an organisation should pursue all tasks with the idea that they can be accomplished in a superior performance from its people in whatever they do".

Part of the foundation for a successful system of management is a philosophy that is consciously thought through, clearly spelled out and consistently acted out in practice.

Wal-Mart

Mr Samuel Walton built WAL-MART into the world's No. 1 corporation with the largest sales turnover of $389 billion and the largest workforce of 1,707,000 in the world, by motivating his people with a great sense of humour, communicating everything with his people including productivity and profits, sharing profits with his people. The United States of America is a fantastic country nurtured by the great American Dream, where an individual can go from rags to riches, from nobody to somebody, from the log cabin to the White House where you can realise your maximum potential by sheer merit, guts and hard work. Samuel Walton was one such. The creator of Wal-Mart stores triumphed with the folksy dedication to giving customers what they want; low prices, a modicum of service by employees who care because they share the company ideals as well as its profits.

Global Human Growth Model: I have a dream

Lastly, we must strive to promote and achieve human growth in India and the world through three fundamental pillars.

1. Education for all
2. Employment for all
3. Energising every human being to realise his/her maximum potential

But, we have a world in spite of all the progress, in which 1/4th are illiterates; 1/5th are poor and hungry, 1/3rd unemployed or under employed and 2/3rd unable to reach their potential. We must change this world and take the long hard difficult road, almost an impossible task and pull ourselves up by our bootstraps in order to tackle the problems of poverty, unemployment and illiteracy by understanding, accepting and implementing the concept and philosophy of human growth and rebuild a new world human order, by educating every individual to realise his/her maximum potential and re-engineer a new individual — educated, employed, energised, who is capable of contributing to the development of his family, organisation, society, nation and the world.

This is the greatest challenge facing the people and the leaders of the world in the 21st Century. If we succeed in educating, employing and energising every human to realise his/her maximum potential, we shall succeed in exceeding the gross global product by 30 times the current aggregate GNPs of the countries of the world.

In short, this is not only the purpose of business but also the purpose of life itself.

In 1967, I requested Dr. V.V. Giri, President of India to write a foreword for my first book, 'Dynamic Personnel Administration'. Dr. Giri said after going through my book, "You have really written a tome and I accept your invitation to write the foreword". Then Dr. Giri exhorted me to think about the problems of the people of India like poverty and unemployment and conduct some research and come up with some solutions. That led me to conduct research not only in India but around the world which led to the publication of my book, "Global Human Growth Model". I presented my Global Model at the 10th World Productivity Congress by the World Confederation of National Productivity Councils in Santiago, Chile in 1997, where I was honoured with a World Productivity Fellowship.

Global Recession 2008

The sordid sad saga of financial meltdown and recession in USA has led to the current global recession resulting in a loss of millions of jobs and trillions of dollars and human misery and suffering. This crisis raises some fundamental questions about business, professional management and social economic development. What is the purpose of business? What is the purpose of global business? What is the role of global management? In short, what is the purpose of life itself?

What is the purpose of Business and the role of Global Management?

II. GLIMPSES OF GLOBAL BUSINESS MANAGEMENT

Now I would like to provide a peek into the all stars of Global Business, so that the reader gets an idea of the complexity, sophistication and enormity of global management, before we turn to their evolution, concept, definition and theory and practice of global management, which is truly dynamic.

The Global Fortune 500-2008

For the past 14 years, the Global Fortune 500 has been the premier list of the world's largest companies in terms of revenue, profits, assets and employees in 2007. Altogether the giants grew a phenomenal 13% to $ 23.6 trillion and set the bar higher to make the list. Companies now must produce a record $ 16.7 billion revenues up 12% from last year. However profits grew less spectacularly at only 3.9%, as opposed to 27% last year, to 1.6 trillion, in view of the financial crises.

The majority of the top 500 companies come from USA (153) and the table below gives the details.

TABLE 1
Countries with Global Companies

USA	153	Denmark	2
Britain	35	Australia	8
Japan	64	Austria	2
China	29	Belgium	6
France	39	Brazil	5
Germany	37	Finland	2
Netherlands	13	Mexico	5
South Korea	15	Norway	2
Switzerland	14	Russia	5
Spain	11	Sweden	6
India	7	Thailand, Turkey	1 each
Taiwan	6	Saudi Arabia	1
Italy	10	Malaysia, Luxemberg	1 each
Ireland	2	Poland, Portugal	1 each
Canada	14	Singapore	1

A falling dollar became an advantage to non-USA companies, especially, those riding the oil and commodities boom by boosting their revenues and profits when currency conversion came into play. Consequently the list shows the fewest American Companies (153 as against more than 200 last year) in more than a decade and confirms the rising prominence of the emerging market. Less than 10 years ago, India, Mexico and Russia posted only one company on the Global 500. This year the list includes seven from India and five firms each from Mexico and Russia.

TABLE 2
Top Ten Global Companies — 2008

Sl.No.	*Name*	*Revenue In billion*	*Profit In billion*	*Employees*
1.	Wal-Mart (US)	$ 378,799	$ 12,731	2,055,000(1)
2.	Exxon Mobil (US)	$ 372,824	$ 40,610	107,000(154)
3.	Royal Dutch Shell (The Netherlands)	$ 355,782	$ 31,331	104,000(161)
4.	British Petroleum (BP) (Britain)	$ 291,438	$ 20,845	97,600(180)
5.	Toyota Motor (Japan)	$ 230,200	$ 15,042	316,121(29)
6.	Chevron (USA)	$ 210,783	$ 18,688	65,035 (262)
7.	ING Group (Netherlands)	$ 201,516	$ 12,648	120,282(135)
8.	Total (France)	$ 187,279	$ 18,041	96,442(181)
9.	General Motors (US)	$ 182,347	$ 38,732	266,000(40)
10.	Conoco Phillips (US)	$ 178,558	$ 11,891	32,600 (389)

Fortune observes : A year of record oil prices wasn't enough for Exxon Mobil (No.2) to unseat WAL-MART, which is No. 1 (for the fifth year) at $ 379 billion revenues which is quite remarkable for a retail company to lead the list. Due to very high spiraling oil prices, the oil companies, Exxon Mobil, Shell, BP Chevron, Conoco Philips, Total, etc., have acquitted

1. Fortune Global Fortune 500, Volume 158, Number 2, Time and of Life Publication, August 25, 2008, pp. 82 and Fl-F-37.
2. Fortune, *Ibid.*

themselves creditably not only in terms of revenues but also in terms of profits. Toyota No. (5) has outpaced General Motors (GM) (No.9) for the first time ever. GM, which was No. 1 for more than a decade, has the dubious distinction of losing the most money ($38,732 billion) in this year's list.

Exxon Mobil has achieved No. 1 position in terms of profits, followed by Shell (31 BP) (20 billion) assisted by spiralling oil prices. In spite of difficult conditions in the Auto industry, Toyota has done well with $ 15 billion profits.

Employment

Let us take a look at the biggest employers in Fortune Global 500.

TABLE 3
Top Ten Global Employers — 2008

Sl.No.	*Name*	*No of Employees*
1.	Wal-Mart (US)	2,055,000
2.	State Grid (China)	1,486,000
3.	China National Petroleum (China)	1,117,345
4.	US Postal Service (US)	785,929
5.	Sinopec (China)	634,011
6.	Han Hai Precision Industry (Taiwan)	550,000
7.	Carre Four (France)	490,042
8.	Deutsche Post (Germany)	475,100
9.	Agricultural Bank of China (China)	447,519
10.	Gazdron (Russia)	436,096

WAL-MART is the clear leader in employing 2,055,000, the highest number of employees, who are called associates who play a very prominent role in the growth of their company and also share the profits of the company and who realise that in the growth of WAL-MART lies the growth of associates, most of whom are share holders of the company also. It is interesting to note that the top auto companies of USA GM ($ 2.5), Ford ($ 3.4 Bil) and Germany, Diamler Chrysler $ 3.4 Bil) have not done well in terms of profit in 2004.

What is extremely noteworthy is the performance of WAL-MART, not only is the No. 1 company in the world in terms of revenue, but is also No. 1 in terms of employment, employing and managing 25,00,000 employees. Despite its philosophy of "Everyday Low Prices" WAL-MART has managed well to achieve a profit level of $ 10 billion in retailing where low margins rule the market place.

In another Fortune study of the most admired companies, WAL-MART emerged at the top as the most admired company in the world. It is indeed rare that a company scored the top position in terms of revenue and in terms of employment, as well as the most admired company in the world.

Fortune ranks the most admired companies on the basis of nine criteria which are :

(1) Globalness (2) Innovation (3) Quality of management (4) Employee talent (5) Financial soundness (6) Use of corporate assets (7) Long-term investment value (8) Social responsibility and (9) Quality of products and services.

Assets

Let us turn to the assets and biggest companies in terms of assets.

TABLE 4
Top Ten Global Asset Companies — 2008

Sl.No.	Name of Company	Assets (in trillions)
1.	Royal Bank of Scotland (Britain)	$ 3,783,155
2.	Deutsche Bank (Germany)	$ 2,953,873
3.	BNP Paribas (France)	$ 2,477,395
4.	Barclays (Britain)	$ 2,443,170
5.	HSBC Holdings (Britain)	$ 2,354,266
6.	Credit Agricole (France)	$ 2,252,835
7.	CITI Group (US)	$ 2,187,631
8.	UBS (Switzerland)	$ 2,007,346
9.	Mitsubishi Financial Group (Japan)	$ 1,938,944
10.	ING Group (Netherlands)	$ 1,918,969

In 2004, Citi Group (USA) was No. 1 in terms of assets at $ 1,484 trillion, but in 2008 to now reduced to 7th position with $ 2,187 trillion. Royal Bank of Scotland which was No.9 with $ 1,120 trillion, has moved up to No. 1 position, almost tripling its assets at 3,783 trillion, followed by Deutsche Bank (Germany) and BNP Paribas (France).

It is interesting to note that USA has only one company (city) in the top ten asset companies in the world.

GLOBAL MOST ADMIRED COMPANIES

Most Admired Companies of The World

1. WAL-MART (General Merchandisers)
2. G.E (Electronics)
3. Microsoft (Software Computer)
4. Berkshire Hathaway (Insurance Property)
5. Home Depot (Speciality Retailer)
6. Johnson & Johnson (Pharmaceuticals)
7. Fedex (Mall Freight Delivery)
8. Citi Group (Mega Banks)
9. Intel (Semi Conductors)
10. CISCO (Network Communicators)

It is very interesting that WAL-MART emerged at the top as the most admired company in the world in addition to No. 1 in revenue and No.1 in terms of employment. It is indeed rare that one company comes out at the top in 3 categories.

Fortune ranks the most admired companies on the basis of the nine criteria — (1) Globalness (2) Innovation (3) Quality of Management (4) Employee talent (5) Financial soundness (6) Use of corporate assets (7) Long-term investment value (8) Social responsibility and (9) Quality of products and services.

INDIAN COMPANIES

TABLE 5
Top Seven Indian Companies in Global Fortune – 500

Sl.No.	Name	Rank	Revenue in Billions	Profits in Billions
1.	Indian Oil	116 (170-2004)	$ 57,427	$ 1,964(366)
2.	Reliance Industries	206 (417)	$ 35,914	$ 4,847(103)
3.	Bharat Petroleum	287 (429)	$ 27,872	439 (433)
4.	Hindustan Petroleum	290 (436)	$ 27,717	338 (446)
5.	Tata Steel	315 (New)	$ 25,717	3,000 (186)
6.	Oil and Natural Gas	335 (454)	$ 24,032	4,934 (102)
7.	State Bank of India	380 (New)	$ 22,402	2,225 (232)

TOP SEVEN INDIAN COMPANIES IN THE FORTUNE GLOBAL 500

All the Indian companies have moved up the ranks as shown in the brackets, which represents their rank in 2004. Tata Steel, is the new entrant with its acquisition of Corus, as well as State Bank of India.

Reliance Group is the first private sector company to figure in the Fortune Global 500 since 2003, when it was ranked the lowest among Indian companies. But since 2004, it has risen spectacularly to the second position among the Indian companies.

However, Mr. Anil Ambani, put it in proper perspective. When somebody told him that Reliance is No. 1 in India, he is reported to have told "yes", we may be big in India, but Reliance is a pigmy when compared to the big MNCs. True, India has a long way to go. Aditya Birla's son, Kumarmangalam Birla has expressed his desire to figure in the Fortune 500. But most of the Indian entrepreneurs have never entertained such ambitions that they want to become one of the top ten in the world, let alone No. 1 in the world.

However, Mittal Steel owned by the richest Indian in the world, Mr. L. N. Mittal, who built his steel business in Indonesia, expanded in U.K., East European Countries, is ranked 253 in the 2004 Fortune Global 500. But in the year 2004, Mittal Steel scored the biggest rise in revenues – 310% to $ 22, 197 million. Mr. Mittal wishes to build Mittal Steel into the top steel company in the world.

In 2008, that honour was won by another Indian Company Tata Steel (No.315) which entered the roster with $ 25.7 billion in sales and earned the honour of earning the largest revenue increase on the list — a staggering 353% — after it acquired Anglo-Dutch Corus.

III. GLOBAL MANAGEMENT PHILOSOPHIES AND STRATEGIES

The million dollar mystery is how do they manage these companies so successfully, so productively, so profitably and so effectively year and after year, grow them from a local company into a national company and then into a multinational and now a global company with billion dollar assets, hundreds of billions of dollar revenues, hundreds of thousands of employees, thousands of multinational, multiracial managerial force, thousands of laws of hundreds of countries around the world. This is indeed a great challenge to manage and manage successfully and build a great business and a global corporation. Let us turn to this great challenge and examine briefly how the managers, the great organisers, manage the great companies and take a peek at the global management practice.

VISION AT&T

American Telephone & Telegraphic became the top company in America, because its founder, Theodore Vail had a vision. "I want to develop telephonic communication system whereby any person could speak to any other person anywhere in the world, quickly, cheaply and satisfactorily". The research, design and development team along with managers and employees worked hard over the years to convert the founder's dream like vision into a reality. Today, we can speak to any person any where in the world quickly, cheaply and satisfactorily. AT & T became so big that Government of America had to break into several companies to reduce AT&T's monopoly in the Telecommunication business. A great vision is a great motivator in building a great business.

GM PHILOSOPHY

People–Asset of GM

The long-term Chairman of General Motors, Alfred P. Sloan Jr. observed "In building autos, everything, *i.e.*, capital, technology, mass assembly line, production, etc., are the same. But what makes the big difference between GM and others is our people. Our people may not figure on our balance sheet but they are the biggest asset of GM. Attracting capable and competent people, training and developing them and motivating them to realise their maximum potential and helping them to grow in the organisation and also grow GM to its maximum stature required great investment in people and thus, converting them into the greatest asset of GM".

A New Marketing Strategy

When a customer asked Mr. Ford for a red-coloured car, Mr. Ford is reported to have said, "Yes you can have any colour of the car as long as it is black." Ford lost its leadership in American Auto industry to GM, because GM realised that there were three distinct income groups in America and that GM must cater their products to these different income groups. GM produced Chevrolet for the low income group/Oldsmobile, Pontiac and Buick for the middle income group and Cadillac for the upper income group. The new marketing strategy of GM enabled it to capture the major market share and become the No. 1 company, not only in America but also in the whole world.

Management Principle

Alfred Sloan Jr. evolved the management principle of centralised policymaking with decentralised administration, which has helped large multinational companies to implement their policies in a more efficient and effective manner through the proper delegation of authority and responsibility. All the multinational companies more or less operate on this principle all over the world and manage their operations successfully.

Mass Customisation

GM also introduced mass customisation, where the customer can choose various options, accessories and car colours and each car is built according to customers' needs, preferences, tastes and lifestyle. This principle helped GM to become the leader not only in the auto industry in USA but also in the whole world.

GE & High Fliers

Jack Welch who developed GE into a global company with over 150 billions in revenue, learnt an important lesson from his senior Vice President, who spent hours with Jack Welch and persuaded him to stay with GE, Jack Welch learnt an important lesson in management and implemented this lesson when he became the CEO of GE. The first thing he did as the CEO, was to go around all the divisions and companies in GE to identify the people with potential and who are the high performers and the high fliers. He implemented this policy in GE by asking all the CEO's of GE to identify three groups of people in their organisation (1) High performers (2) Normal performers (3) Poor performers. High fliers were encouraged to do even better and take the company to higher revenue and profits, normal performers were motivated to continue their good work and move into the high flier category whenever possible. Poor performers were forced to improve their performance and reach normal levels or to leave the company.

In 20 years, GE under Jack moved into a $ 100 billion company and one of the five in Fortune 500 and double digit growth every year became a norm for GE under Jack Welch.

When Jeff Immelt took over from Jack Welch on a day when America faced the 9/11 crisis and when everything was down, including the economy and the stock market, Immelt addressed a press conference and assured the Americans that GE will continue on its track record of double digit growth. His statement had a remarkable impact on the economy and the stock market started moving up due to GE's assurances.

M&A

Jack Welch triggered GE's double digit growth through a systematic program of mergers and acquisitions and moved GE from an electronic company into a diversified financial one with GE Capital, GE Medical and television, insurance, etc., with a careful strategy of diversification. GE emerged into a global company with global business with a complete range of diversified products and services.

MATSUSHITA

New Industrial Philisophy

Konusuke Matsushita formulated a new industrial philosophy for Japan of producing high quality of products at very reasonable prices, so that the customers will not think before buying Japanese merchandise and products. Before Matsushita, Japan was known for its imitation products of poor quality. But it was Matsushita who started producing products: radios

T.V. VCRs, household appliances, etc., of high quality and offering them at very reasonable prices. Soon Sony, Hitachi, Casio, Seiko, Citizen and other Japanese companies followed Matsushita's philosophy. The consequence was that National Panasonic and Japanese products captured the world markets in a couple of decades.

We Make Men

Konusuke Matsushita had another greater principle, which he pronounced very eloquently and simply, "We make men before we make products." Matsushita firmly believed in the principle of training, development and educating all his employees with the required skills, habits, knowledge and attitudes to produce products of high quality at reasonable costs by improving the productivity of the people and pass on the saved costs to the customers at reduced prices, all of which helped the Matsushita Industrial Enterprises to become a leader in consumer electronic business in the world, overtaking companies like Philips, GE & Westinghouse, etc.

Customers' Satisfaction

Matsushita realised the value of customers' satisfaction in improving business. He would personally visit the house of a customer after he bought a National radio and enquire about the performance of the radio, reception, sound and band width, etc., and get the customers' feedback and pass on the same to his technical team and factory production team and see that the radio performance was improved to perfection. He introduced the concept of zero defects and zero accidents, later followed by other Japanese companies.

Employee Involvement

He also encouraged all the employees to come up with suggestions to cut costs, to improve productivity, quality and production, etc., The employees of Matsushita generate 4½ million suggestions every year, which helped the companies to grow at a tremendous pace by carrying out the suggestions to improve productivity and to cut costs.

National

Matsushita's dream was not only to build Matsushita into a global company No.1 in consumer electronics but also enable Japan and Japanese companies to capture the global market by following the industrial philosophy of producing high quality products and market them at very reasonable prices.

Glaxo Welcome Strategy

Glaxo Welcome's strategy to become a global company was to establish its presence in every leading and important nation in the world. Glaxo with the assistance of this strategy, has become one of the top companies in the pharmaceutical industry in the world and operates in more than 100 countries of the world.

Glaxo occupies a top place in profits in the pharmaceutical industry in the world.

Health care and health awareness among the people of the world is enhanced by Glaxo and other pharmaceutical companies and their research and development efforts in coming up with medicines to cure common diseases of the people and by informing and educating people on how to prevent diseases like diabetes, obesity, strokes, heart attacks, cancer, etc., in that, the life span of people all over the world has improved, even in Africa and Asia.

Citi Bank

Citi Bank is the first trillion dollar enterprise, after acquiring the Travels group, and be repositioning as Citigroup with its creative aggressive retail strategy CITI group has learnt to manage a multi national managerial force and economic growth by financing good ideas and feasible projects, not just insist on collateral.

Citi Bank created the Citi Bank man, whereby every employee and manager live by the Citi Bank philosophy and principles, all of which contributes to the growth of Citi groups and Citi Bank all over the world.

This is achieved by establishing training objectives and following the systems approach from (1) identification of needs, evaluation of training effectiveness and analysis of operational impact (2) by regrouping in a centrally managed team, the training technicians of the banks and (3) establishing an independent quality control agency, whose function is to audit training.

The training effort operates from a three-pronged base. One group designs and develops training; another group assesses needs and evaluates training effectiveness and the third group manages the tested and approved ongoing training activities.

IBM Philosophy

IBM is the top company in the computer industry. Thomas J. Watson Sr. states the IBM Philosophy.

1. IBM believes in superior performance from every individual
2. IBM believes in superior customer service
3. IBM believes in superior customers satisfaction.

Customers service and customers satisfaction aided by superior individual performance has propelled IBM to the No. 1 position in the computer industry, which has brought about a great information revolution, which has helped companies and countries to grow fast by providing tools that accelerate problem solving and decision making.

SHELL MODEL — SPOTTING POTENTIAL

Shell is the second largest oil company in the world, which has done considerable amount of research to evolve a methodology to spot the potential and the ultimate potential of the people working in Shell companies around the world. They formed a Project Team comprising Prof. Van Lennep of Utrecht University and Dr. Mueller, a senior executive of Shell to formulate a methodology to spot the potential of people, who are likely to become the top executives of Shell.

The Team used three research methods over a period of three years. First, they studied the leaders in all walks of life-political , social, cultural, etc., in order to identify the qualities that helped them to become leaders in their chosen field of activity. Second, they studied the performance appraisals of about 10 years to identify the qualities that superiors looked for in their people, when they wanted to promote them to higher positions in Shell. Third, they interviewed General Managers, Directors, Managing Directors and Chairman of Shell companies and told the Team the qualities that helped them to get promotions in their careers to become top executives with a view to projecting the kind of people who are likely to become top executives at Shell in the future, and the kind of attributes or traits they possess to succeed in a large organisation like Shell.

The Team after their research project of three years, came up with 3000 qualities, out of which by removing semantic and overlapping, they reduced them to 300 qualities, after further rationalisation and discussion with the top executives, they finally came up with only 5 qualities which are the following :

1. Helicopter Quality

Prof. Van Lennep coined this term, "Helicopter Quality" after considerable research experience in human potential. Most people approach a problem and solve it from their own special expertise like, a finance manager from a financial angle regardless of the larger consequences.

But the person with Helicopter Quality will rise himself over narrow departmental loyalties and interests and look at the problem from the larger and total company point of view. It is similar to, when you go up in a helicopter, you have a panoramic and larger view of all aspects of the problem, you raise yourself above narrow departmental or divisional interests and try to approach the solution, as to its impact from all angles and from a total company point of view. At the top echelons of the organisation you need people with 'helicopter quality' who solve the problems taking into consideration all aspects of the problem.

2. Power of Analysis

This refers to the quality of the executive's analytical abilities, the power to find out the central problem and minor problems that have contributed, that is half the solution.

3. Sense of Imagination

This refers to looking far ahead of others and selling the possibilities, even dreaming and looking for new opportunities of business before others and drawing plans for the future, so that they can come true. But only dreaming or imagining will not get you there. You need a concrete plan and action to achieve it.

4. Sense of Realism

In addition to the sense of imagination, you must be realistic about your strength and capabilities and weakness as well as that of the organisation. Of course, you can become too realistic, when you become almost pessimistic. Hence, these two qualities look contradictory though they are complementary. In other words, you have to be imaginative without being unrealistic and you have to be realistic, without being unimaginative. Studies of leadership clearly indicate that leaders possess such complementary qualities, though they appear to be contradictory on the face of it.

5. Power of Anticipation

You must be able to anticipate and take the right decision at the right time and prevent losses and damages in your business.

These 5 qualities are part of the Shell Executive Appraisal System, which has two parts. The first part contains the appraisal of how the executive has performed and the second part deals with appraising the executive of the five qualities, that indicates the potential and the ultimate potential of the executive and to prepare him for higher assignments. The Shell system asks the appraiser to evaluate the strengths and weaknesses on an open-ended form and suggest to him higher assignments.

The Shell system has been further modified in the light of their experiences and have added the following 5 qualities like :

1. Achievement Motivation
2. Business Sense
3. Decisiveness
4. Capacity to Motivate
5. Delegation and Communication

So that the executive must be able to motivate himself and others, delegate work and relate to people. The above qualities which refer to the role of an executive, his potential relative to his present position, in Shell is termed as currently estimated potential (CEP), which is the highest possible position that an executive can reach irrespective of the job opportunities. High flyers are those who are given a high CEP grade and are treated like precious commodities. They get postings to different parts of the company, even overseas, to groom them for the career paths projected for them.

Any one's CEP can change, someone's CEP may start high but later plateau off or even worse, crash. In such cases, his career path is adjusted to a less brilliant one, offering fewer job opportunities and lower salaries. Conversely, a late bloomer's CEP is pegged higher, subsequently.

But a higher CEP comes with greater expectations and if the person does not perform as expected, his CEP grade is lowered. The underlying principle in Shell is meritocracy that top executives enjoy.

Singapore Uses Shell System

In November, 1994 in the Singapore Parliament, the then Senior Minister, Mr. Lee Kuan Yew related that the Shell System is the best way to pick people for top jobs, after selecting men for big jobs. Ministers, Civil servants, Statutory Board Chairman and after having asked many CEOs on how they selected top executives. Singapore ministers and top civil servants are all trained in the Shell System and they use the system to spot potential for top jobs in the Singapore Government. Government Ministries have adopted the Shell System for their own needs. The Ministry of Defence, for example, rates HAIR qualities, Helicopter Quality Analytical Powers, Imagination and Sense of Reality.

Power of Anticipation

This refers to the ability to anticipate events and problems before they occur, so that you prepare yourself and the organisation "to cross the bridge, when you come to it" or still better able to prevent it from occurring.

WAL-MART NO. 1 IN THE WORLD

The American Dream

The United States of America is a fantastic country nurtured by the great American Dream, where an individual can go from rags to rich, from nobody to somebody, from the log cabin to the White House, where you can realise your maximum and unique potential by sheer merit, hard work and guts. Samuel Walton was one such, the creator of WAL-MART. He triumphed with folksy dedication to giving customers what they want; low prices, a modicum of service administered by employees who care because they share the same company ideals as well as the profits.

Samuel Walton treated his employees not just as workers, but called them associates as partners by implementing a profit-sharing plan for all the associates which has pretty much been the carrot that kept WAL-MART heading forward. Another important ingredient in WAL-MART partnership from the very beginning is the very unusual willingness to share most of the numbers of business with all the associates. It is the only way they can possibly do their jobs to the best of their abilities "to know what's going on in their business".

Samuel Walton shares a few abiding principles that have enabled WAL-MART to think small in order to grow big and not acting like one.

1. Think one store at a time
2. Communicate, communicate, communicate
3. Keep your ear to the ground
4. Push responsibility and authority—down
5. Force ideas to bubble up
6. Stay as a team, fight bureaucracy

Samuel Walton has followed some rules that have worked for him

1. Commit to your business, believe in it more than anybody else.
2. Share your profits with your associates and treat them as partners.
3. Motivate your partners, by setting high goals, encourage competition.
4. Communicate everything you possibly can to your partners.
5. Appreciate everything you possibly can to your partners.
6. Celebrate your success, find humour in your failures, Don't take yourself too seriously.
7. Listen to everyone in your company and figure out ways to get them talking.
8. Exceed your customers expectation and give them what they want a little more WAL-MART sign : SATISFACTION GUARANTEED.
9. Control your expenses better than your competition.
10. Swim Upstream, go the other way. Ignore the conventional wisdom. WAI-MART's credo is to treat Customer as No. 1 and guarantee his satisfaction.

Learning and lifelong learning and learn from everybody, even competitors. He learnt from the Japanese and the Koreans as to how they motivate their employees by singing company songs.

WAL-MART scours the whole world to find merchandising sources and the motto is 'Buy them cheap, Stack them high and Sell them cheap'. Global sourcing has helped in cutting merchandising costs better than its competitors.

WAL-MART has kept up with the technology through management information systems and satellite systems and using a fleet of planes to locate stores in a more effective manner.

WAL-MART, even after Samuel Walton, has kept up the its spectacular growth to emerge as No. 1 in the whole business world and it is projected that WAL-MART will achieve half trillion dollar revenue in another five years, the first company to achieve such a feat in the world of business.

Indian Scene

The Tatas, Birlas, Mafatlals and now Reliance and the public sector giants like IOC, OIL, GAS, Hindustan Petro, Bharat Petro have all grown in India, but they seem to lack the global initiative and ambition. Recently, the IT enterprises like Infosys, Wipro, HCL, are making more progress in working beyond the borders of India, but they are still small and have a long way to go to leave a mark on the global business.

IV. EVOLUTION OF GLOBAL BUSINESS MANAGEMENT

The story of an enterpreneur struggling to start a very small enterprise with the help of his small savings, establishing it and slowly developing it into a small and medium size company and then succeeding in founding a large and national company. Many entrepreneurs stop at that stage, but there are a few who have a dream and a mission in life to grow the company into a top company in their industry and not only in the country, but also those to the top in the world, driven by their passion, dedication, commitment to achieve their dream. One such dreamer was Konasuke Matsushita and we shall turn to his story to illustrate how global companies are built from humble beginnings.

The Story of Matsushita

Matsushita was forced to give up schooling and start supporting his family after his father died. He started as a wiring technician in an electric light company and rose to become an inspector after eight years, a much sough job after good of wiring workers. Two years earlier, he had married because he felt homeless since he had lost his mother in 1913. While his life was good at the workplace and at home, he suffered from physical disabilities which made him more reflective. But he had nurtured the dream of starting his own small business, making a light socket with considerable pride he showed his first test sample to his supervisor who said, "No, this is no good, it's not even worth showing to the Section Chief. Matsushita was dumbstruck but more determined to pursue his dream, so he took the bold step of resigning on 20-06-1917. I shall let Matsushita tell how he started his new small enterprise with a young wife of two years.

The New Socket

So I was on my own. I was going to manufacture sockets. I had less than one hundred yen to invest in the business, including my severance pay (¥ 33.20), savings withdrawn from my salary each month by the company (¥ 42), and about ¥ 20 in personal savings. Even in those days it was a paltry sum when it came to setting up a business. All you might be able to buy was one machine or one mould. Any reasonable person would have immediately concluded it was worthless and downright impossible. But I was filled with expectant optimism and did not think it crazy at all.

I described my plan to manufacture the socket to a close friend of mine named, Isaburo Hayashi, a former co-worker at the electric light company who was employed as an electrician for a small firm, and invited him to join me. He agreed immediately. Another former co-worker, Nobujiro Morita, who was doing office work at Osaka Electric at the time he heard about my venture, also said he wanted to join us, to which I promptly assented. In addition, Toshio Iue (founder of Sanyo Electric Co., Ltd.), Mumeno's younger brother, who had just graduated from upper elementary school on Awaji Island, was to come and help out.

We had plenty of manpower, but that was all. None of us knew where to purchase materials, how to make a socket, or what price a socket could be sold for. We were starting literally from scratch. Socket bodies were made from an insulation material that we vaguely knew consisted of asphalt, asbestos, and powdered stone; but manufacture of insulatory materials for electrical use was a new field and the companies that produced them kept their methods a closely guarded secret.

I must have looked crazy trying to start a business so much in the dark; but Hayashi and Morita were just as crazy. As destined for failure as our enterprise may have appeared, at that point we were not the least concerned. Since we had only

Sam Walton, made in America, written with John Huey, reviewed in Fortune 29-06-1992, pp. 69-72

¥ 100, and could not afford to waste a bit of it, we did everything ourselves. We began by trying to figure out how to make the material for the insulatory case for the socket, calculating the cost of materials, and investigating methods for making various kinds of fixtures. We made simple metal tools and implements ourselves. Our workshop was in my two-room tenement house located in the eastern part of Osaka. One room was about four square metres, the other about nine square metres. We took out half the elevated floor of the larger room to create a tiny earthen-floored workshop, doing all the work ourselves in order to save the ten or fifteen yen it would have cost to hire carpenters. My wife and I had to sleep in one corner of the smaller room. It was the oddest situation you can imagine, but we were still in high spirits.

One hundred yen capital was obviously not enough. Hayashi had a friend who was an apprentice at a waterproofed fabric factory and a very frugal saver. We heard he had saved almost two hundred yen, so we went to him and asked him to lend us one hundred yen. Hayashi and I did our best to persuade him that our efforts would bear fruit and we would have no trouble returning the money. We were elated when he agreed. Unfortunately, Hayashi's friend died very young. If he were alive to see what his one hundred yen helped to build, I am sure it would make him very happy.

Figuring out how to create the proper mix of ingredients for the insulation was the biggest problem we faced. We scrounged fragments of discarded insulation at a local factory where it was manufactured and tried to analyse them, but to no avail. Finally, we learned that a former co-worker at the Osaka Electric knew how to make the compound. Apparently he had tried to make insulation material not long after leaving Osaka Electric, but without success. Determined to find out, he had got a job at an insulation manufacturing company, learned the method and then quit. He had begun to produce insulatory articles himself, but the business had not gone well and he had given up. When he heard what we were trying to do. he very willingly told us how it should be done, providing the key know-how we had lacked, and at last we were ready to move on to the next step. The other parts of the socket were much easier, and around the middle of October 1917, we finally succeeded in producing a limited number of the new model socket.

The manufacturing hump having been surmounted, our next task was to sell the sockets. Morita, who had had some office experience, undertook the role of salesman. He promptly wrapped up some samples and went off to try to sell them. Since we knew no wholesaler who might purchase them, and had no notion of what price they might bring, we decided to show them to any electrical parts dealer we could find, and give a price that would bring a small margin of profit. All we could do was wait and see. We sent off Morita with great apprehension and waited anxiously for his return.

When he finally came back late in the evening, he was tired out and depressed. He described how he was kept waiting at one dealer after the next, asked to come back later, or told bluntly to take his wares elsewhere. He had been confronted with one unexpected question after another: "When did your company get started? What else do you have besides these sockets?" And the wholesalers apparently distrusted such an anonymous manufacturer, making remarks like, "You've just opened, have you? It's hard to tell whether a novelty socket like yours will sell or not. I'm afraid we cannot order any." Morita had visited one small wholesaler who had expressed no interest in the socket but said if we made other electrical goods of insulation material, he might be able to place an order sometime.

Morita's report was sobering; it was going to be tough going. He persisted in his sales efforts for about ten days, managing to sell only about 100 units, and the proceeds were less than ten yen. The poor reception the socket had met convinced us that it would not sell and that we would have to improve it. But we had no funds to invest in designing a better socket and in attempting to keep the business going. All of us had a more immediate concern; we had to earn our daily bread. Morita and Hayashi's worry began to show, and I was not surprised when they expressed doubt that we would ever succeed. After four months, our total proceeds were only ten yen.

Finally they asked me what I intended to do. Did I have any idea how I was going to get along? Where was I going to get more money? They were close friends and never once pressed me for salaries, but, as they pointed out, their pockets were about as empty as they could get. They proposed that we give up the business and each go back to trying to make a living.

What they said brought me down to earth. It was obviously impossible to continue business as things were; yet I was very reluctant to give up something I had only just begun. I tried to persuade them to stick through the crisis, but since I had no concrete strategy for making the business survive, nor any money to finance it with, my pleas were hardly convincing. They were kind and generous fellows, but both had families to support. I could hardly ask further sacrifices from them. Morita found a new job towards the end of October, and Hayashi returned to the firm he had been working for earlier. Left alone with only Toshio as my assistant, I started again.

Though brought back to where I had started, I still did not think of giving up and trying to find another job. Somehow I felt certain the business would eventually succeed. I concentrated my efforts on building a better model for the socket. We were so poor that in the meanwhile my wife had to make frequent trips to the pawn shop to exchange what good clothes we had for small amounts of cash.

Windfall

The year 1917, was drawing to a close, and we still had no income. Work on the socket went slowly for lack of funds. It looked as if our New Year's celebrations would be lean and dismal.

Then suddenly in the beginning of December, a certain electrical parts wholesaler came to us with an unexpected order for one thousand insulator plates to be used in the bases of electric fans. The order came to us, by a circuitous route, from the manufacturer of the fans, Kawakita Electric, a leading electric company at that time, who had been using insulator plates made of porcelain but had decided to replace them with less breakable plates made of the asbestos-based material used for electrical insulation.

The job was urgent, the wholesaler said, but it was a preliminary order; if the customer liked our product, we could count on a huge additional order amounting to twenty or thirty thousand fan insulator plates a year. He advised us to put the socket aside for the moment and asked us to do our best to fill the fan plate order by the end of the year.

The timing could not have been better. I had reached an impasse in my efforts to remodel the socket. To make the insulator plates we needed little of the ingredients for the insulation compound and a mould. The job required little capital, making it the perfect work to keep us going at that critical stage. I wanted to make sure we would get the additional order even if we had to work night and day. It took a week for a local smith to make the mould, and I went frequently to check on the work and ask the smith to hurry. Once the mould was completed, we made a few sample insulator plates we thought were satisfactory. When I showed them to the wholesaler, he was satisfied, "Now make the rest, fast. If they are good, too, you will get another order for four or five thousand plates, at least."

Toshio and I worked like fiends to manufacture the thousand plates by the end of the year. I say "manufacture," but it was a pretty rudimentary operation. All we had were a mould press and a pot for smelting the insulation compound. It took a great deal of time and labour to make even one plate. Toshio was only fifteen and small for his age. He did the trimming, finishing, and odd jobs, and I concentrated on the moulding. It was our first real job, and we managed to turn out about one hundred a day, delivering the order in full several days before the end of December.

The moulding work gave me considerable confidence in my ability as a craftsman. I could work fast and the finished product was clean and neat. The wholesaler was delighted and assured us Kawakita Electric would be pleased. He promised to bring us a new order.

At the end of the year, we received ¥160 in payment for the thousand fan plates. Including the expense for making the mould, the cost of the insulators per unit was about ¥ 0.08, leaving us with a profit of ¥ 80. This was bounty, indeed, and the first profit we had made in our business. We prayed fervently that Kawakita Electric would like our work and give us further orders for insulator plates that could be produced with such a high profit margin.

Not long after, we learned that Kawakita had been pleased and had placed a new order. After some bargaining over the piece price, we received a second order early in the New Year for two thousand more insulator plates. This work kept the business afloat and, although it involved a product far different from light sockets, it provided reasonable profit and gave us valuable experience. In time, I had the leeway to go back to working on the socket design.

The unexpected things that happened in the days when we were starting our business, I have found, were not miracles. It is a kind of law of nature. The goal one aims for can rarely be reached by a direct road. It is well said that "patience is the better part of valor," for circumstances often change and the way may unexpectedly open up for success in what was previously an unfruitful endeavour. Patience and perseverance, moreover, often win praise from people who can provide help. My socket would not sell, but I was not pessimistic. It gave me a focus for my efforts, and my stick-to-activeness apparently meant something, for it brought the order from Kawakita Electric. But I had to be flexible, too, and ready to accept minor digressions from my goal. Without the temporary work on the fan insulator plates, my business would have failed.

Orders for the insulator plates continued to come in, but I also wanted to work on electrical fixture designs on the side, and our workshop was far too small. We learned that there was a larger house available near the Noda railway station on the Hanshin Line, at a rent of ¥ 16.50 a month. It was a densely populated part of town dominated by family-operated workshops and retail stores. We moved to the larger house on March 7, 1918, and started in again with renewed energy.

As they say, the rest is history. Matsushita Electric continued to expand the enterprise to become No. 1 in consumer electronics and one of the top companies in the world with its philosophy, "We make men before we make products". His philosophy of producing quality goods and selling them at reasonable prices became the cornerstone of Japanese industrial philosophy and propelled Japan to the second economic power after USA. After the IInd World War, he founded the Peace, Happiness and Prosperity Institute (PHP) in 1946, to promote the message of PHP through business enterprise.

Changing Concepts of Management

The science of management deals with planning, organising, directing, co-ordinating and controlling the co-operative efforts of individuals with a view to achieving certain pre-determined ends. Central to the management task is getting things done through people. A study of the evolution of the management concepts as enunciated by the able President of American Management Association, Mr. Lawrence Appley indicates the changing concepts of management regarding "the other fellow"[1]:

1. *Savagery:* The other fellow is my enemy and is to be destroyed.
2. *Slavery:* The other fellow is to be conquered and put at my service.
3. *Servitude:* The other fellow is to serve me for a consideration and ask no more.
4. *Welfare:* The other fellow should be helped up when down, without too much concern for what got him down.
5. *Paternalism:* The other fellow should be cared for, and I will decide to what extent.
6. *Participation:* The other fellow has something to contribute to my efforts and can help me.
7. *Trusteeship:* That for which I am responsible is not mine. I am developing and administering it for the benefit of others.
8. *Statesmanship:* The other fellow is capable of being far more than he is, and it is my responsibility to help him develop to his fullest potential.

The third emerging concept is that personnel administration is a profit-cum-growth engineering function. In a recent study conducted by National Industrial Conference Board on personnel managers and their functions, it was found that many personnel executives expressed the opinion that their functions directly contribute to company profitability and growth. Some years ago, Mr. Lawrence A. Appley wrote: "Management is the development of people and not the direction of things..............management and personnel administration are one and the same. They should never be separated. Management is personnel administration." Although Mr. Appley knew that there was more to management than just the development of people, he rightly pointed out the dynamic nature of personnel administration and its central importance in management.

1. Matsushita, Quest for prosperity : The life of a Japanese Industrialist : PHP Institute, Tokyo, 1988, pp. 42-48.

STAGES OF GROWTH OF A GLOBAL COMPANY

The various stages of growth of a global company is shown in diagram.

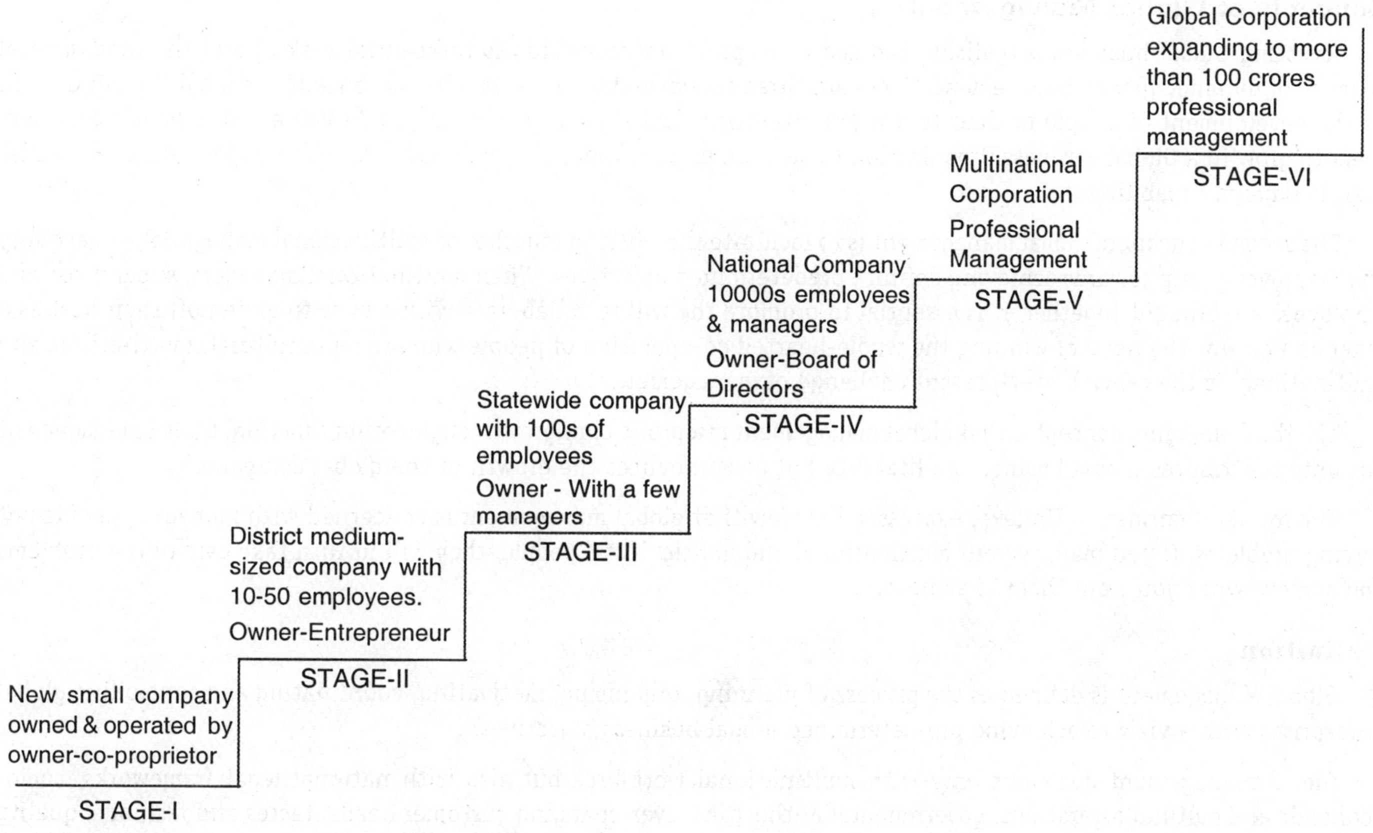

Stages of Growth of a Global Company

So from a single product, emerged with less than 10 workers the enterprise expands to a small medium-sized company to district medium-sized company, then to become a state-wide company and then to a national company with 100s of workers and then to a multinational company with business in several countries and finally emerges as the Global Company with operations all over the world.

What is a Global Company?

We can identify two types of Global Company. First in its purest form, the global company is defined as a company operating in all the countries, 240 of them at the last count. However, we do not have such a global company at the moment in the world. But we do have companies which operate in 120-160 countries of the world. There are also large companies like Glaxo, Smithkline, whose philosophy is that they would like their presence in all the large and important countries of the world.

The second form is that the Global Company sells its products or services in almost all the countries of the world which is probably the most prevalent form of global company at the moment.

CONCEPT AND DEFINITION OF GLOBAL MANAGEMENT

The art and science of management deals with planning, organising, directing, co-ordinating and controlling the co-operative efforts of individuals with a view to achieving certain predetermined ends. Central to the management task is getting things done through people. A study of the evolution of the management concepts as enunciated by the former

President of American Management Association Mr. Lawrence Appley indicates the changing aspects of management regarding "the other fellow"[1]

Concepts of Global Management

Assisting Global business is realising the last concept of statesmanship is the central task of and the fundamental purpose of dynamic global management. There are three fundamental concepts. First is concept of Global Human Growth — the development of people to their fullest potentialities. Global management must add value to the people and help them to grow in a Global Business Organisation to such an extent where they will have complete opportunities to realise their maximum capabilities.

The second concept of global management is to facilitate the working together of multinational managerial, supervisory and employee group towards achieving definite predetermined objectives. When multinational managers, supervisors and employees are brought together, it is essential to promote the will to collaborate with a view to giving off their best as a team or a group. The need of winning the whole-hearted co-operation of people who are multicultural, multi-ethnic and multinational is the central, ever-present challenge of management.

The third emerging concept is that global management is a profit-cum-growth engineering function. Global management not only contributes global business profitability but also enhances the growth of the global company.

The former Chairman of Unilever expressed his view that global management is concerned with managing people not solving problems. If you manage your multinational and multicultural people, they will in turn take care of the problems and achieve what you want them to achieve.

Definition

Global Management is defined as the process of planning, organising, motivating, coordinating and controlling global enterprises with a view to achieving pre-determined global business objectives.

Global management deals not only with multinational workforce but also with national legal frameworks, socio-economic and cultural aspirations, governmental authorities, ever-changing customer needs, tastes and fashions, quality of life and quality of working life issues, climate change, different trade unions and a whole host of issues.

Sometimes, you wonder how the global company manages the global enterprise with all its complexity, diversity and sophistication and some attribute it to the magic of multinational company management. There is no magic or secret of success. It is 99% hard, smart and systematic work and only 1% luck. Perhaps the successful ones make their own luck.

But the key to success in global management was pointed out by Mr. Jeffey Robert Immelt, Chairman & CEO of GE and one of the world's most admired business leaders and a worthy successor to Jack Welch, and who has transformed GE into a $165 billion powerhouse when he talks about his succession to the Chairmanship of GE.

"People get a chance like this not because of what they know but because of how fast people think they can learn. May be Jack and the GE board thought that I am a good learner." The mantra is : "We want to see the best in people, we want people to succeed. So we want to be fair and open with everybody. A lot of people, I would say almost everybody gets a second chance to do well and to perform".

The key is learning and lifelong learning because each day there are numerous challenges and issues and you keep learning how to tackle them and solve them and learn how to help others to learn so that they can give off their best.

Mr. Samuel Walton, who founded Wal-Mart and developed it into No. 1, $379 billion behemoth was a great learner. Any new store or format of retailing opened anywhere in US or Europe or Japan, he would go and study and write copious notes, talking to the salesperson, cashiers and customers about the new store.

The most important thing is to learn how to keep ahead of the pack!

1. Curtis Gager, "Management throughout History" on H.B. Maynand, *Top Management Handbook,* (New York, McGraw-Hill Book Company, Inc. 1960) p. 69.

Process of Globalisation

Shell identified three important trends in business at the beginning of the 21st century (1) Globalisation (2) Diversification (3) Individualisation.

Globalisation

Everybody wants to go global, what with all the progress in science, technology, management, information, technology transportation, instant communication, capabilities, automation, robotics, high productivity, new customer needs and lifestyle changes, gender equality, quality of life and quality of working life, 24-hour shopping, export and import of ideas and outlandish ideas, computers and Internet. In the global village everything seems possible, people have open attitudes and accept new ides and influences.

Diversification

Expansion through diversification of products, services, markets and downstream and upstreams is the key to progress, growth and profits. Acquisition and mergers and conglomeration have shown the route to faster growth than organic growth. Big companies are always looking for new opportunities of diversification.

Individualisation

An individual can change the world with his idea. An individual can make or mar the business. He is the fountain of creativity and innovation. A Samuel Walton can transform a small company from God knows where into a top company in the world with 2 million employees. In business history, how many are there who can employ a million people? In the development lies the development of not only the companies but also countries.

In the practice of global management it was Jack Welch, Former Chairman of GE, who wanted all the Presidents of various companies around the world to take a close look at the performance of all the people in order to identify three kinds of people: (1) High Performers (2) Normal Performers (3) Poor Performers. While encouraging the high performers by patting then on their back, he would try to move the normal performers to high performance and move the poor performers into the normal category. The exercise was most important to the continuous success and expansion of GE from a 50-billion to 130-billion empire.

Global management is global in prospective, national in operation and individual in approach.

VI. GLOBAL BUSINESS TRAITS

The study of global business denotes that there are some general traits that have helped them to grow and succeed on the global scene:

1. A unique and distinctive management philosophy, vision and mission.
2. Their key asset is their people and their potential fulfillment.
3. Customer is the King, customer relations, service and satisfaction are the key to their success.
4. They dare to experiment and take new initiatives and are not afraid to chart their new course
5. Learning is lifelong with no cut-off point.
6. High productivity, quality and profits have helped them to add value to their business, resources, people and countries.

Challenges

Global business faces many challenges, some new and some old. The gender issue, age issue, race and affirmative action, outsourcing strategy and managing a multinational, multicultural and multiracial people around the world has become so complex, sophisticated and demanding that global entrepreneurs and managers have to learn to find new-creative and innovative solutions with the advancing knowledge of service, technology and management and more important, the changing lifestyles of customers around the world.

+++

2 Philosophy of Global Management

The chapter is discussed under the following headings :
• What is Philosophy of Management • Management Philosophy of General Motors • Exxon Mobil Philosophy • Wal-Mart - A few abiding principles of Walton • Matsushita Philosophy of Management • Shell Philosophy

1. WHAT IS PHILOSOPHY OF MANAGEMENT

Every organisation regardless of its size, must have a corporate philosophy, usually influenced and enunciated by the founder of the corporation.

Generally, the corporate philosophy represents the basic vision of the founder or his close followers and the objectives.

It represents the mission of the corporation.

It represents the management principles of the organisation.

It provides the guidelines to the formulation of policies, programmes and procedures and their implementation throughout the organisation.

It highlights the code of conduct for every individual in the organisation.

It is an indicator of certain uniqueness of the organisation.

It is the road map of action, development and progress.

It represents the dreams, hopes and aspirations of the dynamic founder.

Great organisers not only enunciate their unique philosophy of business but also live and swear by it and also ensure that everybody in the organisation, in whichever part of the world, live and operate by the philosophy of the organisation and thus, make it a living corporate philosophy.

We would here like to share with our readers the real philosophies of six great organisations around the world as models of management philosophies, beginning with General Motors, which was No. 1 for several years in the Fortune Global 500 and Fortune American Companies.

2. GM's OPERATING PHILOSOPHY

General Motors operating philosophy is based on the concept of the importance of people. Fundamentally, all business enterprises are composed of opportunities, facilities and people.

It is only in its people that a business organisation is unique. The way its people are organised to work together makes it unique.

The operating philosophy based on this concept was formulated by General Motors Management in the early 1920's; that philosophy has been maintained and developed as a guide for its operation ever since.

Expressed in formal terms, the philosophy is, "Decentralised operation with responsibilities with co-ordinated control." A simpler way of expressing it is "Give a man a clear-cut job to do and let him do it".

Under this philosophy the overall objectives and principles are determined by the top management level, based on the information flowing up from all levels of the organisation. These are the policies, the "whys and wherefores" but the task of carrying them on that is "the how" is the men down the line".

I. Management Philosophy of General Motors (GM)[1]

"In GM, the personnel philosophy is an integral part of the management philosophy," says Mr. J.H. Miller, Executive Vice-President, Personnel and can be expressed in a single phrase: 'the importance of people.' He adds: 'Management objectives are achieved through people. Our convictions concerning the importance of people are reflected in our basic personnel objective of treating all employees fairly, whether hourly or salaried, whether 'represented or not represented by unions. We believe that meeting this objective required satisfying the inherent need of all people to be recognised as individuals.' Alfred P. Sloan Jr., a former Chairman of GM, observed very aptly: 'Most businesses are alike except as to people: there is the difference. The most important single asset of GM is the men and women who make up its organisation.'

More specifically, GM's philosophy towards ED is expressed in the following extracts:

(i) Some beliefs, viewpoints, and practices which have characterised and/or contributed to the success of GM's approach to Management Development and Utilisation.

A. Employees have a basic responsibility for their own development.

B. Historically, line managers in GM have accepted management development as an integral part of their responsibility.

C. Historically, top management in GM has given top priority to building and maintaining the management organisation. An increasing amount of time and attention is being given to reviewing management — personnel and to the development of personnel with management potential.

D. General Motors' method of decentralised operation has contributed to both the number and quality of management development opportunities in the corporation.

E. Management is responsible, consistent with the needs of the business, for providing salaried employees with opportunities for individual growth and development.

F. Management is responsible for stimulating, adding, and encouraging employees to utilise the training and development opportunities made available to them.

G. Employee development is a process with many contributing factors. One of the most important factors in the process is job experience. The most important ingredient in job experience is good supervision.

H. Management is responsible for the timely and selective use of formal training and development activities to supplement and accelerate employee growth and development on the job, and to provide development opportunities which go beyond those present on the job.

I. It is the Corporation policy to fill vacancies from within the organisation, whenever possible, by the transfer or promotion of salaried employees who are qualified, on the basis of their performance and ability. Implicit in this policy is the responsibility of divisional and staff management to produce an adequate supply of qualified personnel to make this policy function effective at all levels of responsibility.

(ii) Job experience as the basic ingredient in General Motors approach to Management Development and the Evaluation of Management Potential.

A. As a Means of Development

1. Historically, GM has relied on job experience as the principal means of developing managers.
2. The great bulk of such experience is provided in the normal course of filling job vacancies.

---

1. We are extremely grateful to General Motors for their kindness in providing this material.

3. In selecting employees to fill vacancies, GM management has historically given consideration not only to the requirements of the job, but also to the development needs of the individuals.
4. Lateral and rotational type moves are used on a selective basis to provide a supplemental means of utilising job experience as a developmental tool.
5. Changes in job responsibilities are utilised to broaden the employee's background and/or stimulate growth through changed or increased responsibilities.

B. As a Means of Evaluating Management Potential

1. Demonstrated ability through job performance is considered to be the best single predictor of potential for advancement.
2. Following each change in job responsibilities, the employee's performance should be observed for a period of time and then evaluated.
3. Each evaluation should lead to a reassessment of the experiences that the employee needs most as the next step in his overall development. (Note that the next step may not always be practical in terms of the needs of the organisation).
4. Each evaluation should lead to a reassessment of the employee's abilities in terms of how far he most likely can advance in the organisation.
5. As the employee is exposed to more and more experiences, and his performance observed over longer periods of time, judgements about the employee's abilities should be more and more valid. These judgements may or may not agree with the previous evaluation made with less opportunity to observe the employee.

These illustrations could serve as models in evolving philosophy in the area of executive development, to become operating guidelines for public undertakings.

They then must live by the philosophy.

3. EXXON PHILOSOPHY OF MANAGEMENT

Mr. Michael Haider, former Chairman of Exxon, the largest oil company in the world, observed the key to the success of Exxon:

"In the life of a corporation, today's success is largely a product of three types of executive actions taken yesterday: selecting the right people; placing them in the right jobs; and seeing to it that they were able to grow to meet their own needs and those of the organisation. This activity is not a programme in the usual sense, any more than selling or making profits are programmes. It has no fixed dimensions, no time-table, no cut-off point."

How seriously he regards this activity, Mr. Haider points out, is indicated by the fact that he assumes the executive development function as his personal responsibility. He and four Executive Vice-presidents of the company acting as a Committee, met 37 times a year to review the company's human resources.

This Committee is, "involved in a continuing examination of the management throughout the Jersey Organisation (later know an Exxon)... Once a year the Chief Executive Officers of the larger affiliates meets with the Committee and reviews in depth his company's development activities and its replacement situation and appraises the performance and potential of all his key management personnel. He goes over his replacement tables, his plans for rotational assignments, and the specific steps being taken to increase the effectiveness of the organisation.

Yes, top executives and indeed all executives must consciously develop this habit of looking closely at their people and their potential and make a generous contribution of their time and effort to make the budding flowers really bloom.

4. WAL-MART — A FEW ABIDING PRINCIPLES

The American Dream

The United States of America is a fantastic country nurtured by the great American Dream, where an individual can go from rags to riches, from nobody to somebody, from the log cabin to the White House, where you can realise your potential by sheer merit, guts and hard work. Mr. Samuel Walton was one such; the creator of Wal-Mart Stores, he triumphed with a folksy dedication to giving customers what they want; low prices and a modicum of service, administered by employees who care because they share the company ideals as well as its profits. In his memoir, *Sam Walton : Made in America*, written with Fortune senior editor, John Huey, "Mr. Sam" shares his views of corporate America, retailing, management.[2]

Sharing Information and Profits

We do not pretend to have invented the idea of a strong corporate culture. We are constantly doing crazy things to capture the attention of our folks and lead them to think up surprises of their own. We like to see them do wild things in the stores, things that are fun for the customers and fun for the associates. If you're committed to the Wal-Mart partnership and its core values, the culture encourages you to think up all sorts of things to break the mould and fight monotony.

I have a cheer, I lead whenever I visit a store. For those of you who don't know, it goes like this:

— Give me a W!
— Give me an A
— Give me an L!
— Give me a Squiggly!

(Here, everybody sort of does the twist)

— Give me an M!
— Give me an A!
— Give me an R!
— Give me a T!
— What's that spell?
— Wal-Mart
— Who's No. 1?
— The Customer

And if I'm leading the cheer, you'd better believe we do it loud. My feeling is that just because we work so hard, we don't have to go around with long faces all the time, taking ourselves seriously, pretending we are lost in thought over weighty problems. At Wal-Mart, if you have some important business problem on your mind, you should be bringing it out in the open, so we can all try to solve it together. But while we're doing all this work we like to have a good time. It's sort of a "whistle while you work" philosophy, and we not only have a heck of a good time with it, we work better because of it.

From the very start we would get all our managers together once a week and critique ourselves — that was really our buying organisation, a bunch of store managers getting together early Saturday morning, may be in Bentonville, or maybe in some motel room somewhere. We would review what we had bought and see how many dollars we had committed to it. We would plan promotions and plan the items we intended to buy.

And it worked so well that over the years, as we grew and built the company, it just became part of our culture. I guess that was the forerunner of our Saturday morning meetings (where company managers get together and review what they've seen in the stores that week). When we made a bad mistake — whether it was myself or anybody else — we talked about it, admitted it, tried to figure out how to correct it, and then moved on to the next day's work.

2. *Sam Walton : Made in America,* written with John Huey, reviewed in Fortune, 29.6.1972, pp. 69-72.

In the beginning, I was so chintzy I really didn't pay my employees very well. The managers were fine. From the time we started branching out into more stores, we always had a partnership with the store managers. Those guys all had a piece of their stores' profits from the beginning.

Back then, though, I was so obsessed with turning in a profit margin of 6% or higher that I ignored some of the basic needs of our people, and I feel bad about it. The larger truth that I failed to see turned out to be another of those paradoxes — like the discounters' principle of the less you charge, the more you'll earn. And here it is: The more you share profits with your associates — whether it's in stock discounts — the more profit will acrrue to the company. Why? Because the way management treats the associates is exactly how the associates will then treat the customers. Satisfied, loyal, repeat customers are the heart of Wal-Mart's spectacular profit margins, and those customers are loyal to us because our associates treat them better than salespeople in other stores do.

In 1971, we took our first big step: We corrected my big error of the year before (when a profit-sharing scheme was offered to management employees only) and started a profit-sharing plan for all the associates. I guess it's the move we made that I'm proudest of, for a number of reasons. Profit sharing has pretty much been the carrot that's kept Wal-Mart headed forward.

Another important ingredient that has been in the Wal-Mart partnership from the very beginning has been our very unusual willingness to share most of the numbers, of our business with all the associates. It's the only way they can possibly do their jobs to the best of their abilities — to know what's going on in their business. If I was a little slow to pick up on sharing the profits, we were among the first in our industry — and are still way out front of almost everybody — with the idea of empowering our associates by running the business practically as an open book.

Everything about us gets to the outside. In our individual stores, we show them their store's profit, their store's purchases, their store's sales, and their store's markdowns. We show them all that on a regular basis, I'm not talking about just the managers and the assistant managers. We share that information with every associate, every hourly, every part-time employee in the stores. Obviously, some of that information flows to the street. But I just believe the value of sharing it with our associates is much greater than any downside there may be to sharing it with folks on the outside. It doesn't seem to have hurt us much so far.

Here's the point: The bigger Wal-Mart gets, the more essential it is that we think small. Because that's exactly how we have become a huge corporation — by not acting like one. Above all, we are small-town merchants. For several decades now we've worked hard at building a company that's simple and streamlined and takes its directions from the grass roots.

A Few Abiding Principles

For my whole career in retail, I have stuck by one guiding principle: The secret of successful retailing is to give your customers what they want. And really, if you think about it from your point of view as a customer, you want everything: a wide assortment of good quality merchandise; the lowest possible prices; guaranteed satisfaction with what you buy: friendly knowledgeable service; convenient hours; free parking; a pleasant shopping experience.

Here are six of the more important ways we at Wal-Mart try to think small:

Think one store at a time: That sounds easy enough, but it's something we've constantly had to stay on top of.

Communicate, communicate, communicate: If you had to boil down the Wal-Mart system to one single idea, it would probably be communication because it is one of the real keys to our success. What good is figuring out a better way to sell beach towels if you aren't going to tell everybody in your company about it?

Keep your ear to the ground: A computer is not — and will never be — a substitute for getting out in your stores and learning what's going on. In other words, a computer can tell you down to the dime what you've sold. But it can never tell you how much you could have sold. That's why we at Wal-Mart are just absolute fanatics about our managers and buyers getting out of their chairs here in Bentonville and getting out into those stores. We have 3 airplanes — only one of them a jet, I'm proud to say — and that's why they're there. We stay in the air to keep our ear to the ground.

Push responsibility — and authority — down: The bigger we get as a company, the more important it becomes to shift responsibility and authority towards the front lines, toward that department manager who's stocking the shelves and talking to the customer

Force ideas to bubble up: This goes hand-in-hand with pushing responsibility down We're always looking for new ways to encourage our associates out in the stores to push their ideas up through the system. We do a lot of this at Saturday morning meetings. We invite associates who have thought up something that's really worked well for their store — a particular item or a particular display — to come share those ideas with us.

Stay lean, fight bureaucracy: Any time a company grows as fast as Wal-Mart has, pockets of duplication are going to build up, and there will be areas of the business that we may no longer need. No boss or employee really likes to dwell on such matters. It's only human nature not to want to have your job, or the jobs of the people who work for you,' eliminated. But it is absolutely the responsibility of a company's top management to be thinking about this issue all the time — to ensure a sound future for the overall company.

A lot of first-time visitors are kind of shocked by our executive offices. Most people say my office, and those of all the other Wal-Mart executives, look like something you'd find in a truck terminal. Were in a one-storey office-warehouse building. The offices aren't real big, and the walls are covered with inexpensive panelling. We-never had fancy furniture or thick carpets, or suites with bars for our executives. I like them just as they are. We sure as heck won't win any interior decorating awards, but they're all we need, and they must be working fine. Just ask our shareholders.

I guess one reason I feel so strongly about not letting egos get out of control around Wal-Mart is that a lot of bureaucracy is really the product of some empire builder's ego. Some folks have a tendency to build up big staff around them to emphasise their own importance, and we don't need any of that at Wal-Mart. If you're not serving the customer or supporting the folks who do, we don't need you. When we're thinking small, that's another thing we're always on the lookout for: big egos. You don't have to have a small ego to work here, but you'd better know how to make it look small, or you might wind up in trouble.

So you see what I mean when I say you have to think small to grow big.

The Beauty of Competition

Competition is actually the reason I love retailing so much. The Wal-Mart story is just another chapter in the history of competition — a great chapter, mind you, but it's all part of evolution of the industry. There are ways of a challenger coming along.

Right now, I see a lot of new challengers coming from offshore with some very sophisticated programmes. Some of the emerging competition in this country who have come from Holland, Germany, and France are close watching. And it won't be long before we have a wave of Japanese retail concepts arriving. I don't know if Wal-Mart can truly maintain a leadership position by just staying in this country. I think we're going to have to become a more international company in the not-too-distant future. We've created an international division in the company, and we have a joint venture with a Mexican company called Cifra for the development of Club Aurera, a whole club concept.

And really, I don't have any desire that Wal-Mart will stay the course and reach $ 100 billion in sales before the year 2000.

There are lessons in what's happened at Wal-Mart that go beyond retail and apply to many other businesses. Recently, I don't think there's any doubt that a lot of American management has bent over too far towards taking care of itself first and worrying about everybody else later.

The Japanese are right on this point: You can't create a team spirit when the situation is so one-sided, when management gets so much and workers get so little of the pie. It's obvious that most companies would be much better served by basing managers' pay on the performance of the company or return on investment to the shareholders or some yardstick that clearly takes into account how well they're doing their job. And the formula has to make sure that profits are divided fairly among workers, management, and stockholders, according to their contribution and risks.

At Wal-Mart, we've always paid our executives less than industry standards, sometimes maybe too much less. But we've always rewarded them with stock bonuses and other incentives related directly to the performance of the company.

In the global economy, successful business is going to do just what Wal-Mart is always trying to do: give more and more responsibility for making decisions to the people who are actually on the firing line, those who deal with the customers every day. Good management is going to start listening to the ideas of these line soldiers, pooling these ideas and disseminating them around their organisations so that people can act on them. That's the way the successful companies out there already are doing it, the 3Ms, the Hewlett-Packards, the Wal-Marts. Great ideas come from everywhere if you just listen and look for them.

We can turn the whole world around just the way we've done it in retail. We can do it better than the Japanese because were more innovative, we're more creative. We can compete with labour in Bangladesh or wherever because we have better technology, which can give us more efficient equipment. We can get beyond a lot of our old adversarial relationships and establish win-win partnerships with our suppliers and our workers, which will leave us with more energy and talent to focus on the important thing: meeting the needs of our customers. But all this requires overcoming one of the most powerful forces in human nature: the resistance to change. To succeed in this world, you have to change all the time.

When you look at what's happened to the American auto industry, it's tempting to want to treat the Japanese unfairly — the way they treat with their protectionist laws. But I don't think we should counter with protectionism because it doesn't address the real problem: The quality of our product doesn't compete with that of the Japanese. The challenge is a great one for management. What they have to do is build a partnership with their people.

But if American management is going to say to their workers that we're all in this together, they're going to have to stop this foolishness of paying themselves \$3 million and \$ 4 million bonuses every year and riding around everywhere in limos and corporate jets like they're so much better than everybody else.

I'm not saying every company should necessarily be as chintzy as Wal-Mart. Everybody's not in the discount business, consumed by trying to save every possible dollar for their customers. But I wonder if a lot of these companies wouldn't do just as well if their executives lived a little more like real folks. A lot of people think it's crazy of me to fly coach whenever I go on a commercial flight, and may be I do overdo it a little bit. But I feel like it's up to me as a leader to set an example. It's not fair for me to ride one way and ask everybody else to ride another way. The minute you do that, you start building resentment and your whole team idea begins to strain at the seams.

Finally, a lot of folks ask me two related questions all the time. The first one is, could a Wal-Mart type story still occur in this day and age? My answer is of course it could happen again. Somewhere out there right now there's someone — probably hundreds of thousands of someones — with enough good ideas to go all the way. It's all a matter of attitude and the capacity to constantly study and question the management of the business.

The second question is, if I were a young man or woman starting out today with the same sort of talents and energies and aspirations that I had 50 years ago, what would I do? The answer to that is a little harder to figure out. I don't know exactly what I would do today, but I feel pretty sure I would be selling something, and I expect it would be at the retail level, where I could relate directly to the customers off the street. Probably, some kind of speciality maybe, or something like the Gap — even the Body Shop.

Anyway, the next time some overeager, slightly eccentric shopkeeper opens up a business in your neck of the woods, before you write him off too quickly, remember that two old codgers once gave me 60 days to last in my dime store down in Fayetteville. Go, check the new store out. See what they've got to offer, see how they treat you, and decide for yourself if you ever want to go back. Because this is what it's really all about. In this free country of ours, that shopkeeper's success is entirely up to you: the customer.

5. MATSUSHITA PHILOSOPHY OF AUTONOMOUS MANAGEMENT

Japanese Dream

Konosuke Matsushita (1894 - 1989), the founder of the Matsushita Electrical Industries in 1918, with his wife and brother-in-law in Japan, is hailed as the father of the modern industrial philosophy, which has propelled not only Matsushita Electric to No. 1 position in consumer electronics, but also Japan Inc. into its prominent position in the world Mr. Matsushita was an original and thought, expressed and achieved in an original fashion. The story of how he arrived at the unique Japanese industrial philosophy is told in many books, articles etc. but bears repetition one more time here. After the devastation of Japan in the Second World War and his company was taken on by the Occupation Army, Matsushita, walking in Osaka, came upon a poor beggar filling his stomach at the public tap, since he did not have any money to buy even a bowl of rice. This apparently ordinary event led to an extraordinary train of thought in the mind of Matsushita. He said to himself that this is a very interesting phenomenon, something to be learned from the simple event. This water, though free to the beggar and the public, costs money to the Government to store, to clean, to transport through pipelines to all places in Japan. The quality of water is good, and is made available to the citizens at very cheap price and free to the public at the public taps, so that even a beggar is not afraid to walk up to the tap and drink water to fill his stomach, since it is free to him. Matsushita said that Japanese business could learn from this example and if Japan wants to develop its industry and business, they must produce goods of good quality at very reasonable prices, so reasonable that the customers not only in Japan, but all over the world would not have to think twice to buy Japanese goods. Good quality, reasonable prices, much lower than competitors', and an abundant production and supply to the market are the key to Japanese business resurgence, from the demolition of the Second World War. Mind you, this was at a time, when Japanese goods meant copy cats, imitation goods of very poor quality and quality means that it must be from Germany, UK, USA, Holland, Switzerland, France, etc.

To the eternal credit of Matsushita, he transported his dream and philosophy to the world through his Matsushita Electric in just 25 years, which was emulated by the other Japanese companies soon to become household names not only in Japan but all over the world.

His simple philosophy stated the central role of people and he declared: "We make men, before we make products." He was evangelical in his sublime faith in his people and their potential and abilities. He took great legendary interest in developing all his people. Though he had to drop out of school at the age of nine to support his family by working as an apprentice, he had great respect for knowledge and educated himself and sought to share his knowledge, experience and experiments through his morning briefing meetings with all his employees. He would address the meetings himself everyday, sharing his views on various matters of concern to his employees and the company. He was quite far sighted and had two of his secretaries to take down the notes of his talks, which he would correct himself and approve one version! Now the PHP Institute has bought out 45 volumes based on his talks at the morning meetings, which are a treasure trove of not only his thinking but also Japanese management philosophy, principles, practices.

PRINCIPLES

In developing his people and business around the world, he preached and practiced three principles (1) Omoyari — concern for others; (2) Shuchi — collective wisdom of all employees; and (3) Sunao mind — an open mind, receptive to all new ideas, concepts and technologies. Through his philosophy, he was not only interested in the expansion but also in world peace, happiness and prosperity. To achieve the latter, he founded the PHP Institute, standing for peace and happiness through prosperity. In April 1987, at the age of 93, Konosuke Matsushita wrote in a PHP publication about:

For a Better Tomorrow

"A noted political scientist once remarked that all realistic political philosophers are premised on the notion that man is inherently evil. Machiavelli's The Prince, of course. is the example *par excellence,* but there are many others. Plato's idea of the 'philosopher king.' As developed in the Republic, and the Confucian ideal of the government by the sages both being expressly elitist, assume at the very least the people's inability to govern themselves.

Such thinkers may be brilliant, but they are wrong. Man is not evil by nature, nor is he foolish. People are weak at times and fail to follow their conscience, and too often they are lured by malignant temptations, but there are few whose heart is not basically good and few who cannot follow the dictates of reason to control harmful desires.

It is true that human history can be read as chronicle of one tragedy after another — wars, atrocities, persecution, starvation, and more. But man has also continued to grow and progress, both materially and spiritually. Science and technology have given us the leeway to grow in creativity. And through the ages the great religions have helped more and more people attain peace of mind. Or think of how greatly literary and artistic masterpieces enrich our lives, and how much philosophers and thinkers have done to help us understand ourselves.

I believe that man is a free agent responsible for his own destiny. He has a choice: he can either become one with the God of love and goodness or sell his soul to Satan, the lord of evil. One leads to peace and happiness, while the other draws us toward chaos and self-destruction. Individually, most of us find ourselves wandering somewhere between the two; in the same way, the human race as a whole now seems to stand at a crossroads between heaven and hell.

The threat of nuclear war casts a pall over the world, while military tensions, political disputes, economic friction, and North-South disparities continue to tear away at the stability in international relations. Internally, nations are constantly fighting unemployment, inflation, social or political unrest, starvation, poverty, crime, pollution, or all of these. It is appalling to realise how close to the edge of disaster we are. No one can say what is going to happen to our world, even before the arrival of the third millennium. The very survival of mankind is now in the balance.

At this critical juncture in the history of our civilisation, we need to get back our confidence in the essential rightness of human wisdom. We must reassure ourselves that we have the capacity to bring our material and intellectual resources to bear on finding solutions to the problems confronting our world. It is always easier to rally our forces in the face of a crisis, but we must not let the sense of crisis overwhelm us with unnecessary pessimism, for that leads to despair and immobility. Let us never lose hope for the future. Let us believe that the popular will ultimately govern the course of human affairs, and that because it is essentially good, the will of the people will prevail and lead the world into a new and better era.

Wishful thinking is useless, and platitudes about peace are mere verbiage. What we need is action derived from concerned optimism and collective wisdom if we are to bequeath a happy, peaceful world to our children and grandchildren in the twenty-first century. It was this belief that led me to establish PHP Institute more than forty years ago. I am all too aware of the long road still ahead, but also know that there are many individuals and groups around the world who share our ideals and are working toward similar goals. I hope the day will some day come when we can join hands with those people in a concerted effort to build a new world of peace, happiness, and prosperity.

How he practised his concept of collective wisdom — Shuchi — in solving tough business problems is explained by Mr. Morimasa Ogawa, the President of Matsushita Electric, North America in his book:[3]

"Five years after the subsidiary had been established, I am ashamed to admit that the new company was not succeeding. The first oil crisis had just occurred. The oil-producing countries had united and increased the price of oil. The civilisation built on cheap oil was shaken to its core, and there were rumours that Japan's oil supplies might be cut-off. Since a large part of our sales was of equipment that ran on oil and propane gas, we were more than a little worried. The company had been at a high break-even point and reduced sales would mean a severe deficit.

At this time, I was the Managing Director. One day, Konosuke Matsushita dropped in for a visit. It has been a long time since he'd been there and he wanted to talk to us. It wasn't the best time for him to come, but there was nothing I could do about it.

First he visited the factory and was very pleased, looking with amazement at the huge boilers being manufactured. It was later, when we sat down to talk, that the roof caved in. I will never forget that conversation with Matsushita.

3. Morimasa Ogawa, Pana Management Kyoto, PHP Institute, Inc. 1991. pp. 134-137.

"The factory and the merchandise look great," he said. "How are operations?" Nervously, I answered, "Not very good. Sales have dropped because of the oil crisis."

"Not very good? What do you mean?"

"We're running at a bit of a loss," I fumbled.

"By how much?" "Nine billion."

"What? I could understand if sales were zero and the deficit was in personnel costs, but you've got sales of ¥100 billion and are ¥9 billion in the red. You mean to tell me we've got a company like this in the Matsushita Group? Responsibility for running a mess like this lies with you and the executives under you. The head office must also take responsibility for letting this go. It's all because the head office lent you that ¥20 billion.

Tomorrow, I'm going to talk to them about getting it back. That's all, Ogawa. Whip this thing back into shape!"

For the moment I was speechless, but then I ran after him. "Mr. Matsushita, that would mean disaster for us! It's five days to payday. At the end of the month we have to pay for materials and parts. If you take that ¥20 billion back now, we won't be able to pay for them."

"That's right," he remarked. "You won't be able to pay the wages and the subcontractors' fees. You have to pay the cafeteria cooks, too. But I'm not going to lend you any money if you and your colleagues are going to run an operation like this. I'm pulling your loan tomorrow."

"But then we won't be able to do anything. We'll go bankrupt."

"What are you talking about ? You've got 4.000 superb employees working here. Talk it over with them, get their ideas, and come up with a reconstruction plan that will work. I know you have confidence in this company, but confidence isn't enough. You have to come up with a plan that a banker would approve of, one that would make him think, 'This looks like a good operation. If we lend it money, we're sure to get it back. If you can get a plan like that together, I'll write a letter of recommendation to Sumitomo Bank for you. With that letter, they're sure to give you a ¥20 billion loan using the land, buildings, and equipment here as collateral. Now, get to work."

We had gone to the head office for that ¥20 billion loan to cover operating expenses because business had been sluggish, our internal reserves low and our dependence on seasonal products high. The rules of the division system required that we pay interest on the loan comparable to what we would pay to a bank. We often extort interest and even make a profit off a subsidiary struggling under a heavy financial burden. Five years before, Matsushita had impressed me as a compassionate person when he apologised to the chef for not eating all his food, but now he appeared more like a ruthless demon.

I didn't have time to get absorbed in my emotions, however. Matsushita called all the managers and executives together and reprimanded us sharply: "You 're working under the Matsushita name, but this is no Matsushita company. If you can't rebuild this company, it will collapse and everyone will have to be laid off. If that happens, you managers have to find jobs for each one of our employees and then figure out what to do about yourselves." He went on with the usual advice we'd heard a thousand times. "If each of the sections of each department can show just a little profit in its accounting, the company as a whole, will get back on its feet. Get down to the section level and make sure you bring together the wisdom of each and every employee. Tell the sales departments in every division to research products that will bring a 50% increase in sales in the next three years. Have R & D devote themselves to achieving that goal. If the goods don't sell, have everyone get out and sell them. Take the 10% excess staff and equipment and find a project for them to work on. Take 1% of sales and invest it in new activity. Uncover the buried losses and turn them into a 2% profit. We can turn this company around and make it into a winner. The wisdom and knowledge to do this can be found in the workplace."

There was nothing unusual in what he told us, but putting it into practice was not going to be easy. The ideas everyone came up with, however, far exceeded my expectations. That year we still ran a big deficit, but when I retired five-years later, the company was in good shape, one that could call itself a Matsushita subsidiary.

It wasn't me that got that company back on track. It was the result of all the knowledge and ideas of the employees pooled together. I realised that the source of it all lay in the rigor of Konosuke Matsushita's attitude towards work. It was he who shattered our belief that the source of the trouble was outside the company, and who drove us to do better.

It is important that managers, from the moment they embark on their leadership careers, cultivate both a compassion for others and an attitude of discipline in the workplace. If you are strict with your people and lax in your own attitude toward work, the results will be disastrous.

Mr. Matsushita was a highly pragmatic and tough leader with a highly humanistic philosophy of business, which is explained at the Third Panasonic Australia Management Policy Meeting in April/May 1990 by Mr. Toru Yamaguchi, Executive Director & Member of the Board of PHP Institute and Dr. Robert J. J. Wargo, Executive Director and Member of the Board of PHP Institute:[4]

PHP — Peace and Happiness through Prosperity

"Mr. Matsushita founded PHP Institute 44 years ago on 3 November 1946. As you all know, Japan surrendered in August 1945, thus, ending the Second World War. The defeat brought unimaginable difficulties for the Japanese people. No one had enough to eat. Many homes had been destroyed by bombing. Many streets of the cities were filled with homeless people. There was a great deal of spiritual and psychological confusion in the war's aftermath.

"Konosuke Matsushita's life too had undergone a great change. The Matsushita Electric business that he had carefully built up for 27 years faced its greatest crisis. The occupation placed a larger number of restrictions on business operations, and Mr. Matsushita confronted a series of disappointments as he wondered how he could keep the company together and how he could protect the livelihood of his employees.

What Mr. Matsushita was thinking at that time can be gleaned from his comments to me when he was working on an article that a magazine had asked him to write seven or eight years ago. "When I think about it now those certainly were tough times. But I looked around me and thought of all those people, there were so many, who had died in the war or had lost their families, and I felt that compared to them I was pretty lucky... I was still alive. I felt that if I just keep working, we'd pull through, and maybe for that reason I didn't think that things were really that bad." All Japan was devastated but Mr. Matsushita was bothered by one simple important question.

"People always want peace and happiness but they are always fighting with each other, hurting each other, always suffering the pains of unhappiness and poverty. Is this man's basic nature? If it is, then what is the material and spiritual progress that humankind has made since it came out of the caves?"

Mr. Matsushita was 50 at the time and all his experience in business had been based on his experience in life, a continuous process of asking questions and searching for answers. It was his conclusion that "man is endowed with the essential nature for creating unlimited prosperity, peace and happiness."

But the question still remained : "Why do people fight and hurt each other and why do they languish in poverty?" That's why Mr. Matsushita came up with the idea of meeting together with others, getting their ideas on these questions, and giving his own ideas so that they could thrash them out. Thus, PHP Institute was set up just 14 months after the end of the war. He told me many times. "If it hadn't been for the great confusion that existed after the war, PHP Institute might never even have been thought of."

Spiritual Prosperity

PHP stands for peace and happiness through prosperity. But prosperity here does not just mean material prosperity, having a lot of goods. It includes a prosperity of the mind, spiritual abundance. It is the prosperity of the tangible and the intangible, where someone is wealthy both materially and spiritually. The realisation of that prosperity will bring true peace and happiness.

4. Toru Yamaguchi, PHP, Peace and Happiness through Prosperity, and Dr. Robert J.J. Wargo, Humanistic Management Australian PHP Seminar, April/May 1990, Panasonic Australia Pvt. Ltd. North Ryde NSW.

But how does one achieve prosperity in both mind and body? Answering that question is one of the main missions of PHP Institute, and Konosuke Matsushita, at the same time that he was busy with the demands of business, was a driving force of the institute.

In a study group, Mr. Matsushita would begin by getting people to think about the very core, the very essence of an idea. Then, he would take into consideration how prosperity was to be obtained in any number of areas, management, of course, the economy, politics and government, foreign policy, education, society, all the fields in which human beings live and work together in Japan and in the world as a whole. The results of all those meetings are contained in more than 40 books and hundreds of articles. But running through every one of them is a single thread, Mr. Matsushita's faith in what he termed SHUCHI or collective wisdom. It was his hope and conviction that "the wisdom of everyone can be brought together to provide an understanding of the very essence of humanity, to realise a true prosperity which is balanced in the material and the spiritual, to build a peaceful and happy society, and to make this world a better place to live."

Konosuke Matsushita and two other people started Matsushita Electric in 1918. That has now grown into an international corporation with 2,00,000 employees. What is the secret of that success?

Fortunately, 20 years ago Konosuke Matsushita took the trouble to analyse his success in management and isolated the following relevant factors:

1. He had good staff
2. His policies were clear
3. He upheld an ideal to which we strive
4. His chosen field of electrical appliances was appropriate of the time
5. He did not allow factions to form within his company
6. He followed a policy of open management
7. He worked towards a system of management by all employees
8. He regarded the company as a public institution

Using this analysis as a basic framework, I would like to concentrate on a discussion of five crucial points relating to the success in enterprise management and enterprise development.

The most important requirement for good management is to clarify the management philosophy, goals, and ideals of the company. The manager of a company must be clear in his own mind about what the purpose of his company is, what its ideals are, how he intends to conduct business, and what concrete goals he should establish for it in the ensuing years. Sound business development is dependent on having such a well-thought-out management plan, for without such a plan one cannot use personnel, technology and capital to their full potential.

Enriching Lives

After many years of working by his own common sense. Mr. Matsushita came to realise the higher goal for manufacturing. He thought man can be happy only when he has both spiritual and material wealth. Neither one by itself brings happiness to man. Religion aims at the spiritual enrichment of man, but what about business?

Even though business strives to create the material goods and wealth indispensable to human life, it is not accorded as much respect as religious activity. Yet this is strange, for while religion promotes the happiness of man. It is business that provides the material goods that maintain human life and as such it too is indispensable for human happiness. Doesn't that make it a noble activity also?

Business is in fact a very noble activity because it brings pleasure and happiness to people. And if business people would think about their profession in this light, it would give new meaning to their work and strengthen their sense of worth. Thus, Konosuke Matsushita came to the conclusion that the mission of an industrialist is to remove poverty from this world by manufacturing as many quality products as possible to make everyone's life prosperous.

Since that time, Mr. Matsushita had made this mission the basic policy of his company's management and has constantly emphasised its importance to his employees. His employees were influenced by this philosophy and in turn found a sense of mission and meaning in their jobs.

In other words, you might say that a soul had been put into the company's management giving it renewed strength and leading to vigorous development. Mr. Matsushita not only established a clear overall management philosophy and proclaimed the concept that enterprise management is noble work, on the operational level he also established specific goals for the corporation at regular intervals or when the business climate made this necessary. This attention to specific goals is one of the indispensable keys to success in management.

Setting Goals

He carefully but boldly presented concrete goals to all his employees, covering such diverse areas as individual work objectives for the next month, specific company objectives for the next one, five, and 10-year periods, sales volume goals and so on.

In 1956, Mr. Matsushita made an announcement to his employees that he would like his company's sales to reach 80 billion yen in five years. This announcement surprised not only the public, but also the employees of Matsushita Electric, because its sales at that time were only a little more than 20 billion yen and it seemed almost impossible to quadruple that figure in five years. Yet the goal was achieved, in four years the sales amounted to more than 80 billion yen, and they climbed to more than 100 billion by the end of the fifth year.

The speech which Mr. Matsushita addressed to all the employees in 1960, had still greater impact on them. At that time he announced that he would adopt a five-day work week, five years later in 1965. The employees welcomed this idea but at the same time felt uneasy about it. No other Japanese company at that time had adopted this system, and they suspected that the five-day work week would simply mean more work in the long run since sales targets would not be lowered. Matsushita's union opposed the president's proposal at first because they did not know what it implied and felt that it might merely be a fine sounding device to exploit them. What happened? The five-day work week was initiated in 1965, as planned and was a roaring success. Because of the diligence, co-operation, and ingenuity of the employees, the new system operated smoothly, with no intensification of labour. Yet, at the same time there was an actual increase in sales. By adopting the system, all came to enjoy a more comfortable, prosperous life.

Thus, Mr. Matsushita had been constantly presentind concrete goals to his employees. Why is this so important? Because employees who are given definite goals will clearly understand what they should concentrate their talents on. They know what is expected and the standards by which they will be measured. Nothing is more frustrating for a person than not to have their efforts properly evaluated. The way to motivate employees to work hard is to present them with a definite goal and indicate precisely where their efforts should be directed.

Good management requires something more: a vision or ideal of what the company is and should be. In addition to a short-term view of the company, it is important for a good manager to have a well-defined long range goals for the company: what it should be like in the distant future; what contributions it should make to society; what is its ultimate role? In other words, the manager must have a vision of what the company should be 100 or even 200 years hence.

When Mr. Matsushita established his basic management philosophy, he also had a vision which seemed too great for an enterprise with only about 1,000 employees. He exhorted his employees to help him transform Japan into a paradise on earth. He did this because he knew that a human being must have an ideal to live by if he is to achieve self-satisfaction, for only when he has an ideal will he strive to improve himself and develop his potential to the full. Without an ideal to guide him, man is apt to dissipate his energies and go bad.

Sharing Visions

It is just as important for a company to have an ideal. When an enterprise has an ideal which commands respect and is accepted by all, each employee tries to improve himself and bring his talents into full play. Mr. Matsushita always tried to give his employees something to work and live for by sharing with them his vision for the company.

Thus, we can see that all three, a management philosophy, a goal, and an ideal or vision, are the indispensable factors for success in enterprise management. All three things must work together to make a positive contribution to the happiness of mankind as well as the peace and prosperity of society. If these ideas are perverted to serve selfish ends, oppose justice and truth, damage the happiness of human beings, and destroy the peace and prosperity of society, the company will quickly be faced with ruin and its manager chastised.

The next key to success is to think of an enterprise as a public institution. In a capitalist society, organisations financed by national or local government are generally referred to as 'public' companies, as opposed to those non-official or 'private' firms that are not government owned. In terms of the origin of the funding, both individual owned small businesses and corporations with many stockholders are regarded as private enterprises.

Yet even though they are private enterprises in the formal legal sense, they all should be considered to be essentially public since the *raison d'etre* for any enterprise is the contribution it makes to improve the life of the community.

The land and facilities that a company owns or leases as well as the "people, materials and monies' which are indispensable to its operations can be said to belong formally or legally to the private enterprise in some sense, but they can equally well be regarded as ultimately belonging to the nation and its people in common. It is only for the sake of convenience and in order to make management more effective and efficient that private enterprise is permitted to possess them and use them for its operations.

Because Mr. Matsushita thought of the corporation as an instrument for public service, he could manage its operations with increased confidence. As Matsushita employees also came to think of the company as a public enterprise whose purpose was to serve the public, they began to regard their work as a mission.

Open Book

The third key to success is open management. Soon after Mr. Matsushita started his own business, when his company was still an individually managed, small company with only about 10 employees, he separated the company accounts from the family accounts. He gave full accounts of the balance sheet to the employees every month to keep them apprised of monthly sales and profits.

Since at the time his company was under private management with no stockholders to answer to, he was not required to open his books to the public. Yet, he spontaneously decided to make the figures known to all his employees. When they heard the report about the amount of profit at the end of the month, they thought to themselves, "That's good, I'll work even harder next month to better the record." The employee finds pleasure, self-satisfaction and purpose in working for his company, and he comes to have enthusiasm which prompts him to work harder.

A system of open management does not give the manager any opportunity to do something dishonest with impunity, for he cannot hide his deeds. Therefore it serves as a self-control mechanism for managers who are, after all human. Any manager can do something dishonest if he has a mind to. However morally upright a manager may be, he may unconsciously mix public and private matters, and when he does not he will have done something improper. Whether done unconsciously or deliberately, the result is the same and the employees will never be able to forgive or respect such a manager.

Confidence between him and his employees will be lost and unless restored, the company will eventually be brought to ruin.

The reason Matsushita Electric has made such remarkable progress and that Konosuke Matsushita was so highly respected by all his employees today is that he had been hard on himself and most careful to avoid even the faintest hint of managerial misconduct. Such a dedicated and morally upright attitude on the part of a manager sends a persuasive message to his employees: they too must be careful to act properly at all times.

Mr. Matsushita himself pointed out 20 years ago that having a good staff was one of the factors of Matsushita Electric's success. I think that we can say that through his practice of open management, he trained his employees to be a good staff.

It was not simply a matter of the company hiring a good staff to begin with.

Collective Wisdom

The fourth key point to success in management is SHUCHI. SHUCHI means 'wisdom of many people' or 'collective wisdom'. It is very important for corporate management to be based on the collective wisdom of all its employees.

There are many distinguished managers who always think things out for and by themselves, decide by themselves, and act by themselves. They may be dramatically successful for a while, but in the long-term view such dictatorial managers find difficulty in being truly successful at management.

A dictatorial manager simply does not feel the need for talented employees with decision-making skills, and so good human resources do not gather about him. Moreover, he will not take the time or trouble to develop the talents of any employees who do happen to be under him. He wants people to simply follow his orders, nothing more.

No matter how much education and knowledge a manager may have or however great his ability may be, he is still only a single individual whose wisdom has very finite bounds. If he judges things solely in terms of his limited perception and knowledge, he will never understand the realities of the problems facing him or the true nature of management. If the knowledge and insight collected from many people is synthesised into a whole to create a body of collective wisdom, the company will certainly prosper and develop.

In managing his company, Konosuke Matsushita always considered it most important to lisen to as many people as possible before making decisions. He, thus, put this principle of management based on SHUCHI into actual practice on a daily basis.

To collect wisdom does not mean, however, to manage a company by majority rule. It is not enough to gather many people together and let them voice their opinions. People should offer their best judgements without regard to their own interest and feelings; they must strive to understand what is correct and work towards a reasonable solution through serious discussion. SHUCHI is produced only through such a process of cooperative striving for objectivity.

To collect wisdom by consulting with one's employees is a good way to increase employee morale and motivation. People always feel happy when they are given an opportunity to express their opinions to others and they feel even more pleased and proud when it is a manager or supervisor who is soliciting their opinion. Employees will actively suggest improvements in company operations to a manager who demands collective wisdom. Such active participation brings about "management by all". The fruits of such management are better products, better service, greater acceptance by customers and ultimately, a healthier pattern growth for the company.

Adaptable Mind

The fifth key point to enterprise development is for a manager himself to try his best to have a SUNAO mind.

SUNAO in Japanese is generally considered to be a term that implies meekness or tractability, and is generally used to describe a person who is obedient, listens to whatever others say, and acts as he is told regardless of whether it is good or bad. Obedience to the will of a superior is certainly one thing we mean by the term but it by no means exhausts the meaning of the term as PHP uses it. The SUNAO mind, as we at PHP understand it, has very definite positive qualities as well, applicable equally to managers and subordinates.

A SUNAO mind is serene without being vacuous. What is meant is that a SUNAO mind is unflappable and supremely adaptable. It is a mind that enables you to see things as they actually are without clinging to preconceived notions. The SUNAO mind engenders the ability to understand the reality of things, because it requires that your deliberations fit the facts to accord with a pre-established pattern of thinking. Managers who lack the SUNAO mind are often swayed by their own interests when they act or make a decision. This cannot be tolerated, for such behaviour will inevitably lead to corporate failures. A manager cannot function as a manager unless he can assess data calmly and make sucessful projections.

Since managers, like all human beings, have prejudices and preconceived ideas and tend to adhere to one way of thinking out of habit, it is all the more necessary, for them to cultivate a SUNAO mind, so they can judge situations accurately and discern the path to success for their companies.

A manager has only two choices: to manage his company on the basis of personal interests and as a result lead his company into bankruptcy, or to cultivate a SUNAO mind to ensure successful management and healthy growth for his company.

These then are the five key points to success in enterprise management.

1. To have a clear management philosophy, clear goals, and a definite ideal
2. To manage a company with the full realisation that every enterprise is a public enterprise
3. To practice 'open management'
4. To collect the wisdom of many
5. Try to acquire a SUNAO mind

HUMANISTIC MANAGEMENT

Konosuke Matsushita was, without doubt, one of the most successful entrepreneurs and most admired managers of the 20th century. Yet it seems that one of the most important factors contributing to his success was an almost total lack of self-confidence. Now that sounds absurd but he had no education to speak of, he had little schooling, no money and no family to rely on. His genius was to take those defects and turn them into assets.

He realised that by himself he could not do everything. He didn't think of himself as a genius. Because he needed help he was willing to listen. That's the basis of Matsushita's whole philosophy. His willingness to listen is the core of "management by all".

Mr. Matsushita was a man who always tried to boil things down to their essence. He wasn't going to get entangled in detail. But he also wouldn't let go until he had gotten to the essence of things.

If you were in business you had an obligation to society if only because if it weren't for that society, you would not have the trained people to use. There would not be the infrastructure that allows you to make your sales and extend your business.

As a company you have to contribute to that society. If you produce good quality products and if you're concerned not only for yourself but for your customers and you have a higher goal, you will certainly be rewarded through profits.

Rational humanistic management is what we're talking about. If your management is not rational, you're going to fail. You have to have an accounting system, a hierarchy, all the paraphernalia concerned with staying alive in business, that is making a profit. Rationality is getting people to work together, pooling their resources efficiently.

But to be really efficient, a company must also have a humanistic orientation. Companies are people. They are not infrastructures. If you don't have people who know how to use machinery, investment in infrastructure is just wasted. It will go to rust, unless people work together to make the best use of it. Matsushita believed you should make full use of everything including people. That's precisely why he insisted that you can't treat people simply as if they were machines or pieces of equipment.

Every human being has the capacity to think, be creative and be a manager, no matter what his or her position in the company. That's the point about management by all, that's the point about collective wisdom.

People are beings, robots are not. You can't have collective wisdom unless you have human beings. Robots don't give it to you. They'll do what they're told. Machines may be able to apply 450 tonnes of pressure to form complex shapes, but they need human beings to arrange them into efficient instruments of production. Human beings are not tools, but tool users. That is the core of the humanistic standpoint.

Developing Potential

Overall, the plan is geared to getting the best out of each human being and to make sure that each human being has the chance, too, to expand his or her own potential, the more value you are to the company and to yourself. The more the company thinks in terms of developing co-operation among you, the more successful it can be, the more it can really implement Matsushita's goal, namely, eventually to make products as cheap as water.

What makes Matsushita any different from a lot of other successful companies? It is not "Japanese management." I don't believe there is such a thing. There's good management, there is bad management. Matsushita's general principles generate a very good management style. These management principles are not designed simply to make money. There is much more at stake than that. Matsushita believed that to make management effective and humanistic, you really had to go back to the essence — what is a human being, what is the nature of business, what does profit mean?

Everyone has to be responsible for their own 'store', everyone must have a profit-loss (P/L) type accountability. You have to have the notion that even if you are sweeping the floor, you can start thinking like a manager. "How can my job be done more efficiently?" "How can it contribute to the overall efficiency of the company?" These are the questions you must ask.

Creativity can be put back into the assembly line as well as into the sales force. As sales people, you are dealing with customers. You are providing the information that the people on the production line need in order to produce products people want. You supply the information.

Taking Responsibility

When you read accounts of Mr. Matsushita's daily routine, you find that he was constantly calling up the first production and plant people, then all the people in the sales divisions of the various parts of the company. He would scream at them when they weren't making their targets, but he immediately asked them about the people who were working for them and he would be harder on his managers for not treating their people properly than anything else. Then he would acknowledge suggestions that had been implemented for the good of the customers.

You have a responsibility not only to yourselves, but also to the society. It's hard to bring about that revolution in consciousness within yourself. You have to reassess yourself, it's not much what the people up on top think of you in the company so much as what you yourself think. Mr. Matsushita constantly applied rational humanistic thinking in all matters, great and small. If you're going to tongue-lash your subordinates for a mistake, ask have I given them the information I should have given them? Have I really given them all the guidance they really should have? Is bawling them out the only way to help them along? And if you think in that direction, you've trained yourself too."

6. SHELL PHILOSOPHY OF MANAGEMENT

The European Dream — The Shell Model

The Shell Oil is the second largest oil company in the world, is one of the few companies in the world which has done considerable amount of research to evolve a methodology to spot the potential and the ultimate potential of people working in Shell companies around the world. More than a quarter century ago. Shell wanted to find out who, among hundreds of thousands of people employed in more than 80 countries, are likely to become the top executives and members of the Board of Directors of Shell headquarters. They organised a global project, the top Shell executive at Shell Center in London explained to me, to formulate a methodology which could be used to spot the potential and ultimate potential of their people. They hired Prof Van Lennep of the Utrecht University and put one of their senior executives, Dr Mueller in a Project Team to spot potential. The Team used three research methods over a period of nearly 3 years. First, they studied leaders in all walks of life, political, social, cultural, religious, sports, etc. in order to identify the qualities that helped them to become leaders in their chosen fields of activity. Second, they studied the performance appraisals of about 10 years in Shell to identify the qualities, that superiors looked for in their people, when they wanted to promote them to higher assignments. Third, they interviewed general managers, directors, managing directors, chairmen of all

Shell companies around the world and asked them to look back on their careers in Shell and tell the team the qualities that helped them to get promotions in their careers and helped them to become top executives, with a view to projecting the kind of people who are likely to become the top executives of Shell in the future and the kind of attributes or traits they should possess to succeed in a large organisation like Shell.

The Team, after their research project of three years, came up with 3,000 qualities, out of which by removing semantics and overlapping they reduced them to 300 qualities. After further rationalisation and discussions with top executives, they finally came up only 5 qualities, which are the following:[5]

1. Helicopter Quality

Prof. Van Lennep coined this term, after his considerable research experience in human potential. Most people, when asked to solve a problem, try to solve the problem of bonus from the angle of their expertise. Suppose you are finance executive and you are likely to solve the problem from the finance expertise and probably suggest that 10% performance bonus is only possible because of financial constraints. He is not worried about how this would affect employees, who are looking at a higher bonus. He is not worried about the production, labour relations, quality assurance, human relations and motivation points of view. He is only interested in controlling costs from his finance angle.

The Industrial Relations Executive may suggest a 15% bonus because that would boost the morale and reduce tension on the shop floor. He is not worried whether the company can afford it or not.

But the person with helicopter quality is not likely to approach the problem only from the finance or labour relations angles or expertise. But he will raise himself over narrow departmental loyalties and interests, and look at the problem from the larger and total company point of view, like when you go up in a helicopter, you have a panoramic view and larger view of all aspects of the problem, you raise yourself above narrow departmental or divisional interests and try to approach the solution, as to its impact from all angles and from the total company point of view. At the top echelons of the organisation, you need people with helicopter quality, so that they solve a problem taking into consideration all aspects of the problem and arrive at the percentage of bonus, that would satisfy the employees, without sacrificing the interests of the company.

2. Power of Analysis

This refers to the quality of the executive's analytical abilities, the power to analyse and find out the central problem and the minor problems that have contributed to the central problems, not carried away by superficial symptoms. If you can diagnose the problem accurately, that is half the solution.

3. Sense of Imagination

This quality refers to looking far ahead of others and seeing the possibilities, even dreaming and looking for new opportunities of business before others and drawing plans for the future, so that they can come true. But only imagining or dreaming will not get you there. You need a concrete plan and action to achieve.

4. Sense of Realism

In addition to sense of imagination, you must be realistic, about your strengths and capabilities and weaknesses as well as that of the organisation. Of course, you can become too realistic, when you become almost pessimistic. Hence, these two qualities look contradictory, though they are complementary. In other words, you have to be imaginative, without being unrealistic and you have to be realistic, without being unimaginative. Studies of leadership clearly indicate that leaders seem to possess such complementary qualities through they appear to be contradictory on the face of it.

5. Power of Anticipation

This refers to the ability to anticipate events and problems before they occur, so that either you prepare yourself and the organisation "to cross the bridge, when you come to it" or, still better, able to prevent them from occurring.

5. Mr. Rudrabasavaraj, Executive Performance Appraisal, National Institute of Labour Management, Bombay, 1978.

Prof. Van Lennep also opined that either people have the helicopter quality or they don't, if they don't, nothing can be done to build this quality in them. This was a little disturbing. The Committee said that Shell had to look for these qualities, when they are in the age group of 28-35 years, since it would take a good 20-25 years for a young executive to reach his ultimate potential of a Managing Director. His career development has to be orchestrated very systematically over this period, through training at every level and function, rotational and on-the-job-training development experiences, promotions, performance appraisal, more responsibilities and challenges. Only a few emerge successfully through the development hurdles to realise their ultimate potential.

The Team, the Shell executives in London explained to me, suggested that these five qualities must become a part of the executive performance appraisal system, which contains two parts. The first part of the appraisal contains the appraisal of how he has performed over the last 12 months. The second part talks about the potential and ultimate potential. appraising the executive on the five qualities, that indicate the potential and ultimate potential of the individual. The Shell System asks the appraiser, to evaluate the strengths and weaknesses on an open-ended form and to suggest a plan of training, that the executive needs to attend and career moves and on-the-job development experiences to challenge and test the executive and to prepare him for higher assignments. The Shell System has been further modified in the light of their experiences, which we shall present later. The Shell System is a very sound system of identifying the potential of people and developing them. Many European MNCs and others around the world have adapted the Shell System to suit their own situation and have needs and successfully implemented them.

One of the countries, which adapted and used the Shell System quite successfully is the Singapore Government, which is greatly interested in spotting the potential of their people and maximise and help the people to achieve their potential.

In November 1994, in the Singapore Parliament, the Senior Minister, Mr. Lee Kuan Yew, singled the Shell System as the best way to pick people for top jobs. The Straits Times reported on the current Shell System as well as how it is adapted by the Singapore government[6].

"Senior Minister Lee Kuan Yew said in Parliament that after having spent 40 years selecting men for big jobs — ministers, civil servants, statutory board chairmen — and having asked many CEOs on how they selected top executives, he found that Shell, the multinational oil company, had the best system.

He said Shell assessed a person's "helicopter quality" rating three attributes: power of analysis, sense of reality and imagination.

He elaborated. "Power of analysis — logical grasp of the facts, basic points, extracting the principles. But that's not enough. They must have a sense of reality of what is possible".

"But if you are just realistic, you become pedestrian, plebian. You will fail. And therefore you must be able to soar above the reality and say, "This is also possible" — a sense of imagination."

Helicopter vision is so important that Shell managers are fond of saying that Executive A's helicopter is flying very high or that Executive B's helicopter has failed to take off. They are talking about someone's ability to see the big picture. People with good helicopter vision can look at a problem from a higher vantage point without ignoring relevant details.

While helicopter vision is only one attribute Shell looks for, it is particularly prized in the organisation. Government ministries have adapted the Shell System for their own needs. The Ministry of Defence, for example, rates HAIR qualities— helicopter vision, analytical powers, imagination and sense of reality.

Potential in Shell is termed Currently Estimated Potential (CEP), which is the highest possible position that an executive can reach irrespective of job opportunities. High-flyers are those given a high CEP grade and are treated like precious commodity. They get postings to different parts of the company, even overseas, to groom them for the career paths projected for them.

For example, if someone has the CEP of a chairman, the company spends the next 20 years exposing him to different areas of work to prepare him fully for the job. But since views on someone's potential can differ among supervisors, about six managers who have worked with the executive grade him together.

6. Rohaniah Saini, Picking Top Talents — The Shell Way, Life. *The Straits Times*, 11-11-94. p. 20.

Anyone's CEP can change. Someone's CEP may start high but later plateau off or even worse, crash. In such cases, his career path is adjusted to a less brilliant one, offering fewer job opportunities and lower salaries. Conversely, a late-bloomer's CEP is pegged higher subsequently.

Not only are the philosophies unique and living management and corporate philosophers, they also represent as a model for other organisations around the world. In every successful organisation you will find a dynamic corporate philosophy. If the management deviates from their philosophy, you see a decline in the fortunes of such a corporation. Each of the above organisation have succeeded in creating an unique BM man, WAL-MART man, MATSUSHITA man, SHELL man who have imbibed the principles of the philosophy and practice it in their daily activities.

3 Strategy of Global Management

The chapter is discussed under the following headings :
• Definition of Strategy • Strategic Management Process • Business Strategy • Seven S Model • Virgin Case of Strategy Implementation • 5 Day Week in Matsushita, Day Week In Matsushita • Everyday low at Wal-Mart

The word "Strategy" comes from the Greek word "Strategia" meaning the 'art or science of being a General'. Successful Greek Generals realised the value of a strategy as a ground plan of action to fight and win battles. Good Generals not only plan but also act and implement their plans.

General Robert E: Wood, President of Sears, Roebuck, a giant mail order house recognised the importance of strategy. Wood realised that the auto revolution would bring rural population closer to the urban areas. A population no longer confined to the countryside, he reasoned, would abandon the mail order catalogue in favour of a retail store. So he embarked on the long-range strategy of converting to a retail chain. According to Wood, the company made mistakes in the book at first but its carefully laid out plans eventually brought huge success. Business is like war in one respect, the General wrote. If its strategy is correct, any number of tactical errors can be made and yet the enterprise proves successful.[1]

DEFINITION

In 1962, Alfred D. Chandler defined strategy as the, 'determination of the basic long-term goals and objectives of an enterprise and the adoption of courses of action and the allocation of resources necessary for carrying out these goals'.

The following three key elements of Chandler are:

1. Courses of action for attaining objectives.
2. The process of seeking key ideas (instead of routinely implementing policy).
3. How strategy is formulated, not just what the strategy turns out to be.

THE STRATEGIC MANAGEMENT APPROACH

Don Schendel and Charles Hofer created a composite definition of strategic management based on the principle that the overall organisation can be described only if the attainment of objectives is added to policy and strategy as key factors in the strategic management process.

In their synthesis, Hofer and Schendel focused on four key aspects of strategic management.

Fig. 3.1. Strategic Management Process

1. Stephen J. Carrol and Dennis J. Glidden, "The Classical Management Functions : Are they really outdated" Proceedings of the 49th Annual Meeting of American Academy of Management, Aug. 1984, pp. 8, 132-6.

The first is goal setting. The next step is strategy formulation based on these goals. Then to implement the strategy, there is shift from analysis to administration — the task of achieving predetermined goals. The final task, strategic control, gives the managers feedback on their progress. Negative feedback, of course, can throw off a new cycle of strategic planning.

Three Levels of Strategy

There are 3 levels of strategy identified and they are (1) Corporate level strategy, (2) Individual Company Strategy, (3) Functional Strategy.

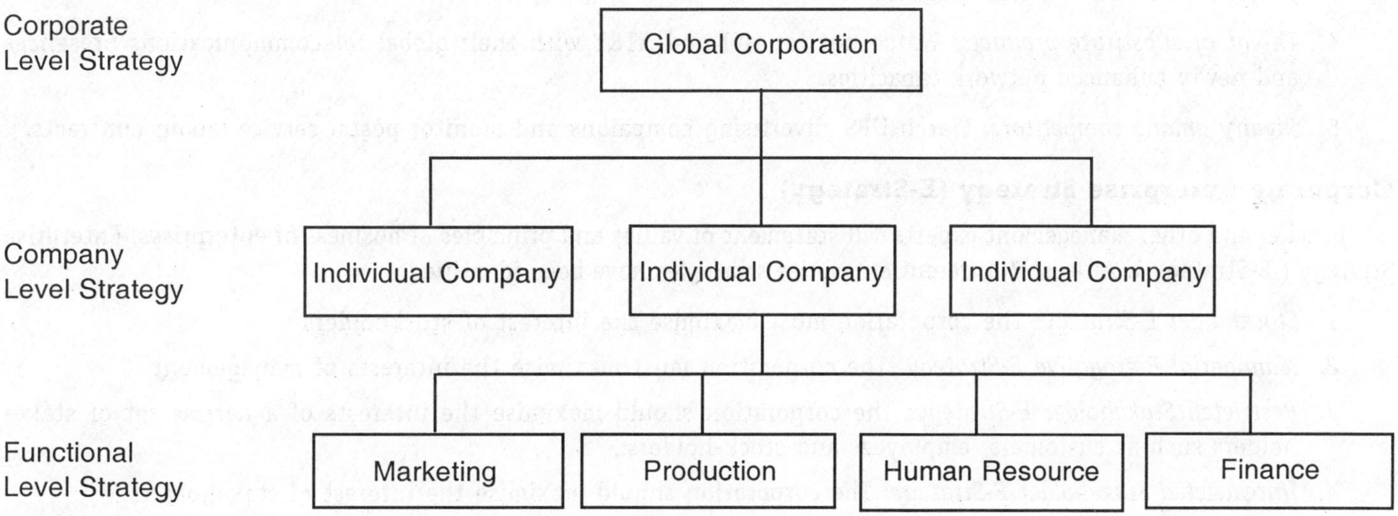

Fig. 3.2. Levels of Strategy

Corporate Level Strategy

This strategy is formulated by top board of directors to manage the operation of business. They are concerned about the kinds of businesses, goals of each business and the allocation of resources.

GE under chairman Jeff Immelt has been extremely successful in managing GE capital, GE electronics, GE medical health care and others with the help of carefully chosen and highly motivated CEOs, who are all high performers.

Individual Company Strategy

This strategy is concerned with managing the operations of a particular company in a line of business. It deals with such questions as; What is the competition in the market? Who are its customers? What products/services should it offer? How to satisfy its customers and expand its market?

Functional Level Strategy

The strategy creates a framework for managers in each function such as marketing, production, etc., to carry out company strategies and corporate strategies. Operational plans follow from functional level strategies.

Five Forces of Corporate Strategy

Micheal Porter, author of *'Competitive Strategy'* observes that an organisation's ability to compete in a given market is determined by the organisation's technical and economic resources, as well as by five environmental forces each of which threatens the organisations venture into a market. The strategic manager, opines Porter, must analyse these forces and propose a programme for influencing or defending against them. The aim is to find a lucrative and defensible niche for the organisation.

In the following list of five forces we use Federal Express as an example, suggesting how each force could influence corporate strategy and what kind of guidance managers would find.

1. *Threat of new entrants:* Keep an eye on what American Airlines and United Airlines might do to expand their cargo services into new markets.
2. *Bargaining power of buyers (customers):* Keep prices within X per cent of UPS and US Postal Service for similar services. Keep new variations on delivery services; next day might not suit everyone's budget.
3. *Bargaining power of suppliers:* Discuss operating plans for acquiring new jet aircraft with Boeing and others to get a favourable aircraft delivery slot.
4. *Threat of substitute products:* Watch out for MCI and AT&T with their global telecommunications presences and newly enhanced network capacities.
5. *Rivalry among competitors:* Watch UPS advertising compaigns and monitor postal service labour contracts.

Corporate Enterprise Strategy (E-Strategy)

Drucker and other management experts call statement of values and principles of business of enterprises, Enterprise Strategy (E-Strategy). At least 7 different enterprise strategies have been identified.

1. *Stockholder E-Strategy:* The corporation must maximise the interest of stockholders.
2. *Managerial Prerogative E-Strategy:* The corporation must maximise the interests of management.
3. *Restricted Stakeholder E-Strategy:* The corporation should maximise the interests of a narrow set of stakeholders such as customers, employees and stock-holders.
4. *Unrestricted Stakeholder E-Strategy:* The corporation should maximise the interest of stakeholders.
5. *Social Harmony E-Strategy:* The corporation should maximise social harmony.
6. *Rawlsion E-Strategy:* The corporation should promote inequality among stakeholders only if inequality results in raising the level of the worst-off stakeholder.
7. *Personal Projects E-Strategy:* The corporation should maximise its ability to enable corporate members to carry out their personal projects.

E-Strategy in Practice

IKEA, a Swedish furniture company, managers have established an entire business around the mission of the company's founder, Ingvar Kamprad to, "create a better everyday life for the majority of the people". Managers at the company have devised a strategy from this mission in which roles of IKEA's suppliers, warehousing, distribution and retailing systems are well-integrated and internally consistent. The strategy is implemented by highly motivated employees who consider themselves part of the IKEA family. They are given generous benefits including paternal leave, and four weeks of vacation after five years of service with the company. At the same time, company executives fly coach and stay in lower priced hotels. So E-Strategy at IKEA combines elements of improving people's lives and relating to family members.

GOOD BUSINESS STRATEGY

Kimiche Ohmae of Japan says that a, "good business strategy is one, by which a company can gain significant ground on its competitors at an acceptable cost to itself. He believes there are four principal ways of doing things :

1. *Focus on key factors of success (KFS):* Ohmae argues that certain functional or operating areas within every business are more critical for success in that particular business environment than others. If you concentrate effort with these areas, and your competitors don't, this is a source of competitive advantage. The problem, of course, is identifying what those key factors for success are.
2. *Build on relative superiority :* When all competitors are seeking to compete on the KFS, a company can exploit any differences in competitive conditions. For example, it can make use of technology or sales net works not in direct competition with its rivals.

3. *Pursue aggressive initiatives:* Frequently, the only way to win against a much larger entrenched competitor is to upset the competitive environment, by undermining the value of KFS-changing the rules of the game by introducing new KFS.

4. *Utilising strategic degree of freedom:* The company can focus on innovation in areas which are "untouched by competitors".

In each of these four methods, the principal concern is to avoid doing the same thing, on the same battleground, as the competition, Ohmae explains.

Ohmae argues that an effective strategic plan takes into account three main players — the company, the customer and the competition, each exerting their own influence. The strategy that ignores competitive reaction is flawed, so is the strategy that does not take into account sufficiently how the customer will react; and so of course, is the strategic plan that does not explore fully the organisation's capacity to implement it.

How do You Achieve Your Objectives?

Implementation is where most strategies fail. Success relies on matching an organisation's resources, culture, structure and people to the strategies which emerge from consideration of the organisation's core competencies and the environment it exists in.

If the strategy is to make the leap from theory to effective implementation the people behind it must:

- Accept uncertainty as a fact of business life.
- Continually look outside the organisation to learn lessons and improve effectiveness.
- Learn from past mistakes and achievements.
- Use unconventional images to communicate strategic initiates.
- Produce short, highly informative strategy documents.
- Regard strategy as a business tool.
- Not allow preconceived ideas to interfere with honest interpretation.
- Distrust immediate consensus.
- Put faith in strong feelings and take risks.
- Assume nothing.
- Break down barriers.
- Involve everyone.
- Look to the future.

THE SEVEN-S MODEL

Based on discussions with consultants, academics, and business leaders, the consulting firm of McKinsey & Co. has proposed the Seven-S Model for successful strategy implementation. McKinsey's consultants found that neglecting any one of seven key factors could make the effort to change a slow, painful, and even doomed process.

Each of these factors is equally important and interacts with all the other factors. Any number of circumstances may dictate which of the factors will be the driving force in the execution of any particular strategy.

Structure. The Seven-S model adds a contemporary perspective to the problem of organisational structure. The McKinsey consultants point out that in today's complex and ever-changing environment, a successful organisation may make temporary structural changes to cope with specific strategic tasks without abandening basic structural divisions throughout the organisation.

Strategy. The Seven-S model emphasises that, in practice, the development strategies pose less of a problem than their execution.

Systems. This category consists of all the formal and informal procedures that allow the organisation to function, including capital budgeting, training, and counting systems. Systems can overpower expressed strategies. Thus, a consumer goods manufacturer might find it impossible to implement a new portfolio strategy if its management information system is not adjusted to produce the necessary cost data by segment, because there would be no way to compare the different segments of the business.

Style. "Style" refers not to personality, but to the pattern of substantive and symbolic *actions* undertaken by top managers. It communicates priorities more clearly than words alone, and may profoundly influence performance. For example, consultants have found that even oil and mineral exploration efforts—surely matters of operational skills and luck more than strategy—benefit from top-management attention. Exploration is more successful in companies whose top managers spend more of their own and the board's time participating in exploration activities, articulate better reasons for exploration, recruit more people with exploration experience, fund exploration more consistently, and have exploration managers report to higher organisational levels.

Staff. Successful organisations view people as valuable resources who should be carefully nurtured, developed, guarded, and allocated. Top managers devote time and energy to planning the progress and participation of existing managers, and use job assignment policies to actively foster the development of new managers. Similarly, new hires are given jobs in the mainstream of the organisation, whether that be marketing or new-product innovation. Talented individuals are assigned mentors, put into fast-track programs, exposed to top management, and rapidly moved into positions of real responsibility.

Skills. The term *skills* refers to those activities organisations do best and for which they are known. For example, Du Pont is known for research, Procter & Gamble for product management, ITT for financial controls, and Hewlett-Packard for innovation and quality. Strategic changes may require organisations to add one or more new skills. Strategic initiatives that require the dismantling or revising of an old skill pose even more difficult implementation problems.

Superordinate GOALS. This refers to guiding concepts, values, and aspirations that unite an organisation in some common purpose. Superordinate goals are often, captured in a mission statement, but they can also be phrased as a simple slogan, such as "new products" at 3M. Superordinate goals have deep meaning within the organisation. They provide a sense of purpose and a certain stability as other, more superficial characteristics of the organisation change. In the case continuation, we will see how some of these Seven-S's work at Sega.

Institutionalising Strategy

To emphasize systems, style, staff, skills, and superordinate goals, we need to look at how strategy is institutionalised. An *institution* is a collection of values, norms, roles, and groups that develops to accomplish a certain goal. The institution of education, for example, developed to prepare children to be productive members of the society. To institutionalise a business strategy, business leaders must also develop a system of values, norms, roles, and groups that will support the accomplishment of strategic goals. So, strategy is institutionalised if it is connected to the culture, the quality system, and the other driving forces in the organisation.

We have seen that the drive toward TQM can be institutionalized. Another aspect of organisational life that is also undergoing increasing institutionalisation is an emphasis on ethics development. Both shift organisational attention from detection and control to co-ordination and strategic impact. The ultimate outcome of this shift in focus is an enhanced quality of work environment for employees and increased quality of products and services for customers.

VIRGIN CASE OF STRATEGY IMPLEMENTATION

Virgin : Headline—Grabbing And Successful

Richard Branson, entrepreneurial owner and founder of Britain's untraditional Virgin group, has fused two dissimilar lines of work—show business and commerce—into a single, extremely profitable enterprise. Virgin group comprises more than 100 companies in 15 countries. It includes Virgin Atlantic, a 12-plane, long-distance carrier; the Virgin Retail group, outlets that sell CDs, videos, and games; Virgin Communications, including a small publishing company, a commercial AM radio station, and a television station; Virgin Interactive Communication, a computer games software publisher; and the Voyager Group, a collection of diverse assets ranging from a hotel chain to a model agency.

Branson's business strategy places him at the forefront as the company's most effective marketing tool. "He has become the world's greatest underdog," commented a London analyst. "He's a great actor." In addition, his strategy also involves making the most of publicity. "If you've got an airline," Branson asserted, "you've got to keep it in the public eye somehow." This he accomplishes through a variety of methods, including headline-grabbing adventures such as crossing the Atlantic Ocean by speedboat and balloon.

Such exploits have served to define Virgin's organisational culture. In addition, morale is boosted by the success of Virgin Atlantic, which had a humble beginning as an upstart airline and was vulnerable to allegedly unfair competitive tactics by rival British Airways (BA). "Being around through the Gulf War, the recession and BA's dirty tricks campaign has been particularly satisfying," Branson remarked. The airline now holds 22 per cent of the transatlantic market. This is less than BA's share, but more than American or United holds. And Virgin is still expanding.

The structure Branson relies on entails his heavy involvement. He believes in taking a hands-on approach, particularly with airlines. At times, he even greets Virgin passengers at airports and asks them how they enjoyed their flights. "Any time that I go out to meet passengers I'm always scribbling things," he commented.

With the airline, in an industry plagued by intense-competition and price wars, survival remains a constant goal. Branson is *therefore cautious.* "There are a lot of big airlines in America that have gone belly-up," he noted. "As airlines get bigger, they sometimes get more vulnerable." *Branson is determined not to let this happen to his airline.*

In recent years, Branson appears to have mellowed with regard to his ambitions. "Before, he wanted to build the biggest entertainment empire in the world," noted Branson's biographer, Mrek Brown.

"Now, the man who has everything, doesn't need more. There is also an element of social crusading in him that needs to be assuaged." Branson has now found at least a degree of contentment. "I have enough money to have my three meals a day, to feed my children, to clothe them, take my holidays and build up and continue to run our companies," he stated. "I have no ambition to build the biggest company in the world."

Branson remains conservative in his lifestyle. He attributes this to his respect for employees. "As a businessman, I think it's very important to set an example for your staff in the way you behave," he said. "You don't drive flashy cars and you choose a wife who isn't into diamond rings and expensive, glitzy clothes." This, he implied, leads to a staff with similar values.

In line with this, as Virgin has grown, Branson has broken operations down into smaller companies of between 50 and 100 people. He believes that each company should occupy separate offices and that employees should be able to take ownership of "their" company. A culture that emphasises individual responsibility in this way enables drastic changes to take place quickly and easily.

The systems within the company are also very supportive of empowerment. For example, through the strong communications system, budgeting is explained to employees, with daily graphs that display performance by area in comparison to area budgets. The hiring system also relies on the empowerment of employees. At one point four junior employees were made responsible for hiring their own replacements when they were promoted.

Virgin offices are extremely informal. With 15-foot ceilings, working fireplaces, and lavish gardens, the building is more like a home than a place of business. Antiques are scattered around, along with plush sofas, intimate family pictures, various plaques, and models of Virgin airplanes. And employees dress casually, in line with the surroundings.

The elements of Virgin's strategy thus clinch the company's success. Under Branson's creative leadership, exciting twists promise to lie ahead.

FIVE-DAY WEEK IN MATSUSHITA

Morimasa Ogawa explains the strategy of Matsushita in introducing five-day work week in Japan which was unheard of in those days.

At the 1960, annual management policy meeting, Matsushita announced his intention to introduce a five-day work week.

Let us look specifically at the features of leadership in business again start with an anecdote from the career of Konosute Matsushita. In the 1960 annual management policy meeting, Matsushita announced his intention to introduce five-day workin five years' time. The announcement was completely unexpected; the five-day workweek was inconceivable in Japan at that time the 7,000 executives assembled were stunned. It took a few members for the applause to begin. I was a group manager at that time. My first reaction was: "If they do that, it's all over for this company. It was not an idea we welcomed. Matsushita explained. "Japan's population won't continue to increase at the current rate. In order to assure Matsushita Electric's growth, we will have to expand into the industrialised — United States and Europe —and most of the manufacturers who have a five-day workweek.

"If we start exporting and continue to work six days a week, we'll find ourselves in trouble because other countries will think Japan is unfair in using poor labour conditions as a weapon. If we're going to export, then we have to conform to the same conditions as the countries to which we export. Only then can we have competitive quality, performance, and prices."

Matsushita also said that having only one day off a week was not really enough time to relax and be with our families. "If you think about it that way, you'll realise that we have to implement a five-day workweek." he said. "Of course, we can't make such a change suddenly. Over the next five years, I want every employee to contribute ideas so that we can figure out how to do the same work in five days that we have been doing in six."

At that time, Japan had a trade deficit, and the yen was stable at ¥360 to the dollar. It was very difficult to export. In a manner far different from that generated by present trade frictions, the United States was helping Japan out as it tried to use exports to establish itself in the international economy. After Matsushita's twenty-minute speech, the whole company became a hive of activity as we set our sights on the five-day workweek. All the production supervisors got their people together to talk about where, what, and how things should be improved so that six-days' worth of work could be done in five. The sales departments studied how they could compress six days of selling into five. The retail departments researched what they could do. Accounting also went to work on this problem of making five equal six. Literally, the entire company tackled the problems of raising productivity and rationalising work.

Our efforts paid off. Five years later, we adopted the five-day workweek, and our corporate performance was better than ever. Within two years, the rest of the electric industry had adopted the five-day workweek.

If we analyse the process by which Matsushita arrived at the decision that unified the thinking of 7,000 managers, who in turn organised, 50,000 employees in instituting this major change in just five years, we can see that he made the following six decisions:

1. The only strategy by which his company could continue to prosper was to enter the world marketplace. This decision was reached after careful observation of the overall situation.
2. The five-day workweek was a basic prerequisite for carrying out this strategy.
3. To obtain his followers assent and co-operation, he explained the circumstances surrounding the decision and the necessity for implementing it.
4. A specific target of five years in which to accomplish the goal was set. If the followers approved of the goal, then leader and followers would have solidarity in realising the plan.
5. The work of actually planning for the goal was left up to the employees. This type of management utilises the knowledge of everyone.
6. Specific plans were devised by the same people who would benefit by them, giving them a strong desire to get the job done. That led to new ideas for the implementation of the plan.

This yields a practical, six-step checklist:

1. Clarify problems and devise concepts (strategy).
2. Determine the basic guidelines for implementing the strategy.
3. Give the followers a detailed explanation of the guidelines.

4. Set up specific goals and cultivate the followers' solidarity toward those goals.
5. Establish a plan mobilising the knowledge of everyone involved and leave the details up to those who will carry it out.
6. Believe in the plan and carry it out with conviction.

Looking back on all the jobs I did in my 28 years at Matsushita Electric, I realise that the ones that succeeded generally followed these procedures. Of those that failed, one or more of the procedures had been overlooked. These six steps may look simple, but they form the basis of leadership in the workplace.

It is important that the leader believes in the goals that are set and make every effort to ensure that they are achieved, but the conditions for success lie in keeping in mind the following guidelines:

1. move ahead boldly
2. remain flexible so that you can cope with changes in circumstances
3. lead the employees under you to maximise their abilities

EVERYDAY LOW PRICES AT WAL-MART

Samuel Walton believed strongly in running a very efficient operation, in controlling costs of merchandising and operations and passing on the benefits to the customers through the strategy of everyday low prices, not just when you have periodic sales. His rule No.9 (among 10 rules of his management) states, "Control your expenses better than your competition. This is where you can always find the competitive advantage. For 25 years running long before Wal-Mart was known as the nation's largest retailer, we ranked No. 1 in our industry for the lowest ratio of expenses of sales. You can make a lot of different mistakes and still recover if you run an efficient operation. Or you can be brilliant and still go out of business if you are not efficient".

Walton made some prophetic words for American business.

"But if American Management is going to say to their workers that we are all in this together, they are going to have to stop this foolishness of paying themselves $ 3 million and $ 4 million bonuses every year and riding around everywhere in limos and corporate jets like they are so much better than everybody else".

"I am not saying every company should necessarily be as chintzy as Wal-Mart. Everybody is not in discount business, consumed by trying to save every possible dollar for their customers. But I wonder if a lot of these companies would not do just as well if their executives lived a little more like real folks. A lot of people think it is crazy of me to fly coach whenever I go on a commercial flight, and may be I do overdo it a little bit. But I feel it is upto me as a leader to set an example. It is not fair for me to ride one way and ask everybody else to ride another way. The minute you do that, you start building resentment and your whole team idea begins to strain at the seams. Walton drove his 20-year-old pick-up truck, no fancy limos for him.

His main strategy was to control and reduce expenses and pass on the benefit to the customers and live up to his other motto "Satisfaction Guaranteed" to the customers, so that the customers made a beeline to his store looking for value of their dollar, contributing to 20% to 30% growth of Wal-Mart every year to reach No.l on the 2008 Fortune Global 500 with a revenue of $ 378 billion and a total associate strength of 2 million.

Earlier in the first chapter of this book, we have already witnessed the certain strategies of Global Companies like GE (Jack Welch's high-fliers) Shell's Spotting talent, Glaxo Simith Kline's Global Business strategies.

Now, let us turn to the next chapter, as to how great leaders lead their people to build their Global business empires.

Leadership of Global Management

The chapter is discussed under the following headings :
• Theories of Leadership • The Essentials of Management Leadership • Managerial Leadership Styles

For a long time it was believed that leaders were born. You could not teach leadership. The theory was that either you were a born leader or you were not. Gradually, over a period of time, a new school of thought emerged, particularly in the military world, that leader can be made and that leadership can be taught through a body of knowledge. In the world of business, the two schools of thought flourish even in modern times, though there is a great body of thought, research and experimentation that suggests that leadership is something that you can acquire through study, training and education. Some leaders and scholars go to the extent of contributing to a new school of thought that all of us possess the qualities of leadership and that anybody and everybody can assume the role of leadership, either by our own initiative and through a set of given circumstances.

We shall discuss the theory and practice of Leadership in Global Management under the following heads :

1. Theory of Leadership
2. Essentials of Management Leadership
3. Managerial/Leadership Styles
4. Shell Model of Leadership
5. Walton's Model
6. Jack Welch Leadership
7. Matsushita Collective Wisdom.

THEORIES OF LEADERSHIP

First, let us turn to the school of thought on leadership currently in vogue.

Modern leadership writers tend to suggest that leadership as a skill or characteristic is distributed generously among the population. "Successful leadership is not dependent on the possession of a single universal pattern of inborn traits and abilities. It seems likely that leadership potential (considering the tremendous variety of situations for which leadership is required) is broadly rather than narrowly distributed in the population," wrote Douglas Macgregor in *The Human Side of Enterprise*. The American Warren Bennis, inspired by Macgregor, has studied leadership throughout his career. Bennis also concludes that each of us contains the capacity for leadership and has leadership experience. He does not suggest that actually translating this into becoming an effective leader is straightforward, but that it can be done, given time and application.

While such arguments are impressively optimistic about human potential, they are disappointed by reality. The dearth of great leaders is increasingly apparent. This suggests that either innate skills are not being effectively developed or that the business world simply does not encourage managers to fulfil their potential as leaders.

The Evolution of Leadership

Leadership thinking has moved rapidly from one theory to another. The main schools of thought can be divided into nine theories.

Great Man Theory

Great Man Theories were the stuff of the late nineteenth and early twentieth centuries, though their residue remains in much popular thinking on the subject. The Great Man Theory is based on the idea that the leader is born with innate, unexplainable and, for mere mortals, incomprehensible leadership skills. They are, therefore, elevated as heroes.

Trait Theory

This Theory continues to fill numerous volumes. If you know who the Great Men are, you can then examine their personalities and behavior to develop traits of leaders. This is plausible, but deeply flawed, for all the books attempting to identify common trait among leaders; there is little correlation.

Power and Influence Theory

This approach chooses to concentrate on the networks of power and influence generated by the leader. It is however, based on the assumption that all roads lead to the leader and negates the role of followers and the strength of organisational culture.

Behaviorist Theory

In some ways the behaviorist school continues to hold sway. It emphasises what leaders actually do rather than their characteristics. Its advocates include Blake and Mouton (creators of the Managerial Grid) and Rensis Likert.

Situational Theory

Situational Theory views leadership as specific to a situation rather than a particular sort of personality. It is based on the plausible notion that different circumstances require different forms of leadership. Its champions include Kenneth Blanchard and Paul Hersey whose influential book, 'Situational Leadership Theory', remains a situationalist manifesto.

Contingency Theory

Developing from Situational Theory, contingency approaches attempt to select situational variables which best indicate the most appropriate leadership style to suit the circumstances.

Transactional Theory

Increasingly fashionable, Transactional Theory places emphasis on the relationship between leaders and followers. It examines the mutual benefit from an exchange-based relationship with the leader offering certain things, such as resources or rewards, in return for others, such as the followers' commitment or acceptance of the leader's authority.

Attribution Theory

This elevates followership to new importances, concentrating on the factors which lie behind the followers' attribution of leadership to a particular leader.

Transformational Theory

While transactional leadership models are based on the extrinsic motivation of an exchange relationship, transformational leadership is based on intrinsic motivation. As such, the emphasis is on commitment rather than compliance from the followers. The transformational leader is, therefore, a proactive, innovative visionary.

The New Leader

"Today's leaders understand that you have to give up control to get results — they act as coaches not as 'the boss'," observes Robert Waterman in 'The Frontiers of Excellence'.

The increasing emphasis in the 1990s, has focussed on leaders as real people managing in a consensus-seeking manner. Instead of seeing leadership as being synonymous with dictatorship, this view sees leadership as a more subtle and humane art. It also breaks down the barrier between leadership and management. Traditionally, in theory at least, the two have been separated. "Men are ripe for intelligent, understanding, personal leadership, they would rather be led than managed," observed Field Marshal Slim. Increasingly, management and leadership are seen as inextricably linked. It is one thing for a leader to propound a grand vision; but this is redundant unless the vision is managed into real achievement. While traditional views of leadership tend eventually to concentrate on vision and charisma, the message now seems to be that charisma is no longer enough to carry leaders through. Indeed, leaders with strong personalities are just as likely to bite the corporate dust (as Bob Horton found to his cost at BP). The new model leaders include people like Barnevik at Asea Brown Boveri, Virgin's Richard Branson, and Jack Welch GE in the United States.

THE ESSENTIALS OF MANAGEMENT LEADERSHIP

Lifelong Learning: Learn, Learn and Learn. Learn Fast, Samuel Walton made it a point to visit any new store with a pad and pen and made copious notes talking to the sales staff, cashiers and managers and come back with ideas.

What Makes Them Tick : Jack Welch learnt that the key to success in management and business is to select and nurture high performers and give them opportunities to succeed, from his own personal experience when his senior Vice-president persuaded Jack not to leave GE, because he did not get right recognition and reward.

Matsushita learns about changing technology, changing tastes of customers, changing business environment, changing aspirations of his own workforce in order to lead his people to realise his vision and dream of building a business empire with the help of people who were more educated and qualified than himself. He was a unique leader and manager who not only dreamt but also converted his dream into reality of uniquely touching his people, who wanted to do everything for their leader. In Matsushita, they have great reverence for him and put him up on a high pedestal. Mr. Jeff Immelt observes, why Jack Welch selected him as the CEO of GE: "People get a chance like this not because of what they know, but because of how fast people think they can learn. Maybe, Jack and the GE Board thought that I am good learner".

What are the attributes of a leader in business?

One list recently compiled is as follows:

1. Integrity
2. Courage
3. Objectivity
4. Ambition
5. Problem Solving
6. Judgement
7. Ability to Communicate
8. Emotional Maturity.

MANAGERIAL LEADERSHIP STYLES

Rensis Likert identified four types of management styles.

The trends of the 1990s, were partly anticipated in the work of psychologist and researcher, Rensis Likert (1903-81). Likert identified four types of management style:

- exploitative authoritarian — management by fear
- benevolent autocracy — top-down but with an emphasis on carrots rather than sticks
- consultative — communication both up and down, with decisions largely coming from the top.
- participative — decision-making in working groups which communicate with each other via individuals who are linking pins, team leaders or others who are also members of one or more other groups.

Beyond these four "systems" Likert also anticipated System 5 where all formal authority had disappeared.

The magic which marks such executives has been analyzed by INSEAD leadership expert, Manfred Kets de Vries, "They go beyond narrow definitions. They have an ability to excite people in their organisations," he says. "They also work extremely hard – leading by example is not dead and are highly resistant to stress. Also, leaders like Branson or Barnevik are very much aware of what their failings are. They make sure that they find good people who can fill these areas."

Leonard Sayles, author of *'Leadership: Managing in Real Organisations' and 'The Working Leader'* is representative of a great deal of the new thinking. Sayles suggests that leadership affects managers at all levels, not simply those in the higher echelons of management. "It is leadership based on work issues, not just people issues, and is very different from the method and style of managing that has evolved from our traditional management principles."

Sayles argues that the leader's role lies in "facilitating co-ordination and integration in order to get work done." Sayles is dismissive of the perennial concept of the great corporate leader. Instead his emphasis is on the leader as the integrator of corporate systems. The leader is a kind of fulcrum "adapting, modifying, adjusting and rearranging the complex task and function interfaces that keep slipping out of alignment." Instead of being centered around vision and inspiration, Sayles regards the leader's key role as integrating the outputs of his or her work unit with those of the rest of the organisation. To Sayles, "Managers who are not leaders can only be failures."

Practise of Leadership

The Shell Model

The Shell Oil is the second largest oil company in the world, is one of the few companies in the world which has done considerable amount of research to evolve a methodology to spot the potential and the ultimate potential of people working in Shell companies around the world. More than a quarter century ago, Shell wanted to find out who, among hundreds of thousands of people employed in more than 80 countries, are likely to become the top executives and members of the Board of Directors of Shell headquarters. They organised a global project, the top Shell executive at Shell Centre in London explained to me, to formulate a methodology which could be used to spot the potential and the ultimate potential of their people. They hired Prof. Van Lennep of the Utrecht University and put one of their senior executives, Dr Mueller in a Project Team to spot potentials. The Team used three research methods over a period of nearly 3 years. First, they studied leaders in all walks of life, political, social, cultural, religious, sports, etc., in order to identify the qualities that helped them to become leaders in their chosen fields of activity. Second, they studied the performance appraisals of about 10 years in Shell to identify the qualities, that superiors looked for in their people, when they wanted to promote them to higher assignments. Third, they interviewed general managers, directors, managing directors, chairmen of all Shell companies around the world and asked them to look back on their careers in Shell and tell the team the qualities that helped them to get promotions in their careers and helped them to become top executives, with a view to projecting the kind of people who are likely to become the top executives of Shell in the future and the kind of attributes or traits they should possess to succeed in a large organisation like Shell.

The Team, after their research project of three years, came up with 3000 qualities, out of which by removing semantics and overlapping they reduced them to 300 qualities. After further rationalisation and discussions with top executives, they finally came up only 5 qualities which are the following:[1]

Helicopter Quality

Prof. Van Lennep coined this term, after his considerable research experience in human potential. Most people, when asked to solve a problem, try to solve the problem of bonus from the angle of their expertise. Suppose you are finance executive and you are likely to solve the problem from the finance expertise and probably suggest that 10% performance bonus is only possible because of financial constraints. He is not worried about how this would affect employees, who are looking at a higher bonus. He is not worried about the production, labour relations, quality assurance, human relations and motivation points of view. He is only interested in controlling costs from his finance angle.

1. Mr. Rudrabasavaraj, Executive Performance Appraisal National Institute of Labour Management, Bombay, 1978.

The Industrial Relations Executive may suggest a 15% bonus because that would boost the morale and reduce tension on the shop floor. He is not worried whether the company can afford it or not.

But the person with helicopter quality is not likely to approach the problem only from the finance or labour relations angles or expertise. But he will raise himself over narrow departmental loyalties and interests, and look at the problem from the larger and total company point of view, like when you go up in a helicopter, you have a panoramic view and larger view of all aspects of the problem, you raise yourself above narrow departmental or divisional interests and try to approach the solution, as to its impact from all angles and from total company point of view. At the top echelons of the organisation, you need people with helicopter quality, so that they solve a problem taking into consideration all aspects of the problem and arrive at the percentage of bonus, that would satisfy the employees, without sacrificing the interests of the company.

Power of Analysis

This refers to the quality of executive's analytical abilities, the power to analyse and find out the central problem and the minor problems that have contributed to the central problems, not carried away by superficial symptoms. If you can diagnose the problem accurately, that is half the solution.

Sense of Imagination

This quality refers to looking far ahead of others and seeing the possibilities, even dreaming and looking for new opportunities of business before others and drawing plans for the future, so that they can come true. But only imagining or dreaming will not get you there. You need a concrete plan and action to achieve.

Sense of Realism

In addition to sense of imagination, you must be realistic, about your strengths and capabilities and weaknesses as well as that of the organisation. Of course, you can become too realistic, when you become almost pessimistic. Hence, these two qualities look contradictory, though they are complimentary. In other words, you have to be imaginative, without being unrealistic and you have to realistic, without being unimaginative. Studies of leadership clearly indicate that leaders seem to possess such complimentary qualities though they appear to be contradictory on the face of it.

Power of Anticipation

This refers to the ability to anticipate events and problems before they occur, so that either you prepare yourself and the organisation "to cross the bridge, when you come to it" or, still better, able to prevent them from occurring.

Prof. Van Lennep also opined that either people have the helicopter quality or they don't. If they don't, nothing can be done to build this quality in them. This was a little disturbing. The Committee said that Shell had to look for these qualities, when they are in the age group of 28-35 years, since it would take a good 20-25 years for a young executive to reach his ultimate potential of a Managing Director. His career development has to be orchestrated very systematically over this period, through training at every level and function, rotational and on-the-job-training development experiences, promotions, performance appraisal, more responsibilities and challenges. Only a few emerge successfully through the development hurdles to realise their ultimate potential.

The Team, the Shell executives in London explained to me, suggested that these five qualities must become a part of the executive performance appraisal system, which contains two parts. The first part of the appraisal contains the appraisal of how he has performed over the last 12 months. The second part talks about the potential and ultimate potential, appraising the executive on the five qualities, that indicate the potential and ultimate potential of the individual. The Shell System asks the appraiser, to evaluate the strengths and weaknesses on an open-ended form and to suggests a plan of training that the executive needs to attend and career moves and on-the-job development experiences to challenge and test the executive and to prepare him for higher assignments. The Shell System has been further modified in the light of their experiences, which we shall present later. The Shell System is a very sound system of identifying the potential of people and developing them. Many European MNCs and others around the world have adapted the Shell System to suit their own situation and needs and have successfully implemented them.

One of the countries, which adapted and used the Shell System quite successfully is the Singapore Government, which is greatly interested in spotting the potential of their people and maximise and help the people to achieve their potential.

In November 1994, in the Singapore Parliament, the Senior Minister, Mr. Lee Kuan Yew, singled the Shell System as the best way to pick people for top jobs. The Straits Times reported on the current Shell System as well as how it is adapted by the Singapore government.

"Senior Minister Lee Kuan Yew said in Parliament that after having spent 40 years selecting men for big jobs — ministers, civil servants, statutory board chairmen — and having asked many CEOs on how they selected top executives, he found that Shell, the multinational oil company, had the best system.

He said Shell assessed a person's "helicopter quality" rating three attributes: power of analysis, sense of reality and imagination.

He elaborated, "Power of analysis — logical grasp of the facts, basic points, extracting the principles. But that's not enough. They must have a sense of reality of what is possible.

"But if you are just realistic, you become pedestrian, plebian. You will fail. And therefore you must be able to soar above the reality and say, "This is also possible" — a sense of imagination."

Helicopter vision is so important that Shell managers are fond of saying that Executive A's helicopter is flying very high or that Executive B's helicopter has failed to take off. They are talking about someone's ability to see the big picture. People with good helicopter vision can look at a problem from a higher vantage point without ignoring relevant details.

While helicopter vision is only one attribute Shell looks for. It is particularly prized in the organisation. Government ministries have adapted the Shell" System for their own needs. The Ministry of Defence, for example, rates HAIR qualities — Helicopter vision, Analytical powers, Imagination and sense of Reality.

Shell's Entry System

Graduates being interviewed for Shell jobs must already have a good helicopter vision. A question Shell managers conducting interviews ask can be: If you are the chairman of Shell in the old days, would you have built a refinery in Pulau Bukom?

Or it can be: Imagine you are Singapore's Prime Minister, what would you do under conditions X, Y, and Z? Candidates are forced to fly their helicopters high for the best bird's eye view. If someone's helicopter is only a low-flying aircraft, his view will be limited.

If someone passes the interview, he goes through a whole day of assessment tests, where again, helicopter vision is measured. In one test, for example, a candidate must put up a proposal to see how he defends and justifies them. Then they give him a fresh scenario and expect him to come up with new solutions on the spot.

Next, the candidate is asked to make a group presentation on another topic with a few other applicants to see how well each works in a team. Next, he has to write an essay and then comes another interview.

Said Mr. Kwan Wai Chong, 32, a job analysis manager with Shell's human resource' department, who went through such a gruelling day in 1990 said: "It was like being put in a washing machine for several cycles and then tumbled dry. But I felt that it was the sort of assessment that was compatible with the sort of company that Shell is."

Shell is not likely to hand the job to pilots preferring to fly alone. In this respect, Shell is the direct opposite of the American computer giant Microsoft, which demands only people who lives and breathes computers and nothing else, in some of its departments.

Says Mr. M. Saravanamuthu, Shell's director of personnel: "Shell needs all-rounded characters — people who were active in games, societies, the arts during their school days. "Looking at how oil companies work, we have to make money, satisfy lobbies, get on with governments, be aware of international sensitivities. We want to be around for another 100 years or more. You cannot survive for very long if you are too narrow and cannot communicate."

Shell, Singapore's largest foreign investor, has been here for 103 years and employs about 2,000 people, 600 of whom are executives. Every year, it recruits about a dozen executives with degrees in diverse disciplines including engineering, business administration, computing, economics and accountancy.

Out of hundreds of job applicants, only one in 15 or one in 20 make it to the interviews. Fewer still make it to the assessment tests.

Appraisal system and career development

Even after someone has landed the job, there is no resting on his laurels. He has to meet increasingly higher job targets and score high marks in his annual report card that measures helicopter quality as well as nine other attributes.

These are:

- power of analysis,
- imagination,
- sense of reality,
- achievement motivation,
- business sense,
- decisiveness,
- capacity to motivate,
- delegation, and
- communication.

So, the executive must be able to break down complex problems, make innovative but practical solutions, motivate himself and others, delegate work and relate to people. The 10 qualities are to rate an executive's potential relative to his peers.

In the past, helicopter vision and the first three qualities were used to rate potential, but in recent years, Shell has introduced the other qualities to rate the person as a whole rather than just his intellectual qualities, said Mr. Saravanamuthu.

Potential in Shell is termed Currently Estimated Potential (CEP), which is the highest possible position that an executive can reach irrespective of job opportunities. High-flyers are those given a high CEP grade and are treated like precious commodity. They get postings to different parts of the company, even overseas, to groom them for the career paths projected for them.

For example, if someone has the CEP as a Chairman, the company spends the next 20 years exposing him to different areas of work to prepare him fully for the job. But since views on someone's potential can differ among supervisors, about six managers who have worked with the executive grade him together.

Anyone's CEP can change. Someone's CEP may start high but later plateau off or even worse, crash. In such cases, his career path is adjusted to a less brilliant one, offering fewer job opportunities and lower salaries. Conversely, a late-bloomer's CEP is pegged higher subsequently.

Samuel Walton's Model

Can Wal-Mart's methods be dedicated? Some rules from Mr. Sam. These rules are not in any way intended to be the Ten Commandments of Business. I always push myself on breaking everybody's rules, and I always favoured the Mavericks who challenged my rules. I have fought them all the way, respected them, and in the end, listened to them a lot more closely than I did the pack who always agreed to everything I said.

Nevertheless, here are some rules that worked for me. Pay special attention to Rule No. 10, and if you interpret it in the right spirit — which applies to you — it could mean simply. Break all the rules.

Rule 1: Commit to your business. Believe in it more than anybody else. I think I overcame every single day my personal shortcomings by sheer passion I brought to my work.

Rule 2: Share your profits with your associates, and treat them as partners. In turn, they will treat you as a partner, and together you all perform beyond your wise expectations.

Rule 3: Motivate your partners. Money and ownership alone aren't enough. Constantly, day by day, think of new and more interesting ways to motivate and challenge your partners. Set high goals, encourage competition, and then keep score. Make bets with outrageous payoffs. If things get stale, cross-pollinate; have managers switch jobs with one another to stay challenged. Keep everybody guessing as to what your next trick is going to be. Don't become too predictable.

Rule 4: Communicate everything you possibly can to your partners. The more they know, the more they'll understand. The more they'll care. Once they care, there's no stopping them. If you don't trust your associates to know what's going on, they know what's going on, they'll know you don't really consider them partners. Information is power, and the gain you get from empowering your associates more than offsets the risk of informing your competitors.

Rule 5: Appreciate everything your associates do for the business. A pay check and a stock option will buy one kind of loyalty. But all of us like to be told how much somebody appreciates what we do for them. We like to hear it often, and especially when we have done something we're really proud of. Nothing else can quite substitute for a few well-chosen, well-timed, sincere words of praise. They're absolutely free — and worth a fortune.

Rule 6: Celebrate your successes. Find some humour in your failures. Don't take yourself so seriously. Loosen up, and everybody around you will loosen up. Have fun. Show enthusiasm — always. When all else fails, put on a costume and sing a silly song. Then make everybody else sing with you. Don't do a hula on Wall Street. It's been done. (By Sam Walton, to pay-off a bet, after underestimating the company's profits.) Think up your own stunt. All of this is more important, and more fun, than you think, and it really fools the competition into thinking. "Why should we take those cornballs at Wal-Mart seriously?"

Rule 7: Listen to everyone in your company. And figure out ways to get them talking. The folks on the front lines — the ones who actually talk to the customer — are the only ones who really know what's going on out there. You'd better find out what they know. This really is what total quality is all about. To push responsibility down in your organisation, and to force good ideas to bubble up within it, you must listen to what your associates are trying to tell you.

Rule 8: Exceed your customer's expectations. If you do, they'll come back over and over. Give them what they want — and a little more. Let them know you appreciate them. Make good on all your mistakes, and don't make excuses — apologise. Stand behind everything you do. The two most important words I ever wrote were on that first Wal-Mart sign: **S**atisfaction **G**uaranteed. They're still up there, and they have made all the difference.

Rule 9: Control your expenses better than your competition. This is where you can always find the competitive advantage. For 25 years running — long before Wal-Mart was known as the nation's largest retailer — we ranked No. 1 in our industry for the lowest ratio of expenses of sales. You can make a lot of different mistakes and still recover if you run an efficient operation. Or you can be brilliant and still go out of business if you're too inefficient.

Rule 10: Swim upstream. Go the other way. Ignore the conventional wisdom. If everybody else is doing it one way, there's good chance you can find your niche by going in exactly the opposite direction. I guess in all my years, the one piece of advice I heard more often than any other was: A town of less than 50,000 population cannot support a discount store for very long.

Jack Welch's Leadership

According to Jack Welch, what leaders do.

1. Leaders upgrade their team, using every encounter as an opportunity to evaluate, each and build self-confidence.
2. Leaders make sure people not only have the vision, they live and breathe it.
3. Leaders get into everyone's skin, exuding positive energy and option.
4. Leaders establish trust with candor, transparency and credit.
5. Leaders have the courage to take more unpopular decisions.
6. Leaders probe and push with a curiosity that borders on skepticism, making sure their questions are answered with action.
7. Leaders inspire risk taking and learning by setting on example.
8. Leaders celebrate.

Matsushita's Collective Wisdom

How he practised his concept of collective wisdom — Shuchi — in solving tough business problems is explained by Mr. Morimasa Ogawa, the President of Matsushita Electric, North America in his book.[2]

"Five years after the subsidiary had been established, I am ashamed to admit that the new company was not succeeding. The first oil crisis had just occurred. The oil-producing countries had united and increased the price of oil. The civilisation built on cheap oil was shaken to its core, and there were rumours that Japan's oil supplies might be cut off. Since a large part of our sales was of equipment that ran on oil and propane gas, we were more than a little worried. The company had been at a high break-even point and reduced sales would mean a severe deficit.

At this time, I was managing director, One day, Konosuke Matsushita dropped in for a visit. It has been a long time since he'd been there and he wanted to talk to us. It wasn't the best time for him to come, but there was nothing I could do about it.

First he visited the factory and was very pleased, looking with amazement at the huge boilers being manufactured. It was later, when we sat down to talk, that the roof caved in. I will never forget that conversation with Matsushita.

"The factory and the merchandise look great," he said. "How are operations?" Nervously, I answered, "Not very good. Sales have dropped because of the oil crisis."

"Not very good? What do you mean?"

"We're running at a bit of a loss," I fumbled.

"By how much?"

"Nine billion."

"What? I could understand if sales were zero and the deficit was in personnel costs, but you've got sales of ¥ 100 billion and are ¥ 9 billion in the red. You mean to tell me we've got a company like this in the Matsushita group? Responsibility for running a mess like this lies with you and the executives under you. The head office must also take responsibility for letting this go. It's all because the head office lent you that ¥ 20 billion.

Tomorrow, I'm going to talk to them about getting it back. That's all, Ogawa. Whip this thing back into shape!"

For the moment I was speechless, but then I ran after him. "Mr. Matsushita, that would mean disaster for us! It's five days to payday. At the end of the month we have to pay for materials and parts. If you take that ¥ 20 billion back now, we won't be able to pay for them."

"That's right," he remarked. "You won't be able to pay the wages and the subcontractors' fees. You have to pay the cafeteria cooks, too. But I'm not going to lend you any money if you and your colleagues are going to run an operation like this. I'm pulling your loan tomorrow."

"But then we won't be able to do anything. We'll go bankrupt."

"What are you talking about? You've got 4,000 superb employees working here. Talk it over with them, get their ideas, and come up with a reconstruction plan that will work. I know you have confidence in this company, but confidence isn't enough. You have to come up with a plan that a banker would approve of one that would make him think. 'This looks like a good operation. If we lend it money, we're sure to get it back.' If you can get a plan like that together. I'll write a letter of recommendation to Sumitomo Bank for you. With that letter, they're sure to give you a ¥ 20 billion loan using the land, buildings, and equipment here as collateral. Now, get to work."

We had gone to the head office for that ¥ 20 billion loan to cover operating expenses because business had been sluggish, our internal reserves low and our dependence on seasonal products high. The rules of the division system required that we pay interest on the loan comparable to what we would pay to a bank. We often extort interest and even

2. Torn Yamaguchi, PHP, Peace and Happiness through Prosperity, and Dr. Robert JJ Wango, Humanistic Management, Australian PHP Seminar, April/May, 1990, Panasonic Australia Phy Ltd, North Ryde NSW.

make a profit of subsidiary struggling under a heavy financial burden. Five years before, Matsushita had impressed me as a compassionate person when he apologised to the chef for not eating all his food, but now he appeared more like a ruthless demon.

I didn't have time to get absorbed in my emotions, however. Matsushita called all the managers and executives together and reprimanded us sharply: "You're working under the Matsushita name, but this is no Matsushita company. If you can't rebuild this company, it will collapse and everyone will have to be laid off. If that happens, you managers have to find jobs for each one of our employees and then figure out what to do about yourselves." He went on with the usual advice we'd heard a thousand times. "If each of the sections of each department can show just a little profit in its accounting, the company as a whole will get back on its feet. Get down to the section level and make sure you bring together the wisdom of each and every employee. Tell the sales departments in every division to research products that will bring a 50% increase in sales in the next three years. Have R&D devote themselves to achieving that goal. If the goods don't sell, have everyone get out and sell them. Take the 10% excess staff and equipment and find a project for them to work on. Take 1% of sales and invest it in a new activity. Uncover the buried losses and turn them into a 2% profit. We can turn this company around and make it into a winner. The wisdom and knowledge to do this can be found in the workplace."

There was nothing unusual in what he told us, but putting it into practice was not going to be easy. The ideas everyone came up with, however, far exceeded my expectations. That year we still ran a big deficit, but when I retired five years later, the company was in good shape, one that could call itself a Matsushita subsidiary.

It wasn't me that got that company back on track. It was the result of all the knowledge and ideas of the employees pooled together. I realised that the source of it all lay in the rigour of Konosuke Matsushita's attitude toward work. It was he who shattered our belief that the source of the trouble was outside the company, and who drove us to do better.

It is important that managers, from the moment they embark on their leadership careers, cultivate both a compassion for-others and an attitude of discipline in the workplace. If you are strict with your people and lax in your own attitude towards work, the results will be disastrous.

PART-II

In Part II we shall turn to a discussion of processes of Global Management such as Planning, Organising, Staffing, Directing, Co-ordinating and Controlling and Evaluating process in the next five chapters. This part gives a detailed picture of how Global Companies "Manage" the above processes in order to achieve their pre-determined goals.

Let us start with the most important process of planning.

They are:

5. Planning
6. Organising
7. Staffing
8. Directing
9. Controlling and Evaluating

5 Planning

The chapter is discussed under the following headings :
• Introduction • Definition and Elements of Planning • Long, Medium and Short-term Plans, Matsushita, GE • Corporate Planning at an MNC • Implementation some Considerations.

INTRODUCTION

In the past, it was easy to prosper with little corporate planning. It was easy to make profits because of the acceleration of demand created by rapid population growth, fast national income growth, and increase in personal income, limited competition and new market opportunities.

Times have changed. Today Global Business is dependent on various institutions like Government agencies, unions, public opinion, transportation, suppliers of vital services, changing market and consumer lifestyles. As a result, business operations are highly influenced by various factors.

More important professionalisation of business and the introduction of professional management have increased the complexity, size and sophistication of management of Global Business and particularly the first and most important process of managing, *i.e.*, Planning.

Information revolution and electronic data processing of large quantity of external information pertinent to business, financial planning complicated by diversification of ownership. Leading institutions, tax planning and minimisation monetary inflation, changing stock markets; growing complexity, specialisation and precision of production planning due to scientific discoveries, new materials and products, high speed manufacture and robotics, sales and distribution and consumer reaction and satisfaction of changing consumer tastes and lifestyles, inventory control, human resources training, development and education, physical facilities planning and research, development and design, etc., have also contributed to the importance of planning the future business operations, instead of letting the future take its own course and chasing the uncertain future.

DEFINITION AND ELEMENTS OF PLANNING

Module 1 — Planning

Planning is the process of setting goals and choosing the means to achieve those goals.

Planning involves selecting missions and objectives, as well as actions to achieve them, which requires decision making, *i.e.*, Choosing course of action from among alternatives.

In designing an environment for effective performance of individuals working together in a group. If the group effort is to be effective, people must know what they are expected to accomplish. This is the function of planning. The most basic of all managerial functions.

Planning also strongly implies managerial creativity and innovation.

Planning bridges the gap from where we are, to where we want to go.

Types of Plans

Plans can be classified as:

1. **Vision:** The Broad Dream
2. **Mission:** Purpose or function or tasks of an enterprise or agency or any part of it. The purpose of university is teaching, research and providing services to the community.
3. **Objectives or Goals:** The ends toward which activity is aimed.
4. **Strategies:** The determination of the basic long-term objectives of an enterprise and adoption of courses of action and allocation of resources necessary to achieve those goals.
5. **Policies:** General statements or understandings that guide or channel thinking in decision making.
6. **Procedures:** Plans that establish a required method of handling future activities.
7. **Rules:** Spell out specific required action or non-actions, allowing no discretions *e.g.*, no smoking.
8. **Programmes:** A complex of goals, policies, procedures, rules, task assignments, steps to be taken, resources to be employed and other elements necessary to carry out a given course of action.
9. **Budgets:** A statement of expected results expressed in numerical terms.

Steps in Planning

(a) Being aware of opportunities
(b) Setting objectives
(c) Considering planning premises
(d) Identifying alternatives
(e) Evaluating alternatives
(f) Choosing an alternative
(g) Formulating supportive plans
(h) Quantifying plans by making budgets.

MBO — Relationship of Objectives and Organisational Hierarchy

1. Vision	Board of Directors
2. Mission	Top Level MGRs
3. Overall objectives (Long-range)	Top Level MGRs
4. Key result areas	Middle Level MGRs
5. Division objectives	Middle Level MGRs
6. Department objectives	First Line MGRs
7. Individual objectives, performance, personal development	First Line MGRs
Hierarchy of Objectives	***Organisational Hierarchy***

Strategic Planning Process Model

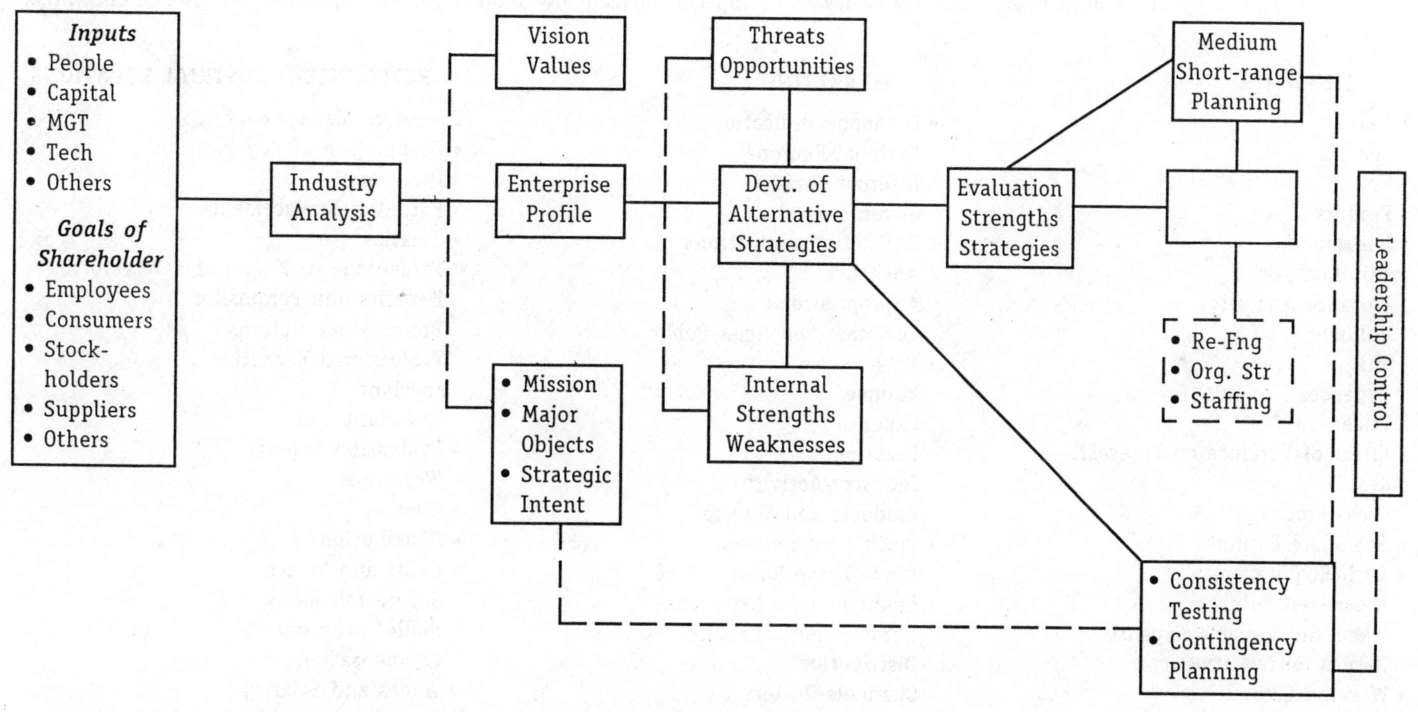

Fig. 5.1

DECISION MAKING

- Is defined as the selection of a course of action from among alternatives.
- Is the core of planning.
- A plan cannot exist unless a decision, a commitment of resources, direction or reputation has been made.
- The process of decision making involves:
  1. Premising
  2. Identifying alternatives
  3. Evaluating alternatives in terms of the goal sought.
  4. Choosing an alternative, *i.e.*, making a decision.
- Rationality in decision making
- Limited or bounded rationality
- Simon — Satisfying – Picking a course of action that is satisfactory or good enough under the circumstances.
- Programmed and unprogrammed decisions.

Illustrative Categories of Operating Information

Past 2-4 years, Current year, Forecast 2-5 years, By Major
t* = most likely regularly reviewed by top management 0 = regular review dependent on type of enterprise;

FINANCIAL

Sales
- List prices
- Net
- Product
- Backlog

Profit Analysis
- Variance Analysis
- Volume
- Mix
- Expenses
- Prices
- Effect of Variance on Forecasts

Sales
- Gross Profits
- • Per Share Earnings
- • Cash Requirements
- Breakeven Point
- Fixed and Variable Expense
- • Return on investment
- • Working Capital
- Current Ratio
- Loan Restrictions
- Line of Credit Utilisation
- • Accounts Receivable
- % Sales
- • Inventories
- Type
- Cost Category
- Product
- Turnover
- % Current Assets
- Product Production Cycle
- • Make or Buy Analysis
- • Property. Plant and Equipment
- Expenditures less Depreciation
- Lease obligations
- % Net Worth
- Ownership
- • Market Movement
- • Shares Traded
- • Principal Stockholders
- Major Market Transactions
- • Other Normal Balance Sheet and Operating Statement Items

MARKETING

- • Economic Indicators
- National-Regional
- International
- Governmental
- Legislation-regulations
- Antitrust
- Appropriations
- Customer-Consumer Public
- • Sales
- Volume
- Expense
- Location
- Industry-Activity
- Products and Services
- • Profit Contribution
- Prices-Lease Rates
- Credit Policies-Experience
- Improvements Required by Market
- Distribution
- Channels-Outlets
- Policies
- Important Competitors-Commercial Intelligence
- Share of Market
- Products, Policies and Plans
- Specific Advantage-Disadvantage
- Sales Management
- Sales Force
- Number
- Location
- Expense
- Compensation Plan
- Training Programme
- • Performance Evaluation
- Sales and Costs per Salesman
- Territory-Customer Penetration
- Advertising and Sales Promotion
- Allocation of Different Marketing Mechanisms

PERSONNEL-INDUSTRIAL RELATIONS

Executive Management
- • Designation of Key Positions
- Incumbent
- Potential Replacement
- • Salaries
- Percentage of Responsible Workforce
- Benefits and Perquisites
- Bonus-Stock Options
- Professional Education
- In-Plant
- Out-Plant
- • Evaluation Reports
- Workforce
- • Number
- • Distribution
- Gains and Losses
- Separation Rates
- Skills Inventory
- Compensation
- • Wages and Salaries
- Classification and Rates
- Paid
- Increase
- Benefits
- Incentive Awards
- Recruiting and Employment
- Requirements
- Sources
- Costs
- Time
- Selection Procedures
- Administration

Ratios of Personnel Staff (No. and Cost) to:
- Workforce
- Other Staff
- Sponsored Activities
- Communications Programme
- Union Labour Relations
- Grievance Policy-Procedure
- Number and Ratio to Employees
- Processing Cost
- Contract Negotiation-Arbitrations Costs
- Time
- Resultant Awards

Fig. 5.2

For Corporate Planning in Larger-size companies

Organisation Product, and/or Geographical categories

remainder reviewed occasionally and available on call; italics = Information less generally maintained or specifically identified.

PRODUCTION

Raw Materials and Supplies
- Performance (Actual vs. Standard)
  - Inventory
  - Price
- Vendor Performance
- Cost Reduction Programme

Production
- • *Capability*
  - Management
  - Manpower
    - Number
    - Skills
  - Machinery and Equipment
    - Current Available
    - Proposed Acquisitions
    - Idle
- Space
- • Schedules
- Lead Time
- Production
  - Lot Sizes
  - In-process Inventory
- Shipping Dates
- • Costs
  - Actual vs. Standard
    - Labor Performance
      - Direct
      - Indirect
    - Scrap and Rework
  - Cost Reduction Programme
    - Engineering
    - Materials
    - Labour

Quality Control Programme
- Inspection
- Yield

RESEARCH AND DEVELOPMENT PRODUCTS

Technology-External Internal
- Knowledge-State of the Art
  - Opportunities
  - Information-Support
- Specific Discoveries-Advances
  - Patents

Product-Research Objective

Professional and Support Personnel
- • Number
- Technical Qualifications-Potentialities
  - Experience
  - Publication
  - Patent
  - Out-Plant Professional Activities
  - Educational Self-Improvement

Projects and Total
- Costs
  - People
  - Space
  - Machinery and Equipment
  - Other
- Schedule of Completion
- Evaluation
  - Number Proposed and Budgeted
  - • Profits Contribution
  - Significant Improvement Existing Products
  - New products
  - In-plant Process and Other Improvement

Space per Person
- Office
- Laboratory
- Other support

Management
- *Special Policies*
- *Separation Rate*
- • Percentage Total Cost to Gross sales

FACILITIES

Physical Characteristics
- Location
- Functions
- Floor Area
  - *Gross*
  - *Circulation*
  - *Structural*
  - *Service*
  - *Net Productive*
- Special Features
- Age

Costs-Total and per Sq-Ft.
- Existing
  - Initial Construction
  - *Rearrangement*
  - Maintenance-Repair
  - Improvements-Additions
- • New
- Project Management
  - Master planning
  - Architectural-Engineering
  - Consultant Services-Other
  - Construction Supervision
- Construction
- Move-in and Related
- • Space Capacity and Vacancy Factor
- People
- Manufacturing-Production
- • Functional Use
- General Administrative
- Direct Productive
- Service and Support
- • Construction Schedules-Budgets
- Master Planning
- A&E-Other Preparatory
- Construction
- Occupancy or Use

Book-Depreciated Value

Fig. 5.3

Note: The assistance of the following individuals in formulating this material is acknowledged with thanks: P. J. Fenchel T.L. Graham (Finance); T.S. Blount (Marketing and Research, Development, Products); T. B. Chamness (Personnel-Industrial Relations): C.W. Goldbeck (Production).

Vice President, Long-Range Planning

Autonetics (A Division of North American Aviation Inc.) 1962

I. Function

Plans and directs the operations and activities of the Long-range Planning Office in accordance with corporate and Autonetics policies for the purpose of developing long-range plans which will achieve optimum growth, stability, and profitability for the Autonetics Division.

II. Company and Relationships

A. Autonetics

1. *Executive Office*—Reports to the Executive Office; assists in the development of Autonetics' policies, plans, and objectives; advises on Long-range Planning performance and other matters affecting the future of Autonetics.
2. *Divisions and Other Staff Offices*—Co-ordinates and integrates the Long-range Planning activities in the various divisions and staff offices.

B. Other NAA Operating Divisions

Confers and co-ordinates with management of other operating divisions on matters of mutual interest.

C. General Offices

Co-ordinates Long-range Planning activities with General Offices executives; obtains their policy guidance and assistance. Furnishes to them reports and information required for their purposes.

III. Responsibilities and Authority

Within the framework of established policy and approved plans and programmes has the responsibility and authority to:

A. Formulate and submit proposals for Long-range objectives, programmes, and plans to the Executive Office for approval.

B. Apply corporate policy as adapted in terms of Autonetics requirements, establish and administer implementing policy and procedures for the development of Autonetics' Long-range plans.

C. Direct the activities of Long-range Planning within the framework of established policy and approved plans and programmes as follows:

1. Determine what data and analysis are needed as a basis for planning; co-ordinate efforts to obtain such data.
2. Analyze domestic and international politico-economic trends and evaluate their effect on the growth and development of Autonetics.
3. Maintain close familiarity with military planning and research efforts and evaluate their probable effect on Autonetics operations.
4. Review commercial market research studies and all proposals for entrance to non-defense markets, and take appropriate action.
5. Co-ordinate efforts to assess technological trends and imminent technological developments within NAA and Autonetics and by competitors, suppliers and customers.
6. Co-ordinate activities to analyse Autonetics' capabilities, limitations alternative uses of Autonetics' resources, including facilities, personnel, production techniques, organisation structure, and finances.

7. Review proposals for investment of NAA capital by Autonetics in relation to risk, estimated earnings, cash flow, returns on investment, and Autonetics' long-range goals and objectives.
8. Direct efforts to determine the trend of competitors' policies and behaviour.
9. Review and approve all Long-range forecasts prepared by Autonetics division and staff offices.
10. Correlate and interpret all data and analyses received, forecast the future competitive environment; propose goals and objectives; and prepare proposed plans to achieve approved Autonetics goals and objectives.
11. Integrate, through co-ordination, Autonetics divisions' plans to ensure that they are in accord with approved long-range plans and objectives.
12. Review all proposals by Autonetics personnel for company mergers, acquisitions, and joint ventures; and recommend such proposals to the appropriate General Offices executives.
13. Control the hiring, developing, evaluating, promoting, and disciplining of employees of the Long-range Planning Office.
14. Direct all other managerial functions necessary to the operations of the Long-range Planning Office, such as: assign responsibilities and authority; determine standards and goals; budget and control departmental operating funds; and advance operational efficiency.

D. Provide Long-range Planning assistance to all Autonetics divisions and staff offices.

E. Represent the Long-range Planning Office in contacts and meetings with customers, representatives of government, industry, and the public

F. Serve on the following Autonetics committees:

Long-range Planning Committee—Chairman
Executive Committee
Management Council
Proposal
Policy Board

Director of Planning

Continental-EMSCO Company (A Division of the Youngstown Sheet and Tube Company) November 1960 *(Reports to Vice President—Special Projects)*

Basic Responsibilities

Provide information to assist Management in formulating long- and short-range goals and plans of the Company. Also assist in the updating of these goals plus general monitoring of attainment.

Co-ordinate activities and prepare special studies centering on acquisition, disposals, joint endeavors, manufacturing rights, and patents.

Serve as resource for determining the acquisition, disposal and movement of physical properties.

Encourage the stimulation of ideas from Management toward broadening Company operations; extract these ideas and follow up on possibilities.

Develop, recommend, and obtain Management approval of plans, procedures, and policies to be followed in implementing diversification programmes.

Perform basic research on diversification, using such sources as American Management Association, National Industrial Conference Board, Research Institute of America, and other points of information.

Perform internal and external economic studies to secure necessary information for over-all planning.

Utilise staff service personnel plus line and committee persons in accumulating and evaluating data.

Analyse the Company's physical properties and personnel capabilities to determine our production span.

In conjunction with staff services, periodically survey performance capabilities of sales, engineering, manufacturing, and service components of the Company.

Conduct an initial survey of the manufacturing organisation's physical properties (facilities, equipment, and tools) and keep information current.

Investigate and determine possibilities of other significant use for our basic products.

Assist in communicating and implementing the diversification decisions of Management during transition periods.

Prepare necessary reports to keep Management informed.

Budgets: Are statements of financial resources set aside for specific activities in a given period of time. They are primarily devices to control an organisation's activities and thus, the important component of planning, programming and principles.

PROCESS OF PLANNING

Generally, there are two basic approaches to the process of planning:

1. Top Down
2. Bottom Up.

Top Down Approach: It is the top management assisted by the planning division, that sets out the plan to be implemented over the organisation.

Bottom Up Approach: Most Global Organisations adopt this approach, whereby the planning process is a year. long process. The V.P. Planning at the headquarters asks each country to prepare the annual plan and submit it by October of the year. The Country Head asks his company's various department heads to prepare a plan for the next year, taking into consideration the market opportunities. All the departments like Production, Marketing, Procurement, H.R. Finance, R&D, etc., prepare the departmental plans and the Country Head discusses these plans with the departmental heads and country planning division and finalises them and send them by October. The V.P. Planning discusses these plans with top management and finalises them by 1st December. Then the finalised corporate plan of the entire corporation is sent to all the country heads for implementation. The country heads call for a corporate planning meeting by the middle of December and educate and inform the heads of department to go ahead and implement the annual plan by staying within the budget and achieve the targets set for the next year. In some cases, global corporations prepare alternative plans and several plans to suit several scenarios in case there are sudden changes in the economic and financial conditions in particular countries or a Global recession like the 2008, financial crisis, which prompt the global companies to change their objectives and plans and bring into operation contingency plans and budgets because of changed circumstances These companies, which are well attuned to the planning process, are well prepared to implement contingency plans and succeed in meeting changed plans.

I believe that one of the great strengths of American business and Americans in general is their ability and keenness to plan ahead, whether it is X-mas shopping, going on a holiday, or financing their higher studies, they are always looking ahead and planning to set aside some money for a holiday buying in post-X-mas sale for gifts next X-mas. One of the great weaknesses of my own countrymen is the lack of planning and until the crisis looms its ugly head no planning is made to prevent or overcome the crisis.

LONG-RANGE AND ANNUAL AT MATSUSHITA AND GE

Role and Definition

Before going into the details it would be worthwhile to look at the role of the business plan in the managerial scheme of things. There is a wide array of management tools and systems available: those related to financing, such as profit-and-loss and balance sheet accounting, management analysis, and cost accounting; those related to production, such as process control, quality control, industrial engineering (IE) and value engineering (VE); and new control methods in fields such as marketing, personnel, education, information, and research and development (R&D). All of these have their own rationales and have been successful in increasing efficiency and competitiveness. But from the viewpoint of overall management of the corporation they are not independent of or in competition with each other, regardless of how they were originally conceived. If not ultimately incorporated into a comprehensive plan, they cannot be used to the full effect and will not make their proper contribution to corporate performance. Thus, the business plan is not just another management tool but the result of taking into account all aspects of management and integrating them into a coherent whole.

Given this comprehensive and integrative character, its role in corporate management becomes immediately apparent:

1. It clarifies what the manager intends to do
2. It determines how management philosophy will be implemented
3. It is a guide for employee action
4. It is a yardstick for measuring the appropriateness or inappropriateness of management activities

Long-range Planning

I explained the concept of strategy in the earlier sections of this chapter. Whether long-range planning is strategic or not is based on the managers' determination and abilities, and the degree to which the environment requires that the corporate strategy be changed.

(1) *Mission, characteristics and time span*: Even if a corporation changes its strategy, there is no guarantee of success. Surveys and analyses cannot possibly provide every grain of necessary information; there will always be unknown factors. Basic strategy changes require large amounts of capital; if the strategy fails the damage to the company may be fatal—with repercussions for employees, the industry, and society. If the corporation finds it necessary to change its strategy, the first thing that it must do is to get a good grasp of what the future holds for the company.

A company's future is determined at least in part by the future of the business environment. As it is impossible to predict the future, we can only speculate as to what that environment will be. Whatever those assumptions, the conclusions that can be reached fall into one of three different types, A, B, and C, as shown in Figures 5.4, 5.5 and 5.6. The graphs estimating corporate growth place growth on the vertical axis and passage of time on the horizontal axis.

Figure 5.4 shows a continuing growth potential situation (Type A—growth market), where the industry's economic conditions are good over a long period of time. When business is good, skilled management can take the corporation above the mean line, and even mediocre management can maintain acceptable performance levels. Such conditions prevailed during Japan's period of rapid economic growth, 1960-72. In this type of situation, long-range

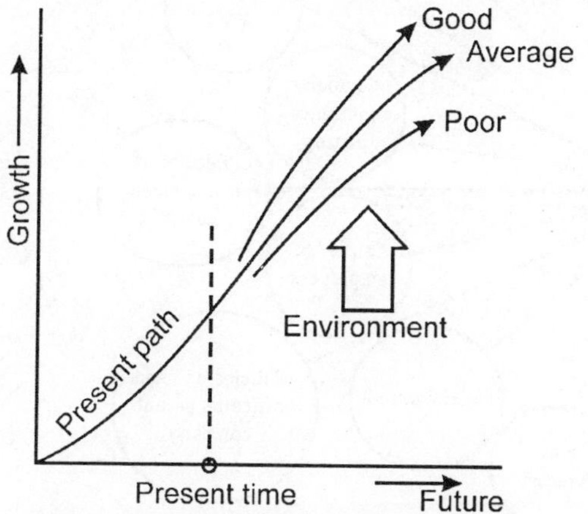

Fig. 5.4. Type A Growth Market

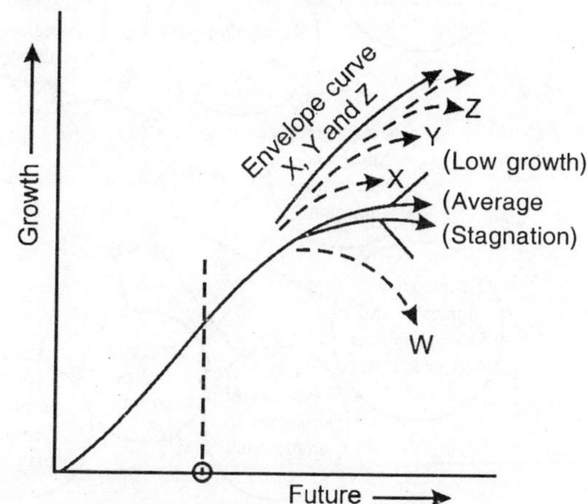

Fig. 5.5. Type B Mature Market

planning consists of merely continuing the present activities. A company does not really need a strategy: all it has to do to succeed is work hard and continue investing.

Figure 5.5 shows a situation in which growth has levelled off in the entire industry. (Type B—mature market). However, the structure of industry is such that aggregate demand is not likely to taper off or disappear.

No corporation can survive a period of low growth or stagnation indefinitely, and must work to increase the growth rate. Severe competition elicits a two-pronged reaction, strengthening both defense and offense. If a new, successful company appears on the scene, a reaction will set in, leading to a few drastic failures like W. This is the logical outcome when the market pie cannot grow.

In such a competitive environment, mediocrity will not survive. The company must pile up a series of successes and must provide the kind of management that will move it along on a steady growth course such as the X, Y, Z envelope shown.

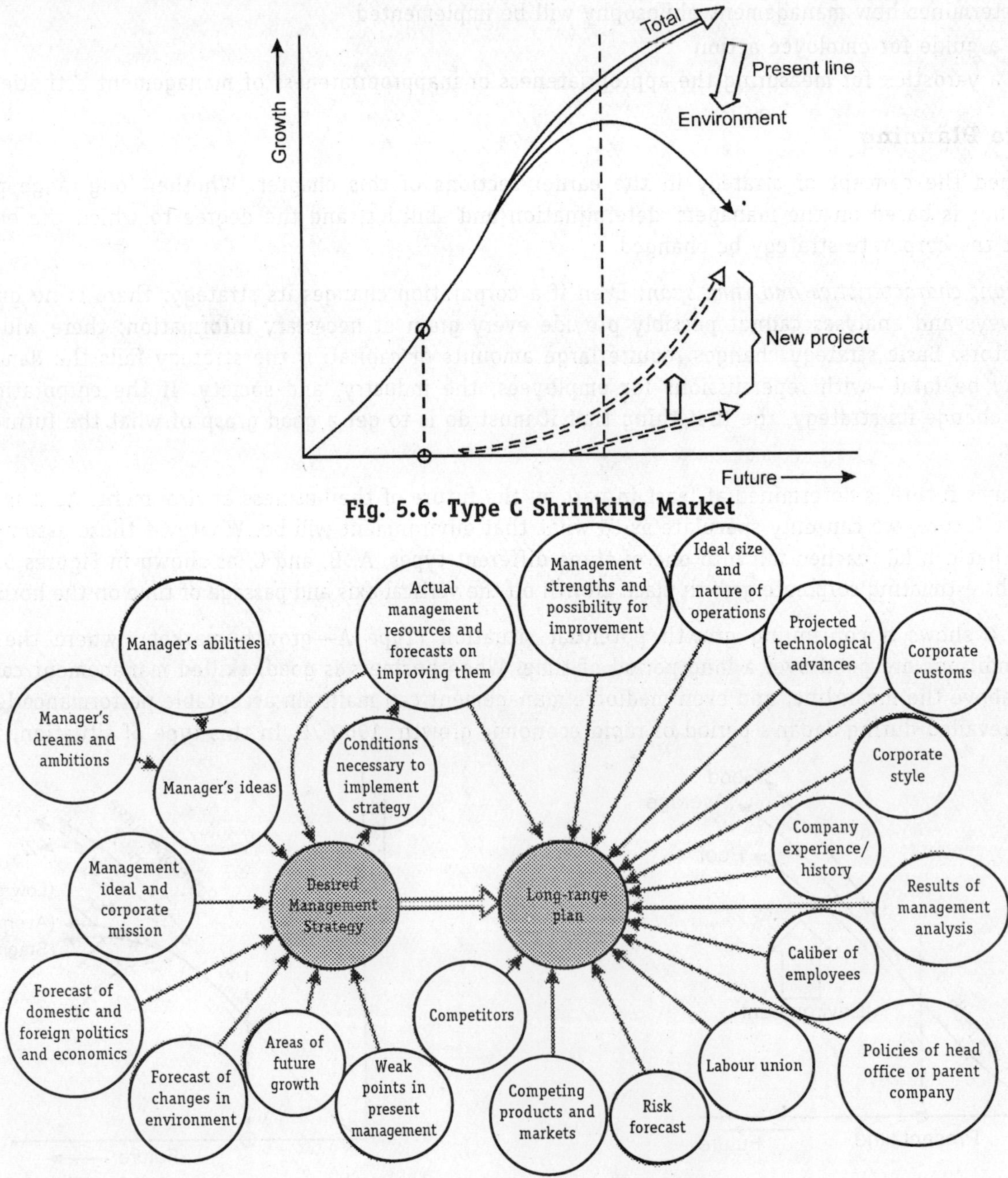

Fig. 5.6. Type C Shrinking Market

Fig. 5.7. Long-range Planning

This is a challenging situation indeed. Matsushita's Electric Iron Division is one that managed to succeed. The electric iron has been in the mature product stage for a long time; total demand has levelled off. Despite the iron division's long history, it maintains an operational performance well above many other Matsushita divisions. Even over the last three years when the home appliance industry in Japan was performing poorly, the iron division registered a 5 per cent growth in sales. The division has created demand by developing new products that are ahead of the competition: steam irons, pants pressers, travel irons, cordless irons, and wrinkle-removers. It has developed networks in overseas markets; it even gets orders from competitors. It has reduced personnel by using robotics and other methods to automate production processes, and continues to make major reforms in both the offensive and defensive aspects of the industry. They have managed to maintain an excellent performance record. The selection of a Type B path is in itself a strategy, but its implementation requires the tactical strength to fight and win every battle in the campaign.

In the Type C (shrinking market) situation, shown in Figure 5.6, forecasts suggest that if the present path of management continues it will lead to decline. If there is no hope for the company to move along a Type B path (surviving in a mature market), then new lines of business should be developed to offset the decline in the company's main field. Inevitably the growth of any core business will peak and then begin to decline. When the decline reaches a certain point, the company must withdraw before it incurs losses. The main question then is where and how to distribute limited management resources. What is required is a strategy survival that involves deciding when and where to fight.

Medium-range Planning

Medium-range planning is often considered in terms of a specific period of time, usually three or five years, and is used in areas ranging from national defense to payments on an automobile. I now want to discuss these plans not only in terms of time, but also in terms of their mission and character.

1. Mission, Character and Time Span

When a corporation sets up a long-range plan for a period of more than five years, it will inevitably lose its timeliness because the business climate will change during that time. The best way to prevent inaccuracy is to institute a medium-range plan with detailed objectives to serve as the first step in the attainment of long-range goals.

While the medium-range plan may seem to be just a check point on the path to long-term goals, it is in fact much more than that. The more expansion and diversification called for in the long-range plan, the more crucial the role of the medium-range plan.

The most important aspect of a medium-range plan is that it seeks to improve the basic constitution of the corporation, and as such is an important part of the company's strategic structure. The medium-range plan becomes a campaign that links the annual plan's tactical strengths with the long-range plan's strategic concepts.

If the long-range plan does not incorporate strategic changes—even if it is just an extension of present policy—it will still have to take into account changes and competition in the business environment. In that case, the medium-range plan becomes more important than the long-range plan because it is the basis for improving the company's overall structure.

If errors in a long-range plan are discovered early, the plan can be redrawn; it can be periodically checked and revised. But the three years of a medium-range plan pass quickly. It is essential that the manager be alert at all times and not try to run the plan on automatic pilot, or the competition could get ahead of him. For this reason, the medium-range plan is the most crucial of the three types of business plan.

2. Content

Marketing, profit, and financial targets are part of any business plan. The medium-range plan gives a detailed schedule for the steps to be taken in the first three years of projects that are crucial to the success of the long-range plan. Such projects might include, for example, construction of a new factory or a second building.

Strengthening the corporation is the basic reason for creating a medium-range plan. Translating that into a concrete plan requires clarifying the following goals:

- Target values and themes for invigorating the Company Schedule and procedures for achieving those targets. Separate procedures for implementing the targets of each department
- Ideas and schedules for each department.
- Most of the measures suggested have to do with the financial sector. For example, if you simply lower the break-even point to 95 per cent of what it is now, you won't be making any major changes and that is not a real strategy. However, if you lower it to 80 per cent, and do that without laying off workers or cutting down operations, then you'll be forced to make drastic changes, such as the following:
- Increase sales by 30 per cent.
- Improve products without raising prices.
- Hold increases in fixed costs to less than 10 per cent, and reduce the fixed cost ratio from 43 to 38 per cent. Maintain variable costs at present levels.
- Hold personnel increases to 3 per cent or less.
- Decrease the size of departments (other than production and engineering).

Annual Planning

A company's annual plan is its strategy for surviving in the real world. Medium-and long-range plans deal with intentions and dreams, whereas the annual plan deals with present conditions. The difference between these plans is that the medium-and long-range plans require no accounting treatment, but the annual plan incorporates strict numerical controls.

1. Mission, Character and Time Span

Ultimately, the results of annual plans must be incorporated on profit-and-loss and balance sheets, on which society bases its evaluation of the corporation and its managers. Wages, bonuses, taxes and stock dividends are paid out according to the results of the annual plan. The annual plan must seek to fully utilise the company's abilities at that time.

However, it also represents the first year of the medium-range plan and the point of departure for the long-range plan. It must thus be in accord with those strategies, even if that means sacrificing short-term profits. Just how much emphasis should be placed on immediate profits, and how much should be sacrificed for the sake of the long-range goals is something that must be decided by the manager. It is in this area that one frequently hears criticism of American management for focussing on short-term profits at the expense of long-term strategy.

The annual plan is a blueprint for short-term battles that most efficiently incorporate tactical strength. It is an operational plan that guides management in the details necessary for success. Management must be concerned with the tactical details of constant day-to-day improvements in procedures whose direction and results are checked annually, so that the achievement of strategic ends is not a hollow success. It is a waste of time to set goals and work towards them only to find that the annual results are poor.

2. Content

Because every member of the corporate organisation is working at all times to fulfil the annual plan's goals, the goals must be worth the effort. If the plan contains nothing more than the level of sales, amount of production, budgets, and profits, it is merely a guideline for top executives.

The annual plan must be more than this. It must be a map that clearly shows everyone how to reach the goals. The more detailed that map, the better. People will look at it and devise ways in which to reach these goals more quickly. In the modern corporation, people are divided into groups, with each group simultaneously working toward separate goals. The annual plan must be prepared so that it fits the needs of each department in the corporation. When this type of plan is put into action, the employees will come up with new ideas and innovations spontaneously. This is the reason I advocate the departmental management system.

3. The Basis of Policymaking

The annual plan constitutes the first year of the medium-range plan and is a plan for achieving specific objectives. There are powerful competitors on the battlefield, and they may break through your lines. That is why we need to develop a plan that forecasts all eventualities. If, for example, we predict a price offensive by a competitor, then we can incorporate into our plan methods of dealing with it, such as discounting or reducing prices, or putting out a new product. Factors that might be considered include such external elements as exchange rates and the availability of financing, and internal problems like production delays or a drop in sales. The annual plan must be drawn up in line with the basic approach provided by the medium-range plan, and it must be able to deal with changes in battle conditions in so far as we are able to forecast them.

4. Pointers for Success

We can see that the success of a plan depends on how suitable it is to the goal, and how quickly it can be acted upon. There are four prerequisites to making an annual plan:

1. The plan must clearly indicate the targets and how they relate to the activity of people in the workplace.
2. Leadership must respond positively and quickly to all changes that occur in the workplace.
3. The job-site leaders must be entrusted with complete authority.
4. Monthly accounting and reviews must be performed as quickly as possible.

The monthly accounting and evaluation should be done three to five days after the closing date. Factors that cause delay should be investigated immediately, and action taken to remedy the situation. No matter how accurate an accounting report, it will be worthless if not used within 10 days. In the departmental management system, people often prepare a preliminary accounting report before the closing date and subject it to examination in departmental meetings to give themselves more flexibility in decision making.

5. Corporate Climate

The most surprising thing for me when I joined Matsushita Electric was that everyone in the company—the people in the engineering department, in personnel, on the assembly lines—knew what the business plan was for their department. Whether or not the goals would be met on time was a major topic of conversation.

The employees are told what the business plan is at the beginning of the period, and are given the results of the monthly accounting at morning assembly. This has imparted to the employees the belief that they are responsible for achieving the goals set down in the business plan. That has now become a corporate custom, and is one of Matsushita Electric's greatest strengths.

I am firmly convinced that implementing autonomous management is the best method of carrying out the mission assigned by the monthly plan and demonstrating the abilities of management to the greatest extent possible.

Three-tiered Business Planning

Because the annual plan constitutes the first year of the medium-range plan and the medium-range plan represents the first three years of the long-range plan, they are all part of the same vision. Some people think the three plans are separate, either because they look different, or because some textbooks treat them as such. If they were separate, then our strategy would lose its foundation and our tactics would lead us in the wrong direction. The annual, medium-range, and long-range plans are valuable precisely because they are in fact a single plan on three connected levels. A business planning table shows how closely integrated the three plans are.

This figure contains, from left to right, the items that must be accomplished to achieve the targets of the long-range plan, the time that it takes to achieve them, and the eventual targets. The first year has conditions that must be met in the annual plan, and the items that must be included up to the third year of the mid-range plan. You can see that this is also a factor analysis (fishbone) diagram (Figure 5.7) describing long-range goals. If the staff members involved and the people on the job use the procedure outlined above, they can compile this type of table and create a strategy that is tactically interconnected and utilises the knowledge of all of the employees. This procedure will also produce tactics that are suited to the overall strategy. Investment in the research sector and surveys of new businesses, for example, make no contribution whatsoever to the annual plan, yet they are crucial items that must be included and actively pursued with annual checks on progress. A financial examination of the plan shows that an estimated ¥10 billion is needed for investment, and a lower-level plan for internal accumulation of ¥4 billion over a period of three and-a-half years is the theme of a new medium-range plan. A similar fishbone chart can also be compiled for this plan. This is an extremely simple method, one that I have found to be very effective.

CORPORATE PLANNING AT GRAND UNION

Plan

In order to attain established objectives, top management must first plan—creatively. It is in this stage that the largest measure of creative thinking is demanded.

Good planning starts with the setting of both near-term and ultimate objectives. Surprisingly, there are more than a few managers who are never quite clear as to what they are driving at and why.

Creative thinking ensures an imaginative approach. Perhaps the best way to clarify the objectives of a company is to visualise what your business should be five, ten, or twenty years from now. What is your best estimate of what the market will be? What share of the market should you have as your objective? What changes may you forecast in the means of production and distribution? In the wants of customers? Should the image your company has created in the minds of your customers be changed?

As you attempt to develop future objectives, thinking in general terms will not suffice.

In our business, for instance, we try to create a specific image that will flash in the minds of housewives whenever they hear the name Grand Union. To be sure, from time to time this image may be modified because of economic and social changes, but always a definite "personality" should be associated with the company's name.

Examples of how objectives may be established and reached may best be drawn from actual experience. In 1947, when I was made head of our organisation, the Grand Union Company already had an excellent reputation. It was the second-oldest food chain in the nation, with 319 stores and annual sales of $ 83 million. (In 1959, sales were over $ 600 million.) Most of these stores, however, were small, neighborhood units. A cumbersome route division, selling door to door, still contributed more than 15 per cent ot our volume.

The revolution in retailing was just moving into high gear. The basic changes that were taking place in the nation's way of life and its "standard of eating" made it imperative that Grand Union's objectives be redefined if the company was to be one of the leaders in this revolution. As early as 1919, the Federal Trade Commission had said:

> Improved marketing facilities and processes are urgently needed ... in village as well as city. Dealers generally recognise this need. Producers are pressing for such improvement. Consumers have demanded that the system of food distribution be simplified and the movement of food be made more direct from field and factory to table.

Yet, it was not until the Depression of the 1930s sparked the development of supermarkets that low-cost, self-service, mass distribution provided the consumer with a much broader variety of merchandise at sharply lowered prices. Then when World War II restrictions were lifted, conversion to the supermarket method of distribution was suddenly accelerated.

At the same time, there were compelling reasons for major changes in the character of the supermarket itself. As we rapidly became a nation on wheels, consumers began to show a preference for one-stop shopping. Also, as the standard of living rose sharply, the housewife's desire for a new freedom from the laborious preparation of meals resulted in a flight from the frying pan to the refrigerator. She moved from in front of the stove to the driver's seat of the family car. This demand for broadened lines of food and precooked, ready-to-serve items resulted in a rapid increase in both lines and kinds of items available to the consumer in the supermarkets.

There was sufficient evidence at hand in the year immediately following the war to cause operators to revise their objectives drastically. Yet, even the most alert food retailers were not imaginative enough to anticipate the scope and pace of this revolution in food retailing.

To take advantage of the immense possibilities opened up by social and economic changes, it was essential for food retailers to accompany - often precede—their customers to the suburbs and, in the transition, to adopt a new personality. The small neighborhood store and the down-town market were quickly replaced by one-stop food palaces with parking for scores and often hundreds of cars. In stocking all the immense variety of products necessary to satisfy consumer demands, new buying, merchandising, and distribution methods were required. And probably more important, these larger food department stores required a different calibre of general manager, trained in new techniques.

Need for Flexibility

This was the challenge which operators faced when I took the helm at Grand Union. My first step was to get away from the distraction of routine and the telephone for a few days. One might say, before advancing I found it necessary to retreat to a quiet spot. In the course of about 10 days, I tried to chart in broad outline Grand Union's new objectives. My first move on returning to the office was to call a meeting of the officers of the company and say to them, "Let's take the position that we haven't worked for the company before—that Grand Union is, in fact, a new company born today."

For the next few weeks, the major efforts of this group were devoted to creative planning. As the group shaped the company's new objectives, a new concept of teamwork developed. This initial planning period also provided an opportunity to decide on shifts in positions on the organisation's team. This process of re-examination has been carried on annually ever since, and sometimes at shorter intervals.

Quarterly, we analyse carefully the trends in different types of stores. Intensive research is carried on continuously in the area of productivity. At periodic intervals, our entire organisation structure, personnel, operating costs, and budgets are studied and revamped.

Not so long ago, this type of review resulted in sweeping changes in our system of store supervision, even though the old system had been working reasonably well.

Just as the individual needs a periodic checkup, so does the corporate body. To put it in another way, some companies go on with the same old daily delivery of oats long after the horse has left the barn and the building has been turned into a garage. Sometimes, too, while the horse is still a consumer of oats, a company is well advised to make plans for servicing its successor.

In this transition in our industry, which has been as swift as the shift from the horse and wagon to the jet, the supermarket of 1947, is already obsolete. And even more sweeping modifications of the supermarket pattern are in the offing. If the principle of self-service and low markups are what the customers demand, why not try it on all household and family use items and why not make these items available all under one roof to food customers? Our Grand-way super discount department stores—some of which do as much business as an entire chain used to deliver— were founded upon this concept of the customers' wants. In the average supermarket, an arbitrary line has been drawn in limiting non-food items to about 900. The Grand-way concept provides for departments stocking about 35,000 family-use items.

When the chief executive adopts a formula or an objective as radically different as the Grand-Way concept, it takes courage as well as imagination to carry it out. Some doubt and honest opposition to new ideas are inevitable. At Grand Union, we resolved this problem by starting the Grand-Way concept on a small scale and by allowing other members of management to participate in the throes and thrills of its development. In effect, we erected a pilot plant which was an interesting, provocative experiment and comparatively inexpensive. If we were wrong, the company would not be badly hurt. Nor would it siphon off money from somebody else's budget. Further, the project was put in the hands of a Vice-President who had come to us from the department-store field and who had some knowledge of the other products we were adding to the line. In this way, a co-operative effort developed and risks were minimised as we examined the possibilities of a major revision of Grand Union's objectives.

In any discussion of planning, one must consider the vast panorama of business motivations included in the simple word "objectives." There is the overall corporate objective of rendering service and making a profit (they go hand in hand).

There is the individual set of personal objectives of the men at the top and down the line. There is the "image," or public relation, objective, the employee-relations objective—to mention but two. Only through an imaginative approach can all these objectives be moulded into a pattern that will inspire an organisation.

Organise

A corporation's objectives can be attained only through the concerted efforts of all its people. The best-thought-out plans cannot be realised without a sound organisation structure. Recruitment, training, and deployment of manpower, however, are areas where textbooks, manuals, and organisation charts must be supplemented by creative thinking and creative (often inspired) leadership.

What kind of human material is necessary for the attainment of objectives? The chief executive must choose with care his fellow travellers on his journey and the segments of the plan to be entrusted to each companion. A good batting average on the selection of the right man at every level is the overriding test of leadership.

To develop leaders at all levels is a never-ending process of recruitment. Quality of talent—rather than quantity—is the chief force that drives the company along the road toward its objectives.

Along with securing the kind of people upon whom a sound structure can be built goes the maximum delegation of responsibility and authority. This does not mean surrender of personal leadership or scrapping basic objectives. There is a fine psychological line between strong-armed dictation and firm insistence on adherence to basic policies.

The man at the top cannot afford to abdicate his fundamental leadership responsibilities, no matter how well-organised the executive complement below him. Leadership is expected of him. People prefer to exercise their own initiative, it is true, but they also respond to inspirational leadership. They want to be loyal not only to something, but to someone.

As business becomes, more complex, there is an increasing tendency to rely on "professional managership." In the briefcase of the professionally trained manager, you will find hypothetical organisation charts, but there is no kit containing inspirational leadership.

Regardless of the growing complexity of our society, personal leadership is still the most priceless asset—and it always will be. A "school for presidents" might be an interesting addition to our educational system, but I suspect a diploma would be no more than a license to attempt to prove that the graduate has qualities of leadership.

In the case of our company, the problem of finding competent executive talent was aggravated by the rapid transition to an organisation of large supermarkets. There simply was no existing reservoir of experienced supermarket executives to draw on back in 1947.

To find such men, Grand Union began a regular programme of college and high school recruitment. Scientifically constructed 3½-hour aptitude tests were inaugurated to screen all executives and clerical personnel. These were supplemented by interviews in which the results of the tests were discussed.

Managing a supermarket these days is a top-management assignment in its own right. The manager has to be acquainted with 5,000 to 6,000 food products. He has to be a specialist in personnel techniques, materials handling, customer and community relations, sales, display, merchandising, warehousing, and budgeting. In the new "super-supers," he may do up to $10 million in annual business at his own location and supervise 200 employees.

Because men must be specially trained for such responsibilities, Grand Union pioneered in the industry with a comprehensive 18 month management-education programme. Then, recognising that the rapidity of change in business would make some of any rules obsolete tomorrow, the company broadened its on-the-job training programme to ensure that executives and store managers would be able to keep up with the latest advances in their fields. Grand Union was also one of the founders of the Advanced Marketing Curriculum at Michigan State University, Cornell University, and the University of Southern California. One of Grand Union's Vice-presidents serves as Chairman of the Task Committee for the retail food industry in this educational programme.

To ensure competence throughout the organisation, the company has training programs for employees at every level. Clerks are given formal courses in operating a check-out counter, stock-keeping, book-keeping, and general courtesy and service to customers. A fully-equipped "classroom on wheels" has been created to give a six-week on-the-spot course to employees of all new stores.

In the deployment of personnel, we at Grand Union have done everything possible to eliminate layers of management. We believe the tendency to introduce additional layers should be combated vigorously; Layers usually grow in a climate of management deficiencies. For example, too often an executive who is a good administrator but isn't imaginative is supplemented with an idea man, and vice versa.

SOME CONSIDERATIONS

Implementation: Procedural Considerations

Companies embarking upon more extensive planning conduct considerable preparatory investigation to determine what they will seek to achieve and how they will go about it. Not all executives are familiar with the fundamental characteristics of the comprehensive planning process. The best method of introducing or extending planning within the existing organisation must be carefully thought out. A "plan for planning" is developed by a small group of high officers within the company.

The first step towards adequate planning is the establishment of a planning climate. Best results are achieved when this begins with the top management—the very top—the Chairman of the Board, the President, the executive Vice-President, and the important Vice-Presidents. They must buy the proposition that planning *perse* and as such is an identifiable, controllable function essential to the health of the enterprise. And they will be completely convinced only if they do a little work on the subject. They must study some of the pertinent literature to familiarise themselves with planning techniques that have been successfully applied in other companies, attend some high-level conferences, take a little time to think and talk about the subject. And they ought to write down their conclusions for everyone to see and improve. Somebody has said, "If you haven't written it out, you haven't thought it out." That is as true of planning as it is of any other fundamental principle.

An experienced consultant can sometimes assist in this initial formulation by bringing to bear a diversity of experience and a disinterested reaction to preliminary proposals. But it is essential that corporate management perform its own analysis and reach its own best conclusions concerning a process so fundamental to the conduct of the business and so intimately a part of its management responsibility.

Corporate planning must then be explained to the rest of management and subsequently throughout the organisation.

As a basic aid, we organized a committee on planning, consisting of the President, the executive Vice-president and all the Vice Presidents, plus a secretary. The committee meets once a week for an hour and a half, and attempts to encourage widespread establishment of objectives, stimulation of plans to meet these objectives, and promote the principle that planning is primarily a line responsibility. It recommends projects, and points out areas where planning is needed. Members discuss the policies and perimeters within which plans should be formulated, foster organisation for planning, and discover and promote the best methods used in modern, successful business enterprise.

People must be made aware of the importance, the necessity, the techniques, and the pay-off, of planning. This is not a simple thing to achieve. Top management belief in planning is not enough. Supervisors and specialists at all levels must accept the fact that planning is a part of their job. And the best way of convincing them is to have them do some actual planning on specific assignment. The subject must be kept alive, also, by the usual techniques of communications and by training techniques.

The principal conclusion has been that planning does not just happen. It must be planned. This is true whether we are talking about short-term planning or long-term planning. In fact, the skills are the same in both cases; only the objectives are different. People who have not first learned to develop good short-term plans are unlikely to produce good long-term plans.

Clearly, comprehensive planning is not established quickly by directive or executive desire. Not only is time needed for organisational preparation, general familiarisation, and preparatory experience, but employee reactions described in the next section can prolong the period of implementation. Executives and supervisory personnel must become accustomed to the demands and consequences of intensified planning. A cardinal principle of successful comprehensive planning is therefore a deliberate policy of gradual implementation—step by step as carefully thought-out in advance.

Almost invariably, haste means waste; objections are accentuated, and acceptance is slower than would otherwise be the case. If a corporate plan, when completed and announced, comes as a surprise and harbinger of unexpected events, it will compound problems of communication between management levels which it should mitigate. Sufficient time is of the essence, and patience a necessary virtue if the frustration frequently experienced by active proponents of planning is to be avoided.

Careful scheduling is as important in the regular conduct of planning as it is in its introduction. At the corporate centre of comprehensive planning and at primary subcenters within the company, master schedules are maintained covering the various stages of preparation, processing, and implementation. Without this information and control, confusion would be the order of the day and successful integration impossible. Scheduling can become sufficiently intricate in larger companies to occupy the full time of one or more persons, but like many management operations of this type, such coordination is more than repaid by the improvements in production performance brought about by increased supervisory efficiency, and the clarification of operational inter-relationships provided to each participating unit. Important "milestone" events are identified, useful correlations and conflicts are noted, and procedure is studied continually for simplification, improvement, and adjustment to meet new conditions.

Improved scheduling techniques, developed in recent years by the military services, are expanding into the industry. By the use of computers, programmes of implementation are studied in much greater detail in advance, and more closely monitored throughout production to determine progress and identify the critical points of productive interdependence where failure to meet any one of several commitments on time will cause disproportionate delay in the completion of the entire project.

Technical management continuously faces the problem of co-ordinating the diverse activities found in the large-scale project. The accuracy of management's estimates for schedules, cost, and manpower often spells the difference between success or failure of a project.. .. Existing management-control systems are based upon gross estimates of total requirements obtained from past experience. Furthermore, these estimates are arrived at independently by individuals responsible for their own increment of work, and there is scant co-ordination (if any) among individuals. The sheer complexity of many large-scale projects limits the use of existing . . . management-control systems such as bars, (or Gantt) charts....

During the past decade, large-scale computers have become generally available and opened the way for more sophisticated systems. Existing management-control systems are essentially manual systems even though machine-processed. Upon installation of a computer, many firms programmed their existing systems of obtaining reports but did nothing to increase the quality of the information. The advent of the high-speed computer permits approaches that express relationships not previously considered feasible because of the time and labour necessary for data processing.

One means of expressing relationships visibly and mathematically is the network. A network model depicts the ordered sequence of events and their inter-relationships in reaching a goal and detailed estimates of elapsed time required between events. The technique utilises time, money, and manpower as variables reflecting planned resource applications and performance specifications. It takes into account alternative options involved in the projection of both physical and intellectual activities. The system detects the expected completion of each event, both singularly and collectively, and determines the paths of critical events. ...

The network concept was first applied to a large-scale system in the Navy Special Project Office (SPO) for the Fleet Ballistic Missile (FBM) programme. The system was called Programme Evaluation Review Technique (PERT). . . . The original concept has proved extremely valuable within the framework for which it was designed, the single dimension of scheduling over time. PERT has been credited with helping to reduce the time required to develop the Polaris FBM programme from 10 years to 5.

The Du Pont Corporation has developed a network system used for the construction of new facilities. This technique is named Critical-path Planning and Scheduling. The General Electric Corporation, too, is experimenting with the network concept to schedule the more complicated manufacturing processes. Other firms such as Aerojet and Lockheed Aircraft are using versions of the PERT system to aid in scheduling.

Plans

In accordance with corporate objectives, each component of the business prepares a plan for the ensuing year, with extensions for each of several additional years. Activities which involve long amortization periods, or for other reasons should be phased out over more than three to five years, are extended further into the future. The plan for the forthcoming fiscal year is sufficiently precise to serve as a specific operational target and criterion of performance.

Naturally, the plan projections for each additional year are progressively less definite, although they will include certain positive commitments or precise forecasts which will extend well into the future.

How far down the levels of administration unit plans are prepared depends on the size and type of business, as well as its particular organisational and operating characteristics. If there is no advantage to be gained in efficiency, exercise of responsibility, evaluation of performance, or training, the programmes of smaller units are not treated separately but are part of the formal plan of a bigger unit. The larger the number of distinct plans, the more time-consuming their collection, processing, correlation, modification, and subsequent review for variances. There is a point of equilibrium between the advantages of widespread participation in the corporate planning process and the cost, delay, and administrative complications of too elaborate a management system.

Ordinarily, the proposed plans of a smaller unit include such information as the expected volume and value of its product or service; costs and profitability; personnel required; machinery, equipment, and spatial facilities needed; and specific programmes of improvement in management-supervision, performance-productivity, morale, organisation, and other matters influencing operating achievement. These plans are not limited to activities which can be quantified and expressed directly and immediately in terms of profit and loss. There are many objectives which are important even though they are less tangible, with deferred benefits for which it is difficult to establish a clear-cut correlation of cause and effect. An example is a programme to gradually change employee disinterest into a constructive attitude which should in time be reflected in profits. "The other [six months' plan] is a 'word plan,' a verbal analysis of his department's strengths and weaknesses and what he proposes to do about each. ('We think that's even more important than the sales budget')".[1]

Except for the first year after the system is inaugurated, these unit plans are not composed *de novo*. They are drawn within a framework of objectives, policies, constraints, and commitments established by the planning and operational experience of earlier years; and they are shaped to a considerable extent by the specific experience of the previous year. Was this prior plan too ambitious as shown by its *post facto* comparison with performance? Were certain aims achieved sooner than anticipated, thus permitting more rapid scheduling? Or was some intended programme of improvement revealed to be so impractical that it should be discontinued, at least for the time being? Have there been changes in corporate objectives which call for modifications in the current plan? Plans provide a basis for comparisons which are impossible if intentions are expressed informally or not at all.

It is worthwhile at this point in our preliminary description of corporate planning to note the benefits derived by each unit in developing an annual plan and projections. Most of these benefits apply equally to the higher levels of management, we shall be discussing shortly. First and foremost, many of the individuals comprising the unit, and especially its responsible head, are stimulated to think ahead. This may seem a formal and elaborate method of promoting forethought, if we assume everyone does this anyway. In some instances, this is certainly the case, but if we review our experience and observations with this characteristic in mind, we find that thinking ahead in a deliberate, organised, and purposeful fashion is as much the exception as the rule. Undoubtedly, most people have thoughts about the future of the organisational unit for which they are responsible; yet not only are these often piecemeal and sporadic, but they may not be translated into a specific programme of attainment with a time schedule of cumulative accomplishment. There is a natural tendency to defer anticipatory decisions until the need becomes self-evident and preparatory action is almost forced by the evolving situation. By this time the advantages

1. Melville C. Branch, *The Corporate Planning Process* (Bombay, Taraporevala Sons and Co. 1967), pp. 46-51 and 191-4.

of forethought are in large part lost. By its very existence, a formal process of organised planning tends to insure that the different units of the business are thinking ahead to the extent of their capability.

Planning also promotes the comprehensive view. The preparation of a unit plan not only necessitates forethought but requires that all significant elements of the unit be identified and considered. Similarly, the corporate plan requires that the various components of the business are integrated and projected in concert. As a consequence of this higher-level examination of interrelationships, the different units of the company are made more aware of what is going on about and above them.

Integration Decision

Corporate management performs the final integration and makes the final decisions. First, it must evaluate each of the major component plans. Is it accurate and consistent within itself? Certainly this is very probably the case, but it is the responsibility of corporate management to confirm by review that there are no significant errors or omissions; the probable penalty to the company of a substantial mistake is too great to ignore. Is each component plan in accord with corporate objectives? For example, if a corporate programme of product diversification has been decided upon, can the efforts to this end be identified within the plans and projections of the major units? If a gradual reduction in overhead costs has been requested, is this apparent in the cost data shown in the proposed plans? Are the capital expenditures requested *in toto* beyond the current capacity of the business? If so, must suggested budgets be reduced or new financing arranged? Are the intentions of some unit relating to personnel or advertising inimical to the general policies of the company? Certain programmes and time schedules may be mutually inconsistent, or combine to produce an undesirable peak load. One decentralised division may want to undertake an increase in wage or salary levels which would, however, create serious personnel problems in other divisions nearby which cannot afford such an increase. Two divisions may have overlooked a co-operative arrangement to their mutual advantage. Or, the company may want to build up a smaller division which has the potentiality of profitable growth and would provide a desirable diversification of sales. Besides the funds they would forego because of the increased allocation to the smaller division, other units of the company may be called upon for indirect support. The over-all view and comprehensive analysis required for such a conclusion are not the province of divisional or group managers. Furthermore, the identification, concentration, and competitive drive which contribute to their own successful performance preclude the broader objectivity requisite to such corporate decisions.

The result of corporate integration may call for modification of the component plans. When this is accomplished, they are combined into a comprehensive plan for the business as a whole which is the performance target for the ensuing fiscal year and the official referent for an additional two to four years. As indicated earlier, the process of planning does not stop with the formal adoption of plans, to be resumed a year later. The major components and their subordinate units adjust their shorter-range objectives as experience and circumstances dictate. In this way, planning is continuous, and current data are available at all times in the event an unforeseen development of major significance requires revision of the corporate plan in midyear. And early identification is more likely in the case of important trends which may call for a reorientation of projections at the next formal review.

As has been described, analysis, integration, and decision are applied throughout the corporate planning procedure from the smallest organisational roots. Each unit, department, and division head has worked his way through to his own conclusions and proposed plan. But the most crucial analyses and far-reaching decisions are made by corporate executives—the apex of the triangle, if we visualise the administrative organisation in this way. These decisions will affect the operations and profitability of the entire business, both immediately and for the future. Whereas a certain percentage of error in planning at lower levels is less consequential because of the smaller size and more limited activities of the units to which it applies, the same average error at the topmost level can create severe and long-lasting difficulties. As will be discussed at some length in subsequent chapters, the performance of the relatively small group of executives comprising top management is vital.

In today's business world, line executives in high positions are hard-pressed to attend to the hundred and one operating demands on their time. The higher their position, the more frequently they must concentrate on operational matters of such importance that they must be resolved at their level of management without delay. The time available to them for longer-range planning is limited. Except in small businesses, they do not formulate and maintain personally the factual background for corporate planning. A flow of information and a system of analysis are organised, in accordance with procedures they approve, to provide the evaluative materials needed for judgement and decision. More and more, small planning staffs are formed to receive and correlate component plans, distill the most indicative data, integrate and analyse these data, project the resulting information into successive stages of future time, and finally present the composite corporate situation and the probable results of alternative courses of actions.

Sound global organisations have long-term plans of 10-30 years duration; Medium-term plan of 5-7 years and short-term annual plan; while the long-and medium-term plans deal with long-term future, vision and mission of where they want to go and want to be 10 or 30 years hence, the annual plan is for immediate implementation, more accurate and urgent for implementation.

When I was in Conference Board in 60s, there was a threat of a nuclear attack from USSR to America, Conference Board did a study on this problem and how American companies were planning to meet this threat. For me, it was very interesting to note that the study, published under the title, 'Nuclear Catastrophe and Survival', revealed that companies planned to meet the threat by having alternate headquarters with all the files of business and executive succession system; if the Chairman is wiped out in the first attack, who will succeed him and various other plans to continue the business on survival.

Now let us turn to the next step in implementing the Plan–Organising.

6 Organising

The Overview of Organisational Design and Structure • The Organisation of General Motors Corporation • Modern Corporate Organisation • Organisational Evolution • The Matrix Model: ABB • Departmental Management in Practice

In the beginning, there is the birth of an idea in the mind of the founder to produce some goods or services needed by the customers and thus, the birth of a new business. The founder essentially does everything like production, marketing financing and making a small profit. When the business grows, he adds a few people to help him in producing more products and selling them. The interest in organising increases with the growth into a small business, then into medium and large in size and it becomes complicated, sophisticated. Only then interest in organisational design and structure surfaces from classical organisation design of scaler chain principle to a contemporary complex structure.

We shall study organising under the following heads:

1. An Overview of Organisational Design and Structure
2. Organisation of General Motors
3. Organisation of Worthington
4. GE's Organisational Revolution
5. ABB : Matrix Model
6. Department Management at Matsushita
7. Downsizing

AN OVERVIEW OF ORGANISATIONAL DESIGN AND STRUCTURE

Definition

An organisation is a pattern of relationships — many interwoven, simultaneous through which people, under the direction of managers, pursue their goals.

These goals are the products of planning, which are ambitious, farreaching & openended.

Managers want to ensure that their organisations can endure for a long time.

Members of an organisation need a stable, understandable framework with in which they can work together towards organisational goals.

The managerial process of organising involves making decisions about creating this kind of framework so that organisations can last from the present well into the future.

Creativity: The ability and power to develop new ideas

Innovation: The use of new ideas

Three Approaches

1. Experience
2. Experimentation
3. Research and Analysis.

Cost-Benefit Anaysis seeks the best ratio of benefit and cost.

MOD-3 ORG

Organisational design is the determination of organisation structure that is most appropriate for the strategy people, technology and tasks of the organisation.

Organisational structure is the way in which an organisation activities are divided, organised and co-ordinated.

Organisational structure is a framework that managers devise for dividing and co-ordinating the activities of the members of an organisation.

Four Building Blocks

1. Divide the total workload into tasks that can logically and comfortably be performed by individuals or groups. This is division of work.
2. Departments combining tasks in a logical and efficient manner. The grouping of employees and tasks is generally referred to as departmentalisation.
3. Hierarchy, specify who reports to whom in the organisation. This linking of department results in an organisational hierarchy.
4. Co-ordination—set up mechanisms for integrating departmental activities into a coherent whole and monitoring the effectivences of that intention. This process is called co-ordination.
5. Division of work—job specialisation—greater productivity.

Adam Smith's Wealth of Nations

A famous passage on specialisation of labour in the manufacture of pins:

Smith wrote:

One man draws the wire

Another straightens it

A third cuts it

A fourth points it

A fifth grinds it at the top for receiving the head.

10 Men working in this fashion made 48,000 pins in one day.

But if they had all worked separately and independently each might at best have produced only 20 pins in a day.

The great advantage of division of labour was by breaking the total job down into small, simple, separate operations in which different workers could specialise, total productivity is multiplied geometrically.

- People believe that the rise of civilisation can be attributed to the division of specialisation, which gave human resources to develop art, science and education.
- Departmentalisation and organisation chart.
- Span of management and control the number of subordinates reporting to a given manager. Also called span of management or span of control.

  Chain of command
- The plan that specifies who reports to whom in an organisation, such reporting lines are prominent features of any organisation chart.
- Hierarchy: A pattern of multiple levels of an organisational structure.

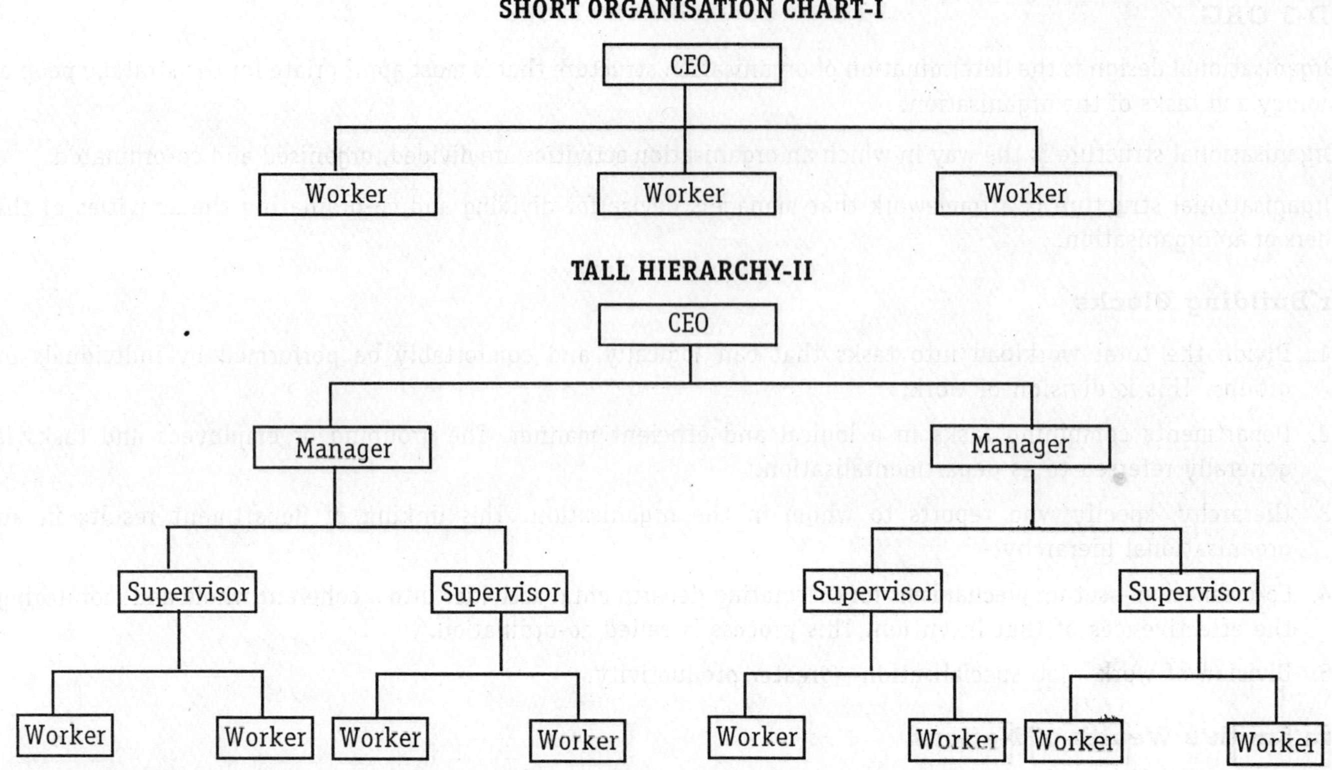

CO-ORDINATION

The interaction of the activities of the separate parts of an organisation to accomplish organisational goals.

Approaches to Effective Co-ordination Method for Managers

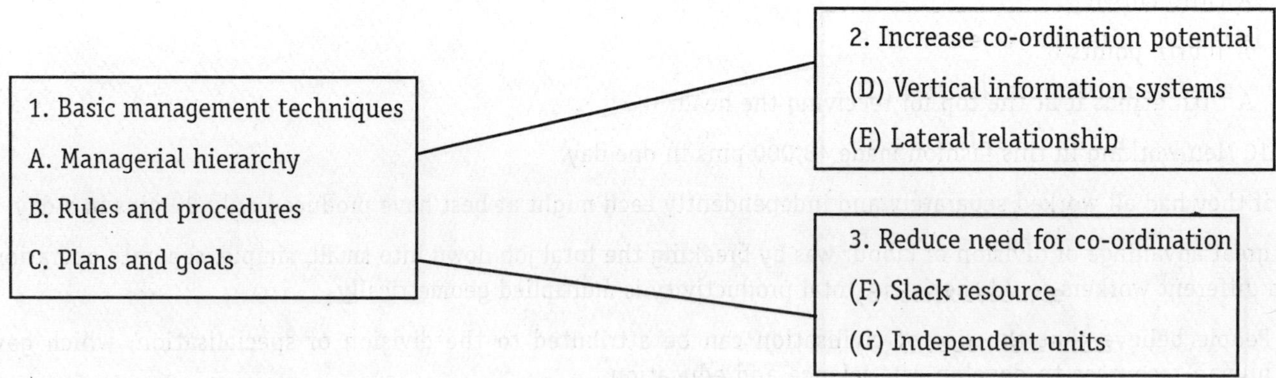

Organisational Design Approach

The classical approach of Max Weber, F.W. Taylor, Fayol

The Task technology approach

(1) Unit a small batch production

(2) Large batch and mass production

(3) Process production

Chemical and pharmaceutical industry

The Environment approach.

(1) Mechanistic system — Bureaucratic organisation
(2) Organic system — Informality, group, open communication.

Downsizing

The formal organisation and informal organisation

Centralisation vs decentralisation of authority—Entrepreneurs

Delegation of power and authority

(1) Reward coercive power (2) Legitimate power (a) Expert power (b) Referrent power

(1) Line authority (2) Staff authority (3) Functional authority.

Types of Organisational Structures

FUNCTIONAL ORGANISATION-III

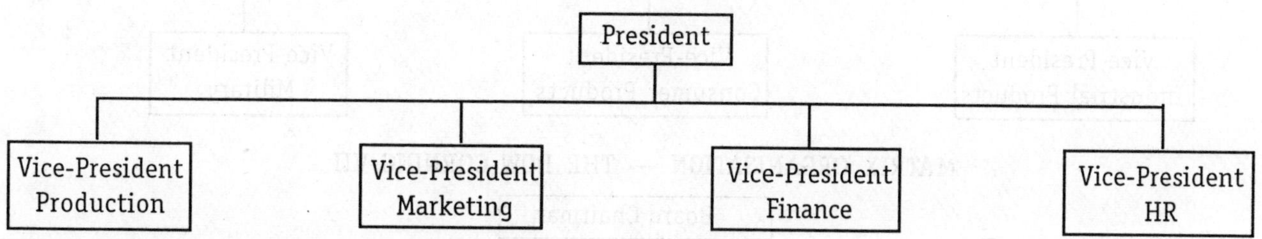

A form of organisation/departmentalisation in which individuals engaged in one functional activity, such as marketing or production, are grouped together.

PRODUCT ORGANISATION-IV

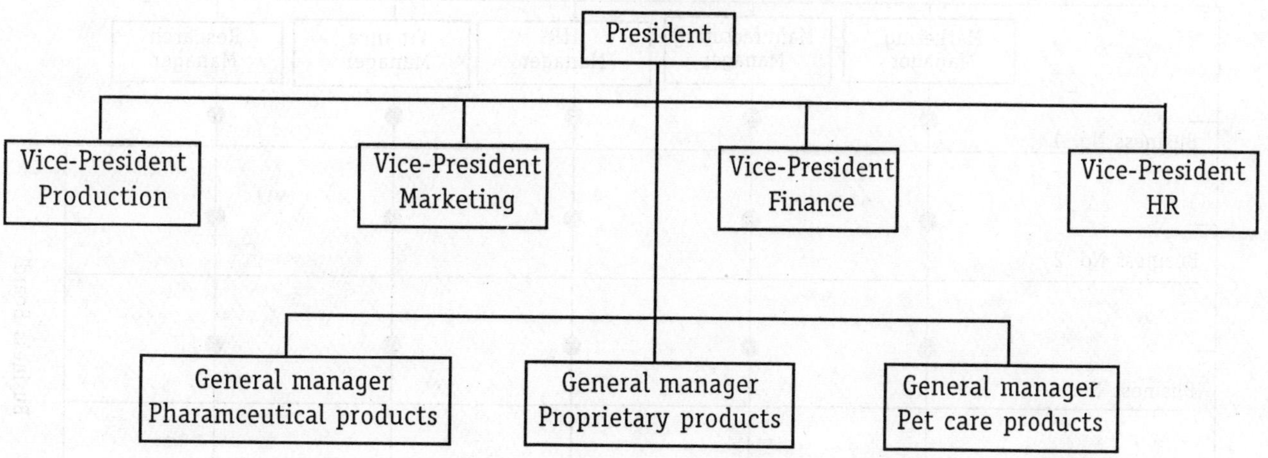

A form of organisation based on product

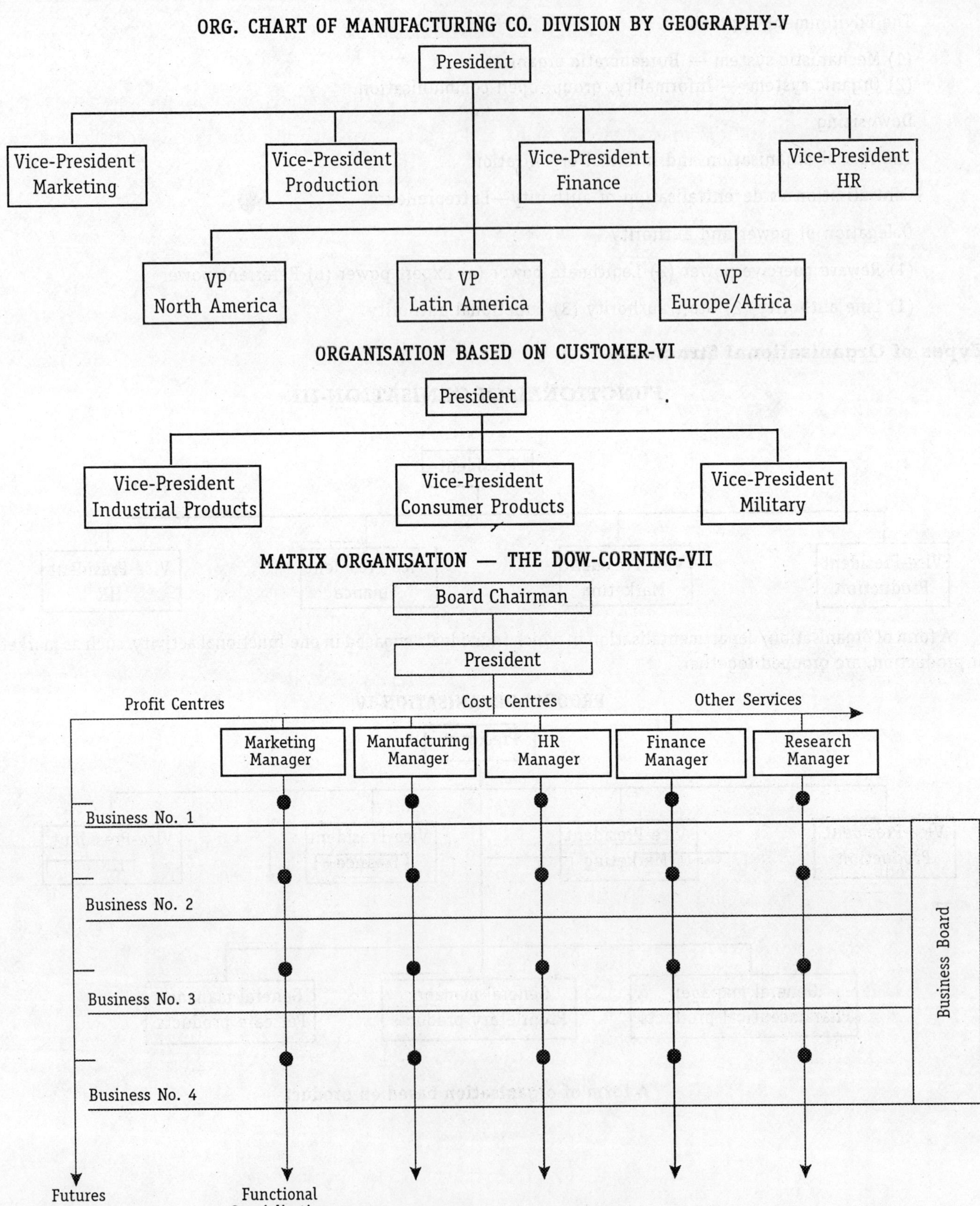

An organisational design in which each emplyee reports to functional or divisional manager and to a project group manager.

MULTIPLE COMMAND SYSTEM

(a) The Virtual Corporation — A New Corporate Model

Today's vs. and strategic alliance may be an early glimpse of the business orgnisation of the future.

In a virtual corporations can share costs, skills, and to global markets, with each parting contributing what its best at.

The key attributes of such an organisation

Technology

Opportunism

Excellence

Core competence

Trust

No borders

(b) Outsourcing-service technologies disaggregated organisation.

(c) FLEXI organisation

(d) Job enrichment — Job enlargement

THE ORGANISATION OF GENERAL MOTORS CORPORATION

General Motors is an operating company composed in the United States of 31 divisions with 119 plants in 70 communities in 18 states. In addition we have one subsidiary operating six plants in Canada, and manufacturing and assembly or warehousing operations in 23 foreign countries. During 1968, total employment averaged about 757,000 men and women. The business is owned by about 1,400,000 shareholders.

Although not directly a part of General Motors there are two large groups of enterprises which are highly essential and related to the business of General Motors. First, the independent retail car and truck dealers who sell our products, and who employ about 350,000 sales and service personnel in the US and Canada. And, second, over 37,000 suppliers in the United States alone, who provide materials and services.

In addition to the five makes of automobiles (Chevrolet, Pontiac, Oldsmobile, Buick and Cadillac), we manufacture in the United States, among other things, trucks and buses, diesel locomotives and engines, heavy-duty off-the-highway earth moving equipment, frigidaire refrigerators and other household appliances, aircraft engines, fractional horsepower motors, etc. we also make automotive parts and accessories for our own divisions and for other manufacturers, as well as service parts for cars in use. In Canada, we manufacture and assemble passenger cars, trucks, buses and automobile engines, frigidaire refrigerators and other household appliances, and automotive parts and accessories.

General Motors defense assignments, in addition to military wheeled vehicles, have included a wide variety of highly technical and complicated equipment such as : Aircraft propellers; Allison turboprop and turboshaft aircraft engines; Sapphire jet engines; light and medium tanks; fighter aircraft; transmissions for tanks; aircraft navigational instruments and bombsights; missiles guidance systems and other missiles components; rapid-fire aircraft weapons, rifles, shells, and many other items.

General Motors was organised in 1908, with the idea of achieving economies and efficiency through mass production. The following ten or twelve years were a period of organisation, of adding to the original nucleus. The 1920 Depression brought this period to an end. Then began a new period of organisation and growth through expansion. Over these years General Motors entered several new fields. For the most part, this was the result of its own research developments. Noteworthy especially is the diesel engine development.

General Motors, operating philosophy is based on the concept of the importance of people. Fundamentally, all business enterprises are composed of opportunities, facilities and people.

It is only in its people that a business organisation is unique. The way its people are organised to work together makes it unique.

The operating philosophy based on this concept was formulated by General Motors management in the early 1920's. That philosophy has been maintained and developed as a guide for its operations ever since.

Expressed in formal terms, the philosophy is "Decentralised Operations and Responsibilities with Co-ordinated Control." A simpler way of expressing it is **"give a man a clearcut job to do and let him do it."**

Under this philosophy, overall objectives and principles are determined at the top management level, based on information flowing up from all levels of the organisation. These are the policies, the "whys and wherefores." But the task of carrying them out, that is, "the how," is up to the men down the line.

Decentralisation of operations and responsibilities means dividing up the job into as many pieces as is practical. It means placing in charge of each piece an executive with complete responsibility for its success or failure. Decentralisation recognises the importance of people. It makes the most effective use of their talents and gives them maximum scope to exercise their initiative and capitalise on their opportunities.

Decentralisation has been the means by which General Motors has retained advantages inherent in well-managed smaller businesses. It provides the flexibility which makes possible changes in operations and the constant improvement in its products in keeping with the needs and desires of its customers.

Co-ordinated control refers to the formulation of overall policy, the framework or area within which the various pieces operate. Under this philosophy, a two-way flow exists at each level of management. On the one hand there is the downward flow of authority derived from established policy. On the other, there is the upward flow of facts and opinion derived from the exercise of individual initiative down the line and which in turn enters into policy considerations, A proper balance of these two flows — the downward flow from authority and the upward flow from initiative — is constantly sought in General Motors.

So far we have described how General Motors evolved into its present form and outlined the philosophy on which the plan of the organisation is based. For a better understanding of how the pieces fit together let us consider the plan of organisation.

Experience shows that an organisation cannot function properly unless each individual knows his place in it and fulfils his duties, and unless those various duties fit into a composite whole. This is essential if a great aggregation of people is to work intelligently together.

In a smaller business the top executive frequently runs the entire operation. He runs the operating end and the policy end. Frequently he is his own staff. In a business of the scope of General Motors no one man makes all of the decisions or performs all of the executive functions that are part of every day's business. Line and staff functions are separate and clearly defined.

In accordance with our concept of decentralisation, each of our divisions and subsidiaries which comprise our operating or line-organisation operates very largely as an independent business. Each consists of a plant or group of plants manufacturing one product or a number of related products.

Each division is under a general manager who is responsible for its success or failure. Subject to certain broad policy controls and to a few phases of the business which are necessarily centralised, the divisions are in large measure self-contained. For example:

Each manufacturing division designs, develops, manufactures and merchandises its own products.

Each division makes its own purchases of materials and component parts —in some cases they are obtained from other divisions and in others from the more than 37,000 outside suppliers. Where divisions buy depends upon who is able to furnish the most suitable product or service at a reasonable price.

Each division develops many of its own manufacturing processes and methods...

Hires and trains its own employes...

Develops and maintains its own operating organisation, including the personnel to run the various phases of its business.

Each division is responsible for being a good neighbour in the community in which it operates — for being a good industrial citizen by making itself an integral part of the community.

Each division is proud of its independence and fully aware of its competitive position, even with other divisions of General Motors.

The general manager of each General Motors division is responsible for building his own organisation, co-ordinating its efforts and planning its progress. However, unlike the manager of a smaller business, the general manager of a General Motors division has available to him the staff facilities and "know-how" of the central organisation.

Our decentralized setup, therefore, combines ability to produce on a large-scale with the flexibility of smaller-scale enterprise. It has the further advantage of giving individual managers and the members of their organisation more freedom of action, affording additional opportunity to a larger number of individuals for development of executive ability and initiative.

In General Motors, operating divisions manufacturing related products are grouped together, for the most part, for better co-ordination. There are five such groups, all of which are under the general supervision of two Executive Vice presidents. Four of these groups are under the direct supervision of a Group Executive who is a Vice president and a member of the Administration Committee, and one group is under the direct supervision of an Executive Vice president.

As shown in Chart 1 below, three of these groups are designated as the Car and Truck, Body and Assembly, and Automotive Components Group, and are under the general supervision of an Executive Vice president. Each of these groups are under the direct supervision of a Group Executive who is a Vice president. Chart. 1 also shows the divisions in each of these groups.

As shown in Chart 2 below, two of these groups are designated as the Overseas Group and Non-Automotive and Defense Group and are also under the general supervision of an Executive Vice-President. The Overseas Group is under the direct supervision of the Executive Vice President and the Divisions comprising the Non-Automotive and Defense Group are under the direct supervision of a Group Executive who is a Vice-President. Chart. 2 also shows the Divisions in each of these groups.

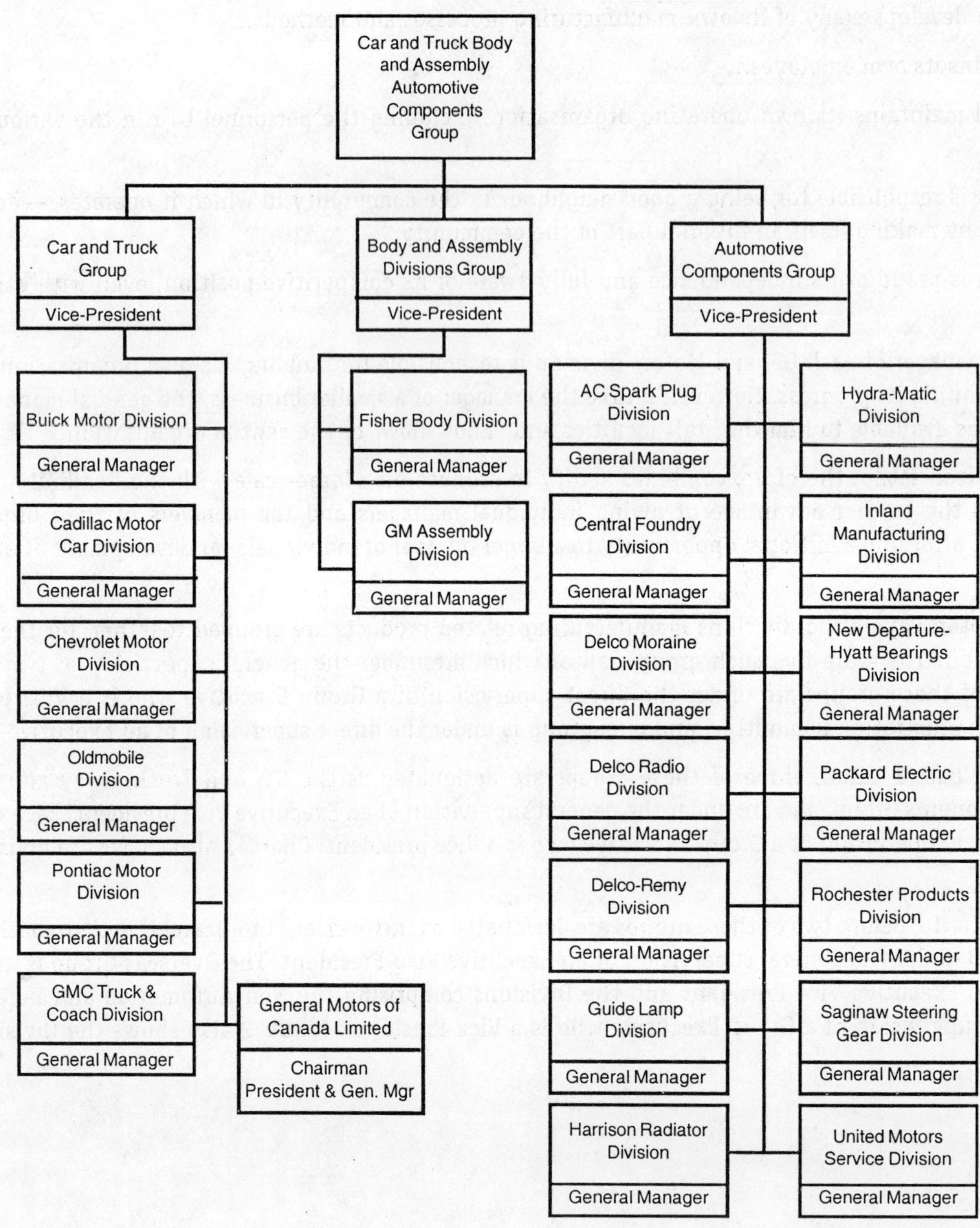
Car and Truck Body and Assembly Automotive Components Group
Car and Truck Group
Vice-President
Body and Assembly Divisions Group
Vice-President
Automotive Components Group
Vice-President
Buick Motor Division
General Manager
Cadillac Motor Car Division
General Manager
Chevrolet Motor Division
General Manager
Oldmobile Division
General Manager
Pontiac Motor Division
General Manager
GMC Truck & Coach Division
General Manager
General Motors of Canada Limited
Chairman President & Gen. Mgr
Fisher Body Division
General Manager
GM Assembly Division
General Manager
AC Spark Plug Division
General Manager
Central Foundry Division
General Manager
Delco Moraine Division
General Manager
Delco Radio Division
General Manager
Delco-Remy Division
General Manager
Guide Lamp Division
General Manager
Harrison Radiator Division
General Manager
Hydra-Matic Division
General Manager
Inland Manufacturing Division
General Manager
New Departure-Hyatt Bearings Division
General Manager
Packard Electric Division
General Manager
Rochester Products Division
General Manager
Saginaw Steering Gear Division
General Manager
United Motors Service Division
General Manager

Chart 1

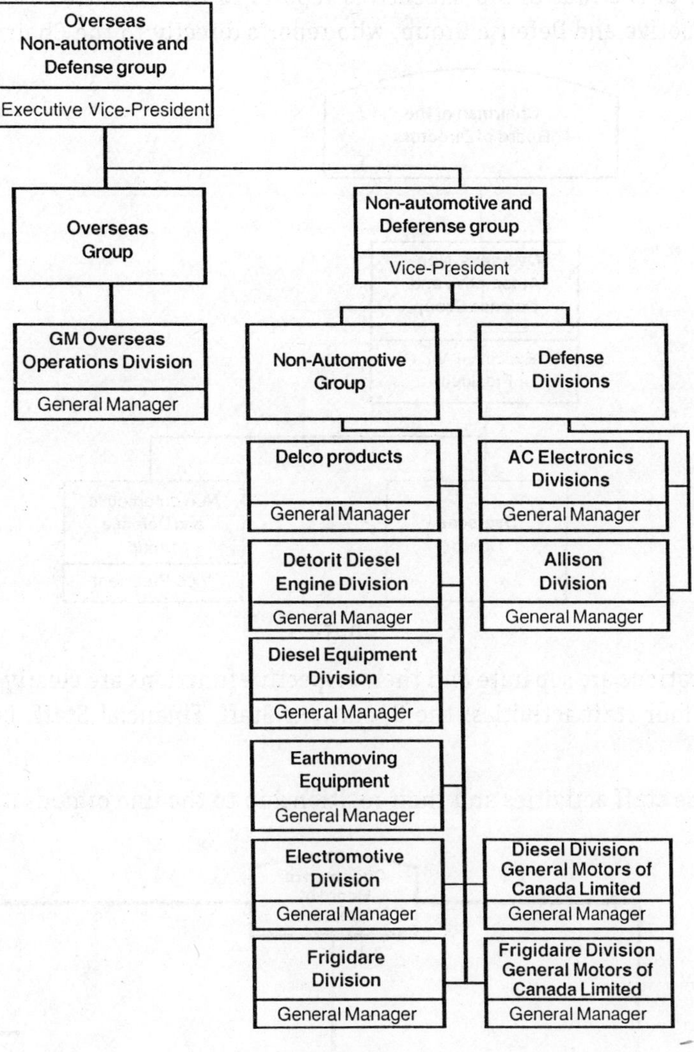

Chart 2

The Group Executive represents General Motors management to, and acts as advisor for, the General Managers of the divisions in his group. In exercising this function he works closely with both the Divisional managers and with the Executive Vice-President to whom he reports. As shown in Chart 3, three of the four Group Executives report to the Executive Vice-President having jurisdiction over the Car and Truck, Body and Assembly, and Automotive Components Group, who reports directly to the President.

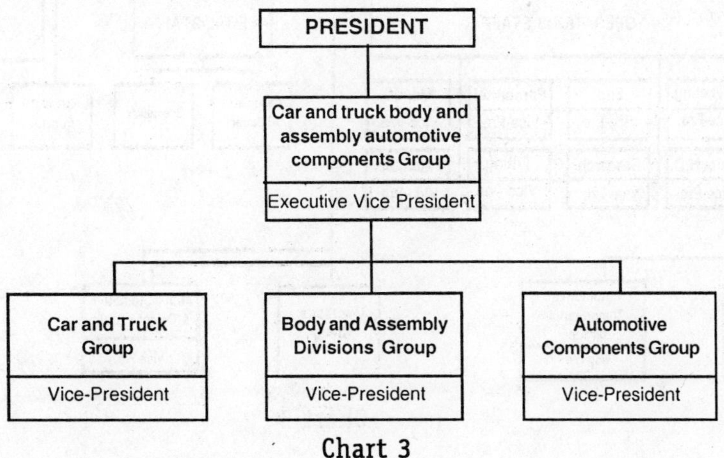

Chart 3

As shown in Chart 4, one of the four Group Executives reports to the Executive Vice-President having jurisdiction over the Overseas, Non-Automotive and Defense Group, who reports directly to the Chairman of the Board.

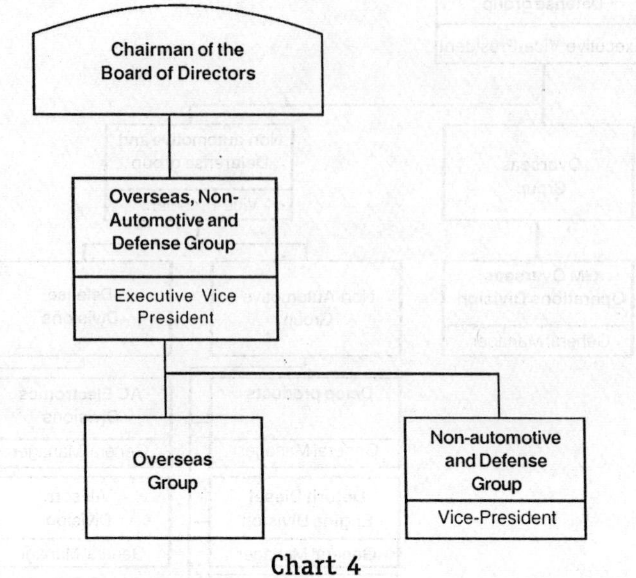

Chart 4

The line and staff organisations are separate and their respective functions are clearly defined. General Motors Central Office organisation includes four staff activities: the Operations Staff, Financial Staff, Legal Staff, and Public Relations Staff.

Chart 5 below shows these staff activities and their relationship to the line organisation:

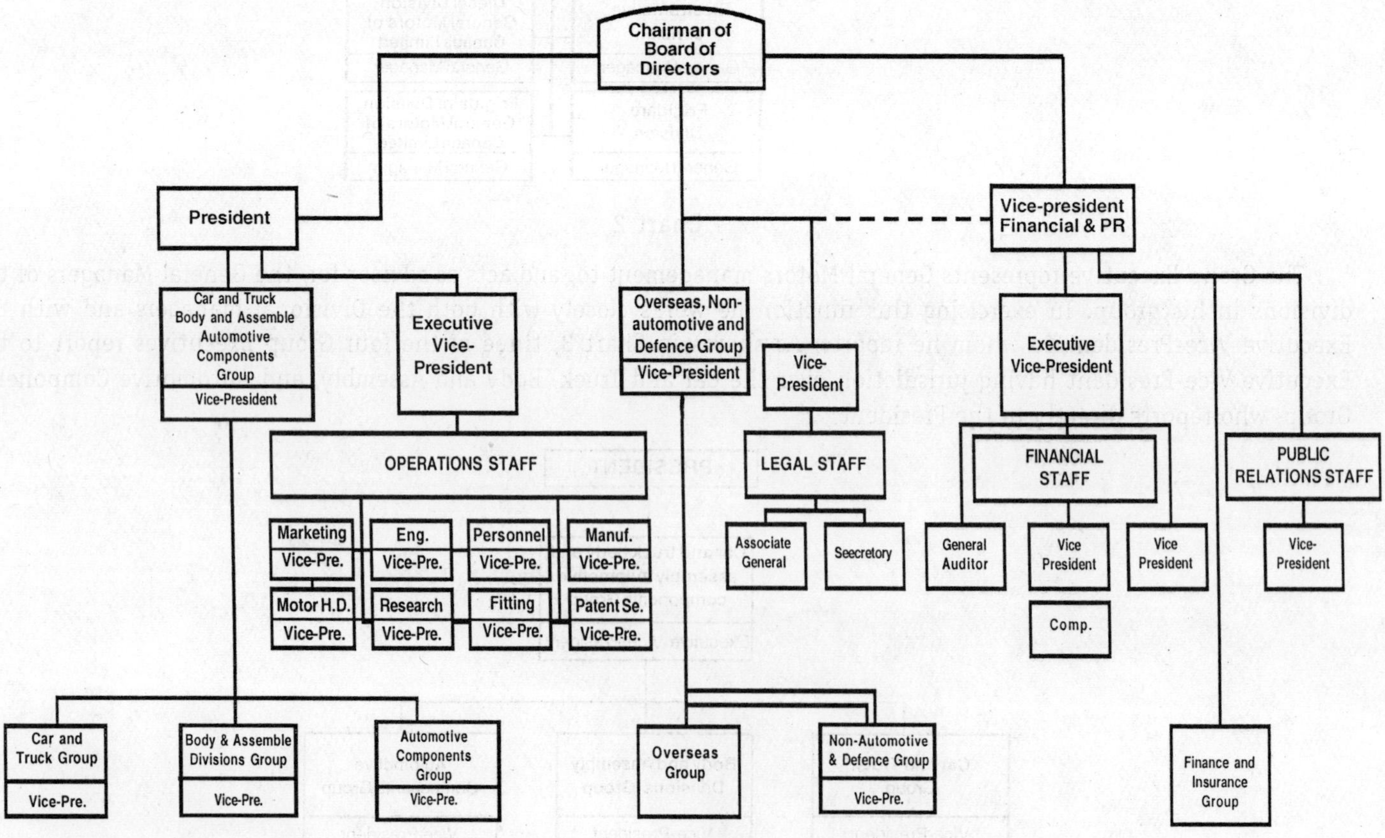

Chairman of Board of Directors
President
Vice-president Financial & PR
Car and Truck Body and Assemble Automotive Components Group
Vice-President
Executive Vice-President
Overseas, Non-automotive and Defence Group
Vice-President
Vice-President
Executive Vice-President
OPERATIONS STAFF
LEGAL STAFF
FINANCIAL STAFF
PUBLIC RELATIONS STAFF
Marketing Vice-Pre.
Eng. Vice-Pre.
Personnel Vice-Pre.
Manuf. Vice-Pre.
Motor H.D. Vice-Pre.
Research Vice-Pre.
Fitting Vice-Pre.
Patent Se. Vice-Pre.
Associate General
Seecretory
General Auditor
Vice President
Vice President
Vice-President
Comp.
Car and Truck Group
Vice-Pre.
Body & Assemble Divisions Group
Vice-Pre.
Automotive Components Group
Vice-Pre.
Overseas Group
Non-Automotive & Defence Group
Vice-Pre.
Finance and Insurance Group

Chart 5

The Operations Staff activities—each headed by a Vice-President of the Corporation who reports directly to the Executive Vice President—Operations Staff, concern themselves with such specialised functions as marketing, styling, engineering, research, manufacturing and personnel. The Patent section is also included under the Operations Staff activities. The executives incharge of these staff serve in an advisory capacity to both the divisional managements and the Corporation Executives.

The Central Office Operations Staff have a dual function. They act as advisors and render services to General Motors top management and the divisions. They also help in the policy formulation function, through their tie-in with the activities of the various policy groups where policy recommendations and suggestions of the various staff are discussed. To illustrate the dual function of these staffs:

The Marketing Staff is concerned with marketing policies and problems and also co-operates with the divisions in the development of effective merchandising and service procedures. Other activities under the direction of the Vice-President in charge of this staff, include advertising and market research, dealer relations, and fleet and government sales.

The Engineering Staff works on the development of forward General Motors engineering policies and co-ordinates the product programmes of divisions. This staff also carries out engineering studies of new products and of new engineering developments for existing products which are beyond the basic research stage. This work is done independently and is supplemental to the engineering programmes of the divisions.

The service function of the Engineering Staff is exemplified by the General Motors Proving Grounds, operated by this staff. Here comparative product tests are made in order to keep management informed about our engineering progress and to assist the individual divisions in their responsibility for the quality and performance of General Motors cars. Other engineering services are provided by the Engineering Staff, benefit all divisions and General Motors as a whole. These include vehicle safety, vehicle testing, engineering standards, experimental fabrication and others.

The Personel Staff deals with policies and problems of personnel administration for both salaried and hourly-rated employes. It also has the responsibility for negotiating and administering over 150 agreements with 17 national labour unions. This phase of the Personnel Staff's activities is necessarily centralised. This staff is also concerned with the development of employe programmes designed to build better relations with and among people in General Motors. This Staff shares in the responsibility for the development and administration of employee benefit plans such as pensions, group insurance, sickness and accident benefits, surgical and hospital coverages. The General Motors Institute is also under the jurisdiction of this staff.

The Manufacturing staff co-ordinates the planning for the inflow of basic materials; handles all matters pertaining to the purchase, lease and disposition of real estate for the divisions; and renders assistance in matters involving construction and alterations.

This staff, through its Manufacturing Development activity, works closely with the divisions, the Engineering and Research Staff, and the Corporation's operating executives on matters dealing with the development and testing of production processes, as well as the improvement of present processes as they are currently being used in the various Divisions. This function constitutes not only the development of the process itself, but also involves the designing and building of necessary machinery and equipment to realise the savings which may accrue from such processes.

The Research Laboratories at the Technical Center are concerned primarily with those more fundamental studies which are the basis for long-range progress and which do not fall within the scope of the development activities of the Engineering Staff, nor of the comparatively shorter-range engineering programmes of the operating divisions.

Fundamental research carried on by General Motors engineers and scientists has resulted in new products and new methods which otherwise would not have been developed. The Research Laboratories also provide advice and assistance to the divisions on current product and processing problems.

The Styling Staff has the responsibility of creating and developing advanced automobile and truck styles. It also works with Car and Body Divisions in presenting to top management the line of bodies to be considered for future model years. In addition, this staff has the responsibility of working with the divisions in creating new appearance trends for all General Motors products.

The other staff activities as shown on Chart 5, are the Financial, Public Relations and Legal Staff.

The Financial Staff plays a vital part in the financial management of the business and has the responsibility of providing top management and the policy-making committees with information on various financial and operational aspects of the business. This staff is under the general direction of the Executive Vice-President—Finance, and, together with the Finance and Insurance Subsidiaries, is under the general supervision of the Vice-Chairman of the Board of Directors.

The Public Relations Staff, also under the general supervision of the Vicechairman, performs a two-fold function with respect to policy. On the one hand it keeps management informed of public attitudes that may have bearing on important policy considerations and, on the other, interprets General Motors policies to the public. Divisions frequently consult with and utilise the services of this staff in connection with their own public relations programmes.

The Legal Staff is under the direction and supervision of the General Counsel who is appointed by the Board of Directors. The by-laws of the Corporation provide that the General Counsel, who is a Vicepresident, has general control of all matters of legal import concerning the Corporation.

The Chairman of the Board of Directors is the Chief Executive Officer of the Corporation. He is directly responsible to the Board of Directors, which in turn is responsible to the shareholders. The President is the Chief Operating Officer of the Corporation.

So far we have traced our line and staff organisations from the divisions to the shareholders. In General Motors it is recognised that policy formulation is separate from administration. Policymaking is the responsibility of two governing committees in the Corporation — the Finance Committee and the Executive Committee. Chart 6 shows the place of these committees on the organisation chart.

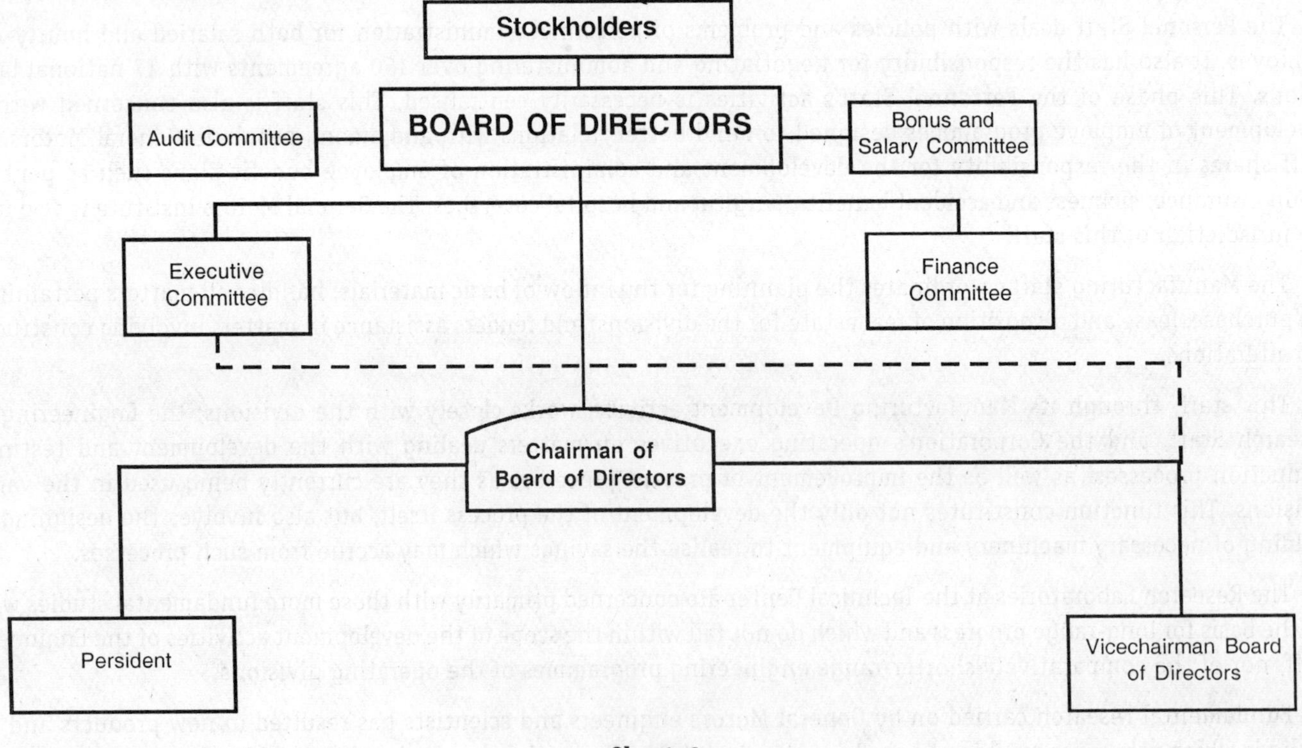

Chart 6

The Finance Committee, appointed by the Board of Directors from its membership, includes members of the Board who do not have operating responsibilities, as well as those who do. This committee is delegated to act for the Board in determining the financial policies and affairs of the Corporation. The Vice-Chairman of the Board of Directors is Chairman of this committee.

The Executive Committee is also composed entirely of members of the Board of Directors. It is delegated to act for the Board in determining operating policies. The Chairman of the Board of Directors is Chairman of this committee. Included in its membership in addition to the Chairman, are the Vice-Chairman of the Board of Directors, the President and the four Executive Vice-Presidents.

These two committees, then, deal with policy at the top level. It should be emphasized that they do not deliberate or establish policy in isolation from the rest of the organisation. Our organisation pattern provides for a channel whereby policy ideas and suggestions filter up from our line and staff organisations. Let us see how this works:

Chart 7, shows the policy groups which work with the Executive Committee—in effect sub-committees—where policy recommendations originate and policy questions are discussed:

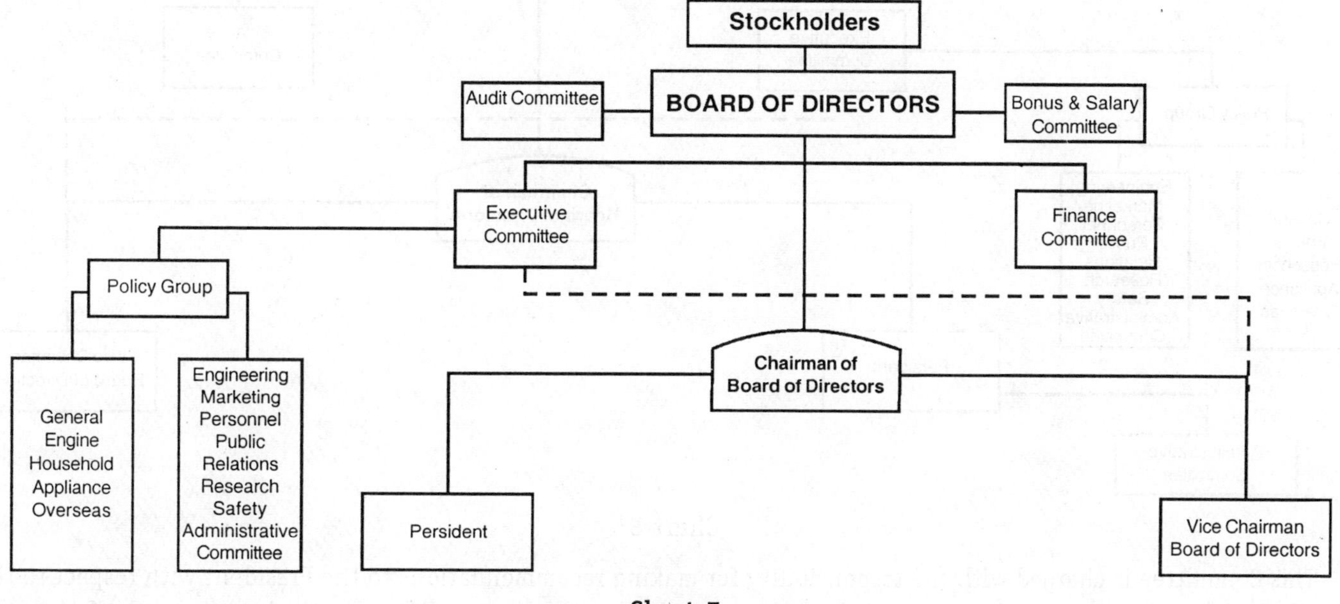

Chart 7

Of these nine policy groups, three are concerned with products or operations. They are:

The other six policy groups have to do with specific functions. The executive in charge of the Central Office Staff whose function is directly related to the interests of the group generally is Chairman of that particular group. The six functional policy groups are:

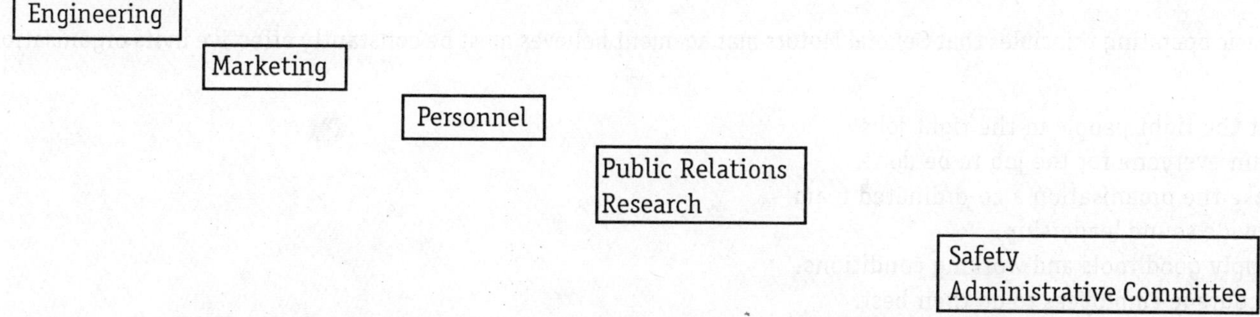

Meetings of these groups are scheduled at regular intervals. Their membership includes top operating executives, and divisional as well as staff executives, whose balanced experience is brought to bear on policy recommendations in the group's particular area. More than that, these groups are the instrumentality whereby policy suggestions and recommendations that come from the line or staff organisations are passed along, if found acceptable, to the Executive Committee.

In addition to the two governing committees, the By-laws of the Corporation provide for an Administration Committee, shown in Chart 8.

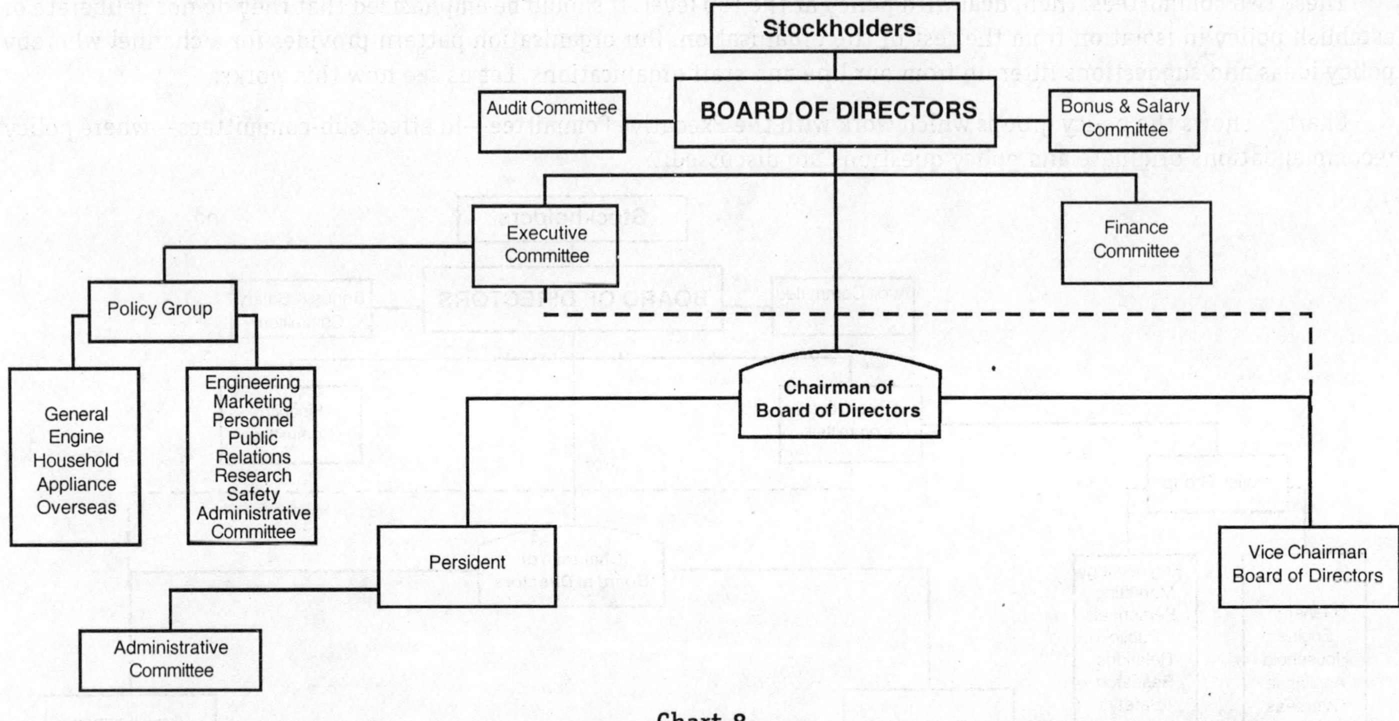

Chart 8

This Committee is charged with the responsibility for making recommendations to the President with respect to the manufacturing and selling activities of the Corporation, and on any other matters affecting the business and affairs of the Corporation that may be referred to it by the President or the Executive Committee. The President is Chairman of this committee. Its membership includes the members of the Executive Committee, the Group Executives, the Vice-President in charge of the Financial Staff, the Car Division General Managers, the General Manager of General Motors of Canada Limited, and the General Managers of the Fisher Body, GM Assembly, GMC Truck and Coach, and Overseas Operations Divisions.

You have now seen the pieces of the General Motors Organisation Chart together with the indication of the line, staff, and policy functions.

You will have noted that it was devised—based on experience over a long period— to fit our own needs. You will have noted, also, that it is patterned to allow for broad participation in the job of management and in policy formulation by the people in the business. The attached complete chart shows all functions in their relation with each other.

The basic operating principles that General Motors management believes must be constantly effective in its organisation, are —

1. Put the right people in the right jobs.
2. Train everyone for the job to be done.
3. Make the organisation a co-ordinated team.
4. Provide sound leadership.
5. Supply good tools and working conditions.
6. Encourage employees to do their best.
7. Maintain our reputation for integrity.

MODERN CORPORATE ORGANISATION

For a large or small company, there is no "perfect" organisation structure. The particular form developed depends on a number of variable factors, such as the type of business, the quality of the management, the degree of specialisation, the objectives of the enterprise, and the method of measuring results. In order to illustrate how a large company is put together, however, let's use as an example the structure of the Warthington organisation at the corporate level of management.

The accompanying Fig. 6.1 shows Worthington's corporate structure. Certain principles of large company organisation are demonstrated. Chief among these are:

1. There is a clear distinction between the "staff" and "line" activities. "The staff functions are portrayed on the middle portion of the chart, while the line groups or operating divisions are shown at the bottom.
2. Both staff and line groups are responsible, ultimately, to the top corporate officers—the board of directors, Chairman and President.
3. The line operating divisions are divided into groups according to type of product activity, with each group responsible to a group Vice-President. The group Vice Presidents report on the activities of their divisions through the President.
4. The corporation's overseas business (shown at the extreme right of the chart), representing its export trade, the operations of its foreign subsidiary companies, and its relations with affiliated companies abroad, is organised under a single officer, a Vice-President of international operations.

The distinction between the staff and line is especially important. The staff functions, headed by Vice Presidents, are the centres of the corporation's specialised skills. They have highly trained personnel—experts in their particular fields of interest—who serve as consultants to the operating divisions. These staff specialists, however, have no authority over what the operating divisions do. Rather, it is their function to assist, advise, and counsel with the operating groups on matters requiring specialised knowledge.

In addition, the corporate staff officers and their specialists work with the divisions in planning further improvements in division operations and in analysing and recommending solutions to difficult problems within their areas of specialisation. They also perform the important services of interpreting corporate policies and of co-ordinating corporate activities on an over-all basis.

Conversely, the line groups function in a strictly operational capacity. They represent the "profit centres" of the corporation, that is the units of the business held responsible for earning a profit from their operations. Because of this responsibility, they are vested with all the authority necessary to achieve their objectives. As previously mentioned, this authority is largely centered in the division general manager.

The group Vice Presidents provide the essential link between the line groups and the corporate staff. They are our chief operating officers. They are the representatives of the divisions at the top-management level and reflect to them the policies, objectives, and interests of the corporation as a whole. As thoroughly experienced "line men," they are responsible for guiding their particular divisions toward the achievement of their goals.

In making a clear separation between our staff and line activities, we believe we have developed a sound organisation structure. To be sure, it has imperfections which we would like to eliminate, and we are constantly on the lookout for ways and means to make further improvements.

Evaluated in total, however, our form of organisation has stood up well in actual practice and successfully weathered the impact of fluctuating economic conditions. It has enabled us to have centralised corporation policies, and yet allowed for the decentralized administration of them. It has placed authority to make decisions where the actions take place, thereby giving us greater agility and speed of decision than would be possible if we had close, centralised control.

For our people at both the staff and line levels, it has provided broad opportunity for continued personal growth and development. And in the case of our operating divisions, it has given them the degree of autonomy they require for the planning necessary to achieve their approved goals.

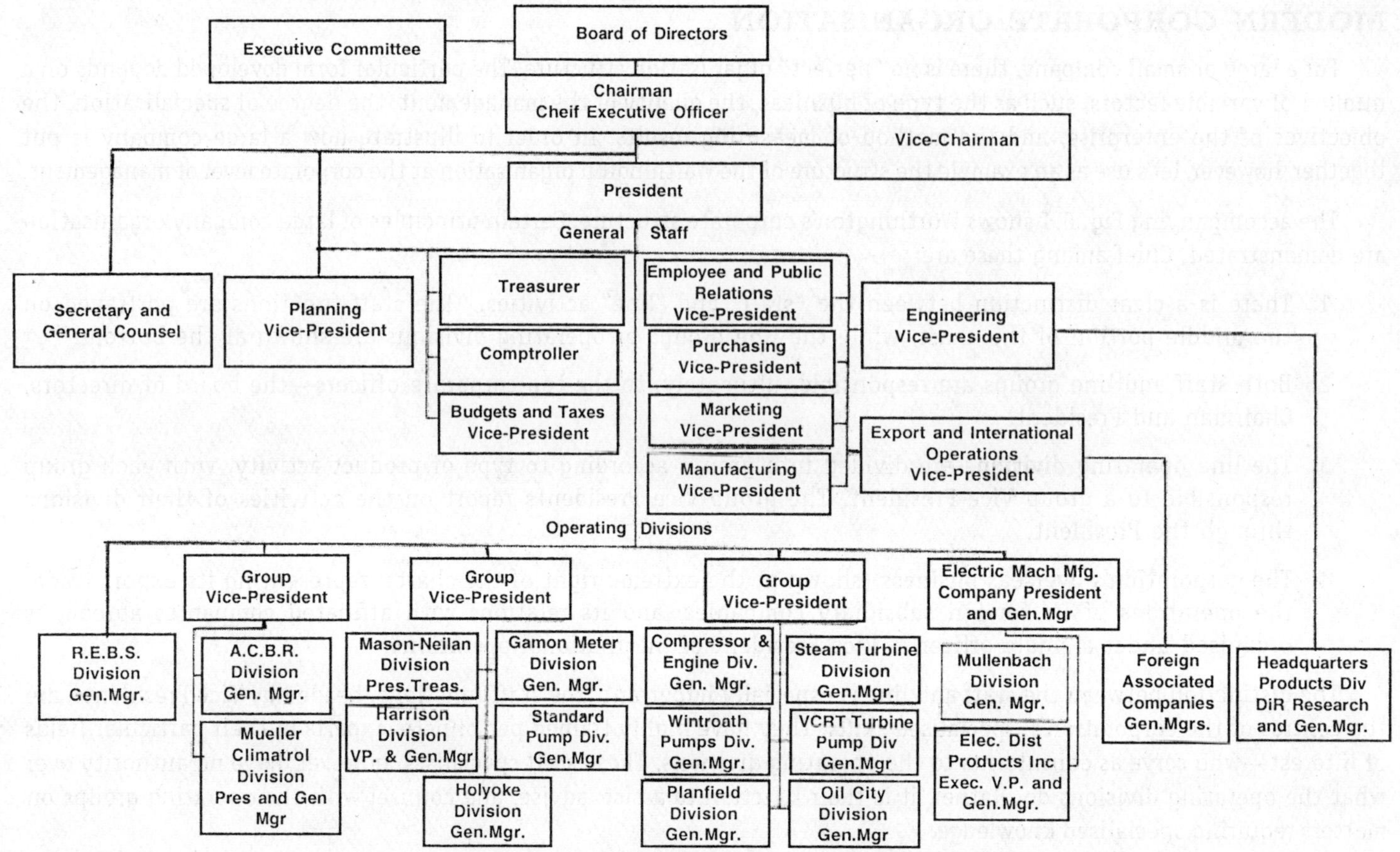

Fig. 6.1. Organisation Structure of the Worthington Corporation

Merely to hold its position in our present-day economy, a business "The emphasis on outputs, on tasks and costs has made organisations more diffuse bodies," says Shaun Tyson of Cranfield School of Management. "The present era has been described as 'post-Fordist' or 'post-modernist' - that is, organisation managers have moved away from thinking of their operational activity as replicating a bureaucratic machine, a rational, non-human monolith which delivers standardised products or services with scant regard for customer choice or competitive rivalry. Instead, work is organised in a more organic way, susceptible to rapid change, and to adjustment albeit within a limited range of options. Banking services, for example, are designed as personal financial advisory services, with most routine withdrawals and regular payments handled by machines; car manufacturers have various specification mixes on offer-, and airlines try to leverage sales through special packages, air miles schemes and the like."

The problems and the challenges were potently mapped out by Larry Hirschhorn and Thomas Gilmore of the Wharton Center for Applied Research in a *Harvard Business Review* article:

The problem is that this traditional organisational map describes a world that no longer exists. New technologies, fast-changing markets, and global competition are revolutionising business relationships. As companies blur their traditional boundaries to respond to this more fluid business environment, the roles that people play at work and the tasks they perform become correspondingly blurred and ambiguous.

However, just because work roles are no longer defined by the formal organisational structure doesn't mean that differences in authority, skill, talent and perspective simply disappear."

What has excited attention in the 1990s, is that organisational theory is being seen to be translated into dynamic business practice. Many accept that the age calls for radical responses, and now there are a growing member of radical role models.

ORGANISATIONAL EVOLUTION

In the US, the modern blueprint for the organisational revolution can be seen at General Electric (GE). When Chief Executive, Jack Welch arrived in 1981, the company was cumbersome and underperforming. Which he has since succeeded in overhauling and realigning it in a way which few thought was possible. Between 1981 and 1990, GE cut the average number of management layers between Welch and the very front line from nine to four. Its headquarters was slashed from 2,100 people to fewer than 1,000. The number of senior executives across the company was cut, first from 700 to 500, and between 1990 and 1994 by another 100. The overall workforce was almost halved.' from 4,04,000 to 220,000. Yet, GE's revenues nearly doubled through this period, from $ 27 billion to $ 40 billion.

Welch has stripped hierarchies away. When he arrived, GE had an average of five or six people reporting to each manager. By the late 1980s, this average had doubled and is now at about 14 - with some units reaching 25 or more. With more people to manage, managers have to manage in a different way using new skills and, increasingly, enabling others to do jobs which were once the sole preserve of management.

THE MATRIX MODEL: ABB

While Jack Welch and GE have grabbed the attention in the United States, Europe's benchmark of the new organisational model is the Swedish-Swiss conglomerate, Asea Brown Boveri (ABB). Under Chief Executive, Percy Barnevik, ABB has set unprecedented standards. Its ability to change itself continually impresses and concerns commentators and ABB managers in equal amounts.

The genesis of ABB began in 1987, when Barnevik, at the time Chief Executive of the Swedish engineering group, ASEA, announced what was then the world's largest cross-border merger between ASEA and the Swiss company, Brown Boveri. Since then ABB has acquired over 70 more companies, assembling a corporate monster worth $30 billion. Its engineering markets include electric power generation and transmission equipment, high speed trains, automation and robots, and environmental control systems.

Barnevik has rigorously rooted out and extinguished any vestiges of bureaucracy in ABB. His straightforward and much quoted rule is that 30 per cent of central staff can be spun off into separate and independent profit centres, another 30 per cent can be transferred to the operational companies as part of their overhead, another 30 per cent can be eliminated as superfluous to requirements and the remaining 10 per cent can be kept on as the minimum required. At ASEA, Barnevik drastically reduced the number of employees at head office from 2,000 to 200.

DEPARTMENTAL MANAGEMENT IN PRACTICE

Management is, in the final analysis, devising plans, implementing those plans, tallying results, and assessing programs and policies. Because the final goal for sales is made explicit in the business plan for every autonomous company and/or division, it is easy to grasp what sort of action will be necessry, and how much will have to be invested to reach the goals. At the departmental level, the specific goals and budgets are usually provided to the management from above. The budgets vary but are divided into general expenses and personnel costs. If the department or section is thought of as a management unit, this simplistic approach will not be sufficient to give an accurate picture of its needs. There are many systems but one I have found that works on this level is to use the concepts of input and output as the basis for determining budgets.

(1) Input : The department consumes management resources to provide some kind of output. The total of all resources used (funds, personnel, equipment, services, etc.) is the input. In addition to the costs of wages, materials, parts, fixed assets, plant and equipment, allocations for staff and administration departments are factored in. The precision of this accounting will vary, but the total input of all the departments should be about equal to the company's aggregate costs.

(2) Output : Output is the result of all resources invested and utilised in the activities of the department (operational input). There are two types of output: (1) tangible output—the total revenue earned for the delivery of products or services to other departments or outside customers, including both sales and allocated budget funds (budget revenue); (2) intangible output—the accomplishment of special tasks by top executives which cannot be expressed in monetary terms.

Sales revenue is the total income from the provision of goods and services to other departments and outside customers. Budget revenue is the funds given to service and administrative (*e.g.* research) departments for those services which cannot be put on a unit transaction basis, but which are performed for the benefit of all employees. The funds are collected from all other departments in proportional increments, which the paying department records as an indirect expense, or part of its input.

When determining output, be it sales or budget income, certain things must be kept in mind.

(1) Sales transaction income must be based on a fair market price for the product or service in order to have a true management system. If the product or service is simply provided at cost, the whole concept of departmental management is meaningless. Actual unit costs have little to do with the price of the product or service in a commercial transaction, but they do, of course, have to be calculated before you can begin a cost-cutting programme.

(2) The amount allocated to the budget cannot be determined simply on the basis of the size of the department or on its past performance. You must clarify the department's assigned responsibilities, set performance goals, and establish the methods and procedures by which the goals will be achieved. Only after putting all these together and considering the overall managerial balance can you effectively set a level for the allocation of revenue, and thus the fees to be charged to the client departments.

(3) Departments with staff functions should also make a detailed analysis of their work, and make sure nothing that could be put on a transaction basis is funded by budget allocations.

One way to evaluate a departmental management unit is to compare its output to input (revenue to costs) to determine profit and profit rate. This resembles conventional budget control, but there is a basic difference. In a budget control system you can take only certain specified actions within the constraints of the budget. In departmental management, however, profit and rate of profit are the basic considerations, so a whole spectrum of options are available. The solutions may range between increasing the input (costs) slightly to achieve large gains in output or reducing the output slightly to cut costs (input). This is the difference between control and management.

It might seem that if all departments did that, overall corporate management would be reduced to chaos. Problems can be alleviated in the planning stages, however, by careful consideration of the overall balance of the departmental management system. What is important is that we take the managerial viewpoint and try to achieve the widest scope for autonomous management activity.

There is output in the completion of normal departmental duties and special tasks. Unfortunately, there is a strong tendency to overemphasize the importance of the monthly accounting of department earnings, but the only reason a department exists is to carry out its assigned tasks. The relationship between task and earnings is like the relationship between function and price or between function and quality in a product. All are necessary to make a good product —a high degree of functionalism, quality, and low cost; so it is in departmental management.

The task output of each department is a reflection of the corporation's management policy. If that policy is perfunctory or poorly conceived, management lacks clarity; if it is specific and concise, it provides leadership to the employees. The sales department cannot be concerned merely with sales figures and departmental profits; it has to formulate clear, specific targets, like ensuring the quality of its sales (as in the promptness of payment and the terms of promissory notes), maintaining an adequate number of retail outlets, and monitoring product inventories.

One of the key points in departmental management is the assignment of output targets. If they are inappropriately assigned, the entire corporation will lack cohesion and the work of the department employees will be meaningless. Output must be determined through discussion between the supervisors and managers in each department and, if possible, in consultation with top management.

What constitutes output from sales and manufacturing departments is obvious, and, therefore, easily calculated. It may require some imagination, though, to define what constitutes output for departments with staff or service functions. If the output or role of the department cannot be calculated precisely, there is no reason for the department to exist. Quantitative evaluations should be devised for all types of output.

(3) Input-output comparison table: Once input and output have been determined, their relationship can be easily understood by drawing up a comparison table similar to a profit and loss statement or balance sheet. This table becomes even more effective by breaking down each item of input and output.

Table 6.1 Input-Output

Input		*Output*	
		Tangible output (Revenue)	*Intangible output (Functions)*
Common Input Direct cost for Job A Allocated costs	Total	Job A	Job A
Common Input Direct costs for job B Allocateed costs	Total	Job B	Job B
	(budget)		

In table 6.1, we match input for A to output A and input for B to output B. Doing this allows us to see how efficient the management is and where improvements are needed.

This Input-Output Table 6.1 can be used for project planning or to examine performance. We should begin, though, by using actual figures to prepare a performance input-output table that will help determine whether the output is appropriate, whether there is any wasteful input, and whether there are any other problems that might have been overlooked. It would be best to have a table that covers the past several years in order to see if the department is improving or getting worse.

The Input-Output Table 6.1 is a tool to help everyone in the department, not just the managers, gain a thorough understanding of the department's progress.

(4) Performance review meetings : Business performance review meetings are conducted in order to compare the actual performance of the department with the business plan. It is essential that all employees participate in the meetings so that everyone has the chance to make suggestions for improvement in the department's operations. Visual aids such as graphs, charts, and progress tables can be used to make the information accessible. Everyone should be allowed the right to speak at these meetings, and should be made to feel comfortable doing so. The meetings should be well-organised.

Downsizing : The 2008, financial crisis has brought in its wake the elimination of certain activities departments and even companies leading to the phenomenon of downsizing or shrinking of the organisation. The auto industry, banking and financial services, transportation, retailing, etc., have witnessed a veritable catharisis and virtual paralysis in the shrinking and closure of companies not only in USA but also leading into a "global recession" taking a toll not only in terms of loss of jobs but also a psychological depression resulting in loss of self esteem, alcoholism, divorce, and permanently lowered standards of living, rising suicide rates. Only recently we have seen two Indian techies in California shooting their children, wife and visiting in-laws and relatives, finally themselves, shocking the entire community there, because of loss of jobs and income and mounting debts.

Good companies while they are forced to downsize, offer outplacement services and training to find alternate employment in the industry or community. Another strategy by great organisations is to provide positions for the downsized in their companies or division elsewhere.

Now, let us turn to the next function of staffing the organisation to achieve enterprise objectives.

7 Staffing

The chapter is discussed under the following headings :
• Scientific Selection • Nature of the Personnel Required • The Nature and Source of Recruitment • Selection Process

Scientific Selection : Placing the Right Man on the Right Job

Alfred P. Sloan Jr. Former Chairman of General Motors, observed very aptly: "Most businesses are all alike except as to people. Buildings, machinery, tooling and markets are largely common instrumentalities available to many. But people, there is the difference; the most important single asset of GM is "the men and women who make up its organisation". In GM, the HR philosophy is an integral part of the management philosophy", says "J.H. Miller, Executive V.P (Personnel) and can be expressed in a single phrase; "the importance of people." He adds: "Management objectives are achieved through people. On *convictions concerning the importance* of people are reflected in our basic personnel objective of training all employees fairly... We believe that meeting this objective requires satisfying the inherent need of all people to be recognised as individuals."

Thomas Watson Sr believed in IBM philosophy's first premise: Respect the individual.[1]

It was Adam Curle, the economist who said that if the underdeveloped countries have remained underdeveloped it is largely because the people are developed having had no opportunity to realise their maximum potential. The maximum utilisation of people and their potential is the key not only of growth of the nations but also of the growth of the organisations.

Mr. Micheal Haider, former Chairman of Exxon reflects on the value of executive development.[2]

"In the life of a corporation, today's success is largely a product of three types of executive actions taken yesterday; 1. Selecting the right people, 2. Placing them in the right job and 3. Seeing to it that they were able to grow to meet both their own needs and those of the organisation. This activity is not a programme in the usual sense, any more than spelling or making profits are programmes. It has no fixed dimensions, no timetable, no cut-off point."

Mr. Henry Ford II Declared in a Statement:

"Executive talent is the most important asset we have. It doesn't appear on our balance sheet, but it will have more important effect on our progress, our profits, and the price of the stock, than any other asset we possess or can acquire nor this asset an expensive one to acquire. It is a bargain everyday of the year, a low cost risk with a high-return potential. If you will give as much thought to the acquisition and development of men/women with top management potential as you do to planning a plant or a product, nothing can stop this company. Fredrick W. Taylor emphasised that scientific selection, in the first place, is the first principle of scientific management.

A former Chairman of Unilever wrote an article in the Harvard Business Review that the essence of management is not solving problems but managing people.

Matsushita believed in the simple philosophy.

Most of the global companies place a great deal of emphasis on scientific selection and acquiring the right kind of people in the first place and allowing them to reach their maximum potential as well as the potential of their organisation. Mr. Samuel Walton would not delegate the responsibility of acquiring good people to Wal-Mart to anybody else almost all of his life. Now we shall distill the research, experiments, and experiences of Global Companies and portray how they go about scientific selection; placing the right person on the right job.

---

1. M.N. Rudrabasavaraj, *Human Factor in Management*, Mumbai, Himalaya Publishing House, 2000.
2. M.N. Rudrabasavaraj, *Executive Development in India*, Mumbai, Himalaya Publishing House, 1997.

SCIENTIFIC SELECTION

The promotion of productive efficiency through an effective utilisation of men and machines is one of the primary objectives of personnel administration and the attainment of this objective largely is contingent upon the function of finding and placing the right man on the right job at the right time in the right place. This poses problems even in the industrially advanced countries of the West, where the employment opportunities in industry and business are vast and this is more so in a country like ours where too many people are chasing too few jobs. In a lighter vein, a wag observed that proper placement is an exception and misplacement is common in our country. In order to avoid the pitfalls of wrong selection and placement, it is necessary to adopt the principle of scientific selection procedure. The use of science and systematic procedures in selection is essential if we want to find the right man for the right job. A wrong man on a wrong job will mar the development and progress of the organisation, even as the right man on the right job will contribute to organisational growth. The function of scientific selection is one of the most important functions of personnel administration and this encompasses the following sub-functions:

1. Determining the nature of the job to be filled.
2. Determining the nature of the personnel required.
3. Determining the nature and sources of recruitment.
4. Selection process: (a) Preliminary interview; (b) Application forms; (c) Reference letters; (d) Group discussion; (e) Interviews; (f) Tests; (g) Physical examination; (h) Selection and placement; (i) Induction; (j) Follow-up.

Policy Framework

Before an examination of the scientific selection procedure, it must be made clear that the personnel administrator must operate within the framework of employment or selection policies. It may be a company's policy to hire only South Indians or North Indians or the close relatives of the employees. Many a company may have a policy of promotion from within and recruitment from within and the objective of this policy is to promote good morale in the organisation. It may be a company policy to hire only high school graduates. Another company may have a policy of hiring only engineering graduates. And the list may be extended endlessly. But it may be sufficient to emphasise that these employment or selection policies will guide the selection process and procedures, which must operate within the policy framework.

Central Employment Office

Another important factor is that all hiring activities may be conducted through a central employment office, a division of personnel administration, which can give the line and top management in a plant the required expertise in hiring. It can keep records and take follow-up measures and use various personnel tools in hiring. It can maintain an organisational balance through an analysis of manpower requirements of the various departments. It can establish a skills inventory along with personnel inventory and plan and forecast manpower requirements. Promotional possibilities and transfer lines may be suggested. Unnecessary waste of other executives' time may be eradicated if all employment enquiries and applications are directed to be routed to the central employment office.

Where a company has branches all over the country and the plants are geographically dispersed it would be good to decentralise hiring procedure and give complete autonomy to plant employment offices to hire. But at the company headquarters may be located the central personnel administration, which would advise the plant's personnel divisions and provide research and other allied services to them.

The Responsibilities of Employment Office

The main responsibilities of the employment offices and selection are enumerated by Northcott.

1. To consider the form and content of the employment policy of the company and advise how best the employees needed may be obtained; to keep in touch with information concerning the general factors affecting the supply of labour and any new trends therein.
2. To this end, to maintain liaison with the Ministry of Labour and with sources of supply, including those other than local.
3. To become conversant with statutory and collectively agreed terms and conditions of employment affecting the company, advise on any that are a functional responsibility and ensure that all are observed.

4. To engage new workers in accordance with a defined functional responsibility which may mean, for example, that the final word in selection may rest with a foreman in the case of a skilled man or formally with the appropriate line executive in every case.
5. In all such instances, to engage new workers, and introduced them into the company's service, assist in placing them where required to the advantage of both the worker and the company, and follow up their progress to ensure that they are becoming both efficient and happy in their work.
6. To transfer workers to meet varying needs of different sections of the establishment or assist in a more satisfactory placement of individuals, carrying out, in particular, the company's policy of promotion.
7. To receive notice from persons who wish to leave and to give notice to such as must be dismissed from the company's service or are no longer necessary to its labour requirements.
8. To interview all employees who leave either voluntarily or on due notice and, in particular, those who leave on pension; in addition, to take necessary action on the death of a worker.
9. To keep records and statistics required:
   (1) by statute and regulation;
   (2) for the due fulfilment of personnel activities and responsibilities;
   (3) for adequate knowledge of each person, including any grading or rating system.
10. In the light of this knowledge, to carry out a company policy of appointments and promotions.
11. To answer inquiries from official sources and from fellow executives, in so doing observing the privacy of records.
12. To afford the fullest opportunities for employees to express their grievances or difficulties.
13. To represent the company on any Governmental or industrial committee concerned with this function.

Having considered the employment or selection policies and responsibilities, as well as the advantages of centralised hiring, let us now turn to the specific; methodology and detailed activities of the already mentioned various sub-functions of the important operative function of personnel procurement. It is appropriate to sound some warning notes here. There are two employment extremes. One is where the recruitment and selection procedures are initated after the notification of an existing vacancy. It is necessary to anticipate and forecast the actual and potential personnel requirements and to initiate procedures to procure personnel in time. The second extreme, is where, as is happening in some industries, enormous number of people are hired now a year or two ahead of time, when the employees will be utilised. For a year or two the employee waits around doing practically nothing, when the plant is erected and the machinery installed. These two extremes ought to be eliminated.

Determining the Nature of the Job to be Filled

This is the first stage in the process of placing the right man on the right job at the right time in the right place, through the adoption of a scientific selection procedure. It is essential for the personnel executive to find out the specific nature of the job to be filled before initiating the process of selection.

The personnel administrator has various tools with which it is possible for him to understand the nature of the job for which the process of procurement is to be initiated. To fill a job effectively, it is necessary to select a candidate, whose actual and potential qualifications match the present and future requirements of the job. So, the first stage of procurement deals with the description of the job to be filled and many problems are created when this aspect is taken for granted or completely ignored.

Job Terms Defined

A 'job' is defined as an assignment of work calling for a set of duties, and conditions that are different from those of other work assignments. A job may include many positions, but a 'position' is a task performed by and related to a particular employee. Whereas the job is impersonal, the position is personal. The term 'station' is somewhat similar to 'position', but there are more positions or stations than jobs in a company. The terms 'occupatation' refers to a group of jobs with common or related characteristics and another term, "job family" is used to indicate the same notion of grouping of similar jobs. Within a job, two or more 'grades' may be identified, where the work assignments may be graded according to skill, difficulty or quality of workmanship. Among clerks, there may be Grade I Clerk, Grade II Clerk, Grade III Clerk, and Grade IV Clerk with varying skills and carrying varying compensation arrangements.

Job Analysis : The personnel tool with which the duties, responsibilities, operations, conditions and organisational aspects of a particular job are studied, specified and clearly enumerated is job analysis. Job analysis is a procedure by which the facts with respect to each job are systematically discovered and noted. From such analyses, general statements are obtained known as job description'. A job description describes the work perfomed, the duties and responsibilities involved, the skill or training required, conditions under which the job is done, relationships with other jobs and personal requirements of the job.

The 'job specification', a product of job analysis and a refined form of job description, may contain the duties of the job and the type of employee required, in terms of skill, education, experience, special aptitudes, etc. The 'job classification' refers to a system of relating jobs with similar or family characteristics into a logical order of groupings. The 'job evaluation' refers to the process whereby the relative values of employees on particular jobs are measured. Job evaluation will be discussed in a later chapter.

Job analysis, also known as job study, is often considered basic in the management of people, because the results of job analysis are so widely used and so distinctly important. This provides complete job information which is useful in the following areas of personnel administration :

1. Recruitment, selection and placement.
2. Transfers, promotions and demotions.
3. Training and development programmes.
4. Wage and salary administrations.
5. Settlement of grievances.
6. Work measurement and method study.
7. Improvement of working conditions.
8. Setting production standards.
9. Increasing productivity.
10. Organisational planning.

Through the job analysis we would like to know what a worker is doing and expected to do on a particular job; how the job is performed; skills required to do the job; the organisational relationships of the job. In short, job analysis provides the following relevant information :

1. Job titles, including alternate or trade nicknames.
2. Number of employees on the job and their organisational relationships.
3. Names of immediate supervisors.
4. Materials, tools and equipment used or worked with.
5. Work or instructions received from and to whom delivered.
6. Salary or wage levels.
7. Hours and conditions of work.
8. Complete list of duties — daily, weekly, monthly, seasonal or casual — and time spent on each.
9. Educational requirements.
10. Experience requirements.
11. Skills, aptitudes and faculties required.
12. Promotional and transfer routes from and to the job.
13. Other information, comments and observations.

Responsibility for Job Analysis: The responsibility for sponsoring a job analyst programme lies with the top management, who usually authorise, the personnel division to execute the programme. The personnel division can train some of its staff to conduct job analysis or they can hire a job analyst from outside to do the job for the division. Very often, particularly in India, the usefulness of a job analysis programme is not realised by the top management and it falls upon the shoulders of the personnel people to 'sell' this programme and its utility value.

In some good companies with good personnel divisions, there may be a small team of specialists headed by a job analyst, who organises, directs, co-ordinates and controls the work of the specialist team. The job analyst may hire specialists or train personnel to become specialists. They may be given proper training in their work about the company, organisation structure, policies and programmes and to get along with line executives, without whose co-operation job analysis becomes very difficult. Where there are trade unions, their co-operation should be sought and they must be consulted and educated as to the purpose and uses of job analysis programme.

Methodology of job analysis : Job information is obtained through three sources: (1) employees on the jobs; (2) supervisors; and (3) managers. Generally, the methods of obtaining information and necessary facts with regard to the job are : (1) Questionnaires; (2) Personal interviews; and (3) Observation.

1. Questionnaire Method is one of the common methods, where a job questionnaire is submitted to each employee and an illustration of a job questionnaire is given below. The job analysts can help the employees in filling the questionnaire and the completed questionnaire may be submitted to the immediate supervisors for their comments and get complete information regarding jobs under their supervision. Questionnaire method is less time consuming and easy. Supervisors and foremen may be given special training and asked to analyse jobs under their supervision.

JOB QUESTIONNAIRE

Title of Position ....

Department .... Section ....

Division .... Data ....

Please read all of the questions before making any entries; then answer each one as briefly as possible, consistent with complete information. Return this description within one week to the Job Analyst, Personnel Department.

Description of Duties

1. What is the general purpose of your work?

2. What duties do you personally perform in the usual course of work? (Say from where you receive your work, what you do with it and where you send it. In answering this question discuss your daily routine.)

3. What duties do you perform only at stated periods, such as weekly, monthly etc.?

4. What occasional duties do you perform at irregular intervals?

5. How many employees do you supervise? (List job names and number of people in each job.)

6. To whom are you directly responsible?

7. What, if any, instructions do you receive as to how the work is to be done and from whom are they received?

Performance of Duties

A. Mental Requirements

8. What is the lowest grade of grammar school, high school, or college education that should be required of a person stating in position?

9. If any special courses are needed in order to perform your duties satisfactorily, name them.

B. Skill

10. What past experience is necessary for a new employee to have in order to learn to perform the duties of your position? Name the kind of experience, where and how it could be obtained and the time required to source it.

11. Having the above education and experience, what would a new employee have yet to learn and how long would it take the employee to obtain sufficient practice in doing the new work to reach the point at which he would be barely satisfactory?

12. In what lower positions could an employee receive training for your position?

13. For what higher position in the company does your present work train you?

14. What, in your opinion, is the most difficult part of your work and why is it difficult?

C. Physical Effort

15. Roughly, what proportions of your time are spent in: standing....%, sitting ....%, moving about ....%, other ....%?

16. What machines or other equipment do you personally operate; regularly or only occasionally?

17. Roughly, what proportion of your time is spent in operating each machine you use? State also what degree of speed is required on each machine.

18. What, if any, are the physical requirements for the proper performance of your duties? (strength, height, dexterity etc.)

19. Please list any other requirements not covered above and any personal qualifications and characteristics which you believe a candidate for your position should have.

20. What is you responsibility for money, securities, or other valuables?

21. What is the nature and extent of your responsibility for the employees under your supervision?

22. Give the nature and extent of any responsibility you may have other than for men and money.

23. What personal dealings with customers do you have in performing the duties of your position? State the nature of your time is spent in dealing with customers.

24. Roughly, what proportion of your time is spent in dealing with customers?

Working Conditions

25. What are your usual working hours?

26. What are the disagreeable features of your work?

Use this space and additional sheets of paper, if necessary, for any special features of your work not covered above, and for answers to questions for which more space is needed.

Your name ....

Years in this position ....

Fig. 7.1

Source: Dale Yoder, *Personnel Management and Industrial Relations, pp. 284-285.*

2. Personal interviews : The job analyst can obtain information through personal interviews with the employees. Although this is more time consuming, the interview may bring out all the relevant information. A trained job analyst knows what to ask and how to get the relevant information. He will interview not only the employees but also the supervisors and managers connected with the jobs under analysis.

3. Observation : The questionnaire and interview methods may be supplemented with independent observation. By observing the worker at work over a period of time, a job analyst can accurately analyse the job and its various components.

A job analyst is careful in using these methods and he is also familiar with analyses of similar jobs. He carefully should avoid describing the employee and his traits and personality and stick to only information concerning the job. The jobs on the surface may appear similar but he should note the distinguishing feature of a job or aim to discover the crucial task in a job. Now all the relevant information concerning a job is ready.

Written job description : After a thorough job study, tentative job descriptions should be written, which may be submitted to various interested supervisors and executives for review, change and final approval. Then, acceptable job descriptions are written out in simple and clear language, avoiding semantics, confusion, ambiguity in sentences. Overestimation or underestimation of job requirments must be avoided. A 'catchall' clause must be used where management will reserve the right to add or delete certain aspects in a job. The job analysis procedures look complicated, but it is a very useful personnel tool in determining the nature of the job to be filled. Now that completes the first stage of personnel procurement, *i.e.*, understanding the nature of the job to be filled; let us now turn to the second stage.

NATURE OF THE PERSONNEL REQUIRED

After the nature of the job is determined, the characteristics of the manpower required to fill the job assume prominence and also the number of employees that must be procured.

Man Specifications

The personal characteristics or 'man' specifications have to be determined and they encompass the following :

A. Physical specifications : Various types and degrees of physical faculties are required for different jobs. For some jobs, such as assembling a TV set, accurate and good vision is required. For a typing job, good finger dexterity and memory are required. For boosting jobs, one has to be strong, thick-set and heavy. To be a cop (policeman) in New York City, you have to be over 6 feet in height and around 165 pounds in weight. So the necessary physical abilities and skills necessary to do the job must be specified. Under physical specifications the following may be mentioned : height, weight, physical abilities like walking, vision, pulling, pushing, finger dexterity, hand steadiness, stamina, etc.

B. Mental specifications : Here the mental processes required to do the job to be filled are specified. This has reference to the following : intelligence, memory, judgement, ability to plan, ability to estimate, to read, to write, to think and concentrate, scientific faculties, arithmetical abilities, etc. Particular types and degrees of mental requirements for different jobs may also be specified.

C. Emotional and Social specifications : There is a growing awareness on the part of the employers that emotional and social characteristics are important although specifying these requirements is not easy. Recent research emphasises the impact of a man's ability to get along with people, his relations with the groups, etc. With the help of research and psychologists, sociologist, and psychoanalysts, some emotional and social specifications are listed. Some of them are : ability to remain calm, social adaptability, personal hygiene, dress, poise, features, etc.

D. Behavioural specifications: This is specified in higher levels of management. Certain management personnel are expected to behave in a certain way. These are not formally listed out, nevertheless these play an important role in selection. The corporate image requires the executive to conduct himself in society in a certain fashion. The status of the individual and prestige of the company help direct the behaviour of executives. With the determination of man specifications and the estimation of manpower requirements, the second stage is completed. Now we proceed to the third stage.

THE NATURE AND SOURCE OF RECRUITMENT

After obtaining information regarding job requirements and manpower requirements and before instituting the selection procedures, it will be necessary to find out the nature of recruitment. The nature of recruitment is dependent upon the nature and stage of economic sophistication of the industrial society. In industrially advanced countries like America, the channels of recruitment tend to be formalised and insitutionalised, *e.g.*, Union, Private Employment Agencies, Public Employment Agencies, etc. But in less advanced countries like our own, there is a tendency to be less formal and non-institutional in character, *e.g.*, friends, relatives, etc. In America, studies have indicated definite recruiting patterns that vary with the size of the firm, the type of workers being sought, and with the structure of the industry. In India also, despite the lack of research studies, one may identify certain definite recruiting trends. Certain industries look for certain types of workers coming from a particular background and from certain regional areas.

It is also recognised that there is a direct correlation between recruiting practices and changing conditions of labour market. According to Professor F. J. Malm, the firm's reactions in its adjustment of recruiting methods to changing labour conditions are influenced by two factors:

1. Firm's position in the labour market : The firm's own size, location and reputation will tend to have a persistent effect on its ability to attract labour. Hindustan Lever, TISCO, TELCO, DCM, Union Carbide, Lakshmi Mills attract an abundant supply of labour, whereas others may not find much response even when they are looking for manpower.

2. The degree of tightness of the labour market : This is a part of the environment within which every firm operates, but its actual effect on any given firm will depend in part on the factors mentioned under : (a) when the market is most loose or when labour supply is abundant, there may be a surplus of applicants at the employer's door; (b) when the market is most 'tight' or when the labour supply is scarce, the employer is likely to resort much more extensively to formal or institutional channels of recruitment and also to imaginative or even unorthodox methods. In West Germany the shortage of labour has forced many an employer to offer various incentives to attract labourers from neighbouring Italy. One company gives a motor cycle to the Italian employee free, so that he may come into Germany to work in the plant in the morning and go home to Italy after work.

In USA, the shortage of manpower is critical in many areas and *Time magazine* reports some unorthodox recruitment procedures : "On posters plastered all over the Lockheed Missiles and Space Co. grounds in Sunnyvale, California, an Indian sends up smoke signals above the caption : 'Spread the Word' ; the word is that Lockheed has an immediate need of 2,000 workers. Douglas Aircraft Co. has been hiring engineers with a $ 1,00,000 savings plan that is above and beyond the normal retirement benefits. In Cincinnati, General Electric is offering present workers, bonuses of upto $ 200 for every new employee they successfully recruit. Monsanto has started running help wanted' advertisements on TV in Dayton. Ford's Lincoln-Mercury assembly plant in St. Louis is using spot radio commercials, has set up portable employment offices at several shopping centres. According to San Francisco's Ampex, the necessity of looking farther afield for technicians has increased its recruitment costs from $ 3,000 to nearly $ 5,000 a man.... Detroit automakers have imported unemployed mountaineers from Appalachia to sweep floors at $ 3 an hour.... Inland Steel has 600 openings for unskilled workers, has had to hire 150 college students just to fill vacancies in its week-end cleaning gangs."

In India, the abundance of human resources poses peculiar problems when we are going through a socio-economic revolution by subjecting recruiting process to informal modes.

The IIPM observes : "The most striking feature in the Indian labour market is the apparent abundance of labour. Yet, despite tremendous unemployment, the right type of labour is not too easy to find. Since new workers are still mainly drawn from the rural population, they take time to adjust themselves to the new life. Sometimes they cannot adjust themselves to the new life and eventually they return to their native villages. Others may return for long spells and some wish to return at least once a year to their homes. Labour turnover and absenteeism, therefore, constitute a continuing problem in the industry. This underlines the need for properly planned recruitment policy in order to minimise the disruption of work by constantly changing personnel. Illiteracy among the working population also raises problems in recruitment and selection."

The Sources of Recruitment

The sources of manpower supply are many and varied and the company must know what and where these are in order to fill their personnel needs. Some organisations have established recruitment policies. It may be a company's policy to hire only the relatives of the employees and one Indian textile mill has a hierarchy of preferences. First they prefer wives or husbands, then sons or daughters, then cousins and then other close relatives. This mill has a policy of intimating its employees of the vacancy or potential vacancy and of inviting employees to recommend a person, who must be his relative. For this purpose the firm uses an Employee Recommendation Form. Many companies have a policy of hiring only friends and relatives. In one US pharmaceutical firm, summer jobs are available only to the childern of the employees and if there are not enough children, only then other students are offered job opportunities. These recruitment policies guide the procedure of hiring and where to look for to fill the vacancies.

There are a variety of sources of recruitment for manual, clerical, sales, professional, technical, and managerial personnel and in USA, the following sources of recruitment are widely used :

1. *Direct hiring :* This has reference to those who come to the door of the company looking for employment. This is a very common source of recruitment. Those firms, which have a good reputation regarding wages working conditions, and other facilities, attract a good number of people, from whom the company may think of selecting some men.

2. *Friends and relatives :* As already pointed out, friends and relatives of employees are another good source of supply and some companies prefer to utilise this source extensively. Often the employee may tell his friend or relative that his company is hiring people and so the word spreads. This is also a popularly used source of recruitment and this is a sort of a recommended labour. Some companies encourage and invite employees to recommend their friends or relatives and the companies feel that this promotes employee loyalty. The employees feel happy at the opportunity of having had a hand in the employment aspect of the company and they are also careful in recommending somebody to the company. There is some sort of preselection available to the company. Companies dependent on this source declare that there is a high degree of morale and loyalty and good group relationships and friendliness among the employees. The work atmosphere appears congenial and even enjoyable.

3. *Advertisements in newspapers* : This is one of the most commonly employed source. The corporation needing manpower to fill certain job, advertises the available job, likely pay, duties and responsibilities of the job—job specification—and also man specifications in a newspaper, magazine or journal and invites applications. But advertisements must be

carefully written giving all relevant data, and they must attract only the right type of people with right qualifications. If the advertisement is vague and general, it may attract hundreds or even thousands of applications, rendering the process of screening time-consuming and costly. The advertisement must clearly state the educational qualifications, experience, and skills necessary to do the job to be filled, with a view to discouraging the unsuitable candidates from applying.

4. ***Unions*** : This is another source of recruitment and in some industries such as the building trades, unions have provided the employer the necessary number of workers. In some industries in U. S. A., the unions have completely taken over the function of hiring semi-skilled and unskilled labour force. There are "hiring halls" of the unions. The union may also advise a worker, where he can find a job. If its member loses his job in one company for some reason, the union may find him a job in another company.

5. ***Public Employment Agencies*** : The United States-Employment Services or 'USES' as it is popularly known, started in 1918, has a network of several state employment services, which act as public employment agencies. In the early years they were not found very useful, but they were, after the passage of the Social Security Act, which provided unemployment compensation to the unemployed for a short time till they found another job. In order to obtain this compensation, the unemployed had to register with USES, providing a roster of all who were unemployed and desired to work. The Second World War gave a strong stimulus to USES, when there was a great demand for all types of manpower.

USES with 1800 offices located all over U.S.A., serves both the worker and the employer by acting as a clearing house for jobs and job information. Counselling, testing, labour market surveys, etc., are some of the services provided by USES. The unemployed register themselves with employment services and USES helps them find jobs with some companies.

6. ***Private Employment Agencies :*** are another important source, which many companies cultivate for hiring purposes. The firms can find suitable men through these private employment agencies. In New York city alone there may be hundreds of such agencies. Usually, they specialise in supplying certain types of personnel and some specialise in clerical and secretarial personnel and others in executives, accountants, engineers, economists, salesmen, dieticians, beauticians, top executives, etc. They usually charge a fee for their services and they may collect the fee either from the applicant or the employer or from both. They also provide employment counselling and guidance service, resume service and other services to the people seeking employment.

7. ***Employers' or Trade Associations :*** Meetings, conferences, seminars, and other social functions organised by these associations are another source through which the firms try to recruit the needed people. A few come to these conferences looking for a change in positions and some others attend to recruit the right man.

8. ***Professional Associations and Journals :*** are yet another source for finding some professional and technical people. Advertising in the professional journals will bring in good response. Again the seminars, symposia, meetings, conferences, and other functions sponsored by the professional associations provide opportunities to recruit professional personnel. Through the journals, the employers can identify some, who contribute articles and papers and who may be tapped.

9. ***Schools and Colleges :*** Recruitment from educational institutions is a popular practice of thousands of firms in U.S.A. For clerical, labour and apprentice help, high schools are extensively used. Many colleges have their own placement offices, through which students find their jobs. The placement office is in touch with various firms and displays employment opportunities on its bulletin board for the benefit of students who may apply for some jobs. Their applications are processed and sent to the companies by the placement office. The companies usually send their recruiters to college or university campus to interview candidates and those who are successful, are invited to the company for further interviews. Schools and colleges are a very widely used recruitment source of the companies. Even in India, many of the leading universities and institutes of management and technology provide a variety of placement services to both of their own students and industries.

10. ***From Other Firms :*** Recruiting personnel from other firms is a popular practice. There are corporations which have made a name for themselves in training and developing people, particularly executives. In the auto industry, they would like to recruit an executive from General Motors. Similarly Dupont, General Electric, Standard Oil, N. J. have an established reputation for good executives and other firms would like to recruit from these corporations.

11. ***Management Consultants :*** Specialised executive selection services are offered to the companies by many consultants. Executive search is a really big and fascinating business in U.S.A. Many firms rely on consultants for executive recruitment. In our country there are many consultancy firms which offer their services to the companies.

12. *Radio and Television* : Through radio and TV many companies recruit their employees and particularly when the labour market is very tight, these sources of recruitment are used much.

13. *Internal Resources* : So far we have only discussed external sources of recruitment. But to many organisations, internal source is the main source of recruitment. Through transfer, promotions and demotions the firms try to fill their personnel needs. Recruitment from within policy is a common policy with many organisations. This policy has many merits. Firstly, it improves the morale of the men. Secondly, it promotes loyalty among men to the organisation. Thirdly, the employer has tried and familiar employees, to evaluate.

But the problem with this policy is that it leads to the danger of "in-breeding". People, when they work for an organisation, develop attitudes and notions that are moulded by the organisation and the danger here is the lack of new initiative, ideas and views. Growth and development of any organisation needs certain amount of exposure to the new ideas and initiative that may come from people who come from outside the organisation. They view the company methods and practices from a new perspective and may contribute views that help in the progress of the firm.

Another danger is that internal source may dry up. It may not be possible to find a certain type of skilled labour within the organisation. Another problem is that promotion based on seniority principle is inherent in this policy of recruitment from within. Seniority alone should not be the criterion for promotions. This aspect, we shall discuss in a later chapter.

14. *Other Sources* : In some areas, churches, fraternal organisations and lodges serve as effective employment agencies. There are some institutions, where deaf, dumb and blind workers are available for employment if you need them.

In India, the popular sources of recruitment are listed by IIPM :

1. Within the organisation.
2. Budli or temporary workers.
3. Employment Agencies.
4. Casual callers.
5. Friends and relatives.
6. Advertisements.
7. Labour Contractors.

To this list may be added radio, management consultants, schools and colleges and other firms.

Many Indian firms, particularly textile mills, employ budli or temporary workers and whenever they need permanent help they turn to these budli employees and make them permanent. There is an advantage here, because the employer knows the worker and his efficiency at work.

Just like USES, we in India have National Employment Service, which has employment exchanges all over the country. These employment exchanges register the names of the candidates, seeking employment and try to place them with some employers. In our country compulsory notification of all vacancies to the employment exchange is required by law. Our employment exchanges are not as high powered as those of the USES, but they serve some useful purpose as an employment agency. For professional and technical personnel the University Employment Bureau or Placement Offices and the Council of Scientific and Industrial Research set up by the Government may also be tapped.

The practice of recruiting through labour contractors, who may themselves be employees, is peculiar to our country. Although this breeds many malpractices as pointed out by even the Royal Commission on Labour and though the Industrial Courts frown upon them, it is still prevalent in some areas, but there is a growing feeling that it needs to be abolished altogether.

In Japan, many firms depend upon University professors, particularly Kayo University and University of Tokyo, to recruit professional, technical and managerial personnel.

Recruitment procedures may be improved, if the personnel executive carefully studies the correlation between sources of labour supply, methods of recruitment and subsequent job performance. The idea is to know from where and through what methods, good and efficient workers can be hired.

After the completion of these three stages—determining (1) the nature of the job to be filled, (2) the nature of personnel required and (3) the nature and sources of recruitment-selection procedures are set in motion to ensure proper selection and placement. Before initiating, selection procedure, a hiring requisition is necessary.

Requisitioning Employees

In case of a vacancy or expected vacancy, the executive or supervisor or foreman in need of help should request the personnel department (or Employment Section) on a 'hiring requisition' form to help him hire the needed personnel. This requisition should give all necessary information about the job, the experience, qualities, skills, and qualifications to be looked for in the applicant. In short a job and man specification must be given. In requisitioning, the line executives must also take into consideration the time factor in recruitment and selection and request for help sufficiently ahead of time. Sufficient time period must be given to the personnel department to employ its scientific selection procedures with a view to hiring the proper personnel. Hasty selections may prove costly to the company in the long run.

It is the duty of the personnel department in its staff advisory capacity to meet the needs of line management by recruiting and screening. There should be close and effective co-operation and collaboration between executives and supervisors on the one hand and personnel division on the other. There is need for good team spirit and team work between line and staff personnel.

After the personnel division knows precisely what kind of man is needed for a particular type of job, it may start its scientific selection procedures.

SELECTION PROCESS

The selection procedures must take into consideration the public policy and operate within the framework of the provisions of the State or Central statutory controls. Public policy may prohibit any kind of discrimination against any person on grounds such as colour, race, sex, creed or caste. Public policy may prohibit employment of children or even women in certain industries or limit the hours when women may work in a plant. Former employees with good standing, who were laid off for some reason, may be considered for employment and in some union-management contracts, management will be required to hire the former employees first and then consider others for employment. Often, employers prefer employees who are known to them and who have a good service record to their credit.

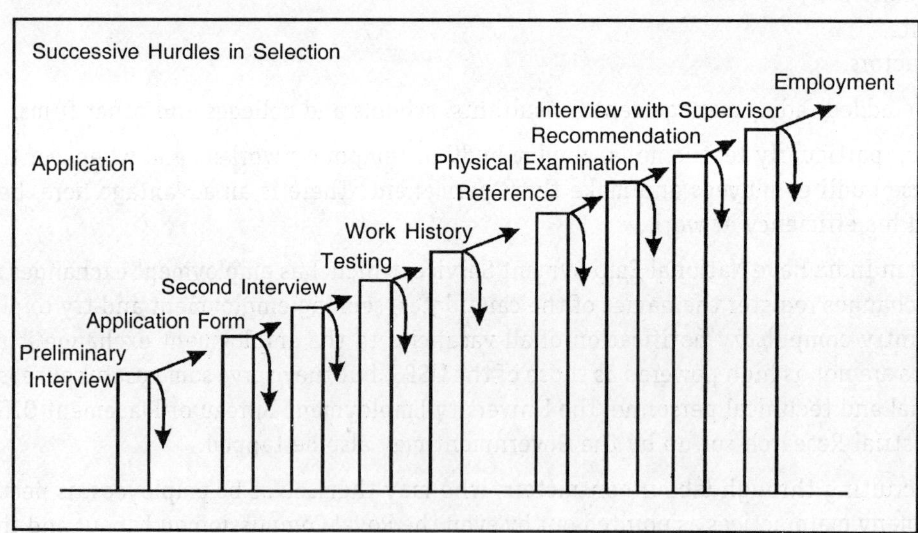

Fig. 7.1. Successive Hurdles in Selection Process

Source: Dale Yoder, *Personnel Management and Industrial Relations, p. 234.*

Within the framework of public policy and company policy, proper selection standards must be prescribed with a view to placing the right person on the right job. The selection process involves a series of obstacles which have to be overcome by the candidates and the winning candidate wins the job. The series of hurdles is well illustrated in the figure 7.1.

Generally a good selection process will include the following steps, which act as a sequence of obstacles to be surmounted by the candidates seeking employment.

1. Preliminary interview
2. Application forms

3. Reference letters
4. Group Discussions
5. Interviews
6. Tests
7. Physical examination
8. Selection and Placement
9. Induction
10. Follow-up.

1. Preliminary Interview

Preliminary interview, which may be conducted by a junior executive in the personnel department, is the first hurdle which a potential candidate has to overcome and it is possible to screen and eliminate unsuitable candidates. For example, if you have a policy of hiring only male employees, any female candidate looking for employment in your plant can be dissuaded from applying for a job and thus save your time and effort and costly processing mechanism. If you are hiring mechanical engineers with B.E.qualification and if a candidate with M.Sc. in production engineering seeks employment, you may tell him that his high qualifications are not necessary for the kind of opening you have in your company and at this stage itself eliminate the candidate because of unsuitability. Or for security reasons, you have a policy not to select foreigners, you can quickly arrive at a decision regarding the unsuitability of the aliens for the job.

But a word of caution is necessary. There is a possibility, in your eagerness to save time-consuming processing procedures, that a potentially good, loyal, and enduring employee may be lost through hasty conclusions at the preliminary interview. Before eliminating a potential applicant, we must make sure he is unsuitable.

Preliminary interview provides the first opportunity for the candidate to know about the company and the job and whether he is suitable or not, the personnel executive must create a good impression of the company on the candidate. It provides an opportunity for the personnel executive to 'sell' the company to the candidate. Even if the candidate does not become a prospective employee, he may become a potential consumer of your product. Besides it never hurts to build the corporate image and the opportunity should not be lightly passed up. Informality, courtesy, kindness, listening patiently and giving relevant information will impress the candidate very much. Rudeness and discourtesy will make you lose not only a potential employee, but a potential consumer also. If a candidate is found suitable, an application blank may be given to him to fill in and return.

2. Application Forms

Application forms are widely used everywhere and constitute one of the fundamental media through which information is gathered about the applicant. Quite a few companies in India do not have any application blank, but will ask the applicant to apply on white paper giving details about age, marital status, educational qualifications, work experience, references. But most companies design different application forms for different types of employees—managers, supervisors, employees, etc. and while some application forms are simple, general and easily answerable, some others may require elaborate, complex and detailed information from the applicant.

Reference to nationality, race, caste, religion, and even place of birth has been regarded as evidence of discriminatory attitudes and the fair employment practice regulations have required the employers to delete any such references. In some instances, requiring photographs may be objectionable.

Generally the information sought to be gathered through the applications refers to the following:

1. Name of the applicant, his address, telephone number.
2. Personal information such as sex, marital status, number of children, other dependants, if any, parent's names and their occupation and birthplaces.
3. Education.
4. Physical characteristics, such as height, weight, health, vision, other defects.
5. Experience, usually with the past three or four employers.
6. Hobbies and interests.

7. Membership of Associations.
8. Financial status.
9. Statement of purpose.
10. References — personal and business.
11. Wages and salary required.
12. Comments and remarks.

The crucial factors, generally, are education, employment record, place of residence, sex, etc.

Weighted application forms : Application forms may be designed to serve as highly effective preliminary screening device. By careful study, such items as age, education, dependants, earnings, and years on previous jobs may be found to be closely correlated with success in the job for which the candidates are applying. On the basis of past experience, a scoring system may be provided for all such items and a *cutting score* may be established for the total. Such a weighted application form may quicken the process of recruitment and selections.

Professor Yoder observes : "In a somewhat similar procedure, six biographical items have been identified as 'knock-out-factors' in a preliminary screening programme for salesmen. They include instability of residence, failure in business within two years, divorce or separation within two years, excessive personal indebtedness, too high a standard of living, and unexplained gaps in the employment record."

Apart from providing information on the applicant, the application forms provide the starting off point for interviews, the basis for reference checking, and also testing. Seldom should applications be the sole cirterion for selecting and seldom they are.

It is just one more hurdle. Often it is possible to screen quite a few candidates on the basis of applications. In a country like India, where too many persons are chasing too few jobs, many will respond to an advertisement, even when they know that they do not possess the qualifications needed to get the job. They hope against hope that the right candidates possessing the needed qualifications may not apply or may not be aware of the opening and in which case the employer may have to settle for candidates with lesser qualifications. Often this is true of experience requirement. Although it may be difficult to find a candidate with seven years' experience, the employer will go ahead and demand seven years' experience in the advertisement. Then when there is no applicant with seven years' experience he may be forced to settle for a chap with four or five years' experience. The usual problem is that the employer may stipulate impossible requirements, particularly in India, where skilled, technical, professional and managerial personnel are in short supply. In the final analysis, he will settle for what is available. There is a need to be realistic in fixing qualification requirements.

It is common in our country to receive hundreds or even thousands of applications in response to an advertisement and many will be found unsuitable by a cursory glance at their applications. Those, who are found to be suitable, may be recruited and invited to face another hurdle— interviews. Before the interviews, the references given by the applicant may be checked in order get some more information from the referees.

3. References

Generally the applicant will be asked to give two or three referees—preferably former employers, or professional acquaintances or friends or professors or famous persons, and the applicant will give the names of those, who may speak well of him. It is possible to get impartial assessment or evaluation of the applicant from some of the referees. Some other referees, in order to avoid any unpleasantness will speak in generalities, which will be of no use to the employer in evaluating the applicant. Hence, many companies do not place much reliance on the referees' letters. In fact Pigors and Myers maintain : "Letters of recommendation are not discussed here since they seem not to be a sound device for getting reliable information. The writers are sometimes more concerned with avoiding disagreeableness than in stating their considered opinion or describing their experience with the candidate." I maintain that contacting the referees has some usefulness, although too much reliance may not be placed and there are some referees, who will give a dispassionate evaluation of the applicant's strengths and weaknesses, which will be useful to the personnel executive and the line executive.

Regarding contacting the previous employers, in some applications, the applicant will be asked whether it is all right to contact his former employers and if the applicant does not want this, his former employers may not be reached. There may be a need to investigate the employment history of the applicant and to check the veracity, accuracy and candour of the applicant.

4. Group Discussion

Next in the sequence of obstacles for the applicant is the group discussion. The group discussion is a method where groups of the job applicants are brought around a conference table and they are given either a case study or a subject for discussion. Any subject, barring religious or political, but mostly topical or relevant subjects are given for group discussion. For instance, if we are hiring management trainees the subject may be the practices of management in Indian industry or the image of an Indian manager or management education in India. Suppose we are hiring a transportation manager the subject may be rural transportation and communication. If we are hiring an economist the subject may be methods to contain inflation or the virtues of the balanced budget. The other variation is to give a short case study highlighting a problem.

It is for the group to analyse, discuss, find solutions and articulate their views, in a completely leaderless situation and they are being observed by a selection panel who judge the group discussion on the basis of such activities as:

1. Initiating the discussion
2. Explaining the problem
3. Providing information
4. Clarifying issues
5. Influencing others
6. Summarising
7. Speaking effectively
8. Mediating arguments among the participants

It gives the opportunity for the selection panel to observe and judge how well the participants can think, analyse problems, substantiate arguments, find solutions, cogently reason and take decisions. Another variation of this method is to ask the participants to rate the others in the group and interestingly it is found that the group will always rate quite objectively who are the No. 1, 2, 3, and nobody will over-rate himself. Still another variation of the method is to ask the participants in the group to write up the summary of the group discussion which gives an opportunity for the selection panel to observe writing abilities of the participants.

Next in the sequence of obstacles for the applicant is the interview.

5. Interviews

Interviewing is the most universally used tool in any selection procedure and interviews are designed to serve in the important areas of employment, training, human relations, and labour relations. In many companies interview may be the only tool used. Interviews may be for a period of five minutes or for sixty minutes. Interviews may be informal and oral or they may be highly planned and carefully conducted.

Invitation for the interview : When a company invites an applicant for an interview at the head office or the plant, some companies meet his travel expenses and some do not. Some meet the applicant's staying expenses also. Executives may be paid first class or air fare, whereas blue collar employees may be given second class fare. According to the type and status, employee's expenses will be met. Then there are many companies that do not defray any expense incurred by the applicant appearing for the interview. Here the ability of the company to defray full or any part of the expenses of the applicant is crucial and its policy is important.

The letter inviting the applicant to appear for the interview must be sent at least three to four weeks ahead of the time of interview, so that the applicant may plan his trip. The interview letter must also state the place of interview and time of interview.

Place of interview : The place of interview in the employment office must be neat, and good-looking and it must create a good impression on the applicants. Many companies provide a lounge for the applicants to sit and relax, while they wait for the interview. Magazines, newspapers and company materials like the house organs, employee handbooks, company reports, etc. may be also displayed for the applicants to browse through. Some companies serve coffee or tea to the candidates.

Time of interview : Generally all the candidates are asked to appear for the interview at the same time. For example, let us say a company invites 10 candidates for the interview and all of them are asked to report for the interview at 9 a. m. at the company office. Even if the interviewer or the interviewing committee or the selection board were to take 10 minutes for each candidate the last of the 10 candidates will have to wait for more than 90 minutes. If the interview takes longer time, the candidates will have to wait for a longer period.

Some companies meet this situation by staggering the interview time in such a way that no candidate will have to wait for more than five minutes. This will call for careful planning of interview time, but this will assist the candidates and also the interviewers.

Some interview rules : Interviews must be planned with care and the interviewers may observe some of the following rules :

1. Be courteous to the candidate and let him feel "at home."
2. Listen attentively and patiently.
3. Do not ask leading or tricky questions.
4. Never argue or interrupt or change the subject abruptly.
5. Ask questions in a simple language understandable to the applicant.
6. Be tactful in asking direct and personal questions.
7. Keep the candidate talking and encourage him to talk.
8. Try to get the relevant information
9. Respect the interests of the candidate.
10. Answer the candidate's questions.
11. Do not 'oversell' the job opportunities in the company.
12. Lead the interview to its conclusion.

Training for Interviewers : To observe all these rules, the interviewer must plan the interview and the questions he is going to ask, with particular care. Many companies train their interviewers in conducting interviews. The interviewers may be asked to beware of their first impressions, hasty inferences, bias, prejudice, likes and dislikes. Despite all the interview techniques, the personal observations and impressions of the interviewer are important in appraising the candidate and this element of subjectivity cannot be eliminated altogether. By pointing out the warning signals, this subjective element can be minimised.

AQ; The Bell Telephone Company at Philadelphia, USA., trains its interviewers with lessons :

1. Establish tentative job qualifications.
2. Review application for employment.
3. Preparation for conducting practice interviews.
4. Conducting practice interviews.
5. Recording the findings.
6. Interpretation of the findings.
7. Introduction of job specifications.
8. Evaluation of findings.
9. Practising the complete interview.

Some companies employ those trained in psychology and psychiatry in the personnel department to interview candidates. Others hire and train people to become expert interviewers.

Purpose of interviews : The primary purpose of the interview is to complete and get the correct picture gained through application forms. It measures the ability of the candidate to speak and present his views, his sociability, poise, appearance, that almost undefinable personality, etc. Through the interview conducted by the employment manager, information about the company policies, programmes and opportunities may be given to the candidate.

There may be just one main interview. In the case of supervisory or managerial personnel more than one interview may be conducted. Interviews are the most widely used personnel tools of selection and some companies may have no other hurdles than this and on the basis of the interview, a candidate may be selected or rejected.

Types of interviews : There are various types of interviews employed by the companies. In India most of the interviews may be oral and informal. Then there are some whose interviews are well-planned and well conducted. The following are the different types of interviews and they are briefly discussed :

1. Informal interview.
2. Formal interview.
3. Planned interview.
4. Patterned Interview
5. Non-directive Interview.
6. Depth Interview.
7. Stress Interview.
8. Group Interview.
9. Panel Interview.

1. *Informal interview :* An informal interview is an oral interview and may take place anywhere. This type of interview is perphaps followed very widely in India. The employer or the manager or the personnel man may ask a few almost inconsequential questions like name, place of birth, names of relatives, etc., either in their respective offices or anywhere outside the plant or company. It is not planned and nobody prepares for it. This interview is used widely when the labour market is tight and when you need workers very badly. In India, a friend or a relative of the employer or manager may take a candidate to the house of the employer or manager, where this type of interview may be conducted. In some instances, the candidate may not open his mouth at all, for his friend or relative may be doing the talking with the employer. The employer or the manager may hire the candidate. This happens not only in our country, but, perhaps, in other countries also.

2. *Formal interview:* Formal interviews may be held in the employment office by the employment officer in a more formal atmosphere, with the help of well-structured questions. The time and place of the interview will be stipulated by the employment office. The formal interview will attempt to elicit the relevant information from the candidate and the interviewer may have a prepared list of questions that he is proposing to ask the candidate

3. *Planned interview :* It is a formal interview, which is carefully planned. Here, the interviewer may have a plan of action worked out in his own mind and he knows how much time he is going to devote to each candidate, what type of information he is seeking and what he proposes to give, how to open the interview and how to close the interview and how to conduct the interview. He may use the plan with some amount of flexibility. He may deviate from his plan, but he knows what he is doing and he can come back to his original plan and continue the interview.

In a planned interview there need not be any waste of time, embarrassing moments of silence, and failure to obtain, some, relevant information.

4. *Patterned interview :* A patterned interview is also a planned interview, but it is more carefully pre-planned to a high degree of accuracy, precision, and exactitude. With the help of job and man specifications, a list of questions and areas will be carefully prepared, and it will act as the interviewer's guide. With the help of this formal list covering all aspects, the interviewer can go down the list of questions, asking one after another and this list is also a memory aid to the interviewer. But the interviewer's guide may be supplemented to gather any other significant information and this is dependent upon the skill of the interviewer.

5. *Non-directive interview :* Non-directive interview or unstructured interview is designed to let the interviewee speak his mind freely. The interviewer has no formal or direct questions, but is all attention to the candidate. He encourages the candidate to talk by a little prodding whenever the candidate is silent. In recent times this type of interview may start off thus: "Mr. Raj, please tell us about yourself after you graduated from high school" and keep the interview going by prodding questions or suggestions.

The idea is to give the candidate complete freedom to "sell" himself, without the encumbrances of the interviewer's questions. But the interviewer must be of a higher calibre and must guide and relate the information to the objective of the interview. Interpreting the information given by the applicant and relating it to the job requirements calls for great skill on the part of the interviewer.

6. *Depth interview :* Depth interview is designed to intensively examine the candidate's background and thinking and to go into considerable detail on particular subjects of an important nature and of special interest to the candidate. For example, if the candidate says that he is interested in tennis, a series of questions may be asked to test the depth of understanding and interest of the candidate : Who was the Wimbledon men's champion in 1965 and women's champion in 1965? Who was responsible for India's victory in the recent Davis Cup match against Brazil? Where was the match played? What are the different types of grips used by tennis players? What are the various types of surfaces on which tennis is played? What is the bounce of the tennis ball like on these different surfaces? How long have you played tennis? Do you like singles, doubles, or mixed doubles play? Similarly great many questions may be asked about tennis to test the candidate's understanding.

The theory is that this gives the interviewer the necessary insight to evaluate and assess the individual candidate and if the candidate is found good in his area of special interest, the chances are that if he likes the given job, he may take serious interest in the job and deliver the goods for the company.

These probing questions must be asked with tact and through exhaustive analysis; it is possible to get a good picture of the candidate.

7. *Stress interview :* This type of interview is designed to test the candidate and his conduct and behaviour by putting him under conditions of stress and strain. The interviewer may start with, "Mr. Raj, we do not think your qualifications and experience are adequate for this position", and watch the reaction of the candidate. A good candidate will not yield, on the contrary he may substantiate why he is qualified to handle the job.

This type of interview is borrowed from the military organisation and this is very useful to test behaviour of individuals when they are faced with disagreeable and trying situations.

8. *Group interview :* The group interview is designed to save a busy executive's time and to see how the candidates react to and against each other. All the candidates may be brought together in the employment office and they may be interviewed.

In another type of group interview, the candidates may be given a topic for discussion and observe who will lead the discussion, how many will participate in the discussion, how each will make his presentation, and how they will react to each other's views and presentation.

9. *Panel interview :* A panel or interviewing board or selection committee may interview the candidate, usually in the case of supervisory and managerial positions. This type of interview pools the collective judgments and wisdom of the panel in the assessment of the candidate and also in questioning the faculties of the candidate.

In the case of executive positions, the candidate may be asked to meet the panel of interviewers individually for a fairly lengthy interview.

In USA., the wives of executives are also interviewed by some companies in order to find out how she would like her husband working for the company in a particular place. If the wife does not like her husband travelling a great deal, the company would like to know that if the job involves extensive travelling. If the wife does not like living in the place where the plant is located, then there will be problems in the home of the candidate and the company would like to know that. The idea is that if the wife is unhappy at home, her husband will also feel unhappy not only at home but also at the office and on the job. That means his efficiency on the job will not be 100% and will be low.

Interview Rating : A method widely accepted in vocational guidance and personnel selection is "The Seven-Point Plan" which provides a framework for listing and examining the important aspects of personality to be sought under the following headings:

Physical Make-up : Health; physique; age; appearance; bearing; speech.

Attainments : Education; occupational training and experience.

Intelligence : Basic and "effective"

Special Aptitudes : Fluency, written and oral; numeracy; organisational ability; administrative skill.

Interests : Intellectual; practical; physically active; social; artistic.

Disposition : Self-reliance; nature; motivation; acceptability.

Circumstances : Domestic; social background and experience; future prospects.

To this may be added position requirements and family background, which would give important relevant information on the upbringing and moulding of his personality, family conditioning, values in life, parental influences. This would act as an interview guide and the candidates may be rated on a five-point rating scale by the selection committee.

It must be admitted that most people do not know the art and skill of interviewing. It must be learnt and practised. Many companies offer courses on selection processes to top executives which are of benefit.

Limitations of interviewing : As earlier pointed out there are certain limitations of interviewing. The subjective element cannot altogether be eliminated. The prejudices, likes, dislikes, first impressions, bias of the interviewer because of his human nature, introduce the subjective element and this may distort the evaluation or assessment of the candidate. The interviewer may unconsciously dislike men with long noses, Brahmins, Negroes, aliens, Jews or Muslims, or Hindus. He may, in our country, dislike quite unconsciously Bengalis, or Punjabis, or Channaiites, etc. This unconscious dislike will show up on the surface in his reception and appraisal of the candidate.

Professor Dale Yoder points out these limitations of interviewing.

"One of the most common types of interviewing errors has been widely described as *halo* or the *halo effect*. It is the tendency to allow one prominent characteristic of the candidate to dominate appraisal of the entire personality, to colour the interviewer's judgment on other traits. If the individual being interviewed has a pleasant voice and speaks well, that quality makes all his other qualifications look better. Any one of many individual characteristics may create the halo—dress, physical appearance, small mannerisms."

"Closely related is what *has been called stereotyping.* The interviewer's experience may have created a close association between some particular trait and a distinctive type of personality. Whenever the interviewer discovers that the trait is present, he tends to ascribe to the interviewee all the other characteristics of the type. The interviewer may, for example, associate red hair with fiery temperament. He may relate a single physical characteristic with racial types. He may stereotype all applicants from Oklahoma as Okies, all those from Minnesota as Scandinavians, all those from Stanford as "eggheads", or all graduates of your *alma mater* as playboys."

Another problem is that same managers believe they are good at character analysis even now and they are guided by their own abilities at character analysis. But this seems to be giving place to systematic selection procedures.

Interpreting information: The information gathered through different types of interviews has to be interpreted and a scoring system may be used. Then interviewers may be asked to rate the interviewees and these may be interpreted with a view to finding the most suitable candidate. A five-point rating scale may be used, such as (1) outstanding, (2) good, (3) above average, (4) below average, (5) unsatisfactory, and total the points in making the final evaluation.

As pointed out earlier, interviews may be the only tool of selection, but most companies supplement the interviews with tests, physical examinations, etc.

6. Tests

Tests are used to gather some more accurate information about the candidate and thus, they supplement the other selection techniques, and they cannot supplant them. Since the First World War, when psychological tests were used by the US. Army to select army personnel, much interest has been shown in USA, in the usage of tests as a selection technique. Tests are not infallible and they depend upon correct construction and interpretation. There are many hazards when tests are used as the sole criterion for selection. But tests are found useful as one of selection techniques. The use of psychological tests is widely prevalent in the West and for their usage it is necessary to get the benefit of specialists. Tests are used in the areas of employment, guidance, promotion, training, placement and transfers.

The use of tests in industry today is not so widespread as the volume of literature on the subject would lead one to believe. Their use has steadily expanded, however, and testing has definitely earned a place in a scientific selection procedure. One survey of personnel practices in business has revealed that 81 per cent of 473 firms having 250 employees or more indicated that they were using one or more tests in hiring. Most smaller firms do not make use of standardised tests, but rely more heavily upon interviews, and background checks. Many have tended to abandon testing in the light of validation requirements made evident by the Supreme Court decision in the Griggs *vs.* Duke Power Company case.

But in India their usage is limited to some of the large established Indian companies and some foreign subsidiaries. Many others do not use any of the tests for the purpose of selection. Some common tests used in the West are as follows :

1. Aptitude tests.
2. Intelligence tests.
3. Mechanical tests.
4. Trade tests.
5. Character tests.
6. Achievement tests.
7. Combination tests.
8. Personality tests.
9. Interest tests.
10. Various tailor-made tests.

The candidate must be assured that the tests are to help the company to assess the candidate and the information will be strictly confidential.

7. Physical Examination

In USA., it is common to give a prospective employee a thorough medical check-up, known as the pre-employment physical examination. If the employee's health is found satisfactory, a job offer is made. This is yet another selection hurdle that has to be surmounted by the candidate. Again there is a need to assure the candidate that his health information will be kept strictly confidential and this will help both the candidate and the company.

Generally the medical examination is both general and thorough, conducted by a qualified doctor and the findings will be interpreted and transmitted by the doctor to the employment office.

In India, physical examinations are not very common for the purpose of selection. But some companies do use these physical examinations and they are used after the employee is hired and only a few give pre-employment physical examination.

8. Selection and Placement

In the selection process, particularly in India, we should not forget to mention the role played by the letters of recommendation and influence. Many candidates are selected mainly on the basis of a recommendation letter from the right individual. Though unfortunate, the letters of recommendation are often a very good passport to a job. And influence plays also a significant role. Without the influence of some godfather, many candidates may not find a job, let alone a decent job. These render the selection process unsystematic and inefficient and in the long run this will reflect on the efficiency, productivity, and profits of the organisation.

In USA., and even with some firms in India the in-basket technique is used in the selection of executives. We are familiar with correspondence separated as incoming and out-going in a basket on the executive desk. Mr. John K. Hemphill, Director of Executive Study, Educational Testing Service writes: "An in-basket test is a collection of documents which presumably have accumulated in the in-basket of a manager and are awaiting his attention. The particular documents in the in-basket constitute the test items. The examinee responds to these test items by taking action as though he were actually on the job, and whatever results he produces in taking the test are his "answers" to the test items." Our research studies in this area have been oriented toward the solution of problems involved in performance measurement on in-basket tests. We have devised systems by which we can score or evaluate the output of a subject. The first system developed yielded measures of his performance in a wide variety of areas, including :

1. The manner in which he analyses the problem.
2. The types of decisions that he makes.
3. The kinds of actions he takes.
4. The way he communicates with others.
5. His method of organising or approaching the work.
6. The amount of initiative he shows in solving problems.

7. The way in which he delegates work.
8. The way in which he interacts with his staff.
9. The amount of consideration displayed toward others.

The in-basket approach is also a useful selection technique and is being used in some companies in India.

Interpreting the findings made through interviews, application blanks, references, tests, personal observation, and physical examinations is the next process of selection, although at each of these selection hurdles, the selection process is taking place. On the basis of the findings, decisions to select or nor to select have to be made. The responsibility for such decisions should rest with the line executives, save in the case of recruitment for the personnel division.

The employee may be, after selection put on a period of probation, after which his employment will be regularised. The new employee needs to be properly placed and here proper matching of the employee with the job is essential. In a case of continuous hiring, and when there is no job opening, but the candidate is a good one, an interim placement may be made, until a suitable job is ready. The newly selected employee may be intimated through a letter of appointment, the terms of appointment and service conditions and when and where he should report to work.

It is necessary to maintain records of rejections also and in case, a rejected candidate applies again for the same job, the records will show that he had been found unsuitable for some specific reason and thus all the elaborate procedures of selection can be avoided. Records of selected candidates should be maintained and into them all additional data regarding service, merit rating, grievances, disciplinary cases, health history, etc., are reported.

9. Induction

The selection procedure does not end once the selection is made, for the new employee has to be inducted into the organisation. The purpose of induction is to educate the employee and provide orientation on the following subjects :

1. Company history, products, processes, and major operations;
2. Company policies, objectives, and regulations;
3. Relation of foremen and personnel department;
4. Rules and regulations regarding wages, hours of work and overtime, safety and accidents, holidays and vacations, methods of reporting tardiness and absences, discipline and grievances, uniforms and clothing, parking, badges and parcels;
5. Economic and recreational services available, insurance plans, pensions, athletic, social, and cultural activities;
6. Opportunities, promotion and transfer, suggestion systems and job stabilisation.

To 'sell' the company to the new employee so that he may feel proud of his association with the company is the primary purpose of induction.

In some companies in USA., induction is done through the 'buddy system' where a senior or older employee inducts the new employee. More conventional is the practice of inducting the new employee through one of the personnel staff. A wide variety of printed material, employee handbooks, pamphlets, picture stories, comics and cartoons, movies and slides are used to educate the new employee about the company. A programme of induction helps the new employee to understand and develop a sense of identification with the company.

10. Follow-up

The objective of a follow-up is to see whether the right man has been placed in the right job or there has been a mistake. This also provides an opportunity for the supervisor or the manager to assess the contribution of the employee and make suggestions, if necessary, to improve his performance. If the new employee is not functioning well, it is necessary to find out his problems. Through interviewing, guidance, and counselling, the problems of the new employee have to be brought into the open and ways and means have to be suggested to eradicate the issues.

If the individual is functioning well in his present capacity and is 'happy' with his job where he has been able to realise his full potentialities, the personnel executive will have had the pleasure of assisting in the placement of the right man on the right job.

The contemporary recruitment, selection, and placement procedures are systematic, professional, and technical in character and they are designed not only to place the right man on the right job but also to see that there is an enduring employee and employer relationship. The personnel administrator's responsibility is to provide a loyal, effective, and enduring work-force to the company and to promote a sense of membership and belongingness in the organisation among the work-force. The long-term association and loyalty of employees to TISCO may be cited as an example. Mr. Bhabha observes : Many of today's workers, foremen, supervisors, and superintendents are the childern of former employees of the Company who earned their livelihood, built their homes, and settled down in the steel city and who have a sense of 'belonging' to Jamshedpur. There must be very few plants in India where there is, for instance, such a sense of personal loyalty to the head of the organisation, Mr. J.R.D. Tata. This is something you cannot help feeling whenever you go around the Steel Works with the Chairman. The newer companies have yet to achieve the same degree of fellowship and sense of partnership and this is where the Personnel Officers have a prominent role to play. Today you cannot, as in the past, wait for many decades for the sense of 'belonging' to be gradually developed. You have got to telescope this process into a short period of years, or even months. And in doing so, you have to achieve one of your primary purposes, which is to relieve the line management men of the burden of looking to the needs, problems and grievances of the workers and imbuing them with a sense of loyalty to the organisation and the will to improve their productivity."

We should like to contrast the scientific selection procedure with some historic selection practices noted by Professor Lundy. "Some of the darkest days in the history of personnel administration occurred when phrenologists, physiognomists, palmists, graphologists, and astrologists were selling their services throughout the business world. Each of these groups specialised in impressive, but unproven, methods of personality evaluation. For example, phrenologists studied the bumps on one's head and judged character accordingly. Franz Gall, the Austrian who proposed the theory of phrenology contended that each of many traits is associited with a particular portion of the brain, and the contour of the skull indicates the prominence of portions of the *pseudoscientific techniques of the* brain and their corresponding traits."

"Physiognomy is quite similar to phrenology, except that the physiognomist judges character by such features, as the shape and size of one's chin, nose, and ears, and the colour of one's eyes and hair. Of all the unsound techniques, physiognomy seems to be the most enduring. How often have you heard red-heads described as short-tempered or people with eyes close together described as cruel or mean ? Many interesting studies have been performed to disprove physiognomy as a valid technique for determining character traits."

"Palmists and graphologists have not been very active in the field of employee selection, but they still can be found at fairs and amusement parks. Palmists claim to be able to judge character and predict one's future by scrutinising the lines of one's hand, while graphologists provide the same type of information by analysing handwriting. Again, the predictability of these techniques has been shown to be no better than chance, though there is a feeling that graphology, if developed more thoroughly, might become a useful approach."

"The most dubious of these pseudoscientific techniques is that of astrology. Not only do the astrologists claim to be able to forsee the future, but they also claim that the position of the stars on one's date of birth determiners one's character and therefore can be used in appraising individuals."

"Although the heading for this section implies that the techniques just discussed are of historic interest only, this represents, unfortunately, just wishful thinking. One can still find medicine men in the field of personnel management. Perhaps with more widespread and improved education in the field, pseudoscientific approaches to problems of personnel management eventually will become extinct."

"One should not conclude from this discussion, however, that such things as appearance and handwriting are, not suitable criteria, but rather their utility is doubtful in the prediction of personality traits. To be sure, in the selection of a chorus girl or a secretary, one might be interested in appearance and handwriting respectively. This is different from hiring or rejecting a machine operator because he has blue eyes, a crewcut, round chin, short upper lip, long nose, or moustache."

Fortunately in modern days, there are more reliable tools available to the men in the field of personnel administration and the selection procedures are more systematic and scientific. It is possible that we may hire once in a while an unsuitable or wrong candidate even after adopting all the scientific selection procedures but the fact is that we leave ourselves wide open to chance and errors if we do not adopt a scientific selection procedure.

The Problem of Discrimination

The problem of discrimination in selection has assumed great importance in modern scientific selection procedure. We find various types of discriminations based on sex, age, race, caste, region, practised in organisations. We find that in certain companies women are not provided employment. In some others minority groups like the Muslims, Christians, etc. may be discriminated against. In some cases age becomes a candidate for discrimination, and older employees are scrupulously avoided. It is also interesting to note that there are companies where Hindus are discriminated against. In the United States, U.K. and other countries black people are discriminated against, and various other minority groups like Chinese, Japanese, West Indians, Puerto Ricans face discrimination. Now the state is interfering in order to prevent such discriminations. It is considered an unfair labour practice. Now in fact, the whole selection procedure and instruments have come under sharp pattack. Now companies are required to justify the instruments in the sense that they are being used for the purpose of scientific selection, objectivity and fairness and not use the instruments with a view to eliminating some groups of people because of their race, caste, religion, region, sex and age. We are sure that even in our country the state will intervene to see that the entire selection instruments and procedures are used fairly, objectively and justly and any discrimination on any ground will be considered not only unfair but illegal also in the very near future.

Scientific selection is one of the most important principles of scientific management and there is enough knowledge and experience to prove that these selection techniques are useful in the recruitment, selection and placement process.

8 Directing

The chapter is discussed under the following headings :
• Introduction • To Nordstrom Way, Directing at IBM - Wartime to Peacetime Expansion • Directing at Bridgeport Machines.

INTRODUCTION

Now we have the vision and mission of the company; drawn up the long range, medium range, and annual plan; designed an organisation structure; placed the right people in the right jobs. Now comes the most crucial task of directing, guiding and assisting people to start implementing the core activities of the company with everybody not only doing their best but also operating productively, effectively and achieving profits for the company. Implementation or going to work is the strong suite of all successful organisations. I had the pleasure of living in Singapore for 15 years consulting with some top organisations in Singapore as well as in various parts of the world. Mr. Lee Kuan Yew, the first Prime Minister, the father of the nation, was a great implementer. If something is to be done, it will be done immediately, not tomorrow. So much so the Government is more efficient than even the best of the private sector or MNCs. If they want to develop an airport, the Government will form a committee with members of departments involved in the project. They are given the task of developing and implementing a plan, they are sent around the world to study the best airports, the best technology, the best expertise. They hire the best expertise with best technology to develop the best airport in the world, better than the best airport. The result, Changi Airport, which has been hailed as the best airport in the world clean, efficient and friendly. The standard set for the efficiency of the airport is : a passenger alights from the plane, goes through immigration and customs, collects his baggage and enters a taxi and leaves the airport all in 10 minutes flat. I used to travel a lot and I would get out of Changi in 5 minutes.

Not once did the Customs ask me to open my bag in all the 20 years, I have used Singapore Airport. Everything in Singapore is world class. Airport, Seaport, Infrastructure, Shopping, Fine arts and culture, etc., so much so you feel that the rest of the world is backward. In Los Angeles, it may take you an hour to get out of the airport.

I was told that Mr. Lee and some of the Government guests were playing golf in Istana and people from the nearby buildings were watching them. Mr. Lee observed this and the next morning an order was sent out to those buildings to close all their windows facing Istana. Pronto, in a day all those windows got closed and nobody was allowed to watch. Some people, after chewing gums, were sticking them on the doors of electric trains and the result was the door would get stuck and wouldn't open. So the chewing gum was banned in Singapore. The point is that things get done yesterday, not tomorrow.

Another organisation which is extremely efficient is the Conference Board in New York. Everything is extremely well-planned and organised and things get done on time. I learnt more about management than by MBA programme, since I could see the excellence in management in the operations. I was involved in a project in Human Resource Management in USA, involving experts who prepared the questionnaire, sent out 11,000 questionnaires to associates and top companies and the project of collecting the completed questionnaires, analysis, interpretation, writing the report by 11 experts and publishing the report in eleven months on schedule. The report is some kind of a Bible to American business who would refer to our report, if they wanted to find out the latest practices in HRM. We would invite our associates to the resorts in Catskills to educate and inform them, out of which came lot of consulting work where Board experts advise associates how to go about implementing new policies and programmes. I was given the task of co-ordinating the project with the experts. It was a great learning experience. The organisation culture was that everybody came early and left on time or a little later and every project was completed on time.

When I joined Conference Board, Mr. Ave Raube, Vice-President of HR Division, briefed me that the associate is the most important person for not only the Board but also to all the staff. Everybody had to inform their secretary where we could be reached whenever the Associate called for something. The Board didn't believe in saying that the expert is out to lunch or in a meeting or something like that.

After this experience in the Board, in my consulting, I would always tell my clients in Indonesia, Singapore, Japan, USA, India or anywhere that if something was bothering them and they wanted to talk to me about it that they could call me anytime, day or night, weekends, holidays, etc., But I found in my 30 years of experience around the world, clients are also very reasonable people and very considerate. They will not talk to you unless it is very important or urgent, from their point of view.

It is interesting to note how Global Companies implement their plans and achieve results.

1. The Nordstrom Way.[1]
2. Directing at IBM.[2]
3. Directing at Matsushita[3]
4. Directing at Bridgeport Machines.[4]

DIRECTORS EMPLOYMENT — THE NORDSTROM WAY

Introduction : The customer pointed out to the Nordstrom salesperson that she had bought a pair of shoes at Bloomingdale's (a competitor) that were too small for her. She liked the style, but Bloomingdale's didn't have her size. After being fitted with the same shoe of the proper size, the customer started to pay for the shoes. The salesperson instead suggested that she merely take the too-small shoes in exchange for the new purchase. When the customer reminded the salesperson that she hadn't bought the first pair at Nord, strom, the salesperson said to her, "if I take these shoes for you, you won't have any reason to return to Bloomingdale's.

Such stories abound when people talk about Nordstrom. *A Sixty Minutes segment* recounted an occasion where a salesperson even changed the type on a customer's car. Such anecdotes underscore the value of empowerment in the corporate arena. Empowerment involves granting employees the freedom and responsibility to do their jobs as they think best, without constantly having to appeal to higher authorities for permission. It enables them to make on-the-spot decisions without getting caught up in bureaucratic red tape. At Nordstrom, empowerment is integral to success in serving customers. Nordstrom is renowned for its empowerment of employees.

Since being founded in 1901, as a shoe store in Seattle, Washington, Nordstrom has developed into one of the country's leading fashion specialty retailers. As of 1992, Nordstrom operated 52 stores scattered through Washington, Oregon, California, Utah, Alaska, Virginia, Maryland, New Jersey, Illinois and Minnesota. During the preceding decade, net sales climbed from $ 769 million to $ 3.4 billion.

Nordstrom management's policy toward employees has made such growth and financial success possible. One way that Nordstrom managers have enfranchised their employees is by using the term "associate" instead of "employee". While on the surface this may seem merely a cosmetic change, the Nordstrom terminology underscores managers' commitment to their people. The company management emphasises *customer satisfaction* as the single overriding goal.

As a corollary, Nordstrom associates are encouraged to pay more attention to their customers' needs than to their bosses' needs. This means that salespeople are free to do whatever they think necessary to serve their customers' needs best. Some salespeople choose to keep a log of their customers' purchases. This is an individual choice not a company policy. The salesperson also determines how much of his or her pay comes from salary or commission. Again, choice is vested in the associate.

---

1. Rudoff F. Bannon, "Directing, Guiding, Leading,' *Top Management Handbook,* pp. 365-71.
2. J. Watson, J.P. Pete Pake, *Fasher, San & Company*, (New York; Banton Books, 1990), pp. 68-69, 133-37 & 151-3.
3. Ogawa, *Pana Management*, pp. 134-7.
4. Stone, *et. al., Management,* p. 43.

Directing at IBM

The IBM School House sat on North Street in the midst of Dad's enterprise, Wrotes Watson Jr, Not many companies had real schools in those days; Dad copied the idea from the Cash and improved upon it greatly. The school's aim was to produce future officers of the company, and Dad always talked to us trainees as if we were colleagues. Everything about the school was meant to inspire loyalty, enthusiasm, and high ideals, which IBM held out as the way to achieve success. The front door had the motto "THINK" written over it in two-foot-high brass letters. Just inside was a granite staircase that was supposed to put students in an aspiring frame of mind as they stepped up to the day's classes. Engraved on the risers were the words:

THINK
OBSERVE
DISCUSS
LISTEN
READ

"In class the first thing we did each morning was to stand up and sing IBM songs. We actually had a songbook, *Songs of the I.B.M.* It opened with "The Star-Spangled Banner," and on the facing page was IBM's own anthem, "Ever Onward." There were dozens of songs in praise of Dad or other executives, set to tunes everybody knew. One of my favourites was to Fred Nichol, who started out as Dad's secretary at the Cash, came with him to IBM, and most recently had been promoted to Vice-President and general manager. Making rousing speeches in praise of my father was one of Nichol's specialities, and his success showed how far loyalty could carry a man at IBM. The song was sung to the tune of "Tramp, Tramp, Tramp, the Boys Are Marching":

V. P. Nichol is a leader,
Working for the I.B.M.
Years ago he started low
Up the ladder he did go
What an inspiration he is to our men!

A lot of outsiders thought our singing custom was odd, but the man in charge of our class didn't make a big deal out of it. He said, "We have these company songs. We think they build morale. Here is the way they go. Mr. O'Flaherty here at the piano will sing it through for you first and then you'll all sing it."

"The teachers were veteran company men, all dressed, as we were, in regulation IBM clothes—dark business suits and white shirts with stiff collars. Dad believed that if you wanted to sell to a businessman, you had to look like one. There was a big picture of Dad looking watchful on the wall behind the lectern. The rest of the classroom was decorated with his slogans, and, as in every office of IBM, there was a "THINK" sign prominently displayed. Magazine cartoonists used to make fun of these signs, and IBM's critics thought they were ridiculous: how could anybody really *think* in a company that was such a one-man show? But to everybody inside, the message was crystal clear: you would sell more machines, and advance faster, if you used your head.

"I used to marvel at how willingly new employees embraced the company spirit. As far as I could tell, nobody made fun of the slogans and songs. Times were different then, and I suppose being earnest didn't seem as corny in 1937 as it does today. And, of course, jobs were awfully hard to come by in the 1930s, so people would put up with a lot. As for me, I was pretty used to the IBM culture because I'd grown up at the source. It only bothered me when Dad let things get out of hand—as in 1936, when he commissioned an IBM *symphony."*

"They gave us twelve weeks to learn everything about the products. We didn't have to worry about scales or meat slicers, because Dad had sold off that division while I was at Brown. In its place he had bought a small company that was trying, without much success, to pioneer the electric typewriter. We studied those and the whole line of time clocks. But the bulk of our course work was on punch-card machines, which were in great demand and already accounted for more than 85 per cent of the revenue of the company."

"At first I was thrilled to get my hands on punch-card machines. I'd grown up around those things, and the basic concept fired my imagination just as it did Dad's. In the history of industrialisation, punch-card machines belong right up there with the Jacquard loom, the cotton gin, and the locomotive. Before punch-cards, accounting and record-keeping were clumsy operations that had to be done manually by clerks. Punch-card systems took away a lot of the drudgery—such as copying ledger entries and writing bills—and they did the work cheaply, reliably, and rapidly. This obviously was the wave of the future, and IBM was starting to attract high-calibre people because the machines were exciting to work with.

"My father always said that those punch-cards were what attracted him to IBM when Charles Flint approached him with the job. He had seen his first punch-card installation while he was still selling cash registers in 1904. A friend of his was using Hollerith machines at Eastman Kodak to keep track of the company's salesmen. The way this worked was pretty simple. Each time a sale was made, all the information about it would get punched onto a single card. Those cards would be sorted and tabulated once a month to yield all sorts of information: what each man had sold, which products were selling best in which regions, and so on. Dad used to make a wonderful sales talk about the punch-card concept. He'd hold one up and say, "You can put a hole in this card representing one dollar—a dollar of sales, perhaps, or a dollar you owe someone. From that point on, you have a permanent record. It can never be erased, and you never have to enter it again. It can be added, subtracted, and multiplied. It can be filed, accumulated, and printed,-all automatically." Dad believed that here was the world's answer to problems of accounting. All he had to do was keep developing this thing and IBM would revolutionise business. Whenever someone would use the term "punch-cards" he would say, "These are *IBM* cards!"

Punch-card machines had become pretty sophisticated by the time I got to Endicott. They could sort 400 cards a minute, print out paychecks and address labels, and duplicate, at very high speed, all of the accounting functions that companies were still doing by hand. I liked the idea that one set of cards enabled a customer to use the same data ten or twelve different ways, and I was pretty sure I'd be able to sell that. However, I quickly found out there was more to IBM school than appreciating what a punch-card was. Everybody had to learn how to program the machines to do specific tasks. This involved arranging wires on a "plugboard," which looked something like an old-fashioned telephone switchboard. We each had a plugboard to work with, and it soon became obvious that I was much better at understanding the potential of the machines than at actually plugging them up. After only two weeks I had to be assigned a tutor so I wouldn't fail. I spent many nights with that guy in the deserted schoolhouse, trying to learn to hook up those little wires.

Before long IBM school felt even worse to me than Carteret or Hun or Brown. Not only was my performance poor, as usual, but I couldn't escape being seen as T. J.'s son. Everyone in the school was trying to guess what Dad wanted done with me— without any regard for what I wanted myself. The head of the school, Garland Briggs, had been headmaster of the Hun School when I was there. Dad had picked him, in his simplistic way, because he needed an educator and Briggs was one he knew. I always thought Briggs was way out of his depth in that job. He had the big idea that it would please Dad if I were elected class President. So he put the other students up to it, even though they all knew I needed tutoring to get by. Unfortunately for me, I lacked the force of character to say, "I won't have this."

Endicott seemed more and more bleak. The place didn't offer much in the way of fun, and even if it had, I felt obliged to behave soberly and responsibly. Usually I ate with my classmates at the hotel; if we went out it cost money, and most of them were poor. Besides, there was no place to go. Endicott's restaurants were working class Italian places, and the food they served always gave me heartburn. Once in a while I'd talk some of the Scandinavians in the class into going skiing for a weekend, but the local slopes weren't very good. Soon I'd be back in my room at the Frederick trying to focus on some big black textbook with a title like *Machine Methods of Accounting*.

"I complained constantly to my college friends outside the IBM school, and Nick Lunken, one of my fraternity brothers, decided I was a sitting duck for a practical joke. He called up one day and said he wanted to fly to Endicott to see me. I was delighted. He said, "If you have any friends in class who might like to have a ride in my airplane, bring them along." So I got the Vice-President of the class and the treasurer, both of whom were trying hard to make their way in IBM. Nick was a little late, and we waited at the Endicott airport, which is very small. Finally, a red plane landed and I could see Nick in the cabin with a huge grin on his face. The door opened and out came a pair of silk legs—really good legs. They looked to me like they were about four yards long. Then the rest of the woman came out, and she was very hot-looking. To this day I don't know how Nick set it up. The woman hopped down and made a beeline for the side of the field, where a kid was standing with a horse. The door of the plane opened again and a racetrack tout came out, a guy in a long blue double-breasted chesterfield coat and black derby. He had a bottle of Scotch in his hand, and my two classmates began backing away from the scene. The woman got on the horse and started galloping around with her skirts up to her hips. Finally Nick stepped out of the plane.

I said, "For God's sake, Nick, what is this?"

"I knew you'd want to meet Grandmother Verne," he said. "She'll get off that horse in a minute, but she's very fond of horses. And this fellow's here in case you want to lay a bet."

I didn't know anything about horse racing. But by then the other two officers of my class were disappearing around the airport building. They didn't want to be connected with whatever terrible thing was going on. I bought Nick and his friends lunch at a hot-dog stand, and it seemed like hours before I could get rid of them. Finally I stood watching the plane disappear, and went resignedly back to my school books.

"About once a month, Dad would show up. The local managers would get tense, because Dad was great at spotting something wrong that no one else had thought of and blowing up about it. No matter what aspect of the business he examined, he insisted on having a hand in the details and was always bristling with ideas and questions, forcing people to be on their toes. Often he gave orders without warning and it could happen at any hour, which meant that managers didn't dare leave their offices or their houses when he was in town. Dad's unpredictability would sometimes produce odd behaviour in people. Garland Briggs, for example, tied himself in knots over whether to leave me at my studies or order me down to the train station to greet my father. Generally I took it upon myself to be there, standing dutifully on that cold platform as the train pulled in, shooting steam.

Dad's favourite spot in Endicott was the IBM Homestead. This was a square old lovely Italian-style house with dark green tiles that originally belonged to the town's founder. Dad had added a long wing with 40 room-and-bath cubicles for guests, and that was where customers would come for one-week courses on how to use punch-card machines. The master suite was always reserved for Dad. From his window he could look out and see it all—the IBM golf courses, the shooting ranges, the country club, and the factory buildings down below. He would inspect the factory during the day—walking through the plant, putting his foot up on the stool of a guy at a drill press, and getting into a conversation that would sometimes last half an hour. Then he'd come out and bark orders to his secretaries based on what he'd heard. Dad was always alert to what the factory man needed. In 1934, after one of these tours, Dad overruled his factory managers and abolished piece-work, saying it distracted people from producing high-quality goods.

At night Dad would go into the Homestead dining room, sit down next to some customer—they all wore badges that said who they were—and start a conversation. When dinner ended more people would draw up to the table and he might have 15 or 20 to talk to. It was easy to see he was a great salesman. His words would come out in a dignified way, he'd make a few simple gestures, and whether they agreed with him or not, people would listen. After a while he'd say, "Gentlemen, let's go into the living room and continue this conversation." He'd talk until one or two in the morning. It was all right for him, but terrible for me if I was there. I was usually bored but I always had to stay to the end because he would feel hurt if I walked out.

There was no better way to learn about IBM than to be present when Dad visited a class. Some of the things he said didn't mean much; he sermonised a lot about self-improvement, as in his letters to me at Brown. But he also told stories to illustrate his management principles. The most important story involved how he learned to sell cash registers. Dad got hired as a salesman for the Cash in Buffalo, New York, in 1896. During his first couple of weeks he failed to close a single sale. Finally he reported this to the branch manager, a tough old-timer named Jack Range, who blew up. He lit into Dad so hard that Dad used to say he was just waiting for the tirade to die down so he could quit. But when Range decided he had pushed my father as far as he could, he suddenly turned friendly. He reassured Dad and offered to help him sell some cash registers. He told Dad, "I'll go out with you, and if we fall down, we'll fall down together." They loaded a big, fancy machine onto the wagon and sold it that same day. Range showed my father how to hit the right notes in talking to businessmen and how to improvise on the canned sales pitch that Patterson required all his salesmen to use. Range let my father watch him close several more sales, until finally Dad caught on.

My father carried that lesson in his bones. He wanted his managers to be on sales calls with a guy three or four times before labeling the man a failure. And he believed that each employee was *entitled* to help from those above. He would say "A manager is an assistant to his men." That personal relationship between the individual and the supervisor became the IBM equivalent of the social contract.

I never disagreed with those lessons Dad taught, but I'd heard them all a hundred times before. Generally I tried to keep my distance during his visits. Although he never said anything about it, I was sure he was unhappy that I wasn't earning top grades. All the same I persevered, and finally school was done. As a sort of graduation, the whole class went to Manhattan to attend the Hundred Percent Club. This was IBM's annual sales convention, one of the morale-building techniques Dad had learned from Patterson. Hundreds of IBM men who had made their quotas were brought to New York, at company expense, for a huge banquet at the Waldorf. There were songs and awards and testimonials as each salesman stood at the podium and said a few words. It went on for hours. At the end I had to give a little speech. On behalf of the new graduates I gave my father a book of yachting prints, and he and I were presented to the audience as the newest members of the IBM Father-Son Club. This was something Dad had founded back in the 1920s, on the firm belief that nepotism was good for the business.

DIRECTING AT IBM — WARTIME TO PEACETIME EXPANSION

IBM's situation in those days was enough to make anybody want a drink. Like hundreds of other businesses, we had to switch as fast as possible from wartime to peacetime production. Dad had no intention of shrinking IBM back down to its prewar size—that would have meant firing his new employees, selling the new factories he was so proud of, and closing the door on some of the returning veterans to whom he felt a deep obligation. Yet, two-thirds of our factory space was devoted to making war material, and that market disappeared the day America won. So how were we supposed to keep all the employees busy and the factories full? Somehow IBM was going to have to sell *three times* as many business machines as before the war.

Dad was surely one of the most positive-thinking and optimistic businessmen who ever lived, but even he worried about this one. There is a record of a meeting in 1944, where he was already leaning on his engineers to develop new products for peacetime. "Supposing the war in Europe ends in three months," he said. "What can we go out and take orders for that we are not taking orders for now?" The engineers called off the names of machines being developed, but Dad said none of them opened up new fields. "What I have got to look for is new-business." he said. "Otherwise, there is no use in talking about keeping all those people employed full time, gentlemen. It is easy to say but hard to do, and I lost a lot of sleep last night just thinking about how we are going to do it." Dad told the engineers that from then on they would have to work a lot faster. Before the war it wasn't unusual for new IBM products to take five years from conception to market. But Dad pointed out that with machine guns, something totally new to IBM, the company had gone from a standing start to full production in a matter of months. "If we can do it on the gun," he said, "we can do it on this apparatus that we know something about." He wasn't just being arbitrary—somehow he sensed correctly that, because of the War, the pace of technological change in American life had permanently accelerated.

One of the things keeping Dad awake at night must have been the memory of the year 1921, when the U.S. economy contracted after World War I and CTR almost went bankrupt. I'm sure he also had unhappy visions of the hundreds and hundreds of accounting machines on rental to the U.S. armed forces. Most of this equipment would be turned back to IBM. Defence contractors who had built up for the war and now had to cut back couldn't be counted on to keep all their machines either. So unless we could find armies of new customers, our warehouses were going to fill up with used machines earning no money, and our factories would have nothing to do.

In the face of the possible calamity, Dad's impulse was always to hire more salesmen. That's just what he proposed around the time I came back from the war. He was determined that IBM should have an office in every state capital, and everybody from Kirk on down was scrambling to expand the sales network as rapidly as possible. In the midst of this we got hit unexpectedly with an avalanche of orders for our products. The post-war recession never materialised. Instead, the U.S. economy boomed because of a huge pent-up demand for consumer goods that nobody had been able to buy during the war—cars, houses, appliances, and clothing. This in turn boosted supporting industries like banking, insurance, and retailing—our big customers. All of them suddenly had rapidly growing record-keeping and accounting needs. We quickly found ourselves in a race to keep up with demand. By the time I joined, Kirk was working 16-hour days.

The first business trip I took with Kirk could well have changed the course of the computer-industry history, if either of us had understood what was in front of our noses. It was a gray day in March, and we went to visit the eniac at the University of Pennsylvania. This was one of the first computers, a giant, primitive number-cruncher for solving scientific problems. It had just gone into operation, making a big name for its inventors, Presper Eckert and John Mauchly. They broke new ground by using electronic circuits instead of electromechanical relays like the ones in our tabulating machines. Dad was very big on supporting projects like ENIAC, more for prestige and philanthropic motives than commercial ones.

During the war IBM and Harvard University had built a gigantic non-electronic computer called the MARK I. It consisted pretty much of two tons of IBM tabulating machines synchronised on a single axle, like looms in a textile mill. The MARK I got a lot of attention as "Harvard's robot super-brain," and was used successfully on top-secret war problems.

Dad heard about Eckert and Mauchly late in the war, when the Navy asked IBM to supply punch-card equipment to assist in getting data in and out of the ENIAC. That gave Kirk and me an entree. But going to see ENIAC was really Kirk's idea. He was curious because there was so much publicity about eniac's ability to make lightning-fast calculations. Another reason he wanted to have a look was that Eckert and Mauchly were talking about filing a patent, causing our lawyers to worry that IBM would have to pay big royalties if the idea of electronic computing ever went anywhere.

"I remember the ENIAC vividly. It was made up of what seemed like acres of vacuum tubes in metal racks. The air was very hot, and I asked Eckert, a trim, urbane man, why that was. He explained, "Because we are sharing this room with eighteen 18,000 radio tubes." They hadn't air-conditioned it. I asked what the machine was doing and Eckert said, "Computing ballistic trajectories." To show us what he meant, he sat down with a pencil and paper and drew the curve an artillery shell follows through the air. He explained that to make maximum use of a gun, you had to be able to calculate where its shell would be at every fraction of a second of its flight. This required a tremendous amount of computation, and ENIAC was doing it in a very short time—less time, in fact, than it would take an actual shell to reach its target. That impressed me. Eckert went on to tell me that computers were the wave of the future. He didn't quite call our punch-card machines dinosaurs, but he said he and Mauchly were going to take the ENIAC patents and go into business. As he talked I got the impression that they thought they were going to push IBM aside pretty quickly. I said, "It's a great idea you have, but you're going to run out of money. Building these things for customers is going to be very expensive."

"The truth was that I reacted to ENIAC the way some people probably reacted to the Wright brothers' airplane: it didn't move me at all. I can't imagine why I didn't think, "Good God, that's the future of the IBM company." But frankly I couldn't see this gigantic, costly, unreliable device as a piece of business equipment. Kirk felt the same way. On the train from Philadelphia back to New York, he said, "Well, that's awfully unwieldy. We could never use anything like that." We both agreed that, even though electronics innovations like radar were attracting a lot of popular attention, this ENIAC was an interesting experiment way off on the sidelines that couldn't possibly affect us. I never stopped to think what would happen if the speed of electronic circuits could be harnessed for commercial use.

Fortunately, this myopia was only temporary. A few weeks later my father and I were wandering around IBM headquarters. Dad always liked to nose around the offices when he had spare time; that afternoon I happened to be along. In a part of the building I'd never seen before we came upon a door labeled "Patent Development." Inside was one of Dad's engineers who had a high-speed punch-card machine hooked up to a box with black metal covers. It looked like a suitcase, only it was about four feet high. I said, "What is this doing?" And the engineer told me, "Multiplying with radio tubes." The machine was tabulating a payroll, a common application for punch cards—wages times number of hours worked, less Social Security deductions, retirement, medical deductions, and so forth, and coming out to net pay for each worker. Then the engineer told me how fast the machine was working. It did its calculation in one tenth of the time it took the punch-card machine to punch out the answer and go on to the next card. The box spent nine tenths of its time waiting, because the electronics were so fast and the mechanics so slow. That impressed me as though somebody had hit me on the head with a hammer, because the multiplier looked like a relatively simple device. I left that room and said, "It's fantastic, what that thing's doing. It's multiplying and coming out with totals, and doing it all with tubes. Dad, we should put this thing on the market! Even if we only sell eight or ten, well be able to advertise the fact that we have the world's first commercial electronic calculator."

"That is how IBM got into electronics. In September, we announced the machine with a full-page ad in the *New York Times.* We called it the IBM 603 Electronic Multiplier. Technically speaking it wasn't a computer—it had no stored programme and processed numbers only as they were fed in from punch-cards. In fact, the 603 was mainly a gimmick—it could calculate at electronic speeds, but that was not very useful because the punch cards couldn't keep up. But in spite of this, the thing caught on. We were hoping to rent out a handful, enough to justify the expense of the ad, but big customers were anxious to get their feet wet with electronics and we sold a hundred of them. Within a year we got past the gimmick stage. We figured out how to make electronic circuits not only multiply but *divide* —a job that was almost prohibitively expensive to do mechanically. At that point electronic calculators became truly useful, and our next machine, the IBM 604, sold by the thousands."

DIRECTING AT MATSUSHITA

Maintain a rigorous attitude toward work

"Five years after the subsidiary had been established, I am ashamed to admit that the new company was not succeeding". "The first oil crisis had just occurred. The oil-producing countries had united and increased the price of oil. The civilisation built on cheap oil was shaken to its core, and there were rumours that Japan's oil supplies might be cut-off. Since a large part of our sales was of equipment that ran on oil and propane gas, we were more than a little worried. The company had been at a high break-even point and reduced sales would mean a severe deficit."

At this time, I was managing director. One day, Konosuke Matsushita dropped in for a visit. It had been a long time since he'd been there and he wanted to talk to us. It wasn't the best time for him to come, but there was nothing I could do about it.

First he visited the factory and was very pleased, looking with amazement at the huge boilers being manufactured. It was later, when we sat down to talk, that the roof caved in. I will never forget that conversation with Matsushita.

"The factory and the merchandise looks great," he said. "How are operations?"

Nervously, I answered, "Not very good. Sales have dropped because of the oil crisis."

"Not very good? What do you mean?"

"We're running at a bit of a loss," I fumbled.

"By how much?"

"Nine billion."

"What?! I could understand if sales were zero and the deficit was in personnel costs, but you've got sales of ¥ 100 billion and are ¥9 billion in the red. You mean to tell me we've got a company like this in the Matsushita group? Responsibility for running a mess like this lies with you and the executives under you. The head office must also take responsibility for letting this go. It's all because the head office lent you that ¥ 20 billion. Tomorrow I'm going to talk to them about getting it back. That's all, Ogawa. Whip this thing back into shape!"

For a moment I was speechless, but then I ran after him. "Mr. Matsushita, that would mean disaster for us! It's five days to payday. At the end of the month we have to pay for materials and parts. If you take that ¥ 20 billion back now, we won't be able to pay for them."

"That's right," he remarked. "You won't be able to pay the wages and the subcontractors' fees. You have to pay the cafeteria cooks, too. But I'm not going to lend you any money if you and your colleagues are going to run an operation like this. I'm pulling your loan tomorrow."

"But then we won't be able to do anything. We'll go bankrupt."

"What are you talking about? You've got 4,000 superb employees working here. Talk it over with them, get their ideas, and come up with a reconstruction plan that will work. I know you have confidence in this company, but confidence isn't enough. You have to come up with a plan that a banker would approve of, one that would make him think, 'This looks like a good operation. If we lend it money, we're sure to get it back.' If you can get a plan like that together, I'll write a letter of recommendation to Sumitomo Bank for you. With that letter, they're sure to give you a ¥20 billion loan using the land, buildings, and equipment here as collateral. Now, get to work."

"We had gone to the head office for that ¥ 20 billion loan to cover operating expenses because business had been sluggish, our internal reserves low, and our dependence on seasonal products high. The rules of the division system required that we pay interest on the loan comparable to what we would pay to a bank. We often complained about the indifference of a head office that would extort interest and even make a profit off a subsidiary struggling under a heavy financial burden. Five years before, Matsushita had impressed me as a compassionate person when he apologised to the chef for not eating all his food, but now he appeared more like a ruthless demon.

"I didn't have time to get absorbed in my emotions, however. Matsushita called all the managers and executives together and reprimanded us sharply: "You're working under the Matsushita name, but this is no Matsushita company. If you can't rebuild this company, it will collapse and everyone will have to be laid off. If that happens, you managers have to find jobs for each one of your employees and then figure out what to do about yourselves." He went on with the usual advice we'd heard a thousand times. "If each of the sections of each department can show just a little profit in its accounting, the company as a whole will get back on its feet. Get down to the section level and make sure you bring together the wisdom of each and every employee. Tell the sales departments in every division to research products that will bring a 50 per cent increase in sales in the next three years. Have R&D devote themselves to achieving that goal. If the goods don't sell, have everyone get out and sell them. Take the 10 per cent excess staff and equipment and find a project for them to work on. Take 1 per cent of sales and invest it in new activity. Uncover the buried losses and turn them into a 2 per cent profit. We can turn this company around and make it into a winner. The wisdom and knowledge to do this can be found in the workplace."

There was nothing unusual in what he told us, but putting it into practice was not going to be easy. The ideas everyone came up with, however, far exceeded my expectations. That year we still ran a big deficit, but when I retired five years later the company was in good shape, one that could call itself a Matsushita subsidiary.

It wasn't me that got that company back on track. It was the result of all the knowledge and ideas of the employees pooled together. I realised that the source of it all lay in the rigor of Konosuke Matsushita's attitude toward work. It was he who shattered our belief that the source of the trouble was outside the company, and who drove us to do better.

It is important that managers, from the moment they embark on their leadership careers, cultivate both a compassion for others and an attitude of discipline in the workplace. If you are strict with your people and lax in your own attitude toward work, the results will be disastrous.

DIRECTING AT BRIDGEPORT MACHINES

Personal Qualifications

It will not be argued, I think, that the personal traits of a given individual are overwhelmingly important in the leadership equation.

Recently, a committee of the Association of Consulting Management Engineers attempted an evaluation of this factor. A brief review of their findings may be helpful to us in providing a systematic approach to the analysis of the personal qualifications of a leader.

The study concluded that there are only three fundamental capacities which provide the basis for all human development and behaviour:

1. The capacity to learn
2. The capacity for feeling
3. The capacity to produce energy

Capacity to Learn. The capacity to learn is based on the functional characteristics of the brain and therefore appears to be inherent; an individual is born with it. Although what he does with it and the extent to which it is developed is a matter of training and education, it has been fairly well-determined that no amount of effort on his or anyone else's part can increase this capacity beyond its inherent limits. The best that he can hope to do is to utilise to the fullest extent that capacity with which he was endowed at birth.

Exceptional mental ability, of course, is a tremendous asset in any form of endeavour. Sometimes, however, its possession leads an individual into technical research activities, which, in turn, tend to develop a degree of specialisation. Such specialisation, more often than not, militates against the development of broad experience and sound judgment in a variety of areas considered to be necessary for anyone in a position of leadership.

For this very reason, the brilliant scholar seldom develops into a position of leadership. He is more likely to achieve success through his own personal contribution, rather than by directing the efforts of others. Kettering, the thinker and scholar, made a contribution to General Motors. But so did Charles E. Wilson, the brilliant manager.

Capacity for Feeling. The next personal qualification for leadership—a capacity for feeling—is an interesting and complex one.

Every newborn animal, including the human animal, starts life interested only in its own comfort. During early infancy, his wants are simply warmth and food. He expects the adults in his environment to supply this warmth and food, and he develops feelings of resentment if these basic needs are neglected.

But modern psychology has shown that as the human animal grows and develops, he learns that he must *give* in order to receive. If an inherent capacity for feeling is present, he learns that almost equal pleasure can be derived from giving and from the response in others that this produces. The degree to which this awakening interest in people is developed is contingent on environment and early parental training.

Since a leader must accomplish his objectives through others, it is obviously important that this capacity for feeling be well developed.

But, as in the capacity to learn, there are two sides to this particular coin. It is quite possible to have the capacity for feeling overdeveloped in positions of leadership.

Consideration for others' interests, to the extent of self-abnegation, produces an unrealistic approach to the problems of life. This, in turn, often leads to ineffectiveness in the world of business. Many otherwise capable men have been unable to attain any real position of leadership, simply because of an inability to fire delinquent subordinates, or even to censure them.

Capacity to Produce Energy. The third factor listed is the capacity to produce energy. Whatever degree of such capacity any individual possesses stems almost solely from the characteristics of his parents. As in the case of capacity to learn, it is inherent, and he can't do anything to increase it. Naturally, this capacity will vary widely between individuals. We all know people who seem to have been born lazy and others who have tremendous energy. There are, of course, an infinite number of degrees between the two extremes.

In the mature person, the two inherent capacities of intellect and energy are used to support the human relations, aims, and ideals which have been developed through the capacity for feeling. Possession of an ample supply of each of these capacities is essential for any individual in a high position of leadership.

Personal Attributes. Personal attributes are derived from the three fundamental capacities. The good leader in business, knowing the *capacities* of his subordinates, can help them to develop these good attributes.

What are the attributes of a leader in business? One list, recently compiled, is as follows:

1. Understanding of people
2. Integrity
3. Courage
4. Objectivity
5. Ambition
6. Problem-solving
7. Judgment
8. Ability to communicate
9. Emotional maturity

Some might wish to add to this list such qualities as ability to promote innovation and assumption of responsibility, but I believe the list above sums up things pretty well.

Concepts of Managing Others

How can we classify the various concepts of leadership? One classification that appears to be both logical and comprehensive is the following:

1. Autocratic
2. Democratic
3. Integrated

The Autocratic Approach : With few exceptions, our old concepts of autocratic management have long since disappeared from the business scene. To many of us, the term "autocratic" creates a picture of the nineteenth-century businessman operating his business entirely by himself in a completely dictatorial and arbitrary way. He does this by giving orders and instructions to subordinates, without consulting anyone else. Of course, such a description is an exaggeration, even of the most headstrong of businessmen of the last century. (Actually, it is quite interesting to read some of the management literature of that period and to realize how far advanced some of the pioneers in the field of scientific management were in their thinking 75 years ago).

However, for our purposes now, the word autocratic is used to define that type of leadership which results from decisions made primarily by one individual, with little or no consultation with other members of the organisation. When we define autocratic in these terms, it is apparent that this type of leadership is still quite in evidence and, under certain conditions, a most effective concept. Yet the drawbacks, as we all know, are obvious.

The Democratic Concept : The "democratic" concept of leadership, as it applies to business and industry, is perhaps best defined as a *committee* type of leadership. The leadership in this case is exercised by the committee chairman. Unlike the autocrat, the committee chairman is responsible for obtaining an objective by utilising the talents, abilities, and experience of the committee members. It is the duty of the Chairman to organise an agenda and to guide the discussion of the committee member.

Controlling and Evaluating

The chapter is Discussed under the following headings :
• Meaning and Definition of Controlling • Steps in the Control process • Key Result Areas (KRAs) • Financial Controls • Budgetary Controls • How Global Companies use Controlling • Profit as a Yardstick Process • Moriamasa OGAWA Evaluates and turns around Hokkaido Operations • How Konosuke Matsushita helps Wholesalers and Agents to overcome their Losses • Controlling Stability at Deere & Co.

MEANING AND DEFINITION OF CONTROL

Management control is the process of ensuring that actual activities conform to planned activities. Control is the most pervasive than planning. Control assists to monitor the effectiveness of their planning, organising and other leading activities. The essential part of the control process is evaluating and taking corrective actions as needed.

Robert J. Mockler's definition of control points out the essential elements of the control process:

Management control is a systematic effort to set performance standards with planning objectives, to design information feedback systems, to compare actual performance with those pre-determined standards to determine whether there are any durations and to measure their significance and to take any action required to assure that all corporate resources are being used in the most effective and efficient way possible in achieving corporate objectives.

Mockler's definition divides control into four steps illustrated in Chart 1.

Chart 1. Basic steps in the Control Process

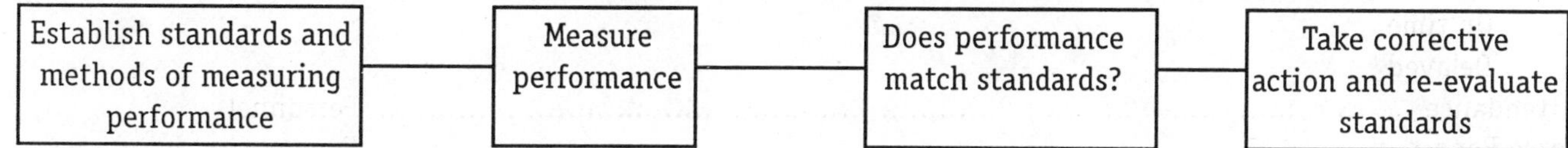

STEPS IN THE CONTROL PROCESS

1. Establish Standards and Methods of Measuring Performance:

Ideally, the goals and objectives established during the planning process will already be stated in clear, measurable terms that include specific deadlines. In an industrial enterprise, standards and measurements could include sales and production targets, work attendance goals, waste produced and recycled, and safety records.

In Service industries, standards and measurements might include the amount of customer waiting time, in line in a bank, the amount of time they have to wait before the telephone is answered, or the number of clients attracted by a revamped advertising campaign.

2. Measure the Performance:

Like all aspects of control, measurement is an ongoing repetitive process. Daily production and sales are measured to see that they are reaching their targets or not, if the performance matches the standards, managers may assure that "everything is under control" and they don't have to intervene actively in the operations.

3. Take Corrective Action:

This step is necessary if the performance falls short of standards and analysis indicates action is required. If the production has not reached the target, because of the shortage of raw materials, the manager takes the corrective action to procure raw materials quickly, so that production can reach targets. The emphasis is to take immediate action to remedy the situation that is coming in the way of meeting targets.

One global company uses the list of major control reports shown in Table 9.1.

Table 9.1 : List of Major Control Reports

Report	Responsibility
Volume	
Invoices issued	Finance and Control
Orders booked	Sales
Total	
Product headings	
Cancellations	
Figured profit	
Moving annual total of	Finance and Control
Total business and new business	
Profit margins	
Report of promising jobs	Sales
Lost business report	Sales
Per cent of new orders to estimates	Sales
Backlog and production schedule	Production
Break-even analysis	Finance and Control
Production costs	
Weekly summary of orders closed	Finance and Control
Cost cards for each job	
Operating performance	
Monthly budget report	Finance and Control
Daily report of jobs shipped	Production
On time	
Delayed	
Attendance	Personnel
Force Report	Personnel
Production machine hours	Finance and Control
Ratios of hours spent on production	
Machines to	
Set up hours	
Tool-repair hours	
Idle time	
Maintenance time	
Finance	
Monthly balance sheet	Finance and Control
Balance sheet comparisons	Finance and Control
Fund flow	Finance and Control
Cash forecasts	Finance and Control
Other elements of company strength	
Merit reviews	Personnel
Grievance committee minutes	Personnel
Safety reports	Personnel
Reports on research and development projects	As assigned

In one of my client groups, the CEOs were required to go to the textile mills in the morning and see that the day's production is going on smoothly to achieve the targets. If there is any shortage of raw materials like cotton, he will initiate action to overcome the problem. The CEO returns to the head office and reports to the President of the group in the afternoon that everything is under control and if the CEO needs money to buy more cotton, he will get the approval of the President or if President's intervention is required in any other matter, he will discuss with the President.

Tea at KPM

The President would meet all the CEOs at 4 pm for tea and he would know what the Group has made in terms of profits (or loss) and he would be brought to speed about what is going on in the management of the Group, which was one of the most successful business groups in India.

Key Result Areas (KRAs)

KRAs are those aspects of the organisation that must function effectively for the organisation to succeed. Exhibit 1 shows the key performance areas for production, marketing, human resources, finance and accounting.

EXHIBIT 1

Standards used in Functional Areas to evaluate Performance

Production	Marketing	HR	Financial Accounting
Quality	Sales Volume	Human Relations	Capital Expenditures
Quality	Sales Expense	Labour Turnover	Inventories
Cost	Advertising Expenditures	Absenteeism	Flow of Capital
Individual Performance	Individual Sales Person's Performance		Liquidity

Source : Hal B. Pickle & Royech, Abramhamson, *Small Business Management* (New York, Wiley, 1990, Chpt. 8.)

Managers must pay a great deal of attention which help define the more detailed control systems and standards in order to achieve organisational objectives.

Financial Controls

Managers use a series of control methods and systems to deal with the differing problems and elements of their organisations. However, financial controls have a special prominence, since money is easy to measure and tally. First, we shall discuss financial statements which provide an insight into the organisation's performance and then we will look at the budgetary controls.

Financial Statements

Financial Statements track the monetary value of goods and services produced and sold. They monitor three major financial conditions of an organisation :

1. *Liquidity:* The ability to convert assets into cash in order to meet current financial requirements.
2. *General Financial Condition:* The long-term balance between debt and equity (assets left after liabilities are deducted)
3. *Profitability:* The ability to earn profits steadily over extended period of time.

Financial statements are widely used by managers, shareholders, banks, investment analysts etc., to evaluate the organisation's performance and health. Managers could compare the organisations current financial statement to past statements and to those of competitors as one measure of how well the organisation is doing over time. They might be able to see trends that require corrective action. Bankers on the other hand, will use the statements to decide whether to invest or not.

The most common financial statements, used by large or small organisations alike are income statements, balance and cash flow statements.

Balance Sheet
RMN METALS
CONSOLIDATED BALANCE SHEET
as of December 31, 2008

Assets	$	$
Current assets	950,000	
Cash		50,000
Marketable securities		3,50,000
Accounts receivables		2,50,000
Inventories		3,00,000
Fixed assets	1,250,000	
Land		50,000
Plant and equipment		1,500,000
Less accumulated depreciation		3,00,000
Liabilities and Net Worth		
Other assets	70,000	
Patents and goodwill		
Total assets	2,270,000	
Current liabilities	600,000	
Accounts payable		4,75,000
Accrued expenses		1,25,000
Long-term liabilities		$600,000
Total liabilities	1,200,000	
NET WORTH	1,070,000	
Commonstock par		850,000
Accumulated retained earnings		220,000
Total liabilities and net worth	2,270,000	

The balance sheet is a picture of what the company owns and what the company owes as on Dec. 31, 2008 and its net worth. What the company owns are assets which range from money in the bank to the goodwill value in the market place. The left side balance sheet list these assets in descending order of liquidity. A distinction is made between current assets and fixed assets. Current assets cover items such as cash, accounts receivable, marketable securities, and inventories — assets that could be turned into cash at a recently predictable value within short time. Fixed assets show the monetary value of the company's plant, equipment, property, patents and other items used on a continuing basis to produce its goods and services.

Liabilities are also made up of two groups: Current liabilities and long-term liabilities. Current liabilities are debts, such as accounts payable, short-term loans and unpaid taxes, that will have to be paid off during the current fiscal period. Long-term liabilities include mortgages, bonds, and other debts that are being paid off gradually.

The company's net worth is the residual value remaining after total liabilities have been subtracted from the total assets.

The widespread use of electronic spreadsheets has made the preparation of balance sheets much easier. In addition, computer packages have been developed specifically to process accounting transactions and prepare the resulting balance sheet and other financial statements.

Income Statement

While the balance sheet describes a company's financial condition at a given point of time, the Income Statement summarises the company's financial performance over a given interval of time. The Income Statement says then "here is how much money we have made over a given period", instead of " here is how much money we are worth now".

Income Statement such as Table 9.2, starts with a figure for gross receipts or sales and subtracts all the cost involved in realising those sales, such as the cost of goods sold, administrative expenses, taxes, interest and other operating expenses. What is left is the net income available for stockholder's dividends or reinvestment in the business.

Table 9.2. The Income Statement

RMN METALS

Statement of Income for the year ended Dec. 31, 2008.

Gross sales		$ 4,289,000
Less returns	$ 789,000	
Net sales		$ 3,500,000
Less cost of sales and operating Expenses		
Cost of goods sold	$ 2,775,000	
Depreciation	$ 1,00,000	
Selling administrative Expenses	$ 75,000	$ 2,950,000
Operating profit		$ 550,000
Other income		$ 15,000
Gross income		$ 5,65,000
Less Interest expense	$ 75,000	
Income before taxes		$ 4,90,000
Less taxes	$ 196,000	
Income after taxes		$ 2,94,000

Cash Flow : Sources and uses of funds :

In addition to the standard balance sheet and income statement, many companies report a statement of cash flow or a statement of sources and uses of funds. These statements show where cash or funds came from during the year (from operations, accounts receivable and sale of investments, etc) and where they are applied (for purchase of equipment, payment of dividends and for reducing accounts payable, etc.,). They show how cash or funds were used rather than how much profit or loss was incurred. In most businesses, cash flow is often more meaningful than income.

BUDGETARY CONTROLS

Budgets are formal quantitative statements of the resources allocated for planned activities over a stipulated periods of time. They are widely used means for planning and controlling activities at every level of the organisation. There are a number of reasons for their extensive usage.

First, budgets are stated in monetary terms, which are easily used as a common denominator for a wide vaniety of activities like hiring and training HR, purchasing equipment, manufacturing, advertising, etc., Second, the monetary aspect of budgets means that they can directly convey information on a key organisational resource - capital - on a key organisational goal - profit.

Third, budgets establish clear and unambiguous standards of performance for a set period, usually a year. At periodic intervals, actual performance will be directly compared with the budget. Deviations can be quickly detected and acted upon. In addition to being a major controlling device, budgets are the major means of co-ordinating activities of the organisation. The interaction between managers and subordinates that takes place during budget development process will help define and integrate the activities of organisation members.

We shall now describe the role of budgets in a control system and the budgeting process.

Responsibility Centre

Control systems can be devised to monitor organisational functions or projects. Controlling a function involves making sure that a specified activity (such as production and sales) is properly carried out. Controlling a project involves making sure that a specified end result is achieved (such as development of new product or completion of a plant) budgets can be used for both types of systems.

Any organisational unit or functional unit headed by a manager who is responsible for the activities of that unit is called Responsibility Centre. Typically responsibility is assigned to a revenue, expenses, profit or investment centre.

Revenue Centres

Are those organisational units in which outputs are measured in monetary terms but are not directly compared to input costs. A sales department is an example of such a unit. Budgets (in the form of sales quotas) are prepared for the revenue centre and figures are compared with sales orders or actual sales. In this way, a useful picture of the effectiveness of the individual sales people or of the centre itself can be determined.

Expense or Cost Centres

Inputs are measured by the control system in monetary terms, but outputs are not. Examples are maintenance, administration, service, research departments. Budgets will be devised only for the input portion of these centres, operation.

Profit Centres

Performance is measured by the numerical difference between revenues (outputs) and expenditure (inputs). Such a measure indicates how well the centre and manager is performing. A profit centre is created whenever an organisational unit is given the responsibility for earning a profit. In a divisionalised organisation, each division is completely responsible for its own product line and separate divisions are considered profit centres.

Investment Centres

The control system again measures the monetary value of inputs and outputs but it also assesses how these outputs compare with the assets employed in producing them, *e.g.*, new plant requires a capital of $ 20 million for building, equipment and working capital. In its first year, the plant has $ 2 million in labour and other expenses and $ 4 million in revenue. But we cannot say the plant has earned a profit of $ 2 million because, we have not covered the depreciation of the building and interest that could have been earned from alternative investment. By assessing these factors as well, the company obtains a much more accurate picture of profitability.

The Budgeting Process

The budgeting process usually begins when managers receive top management's economic forecasts and sales and profit objectives for the coming year, along with a timetable stating when budgets must be completed. The forecasts and objectives provided by top management represent guidelines within which other managers' budgets will be developed.

In a few organisations, the preference is for "top-down" budgeting. Budgets are imposed by top managers with little or no consultation with lower-level managers. Most companies, however, prefer the process of "bottom-up" budgeting. Budgets are prepared, at least initially, by those who must implement them. The budgets are then sent up for approval to higher-level managers.

Bottom-up budgeting has a number of advantages for many organisations. First, supervisors and lower-level department heads have a more intimate view of their needs than do managers at the top, and they can provide more realistic details to support their proposals. They are also less likely to overlook some vital ingredient or hidden flaw that might subsequently impede implementation. Managers are also more strongly motivated to accept and meet budgets they have had a hand in shaping. Finally, morale and satisfaction are usually higher when individuals participate actively in making decisions that affect them.

The process by which lower-level managers participate in developing budgets is similar to the multilevel planning process described in Chapter 10. Supervisors prepare their budget proposals using the guidelines drawn up by upper management. Department heads then review the lower-level budgets and resolve any inconsistencies before compiling them into department budgets. These budgets are then submitted to higher-level managers for approval. The process continues until all budgets are completed, assembled by the controller or budget director, and submitted to the budget committee for further review. Finally, the master budget is sent to the top management (the president, chief executive officer, or board of directors) for approval.

The Role of Budget Personnel. Although developing budgets is the responsibility of managers, they may receive information and technical assistance from the staff of a planning group or from a formal budget department or committee. These groups are likely to exist in large, divisionalised organisations in which the division budget plays a key role in planning, co-ordinating, and controlling activities.

The *budget department,* which generally reports to the corporate controller, provides budget information and assistance to organisational units, designs budget systems and forms, integrates the various departmental proposals into a master budget for the organisation as a whole, and reports on actual performance relative to the budget.

The *budget committee,* made up of senior executives from all functional areas, reviews the individual budgets, reconciles divergent views, alerts or approves the budget proposals, and then refers the integrated package to the board of directors. Later, when the plans have been put into practice, the committee reviews the control reports that monitor progress. In most cases, the budget committee must approve any revisions made during the budget period.

First, information supplied to top management regarding delegated activities is of substantial value only when it can be used *to evaluate the rate of attainment of previously set objectives.* A Chief Executive cannot be really effective unless he has the means of seeing that objectives are reached on schedule.

Second, and equally important, objectives and standards of measuring their achievement must be *understood and accepted throughout an organisation* if they are to serve their purpose of charting a course and facilitating the correction of variances from that course. Their importance, meaning, and use must be understood by the foremen who influence production costs. They must equally be understood by the salesman who makes the ultimate decisions on his calls for the day. To be accepted, objectives and standards of measurement must be reasonable. The Chief Executive cannot assume that a given standard means the same to his subordinates as it means to him. Success depends more on a common understanding of objectives and their necessity than on setting forth details in technical language.

Third, objectives must *reflect hidden as well as obvious potential.* In addition to a fair share of the present market, they should take into consideration expansion of given markets through increased absorption of present products; profitable development of new products; additional products that can be produced by existing facilities; practical plant expansion and sound acquisitions that can help reach specifically determined goals more quickly and economically.

Fourth, they must *provide for periodic review.* Evaluation and measurement cannot wait for the completion of a project. Periodic checks not only indicate lagging performance, but also future difficulties, and sometimes the need for alteration of plans or even adjustment of objectives.

And fifth, they must be *reduced to a common denominator to avoid the confusion* of trying to compare apples with bananas. It is only human for managers at various levels to think in terms applicable to their own operations. For instance, the plant manager, thinking only in terms of total shipments, may push shipments at the end of the month to the detriment of efficient operations. The tendency of salesmen to think in terms of making sales leads to endless questions about prices and credits. What is the common denominator?

HOW GLOBAL COMPANIES USE THE PROCESS OF CONTROLLING?

Profit as a Yardstick

The chief executive must perforce evaluate all performance in terms of profit. A company cannot exist, much less grow, without money; and profit is the only dependable yardstick for measuring growth, although the period for attaining desired profit objectives has certain flexibility.

Profit as a percentage of sales of present products, manufactured with present equipment, fails to take into consideration product obsolescence or the potential of modernized or expanded facilities. At Sun Chemical Corporation, our standards are set in terms of return on investment, which we are constantly seeking to improve. Instead of accepting standards set at lower management levels and translating them at the top into return on investment, we have sought to teach all levels of management to think in terms of the investment which has been entrusted to their stewardship.

As everybody knows, the percentage return on investment can be arrived at simply by dividing the total investment of a business into its net profit before taxes. However, such a short cut does not provide a provocative yardstick because it fails to take into consideration the interrelationship of investment, sales, and net profit before taxes, all of which must be evaluated simultaneously in setting realistic growth goals.

How Global Companies use the Process of Controlling

Accordingly, at Sun, we added the "turnover factor" (sales divided by investment) to arrive at this formula:

$$\frac{\text{Net profit}}{\text{Sales}} \times \frac{\text{Sales}}{\text{Investment}} = \text{return on investment}$$

The mathematical concepts are unchanged, but a new dimension of thinking is added.

For instance, at Sun, a division manager is evaluated and compensated in terms of what he does with the assets that are assigned to his operations. Let us suppose that a new manager of a sluggish division is assigned assets with a net worth of $ 10,000,000, which, at a turnover factor of 2, would yield $ 20,000,000 sales. However, he asks himself, what could be accomplished with 25 per cent more capital invested in local plants, branch offices, or any of several other expansion moves? His market research and cost studies indicate that he could boost his turnover factor to 2.5.

His breakdown looks like this:

Item	*With present investment*	*With additional capital*
Net worth of assigned assets	$ 10,000,000	$ 12,500,000
Total investment	$ 10,000,000	$ 12,500,000
Turnover factor	2	2.5
Sales	$ 20,000,000	$ 31,250,000
Anticipated profit as a percentage of sales	10%	10%
Net profit	$ 20,000,000	$ 3,125,000
Return on investment	20%	25%

This does not take into consideration the added factor that increased volume should produce a higher profit in relation to sales. Of course, added capital is no guarantee of increased return. The point is, without the added element of thinking about sales, profit on sales, and return on investment in one package, middle management seldom gets beyond the point of thinking solely in terms of return on present assets, which is a losing battle against obsolescence.

When a division manager knows what is expected of him—what return he must produce on the assets assigned for his operations and what sales and growth targets he is expected to reach within a given period—his mind is freed of much of the worry that follows such ambiguous instructions as "make as much money as you can."

And top management can concentrate on correction of variances. Top management, however, must also assume the responsibility for analysing and preparing for situations, such as approaching periods of either recession or opportunity, which operating management cannot see in the day to day task of running the business.

Need for Flexibility

This brings us to the sixth criterion of good standards. They must be *flexible* enough to be adjusted quickly to take into consideration both crises and unforeseen opportunities.

A certain degree of practical flexibility should be included among management goals. For instance, it is easy to get boxed in with facilities that operate very efficiently at a high rate of production but become an inflexible burden when market demand slackens; similarly, the efficiency of equipment should also be measured in relation to its adaptability to quick production of new products for full market advantage, as well as low-cost manufacturing of present lines.

When a new top management undertook the task of rebuilding and expanding Sun Chemical, it introduced a basic set of standards which could be applied to:

1. Short-term goals, or those which could be realised in one year
2. Intermediate goals, or those to be attained in from two to five years. Long-term standards came later.

Our primary standards reflected:

Return on investment

Pre-tax profit as a percentage of sales

The company had diverse product lines, most of them with a good growth potential but each of them with its own peculiar market problems. Its products included inks for the packaging industry, newspapers, periodicals, lithographing, and metal decorating, the combined market for which in recent years has kept steady pace with the gross national product; machinery for printing; organic pigments for inks, paints, textiles, cosmetics, floor coverings, plastics, and other such end products; textile chemicals for water repellency, spot and stain resistance, and wash-and-wear qualities; paper and fabric coatings for electrical insulations, closures, aircraft fabrics, and reinforcements; paints, enamels, lacquers, and varnishes for industrial and home use; custom finishes; maintenance coatings; concrete additives for curing, hardening, and damp-proofing; caulking and sealing compounds; and remedial restorations.

STARTING CORRECTIVE ACTION

As previously stated, spotting variations is a primary responsibility of line management. Similarly, corrective action is the line manager's responsibility, with staff guidance called for only when needed.

It is for this reason that top management at Sun Chemical is normally provided only with reports on sales and profits of its various groups. Detailed division reports on sales, profit before taxes, cost of goods, selling expenses, and the like, go only to the group management concerned, except when a critical group variance from standards requires top management examination of the causes. Similarly, branches and each lower management level report only to the control point above them.

This prevents over eager staff members from assuming a dominant role in both planning and operations. The underlying purpose of standards is to permit orderly delegation of responsibility for and measurement of performance.

In a complex business, many activities must proceed without waiting for top management decision or guidance. Measurement against established standards is concerned primarily with appraising current progress to see if line operations are operating effectively and reviewing completed projects as a means for evaluating performance and establishing bases for setting standards for future operations.

Failure to meet objectives beyond a reasonable period requires careful evaluation of the manager concerned. The first step is to make sure that the objectives are clearly understood. If variances continue, the manager should be appraised on the following:

1. Personal performance
   - (a) Knowledge of his field
   - (b) Up-to-date knowledge of his market
   - (c) Acceptance of responsibility
   - (d) Delegation of both responsibility and authority
   - (e) Attitude toward budgets, which represent goals to be achieved through correct use of money, rather than licenses for spending.
2. Relations with others
   - (a) Ability to judge others
   - (b) Promoting teamwork
   - (c) Ability to express ideas clearly
3. Character qualities
   - (a) Intelligence
   - (b) Integrity
   - (c) Drive

(d) Perseverance

(e) Ambition

(f) Cooperation

(g) Moral and civic responsibility, which is a key to basic attitudes.

It is highly important that goals be understood and accepted. This is much more important than keeping a tight rein at all times on the day-to-day activities aimed at achieving these goals. This will be accomplished more efficiently if:

1. Goals are properly identified with individual responsibility.
2. Objectives are agreed to by the person responsible for carrying them out
3. Control procedures require only a limited amount of executive time.

As long as operations progress according to plans, there is no need for staff inquiry or interference. It is only when pronounced or prolonged exceptions are manifest that top management attention is needed.

Once a policy is set and understood, corrective action should become automatic. It is incumbent upon top management in initiating a control programme to provide certain bench marks for corrective action. Broadly speaking, these might include the following actions, either singly or in indicated combinations.

1. *Adjustments to reduce costs and to increase share of market.* Ways of overcoming increased costs of material and labour must be sought constantly. Equal effort must be applied to reducing costs arising out of inefficient facilities and equipment. Repair and maintenance must be carefully weighed along with new capital outlays against operating goals. The industrial engineer may be brought in to provide expert advice. The good manager will attempt to make performance conform to forecasts rather than adjust forecasts to take into account changing conditions which might have been anticipated.

Sales effort must be devoted to reaching established goals despite changing market conditions in preference to cutting back objectives. Sometimes it is wiser to increase selling expenses to achieve volume objectives than to cut costs because sales goals have not been reached.

2. *Modification of objectives and plans where necessary.* Goals and plans for reaching them usually require some revision during the year. Revisions are dictated by the impact of external forces which could not be reasonably foreseen. Revision may be either up or down. If results are substantially above standard, the reasons should be thoroughly studied and used to establish new standards.

3. *Provision of positive motivation.* If performance is to conform to plans, some positive push is often needed. Motivation of subordinates should be carefully studied and kept in adequate balance. Provision of stronger incentives than are necessary not only is wasteful, but tends to lessen their effectiveness at a later time.

4. *Reviewing the direction given to subordinates.* Good communication remains a major problem in modern business. Direction must be given in frames of reference used by the listener. Quite frequently, a subordinate's interpretation of words differs from that of his superior. Hence, managers need to review frequently with subordinates what is wanted and how it is to be obtained.

5. *Periodic evaluation of the qualifications and training of subordinates.* It is the manager's primary responsibility to see that each employee reporting to him is trained and guided to do the best job he is capable of doing and that each employee is put into the job that he can do best.

MATSUSHITA HELPS WHOLESALERS AND AGENTS TO OVERCOME THEIR LOSSES

The household electrical appliance industry had also been drawn into the backwash of recession and the situation looked very grim. As market conditions went from bad to worse, an increasing number of Matsushita Electric sales and wholesale firms began to gointo the red.

"It had been about three years since I became chairman, sales, Matsushita and there had been no opportunity during that time to meet with our sales agents and wholesalers. Their losses were rapidly creating a situation that could only get worse, so I decided it was time to bring them together and try to get to the root of the trouble. I spoke to the top management of the company, and they arranged to invite the presidents of Matsushita Electric sales and wholesale firms from all over the country to a convention in July 1964 at the New Fujiya Hotel in Atami, a hot spring resort south-west of Tokyo. It was the first such gathering to be held since I assumed the chairmanship.

Listening to the reports of our distributors on the state of their businesses, I was shocked by the size of some of their deficits. One company capitalised at ¥5 million was operating at a loss of ¥150 million. This meant it was in the red by thirty times as much as its capital! Ordinarily, such a firm would be considered too risky, but Matsushita Electric had continued to supply it with merchandise. However, far from being apologetic or grateful, the president of the company in question was indignant that his business was showing no profit. The more the agents talked about their problems, the more aware I became of a decidedly critical mood toward Matsushita Electric.

"We have been handling Matsushita products since my father's generation, but we're not making the least bit of profit these days. In fact, we're losing money. What do you think is wrong?"

"In my area, the competition is fierce, and I just can't turn a profit. All I have is a pile of promissory notes, and at least a few of them bounce every day."

Every comment I heard seemed to say that the appliance business was a hopelessly losing proposition. Could this be so? So I asked them, "Are any of you here actually making a profit? If you are, please raise your hand." About 30 people raised their hands. From this I reckoned that about 170 companies must be operating at a loss. The overwhelming majority were in the red, but there were 30 companies that were not. Small as the number might be, it suggested to me that a company could stay in the black if it was well managed, despite the recession. I was dismayed to see so many operating at a deficit, but it was encouraging to observe that a company could cope if only it knew how.

It was not going to be easy to figure out what to do about the majority who were losing money, though. So I plunged into the fray, saying, "I came here today out of a desire to find some way of pulling all of us out of the difficult situation we are in. Please tell me frankly what your problems are. Do not hesitate to tell things as they are. If you think Matsushita Electric's methods need to be changed, say so. They will be remedied at once. I need to know the facts about your situations."

This seemed to open the dam, so to speak. A torrent of complaints and tales of woe poured from people who earlier had spoken hesitantly and tried to soften their complaints. They ceased to mince words. The dealers with heavy losses were especially bitter: "What do you intend to do about our losses? We have followed Matsushita Electric's instructions to the letter. We have put all of our assets and energy into the sale of your company's products. In spite of all this, we're not making any money. Don't you think this is partly your responsibility?"

I felt compelled to say something in our defense. "You may well say that," I countered, "but if this were an ordinary business relationship, your supply of merchandise would have been stopped long ago. Doesn't the fact that Matsushita Electric has continued to supply you without a word of complaint mean that it is a very benevolent—though perhaps too lenient—company? I accept your grievances, but we, too, are in a position to complain. You say that you have suffered, but I wonder if you've really done your utmost."

Still, it was pointless to keep arguing. "Well, there's no point in simply grumbling," I said. The question is, where do we go from here?" I stared at them in dead earnest, and the faces before me were seriousness itself. Matsushita Electric would surely go under if it could not collect its bills from these companies. I made up my mind not to budge from the rostrum until we could find a satisfactory solution. "It doesn't matter how many hours this takes," I told the assembled dealers. "Let's talk it out until we reach a mutual agreement."

The Atami conference had been scheduled to last for two days, but progress was so slow that we agreed to stay another day. As the third day drew to a close, the stream of grievances against Matsushita Electric continued to flow. I decided that the meeting must not be allowed to end on this negative note. I would have to present some kind of conclusion on behalf of Matsushita Electric myself. Taking the rostrum at the end of the meeting on the third day, I spoke as follows:

"Since the day before yesterday I have been listening to your complaints and problems. I have responded and countered your charges from the standpoint of the company. To be quite honest, I feel that you are all at fault in some respects. Over 30 companies among those represented here today are turning a profit. It seems to me that Matsushita Electric has a fairly strong argument against those that are not".

However, we've been hashing this over for three days now, and I think it's time to stop arguing. The more I think this over, the more it seems to me that Matsushita Electric is to blame. Basically, it all comes down to that. We have failed to stand by you as we should. Slump or no slump, there must be some way of successfully beating these problems. Matsushita Electric is at fault for failing to lead you safely out of the crisis. I am truly sorry for this negligence on our part.

You know, I just happened to recall something that happened almost 30 years ago. Matsushita Electric had started making light bulbs, and I went round to your offices trying to sell them. That was a long time ago. Japanese light bulbs were not yet first class in terms of quality or durability. But, I said, consider my light bulbs as you might a young *sumo* wrestler. He may only have a junior rank, but given the chance and the time, he has the promise of becoming a grand champion. I assured you that I would come up with a "grand champion" light bulb if given sometime. I pleaded with you to give my "junior-class" light bulb a try.

At first you were firm. "No. We'll sell your other products, but we don't want any part of your light bulbs." Others were willing to consider the matter: "Lower your prices and we'll sell them." I was audacious enough to continue campaigning on behalf of our light bulb. "If you don't have some patience with these fledgling light bulbs, Japan will never produce first-rate light bulbs of its own," I said. There will be no training ground for their development. Please bear this in mind. I am asking for your help in creating some 'grand champions."

At last my appeals struck a sympathetic chord, and in the end you agreed to carry the light bulbs. Thanks to your sales efforts, the Matsushita light bulb was on its way. In the years that followed we made repeated improvements, and today I am proud to say that our light bulbs have become "grand champions" both in name and reality.

This is the sort of thing that has happened repeatedly in the course of Matsushita's growth. Matsushita Electric has been blessed with devoted service on the part of its sales agents and has benefited immeasurably from your generous support. In light of this, I feel particularly ashamed and sorry that we allowed you to fall into this difficult plight. You gave us a chance when we were small and weak by agreeing to do your best by our products.

As I think back, I realise how much Matsushita Electric owes you. I cannot with any grace say a word against you. I was wrong to observe the situation and form conclusions in total disregard of the favour you have shown us all along. I had simply forgotten, and this is a mistake and a weakness on our part. Beginning now, I hope to make a fresh new start, and I promise you that we will mend our ways."

A wave of emotion overcame me as I spoke, and, moved to the verge of tears, I found I could no longer go on.

When I finally thought to look up at the audience, I was surprised to find that the majority of those assembled had pulled out handkerchiefs and were wiping at their eyes. They sat in utter silence. Never before had I witnessed such a scene.

After my speech, strangely enough, the atmosphere of anger and antipathy that had filled the hall seemed to vanish completely. One after another, the presidents rose to say, "We were at fault too. Let's all turn over a new leaf and try to do better from now on." It was a great relief to see that people really could understand' one another's point of view if they tried. People can find ways of working out their differences and helping meet each other's needs if only they will try to put themselves in the other guy's shoes and frankly discuss the issues at hand. Such is human nature.

So the meeting ended constructively after all. The ensuing effort to bail out our sales subsidiaries and agents, however, turned out to be no easy task. I decided that I would have to get involved directly, and since Hiroshi Yasukawa, national sales manager (later, Vice-President) was ill at the time, I took up the position of acting head to direct affairs at the front line of sales. I undertook a sweeping reform of Matsushita's sales and distribution system. Concretely, this entailed clearly delineating the territories of the regional sales agents to prevent overlap and rationalising the retailer-wholesaler networks for greater efficiency. Another step was to institute a new system of installment credit to facilitate cash transactions between retailers and wholesalers. I spent a great deal of time meeting with the executives and staff of the stores that carried our products explaining my ideas about business and management, on more than one occasion spending four hours at a stretch in such meetings. Through close cooperation, we finally managed to get the Matsushita sales network back on its feet and the future of the whole industry began to look much brighter.

Controlling Stability at Deere & Co.

In the 1860s, John Deere, a blacksmith in Vermont, invented a plough that was able to turn the thick, rich soil of the vast and fertile midwestern U.S. Prairies. Then in 1868, Deere formed company to distribute his ploughs and stressed a philosophy of quality products and customer service. By 1911. that company had evolved into a full-time manufacturer of farm equipment. In 1918, through its purchase of a Waterloo, Iowa-based gasoline engine came instrumental in the conversion of American agriculture from animal to machine power. Through diversification Deere has remained a viable concern, and today Deere stands as the largest producer of farm equipment in the world. In addition, Deere is a major supplier of destruction machinery. Managers emphasise the globalisation of Deere enterprises (including facilities in Mexico, Canada, Spain, France, Australia, and elsewhere) and stable leadership. Deere has had only four, CEOs since 1928.

Although Deere has worked with GM on diesel engines and with NASA on developing metal alloys, agricultural equipment remains its core business. As of 1994, Deere held 35 per cent of the farm tractor market and approximately half of the self-propelled combine market.

During recent years, however, American agriculture has experienced ups and downs. In the United States, for instance, many farmers accrued overwhelming debt burdens in the late 1980s, that compelled them to part with land that had belonged to their families for generations. Some of the land was consolidated into larger farms. Much of it was sold to housing developers.

Even when the industry began to pick up in the early 1990s, few farmers rushed to buy new tractors, combines, or farming equipment. In fact, an article in the *Wall Street Journal* in 1992, reported that the average tractor in the United States was 19 years old. This could be due, at least in part, to the expense of Deere products. Even a modest piece of farm equipment manufactured by Deere can cost as much as a luxury automobile, while the latest, most sophisticated tractors retail for as much as $ 80,000. Deere's fortunes therefore tend to rise and fall with those of the of the farmers. In 1990, for example, Deere posted earnings of $ 411 million—the best in the company's history. In 1991, however, the company suffered a loss of $ 37 million. Then, the industry began to recover in 1992 and 1993, and Deere reported 1993 earnings of $ 184 million. Given such volatility, how does Deere keep going?

One of Deere's strategies involves helping dealers offer incentives, such as price cuts, sales promotions, and low-interest financing through Deere's credit subsidiary. Dealers, hoping to compensate for lost profit through future parts and service business, often end up selling equipment at near cost.

Price incentives and promotional campaigns help Deere create regular demand for its goods. Under ordinary circumstances, farm equipment sales are seasonal–high in the spring and summer but low during the rest of the year. If Deere were to ignore the seasonality of its products, the company might be forced to lay workers off during the off-season or hire extra workers during the on-season. Instead, Deere attempts to even out demand through sales promotions and incentive programmes. For example, to encourage year-round sales. Deere offers incentive merchandise such as furniture and travel awards to debaters who surpass their goals.

When demand dips exceptionally low, as it did in 1991 and early 1992, Deere holds week-long factory shutdowns in place of permanent layoffs. "During the era of market downsizing," explained Al Delattre of Andersen Consulting, "the first thing some companies did was make wide cuts of factories and people without building in performance to allow them to respond to the change in the market." The temporary shutdowns, however, enabled Deere to keep production at a constant, efficient rate, and still remain flexible to the demands of the cyclical market.

Careful control has thus enabled Deere not only to survive but to prosper in a cyclical industry in which extremely narrow profit margins are shared with dealers.

OGAWA TURNS AROUND HOKKAIDO OPERATIONS

"I became manager of the Microwave Oven Division at Matsushita Electric in the mid-1970s. As the microwave oven was still a luxury item with prices over ¥ 100,000. it was a difficult product to sell. We set up a large sales department and divided it into seven sections, one for each region of the country," states ogawa.

"The sales targets for each regional office were roughly proportionate to the population of the region. Although the total number of microwaves sold was larger than predicted, sales in individual regions varied between 70 per cent and 150 per cent of the targets. When we inquired as to the reason for this discrepancy, we were told it was attributable to "regional differences." I couldn't quite accept this excuse. I couldn't see why the same product, sold at the same price and with the same advertising methods, should sell unevenly among people living in different parts of the country. When we pursued the problem, we found conditions particular to each region that caused the salespeople to take issue with the targets. For example, in Hokkaido, Japan's northernmost island, our salespeople told us that they could not meet the target because the Matsushita sales network was still weak, and people in Hokkaido were unfamiliar with microwave ovens. That meant the sales agents had to work much harder than those in other regions. On top of that, there was the size and relative isolation of the region: when the salespeople went out on their rounds, they were often gone for ten days at a stretch. The harsh winters further disrupted sales efforts. Due to these adverse circumstances, the Hokkaido office claimed, their salespeople's job was a lot tougher than that of other districts. Most of the report sounded plausible, so at the time I accepted it.

"When we calculated the profit and loss for each regional office, though, we found that Hokkaido was operating at a deficit of 5 to 10 per cent. I decided to get tough with them. I told them, "Operations in Hokkaido are in the red. while all the other regional offices are showing a profit. You're just too worried about achieving targets. Your office is the supplier and seller of goods from the manufacturer to the retailer— you're a wholesaler. You also have the advantage of being the sole supplier of National microwave ovens. We're leaving the sales in Hokkaido entirely up to you. The regional sales manager should think of himself as a store owner and the staff should think of themselves as shop salespeople, and you should manage your store so that you can pay your salaries."

They said they could see my point, and would try to improve. Thus began what we now call "departmental management."

We decided to practice departmental management—Matsushita's division system in a smaller scale —for all the regional offices. Since each office was treated as an independent outlet, they had to balance their books every month. Each employee understood that if the accounts stayed in the red, their operations would collapse. Even with goods in inventory, if they fell short of funds, they would eventually go bankrupt. Seeing what could happen, the store owner and the salespeople would have to get serious about improving their management. They would have to put their heads together, come up with new ideas, and put them into practice immediately. If business improved, it would be proof of their effectiveness. Once they became aware that their jobs had a clear purpose, they became more interested in their work and more enthusiastic.

The Hokkaido office became the model of autonomous management. I had at first feared a confrontation with them, but instead we were able to forge a relationship of mutual cooperation. The result of this effort was apparent in the improved performance of the Hokkaido region, which soon began pulling its own weight in the division.

I realise now that I was slow in applying the lessons learned in sales to other departments in the division. It was two years after this autonomous-shop style of management had proved so effective in the sales department that I realised the need to put it into practice in other departments. It took some ingenuity on everyone's part to adapt the system to the production, administration and service departments, but that made the effort all the more enjoyable and effective.

Before discussing in detail the departmental management system, we should perhaps put the concept into context and distinguish it from other managerial schemes.

HANDS-ON MANAGEMENT

There are two types of management today. One is management for the future. Also known as strategic management, it includes management techniques to ensure the permanent survival of the company. So important is this kind of management that a failure in strategy cannot be offset by tactical maneuvers. It is extremely difficult to determine how appropriate one's strategy is and how well it is succeeding, so this kind of management is somewhat a cerebral exercise.

The other type of management is management for the present, the hands-on approach that ensures the survival of an enterprise here and now. It is this type of management that I shall now describe in detail.

Management, for the present, is what all employees are doing every day in every department. Since the modern corporation is divided into many departments, sections, and other sub-units, each one is responsible for performing work in their specialised area.

Control *vs.* Management

"When a corporation reaches a certain size, operations have to be implemented through some division of labour. But behind this natural division is another phenomenon of which we are usually not aware: operations come to be carried out in a context of *control* rather than *management.* The person who oversees or controls the operations at a given level holds rank in a supervisory hierarchy. Although in English it is most common to speak of middle and top management, the Japanese term *kanrisha* has more the nuance of "controller," "supervisor," or "overseer." In most cases, the Japanese term seems to be the more accurate description of the way large organisations everywhere conceive of the role of these people.

In departmental management, each department (or section) is seen as an independent unit which is responsible for its own operations. Rather than being controlled from above, it is managed from within. In such an environment, the head of the section or department must transform himself from a mere controller into a true manager. With the right kind of leadership, the workplace comes to life, becoming a place where work is meaningful and fulfilling and where the principle that everyone is responsible for management is put into practice.

Let us look a little more closely at the difference between management and control. Management by control means that a superior gives orders and those under him merely carry them out. In a true management situation, tasks are set in accordance with the worker's own ideas, undertaken by means he devises himself and completed on his own initiative.

The control style of management is fundamentally oppressive, be it intentional or inadvertent. A true management-oriented environment, however, seeks renewal and creativity; it embraces diversity. It makes any endeavour worthwhile and enjoyable.

In a control situation, wages are a remuneration for carrying out orders. Workers who faithfully carry out orders have the right to claim remuneration for their labours, no matter how well or poorly the company is doing. This is only right; but, in a management environment, everyone is aware that their wages are directly connected with the performance of the company in the market-place. In order to earn the money to pay wages, the company must compete to attract customers for its products or services and make a reasonable profit. You cannot do business without thinking of customers, competition, and profit margins. In a control situation, however, the only concern of the workers is fulfilling assigned tasks. These points are outlined in Table 9.3

Table 9.3. Control and Management

Control	*Management*
• Basic motivation for action is to earn out orders from above.	• Basic motivation for action comes from self.
• Subordinates are given authority, encouraged to think for themselves, and to put their ideas into practice.	• Subordinates are forced to carry out policies dictated by their superiors.
• Basically a form of coercion.	• Atmosphere of freedom, and high interest level.
• As long as employee follows orders, the company pays wages.	• Employee has to earn his/her wages.
• Customers, competitors and profits are not the concern of the subordinates.	• Employees must provide service for the customer, work to beat the competition, collect receivables, and post profits.
• Superior subjectively evaluates employees by the degree to which they achieve assigned targets.	• Evaluation is objective based on the input/output relationship.
• Effective leader is one who stands out in front of the troops and directs them.	• Leadership is based on delegation of authority, guidance, and backup.
Daily routine is regulated by strict observance of rules.	• Everyday brings a new challenge.
In terms of your job, that is no need for dreams or vision, strategic thinking is irrelevant.	Dreams, vision and strategic thinking are required. Out of these are born management principles.

Appraisals of performance in a management environment are more objective than those in a control situation. In management, appraisal is based on whether the operations have earned a profit, that is, on the difference between invested capital (input) and returns (output). Thus, self-appraisal is possible, for the balance sheet will show the degree of success or failure. In a control situation, however, the only basis for appraisal is whether the goal has been reached; the work can be judged only by the person who set the goals.

A person in a control situation gives his subordinates instructions on the basis of orders received from above, and he expects his instructions to be carried out to the letter as well. He tends to rule with an iron fast, emphasising adherence to rules and regulations. A manager, on the other hand, gives his subordinates authority and the freedom to work creatively.

How can you bring management back to the worksite? My solution is to assign management objectives in a form suitable to each department and introduce into those departments the managerial concepts of customers, competitors, and profits. By doing so, we come close to the departmental management I advocate, with each department operating as an independent management unit.

PART-III

Part III deals with 5 fundamental critical features of Dynamic Global Management, which herald success or failure of Global Operations.

They are:

10. **Motivation**
11. **Developing Future Management**
12. **Managing Diverse People and Cultures**
13. **Global Human Growth Model**
14. **Dynamics of Global Management**

10 Motivation

The chapter is discussed under the following headings :
• The meaning and definition • The theory and practice of motivation • Wal-Mart: A model in motivation • The Adrian story • Ogawa's philosophy and practice of motivating people.

We shall start with the first critical management process of motivating people to realise and achieve their maximum potential as well as the organisational goals.

THE MEANING AND DEFINITION OF MOTIVATION

In the words of the great Sophocles: "The wonder of wonders is the man/woman and there is no doubt that man/woman is the most dynamic animal. He/she has an infinite capacity to think, to create, to develop, to discover and invent, to produce, feel, to love, to dream, to conquer, to master, to achieve, to give and take, to learn, to live, to respect, to play, to pray as well as to destroy, to hate and to kill. He/she is the most complex being there is. His her behaviour and conduct may also be the most unpredictable. He/she can do infinite good and infinite bad as he/she chooses or as he is led to choose. But above all, he/she is human, although at times his/her conduct and actions may border almost on the inhuman side. He/she is not a machine. He/she is not merely a commodity that can be bought and sold.

This human element is the predominating factor that affects his/her relations with others in business, or society or industry. This human element is perhaps the non-business character that greatly influences his/her business character and the two are inseparable. "The whole human" who comes to the day shift carries with him her both the business character of man/woman, father/mother, husband/wife, brother/sister, etc., the whole person is a complicated human being with various emotions, aspirations, dreams, fears, desires and ambitions, likes and dislikes, prejudices and fads and he/she meets and works with other men/women with similar or dissimilar feelings, emotions and aspirations in a factory or office. There is a constant interaction and interplay of these various dynamic human factors and it is the business of managers to harness these dynamic forces and weld them together to work towards the common goals of the company. The art and science of human relations/human resources and human capital movement after considerable ongoing research, study and experiments, have evolved theories, tools and techniques for management to use in the industrial and business spheres. It is the major duty and responsibility and opportunity of human resources managers to assist and advise top and line management in this vital areas of motivation."

THE THEORY AND PRACTICE OF MOTIVATION

Professor William G. Scott's definition is as follows :

"Human relations is a process of effective motivation of individuals in a given situation in order to achieve a balance of objectives which will yield greater human satisfaction and help accomplish company goals ".

"Human relations is the term commonly applied to the process of focussing the methodology and findings of a number of behavioural science disciplines on human problems. The human relations approach to problem solving is, therefore, labelled *interdisciplinary.* Management uses human relations, to determine a course of action for unravelling problems of human conflict and human satisfactions in business. *Management action through human relations requires the application of behavioural science principles to promote human collaboration and social solidarity within the social system of the business organisation.* Simply stated, human relations is the art and science of accomplishing predetermined company goals, the process of which promotes individual efficiency and satisfaction and group solidarity and effectiveness as well as company productivity, profitability and growth and, in the ultimate analysis, the harmonisation of the interests and aspirations of the company on the one hand and individual and the group on the other."

Human Relations Research

Considerable research on human relations is being carried on by the universities, professional management associations, research institutions, companies in USA, and some in India also.

The famous Hawthorne studies conducted by Professor Elton Mayo and his team of researchers and the findings of those studies represent the core of human relations theory and practice. Several books, that were the result of Mayo's experimentation for a period of more than a decade have remained as the important contributions to human relations literature.[6] It is well-known that many of the concepts and hypotheses that are being tested through the above mentioned researches originated in the field of psychology, sociology and anthropology. An inter-disciplinary approach was evolved and the following Table 10.1 suggests the interdisciplinary framework.

Table 10.1 How Science Becomes Practice in Human Relations

Science	*Techniques*	*A clinical point of view and method*	*Professional practice*
1	2	3	4
Psychology	Applied Psychology		Administration
Sociology	Applied Sociology		
Anthropology	Applied Anthropology	Human Relations	Personnel Relations
Physiology	Applied Physiology		
Engineering	Scientific Management		Labour Relations

Based on F. J. Roethlisberger, "Human Relations: Rare, Medium, or Well done? *Harvard Business Review*, January 1948, p. 103 adapted.

In 1947, the Survey Research Centre, Institute for Social Research of the University of Michigan, initiated a 10-year human relations research based on direct observation of organisations with two major criteria to evaluate the effectiveness of organisations, departments or groups :

1. Productivity per man-hour, or some similar measure of the organisation's success in achieving its productivity goals.
2. Job satisfaction and other satisfactions derived by employees or members of work groups (as determined in most instances through opinion survey questionnaires).

It is found that there is a consistent pattern of motivational principles and their application has is to be associated with higher productivity and job satisfaction, irrespective of the particular companies or industries that have been studied.

Human Relations and Motivation

There is no doubt that motivation is the key to the promotion of proper good human relations. Rensis Likert calls motivation the core of management which shows that *every human being earnestly seeking a secure, friendly and supportive relationship which gives him a sense of worth in face to face groups which are most important to him...a supervisor should strive to treat individuals with dignity and a recognition for their personal worth"*.

It is needless to drive home the point that every individual, regardless of race, colour, rank, status, nationality, caste, deserves respect and recognition of his worth as a human being and craves for them. Deny him these, you have reduced his effectiveness on the job, because he is resentful and he has a deep but justifiable grouse. The ILO team, back in 1950s, pointed out that human relations is the weakest point of management in India. The most serious lacuna in employer-employee relationship in our country is that management, save for a few cases, have largely not succeeded in communicating to the mass of illiterate migrant workers a sense of tremendous challenge, a sense of participation, a sense of national awareness and purpose and the worker has a significant role to play in the terrific transition that is taking place in India. When the worker does not get the necessary constructive guidance and leadership from the management, he turns to

6. F.J. Roethlisberger, Human Relations.

others, who may use him for their own ends. Addressing the Seventeenth Annual Conference of the Indian Institute of Personnel Management held at Coimbatore on March 11-13,1967, Mr. R. S. Pande, Resident Director of TISCO, on the theme of "Maximising the effectiveness of Personnel Management", explained that the industrial worker is an "uncommon child" requiring guidance and leadership from management and through good human relations and proper motivational plans, management must satisfy his needs so that he may become a productive industrial citizen.

Motivation and Human Satisfactions

Life is a search for satisfactions. It is necessary to find out what satisfies the individual and to know something about *what makes man to do what he does.* If the motivations of the individuals can be identified, a good start is made. Various authorities have identified various drives, motives, or needs of the individuals which motivate them and management must strive to satisfy these motivations. It is said that attitudes pave the way for the development of motives and depending on a particular motive, a certain behaviour is chosen. Professor Roethlisberger developed " X " Chart, shown in the Fig. 10.1. to potray the relationship of attitudes and behaviour.

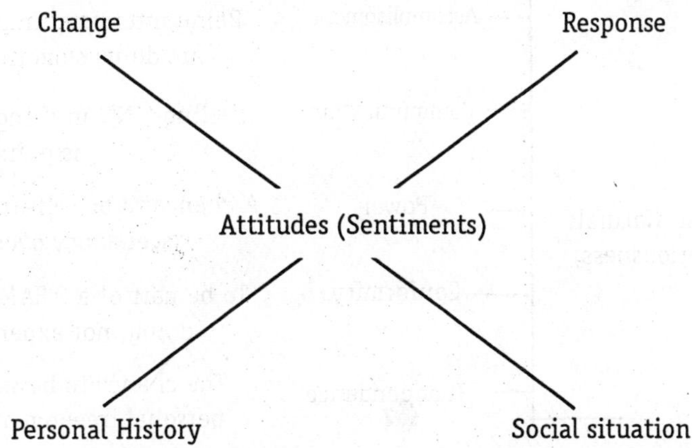

Fig. 10.1. ***The "X" Chart.***

Source: F. J. Roethlisberger, *Management and Morale,* p. 21.

The relationship of attitudes, motives and behaviour are is shown in Fig. 10.2.

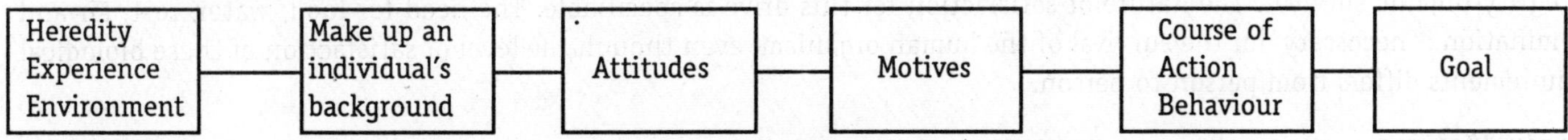

Fig. 10.2. The *Relation of Attitudes, Motives and Behaviour*

According to Professor Scott, motives imply that resulting behaviour will be consciously directed toward a goal. The goal may be viewed as a specific satisfaction for a specific motive. "Motives can be satisfied through numerous forms of activities including religion, education, social service, family life and many more. Of course, work is a channel of satisfaction of a number of learned human motives." Fig. 10.3 shows a system of classification of work motives illustrating their relationship to primary drives, basic drives and their ultimate requirement of satisfaction.

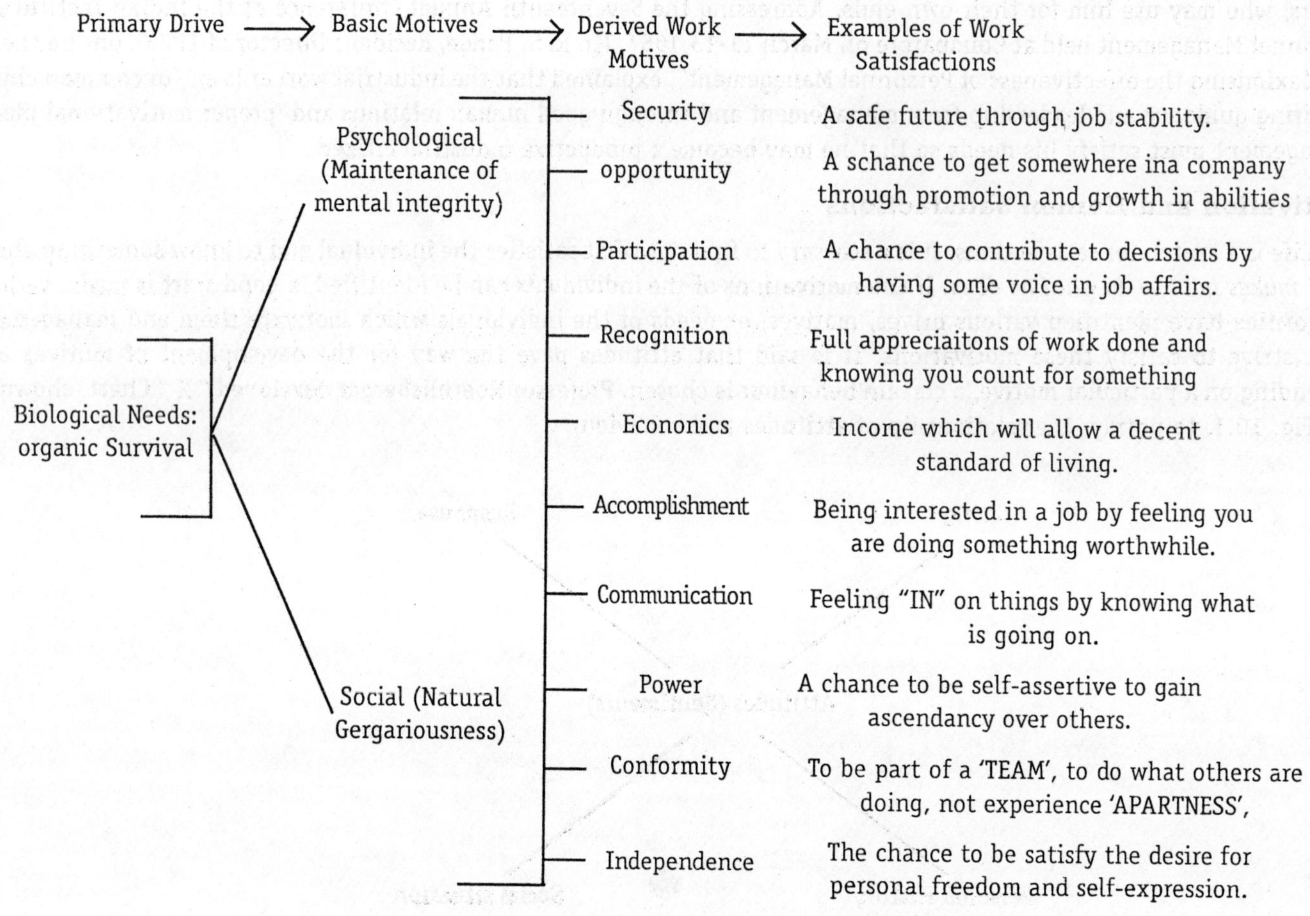

Fig. 10.3. Basic and Derived Work Motives and their Satisfaction.

Primary Drive

The biological drive, already mentioned, requires the satisfaction of these basic needs essential to maintain physiological integrity-organic survival. The nature of satisfaction for this drive is specifiable. The need for food, water, rest, air and elemination is necessary, for the survival of the human organism, even though the level of satisfaction of these biological requirements differs from person to person.

Basic Motives

There are two basic motives — psychological and social. The psychological motive results in a quest by an individual to maintain his mental integrity or balance. The social motive stems from the natural gregariousness of man and his need to associate with his fellow men.

Unlike the biological drive, it is impossible to generalise and predict the specific routes individuals will follow to satisfy these motives. Further, the satisfaction of basic motives is volitional. Although it was said that the social motive is basic for man in general, the example of a hermit or recluse comes to mind immediately to demonstrate the volitional character of this category of motives.

Derived (Work) Motives

This last category provides the richest source of motives underlying human behaviour. The ten derived work motives are only a few of many possible reasons why people work. These motives are derived from the basic social and psychological motives. But they are not connected in a specific way to one or the other basic motives. Who can say with any degree of certainty that the recognition motive is social or psychological in origin? The only possible way to find out is by studying an individual, not by generalising to a whole population.

Derived work motives have the interesting characteristic of being highly dynamic in nature. In this regard, (1) each person at a point in time has a certain hierarchy, a special ordering of importance of the derived motives; and (2) when the motive which is first on his " list" is satisfied, it slips in urgency and another motive takes its place.

Thus, when research studies in worker motives turn up the "Discovery" that money is not on top of the list of motives for a group of employees, the obvious conclusion is not that money is no longer important, money is still vital but it is not the only reason for working. Once the basic income requirement is satisfied, other motives supercede it on the list of motives, for a time at least.

The Requirement of Satisfaction

Management is in part responsible for the satisfaction of derived work motives. The satisfactions are suggestive; and some satisfactions appear to be mutually exclusive of others. Each individual may interpret his requirement for the satisfaction of a particular motive differently. One job of a manager who is attempting to improve his motivational ability is to determine what his subordinates expect in terms of satisfaction for their unique motives.

Generalisations will not accomplish this job, nor will statistical studies of the hierarchy of employee motives. No substitute exists for managerial insight and sensitivity when it comes to perceiving the type of motive satisfaction required by each employee. Understanding individual motives is a day to day task.

Furthermore, motivation is a function which a manager performs in order to get his subordinates to achieve job objectives. It is not merely a management process and there is another side to it — the individual being motivated. Psychologists call individual motivation *a state of tension*. According to Viteles, motivation represents an unsatisfied need which creates a state of tension or disequilibrium causing the individual to move in a goal-directed pattern toward restoring a state of equilibrium by satisfying the need.

Management should be aware that the strength of tensions, and therefore, the strength of motivations vary. John W. Atkinson views motivation strength in the form of an equation:

$$\text{motivation} = f\,(\text{motive} \times \text{expectancy} \times \text{incentive})$$

The strength of motivation to perform an act is a function of:

1. *The strength of the motive* which is the position of a motive in the individual's hierarchy of motives, representing a level of urgency for fulfilment.
2. *Expectancy* which is the probability that the act will obtain the goal.
3. *The Value of the incentive* which is the reward hoped for by obtaining the goal. The greater the rewards, the greater will be the motivational strength, provided the other two factors remain equal.

Scott observes that motivation is not an automatic nor is it a one-sided management process. Individual motivational tensions are social, psychological as well as economic in origin. Knowing that unmet motives, expectancies and value systems of individuals provide management with the concrete information necessary to perform the process of motivation considered in the more traditional sense ". An overall approach to motivation may be visualised in Fig. 10.4.

Key questions, to ask about the employee and yourself

1. What are the employee's attitudes?
2. What are the employee's motives?
3. What is the strength of his motivation?
4. How do I, as a manager, feel about his motives and attitudes?

↓

A motivational problem situation ← Approach to the situation = Manner of handling the problem.

↑

Fig. 10.4. ***An Approach to Motivation***

Key questions to ask about the work situation.

1. What factors in the physical and social job setting are relevant to the solution of this problem?

2. To what extent does the company policy circumscribe actions that might be taken to solve the problem?
3. Are there any outside organisations, like a union, which may affect the problem?

Professor Mee lists the following human drives which are to be satisfied by the management:

1. *Hunger and Security Drive :* Under this are included the human drives to secure food, shelter, security, to avert pain and to gain physical pleasure.
2. *Sex and Family Drive :* In this classification are included the love of the family, the gregarious drive, the drive of worship and sense of duty and the desire to be liked by one's fellow men.
3. *Mastery and Self-esteem Drive :* The drives of mastery and self-esteem as a group classification include the drives for self-respect; rivalry drive; desire to be recognised, respected and liked by the group; the drive of pride; the desire of possession; and the desire of understanding.

From Professor Maslow we have a theory of motivation where he identified a hierarchy of needs as shown in the Fig. 10.5.

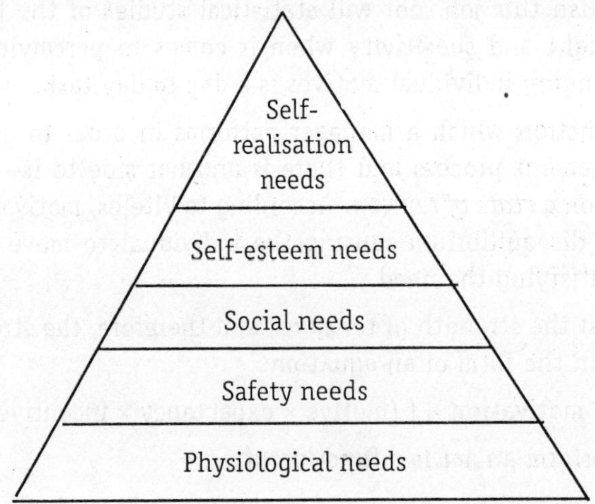

Fig. 10.5. *A Hierarchy of Needs*

First of all, the individual has the basic physiological needs such as food, shelter, clothing, etc. Secondly, he has safety needs such as security, protection, etc. Thirdly, the social needs pertain to the love of the family, recognition from society, and social acceptance. The fourth type are needs for self-respect and self-esteem. The last are the needs for realising the fullest stature of the individual or self-fulfilment. When a person realises his fullest potentialities or has the opportunity to grow to his fullest capabilities, he is satisfied. It satisfies his ego also. This is the theory of needs based on a motivational system of hierarchy propounded by Maslow.

Unsatisfied needs are motivators and a satisfied need ceases to be a motivating force at a given point of time, under a given situation or set of circumstances.

Professor Jucius rightly has observed that "there are many buttons beyond number. And many would give the same response. It is necessary to determine which buttons should be pushed — a compliment, a dollar raise, a smile, a promise of a raise, a new typewriter, a preferred location or a new desk? The theory does not tell an executive which button will provide the best spur under the circumstances".

Jucius also states that differences such as the following must be considered when establishing motivating plans:

1. Personal background
2. Education
3. Age
4. Marital status
5. Financial status
6. Health
7. Political affiliation
8. Religious beliefs
9. Social relationships
10. Psychological make-up
11. Union affiliation
12. Company experiences

Steps of Motivation

Jucius has suggested the following steps of motivation:

1. Size up the situations requiring motivation.
2. Prepare a set of motivating tools.
3. Select and apply the appropriate motivator.
4. Follow up the results of the application.

It is necessary to find out whether the 'pay-off' of motivation has resulted either in higher output or lower costs or greater loyalty, etc.

Rules of Motivation

Jucius lays down five rules of motivation :

1. *Self-interest and Motivation:* People are selfish. When a person realises that his own interests are best served in the attainment of company interests, he is likely to give off his best.
2. *Attainability:* It is necessary to establish goals that are attainable and when such goals are achieved, it leads to employee satisfaction. Unattainable goals frustrate people.
3. *The Human Element :* Motivation appeals to emotions, importance of feelings. The executive, who is most successful as motivator, can trace his success invariably to his skill in dealing with people's feelings. He can bring out the best in people because he makes them feel good, feel significant, feel worthwhile and feel that they are growing.
4. *Individual-Group Relationship:* Motivation must be based upon group as well as individual-centered stimuli. Groups have terrific impact on individuals. Firstly, utilise motivational plans which do not run counter to group forces and secondly, to seek to change constructively the ideas of the group.
5. *Managerial Theory :* Management must base its motivational efforts on sound theory.

How to Handle Human Relations Problems?

The Twin City Chapter of the Society for the Advancement of Management recommend the following approach :

1. Recognise basic individual needs. These include

   (1) recognition as an individual, (2) self-respect, (3) pride, (4) communication, (5) understanding, (6) confidence, (7) opportunity, (8) discipline.
2. Get background information about the individual, through (1) direct methods, such as (a) man-to-man talks, (b) observation, (c) records analysis, (2) indirect methods, such as, (a) testing, (b) interview, (c) attitude surveys.

The Twin City SAM group recommends the following in handling human relations problems :

1. Recognise that individuals are different
2. Gather all information possible on a continuing basis
3. For identical needs two individuals may have to be approached differently
4. All information must be kept confidential
5. Allow time for this in your daily activity
6. Results will not necessarily be immediate or apparent
7. Take immediate action wherever possible
8. Eliminate or change the cause
9. Know each individual so that rapport is established
10. Keep informal notes on each case
11. Separate facts from opinions
12. Don't forget that you are involved and that you may have to change
13. Do let suggestions for change appear to come from the individual

14. Recognise that in some situations action by the supervisor is not appropriate, e.g., husband-wife relationships
15. Do not express moral judgements — be objective
16. Do not express surprise
17. Find out what the individual wants
18. Needs may be changed by changing conditions
19. Ask for assistance from your own or other supervisors and from the staff.

Most human relations approaches emphasise increasing employee motivation through improved communication and through additional participation in solving problems found in the work situation. It is believed that improved morale will result from these practices.

Professor Scott in Fig. 10.6 illustrates that the data supplied by the analytical areas provide management with a basic understanding of human behaviour and organisational processes. With this information, management should have the technical insight necessary for the diagnosis, prevention, or cure of many human problems in business.

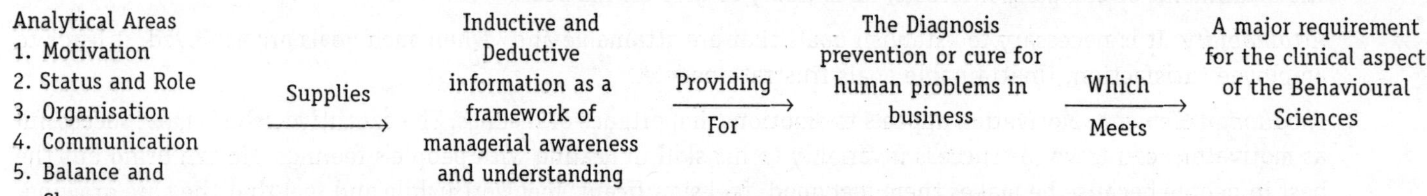

Fig. 10.6. ***Analytical Areas and Clinical Dimensions of Human Relations.***

Mr. Donald R. Shoen lists the following *guides* for a manager in human relations practice:

1. He should understand and accept people as they are.
2. He should be aware and sensitive to another's point of view — along with an ability to maintain his own position.
3. He should be willing to understand and to respond to the feelings and attitudes of others which might not be purely logical from his own frame of reference.
4. He should be aware of himself and appreciate the scope of his influence on others.
5. He should appreciate the social structure or social system in which he is involved.
6. He should be realistic about his authority and status and be aware of how they affect others.
7. He should attempt to predict (although the probability of occurrence of the outcomes he predicts may be low) as to how the organisation will respond to a change he introduces.
8. He should make use of experience and abstract generalisations about social phenomena in taking action.

Management Attitude

Paradoxically enough, often it may be the apathy and non-involvement of management in human relations that may cause many problems. Only when matters come to a head, they realise that they had neglected this vital area. Then there are some who are domineering by nature and to them human relations approaches are an infringement on their own rights and prerogatives. There are some managers who regard labour as a "cost, a commodity" or a machine and not as human beings, then there are "production-centred" or "efficiency-centred" managers, who are concerned only with increasing productivity or efficiency regardless of "the cost in human assets". There is another category of older executive to whom human relations is "a new gimmick" and they cannot cope with this new dimension, " after all I have been handling people all these years."

Most of these types of executives need exposure to human relations approaches, theory, practice, and best of all, "how it is working out in Sam's Company". Here is an area where the personnel administrator fits in perfectly. He must assist executives and supervisors in getting the necessary training, education and exposure to human relation concepts.

Professor Mee offers some examples of common human relationse problems and how to handle them in the following Fig. 10.7.

Problem	*Possible causes*	*Possible action*
1. Absenteeism. 2. Complaints about working conditions. 3. Dirty work and work place. 4. Disloyalty. 5. Complainer spreads discontent. 6. Excessive talking. 7. Insubordination. 8. Misrepresenting the management or company data. 9. Not using safety aids. 10. Plays on job. 11. Quality of work poor. 12. Rumour-spreader. 13. Quitting ahead of 5 p. m. 14. Soldiering. 15. Theft. 16. Wastefulness.	(1) Habit, lack of interest, trouble at home, dissatisfaction with job, transportation trouble. (2) Jealousy, favouritism, actual poor conditions. (3) Lack of interest, carelessness, toleration by management. (4) Discontent, favouritism, lack of recognition. (5) Work conditions, poor wages, lack of recognition, poor leadership. (6) Lack of social outlet, idleness (7) Lack of interest, spite, jealousy, favouritism, personal issue. (8) Ignorance of facts, dissatisfaction. (9) Clownishness, desire to be important to group, lax discipline, not enough work. (10) Lack of knowledge, laziness, desire to exceed piece rate. (11) Jealoulsy, curiosity, desire to seem important. Habit, transportation, lack of washroom facilities, desire to get out, rate too high. (12) Improper time standards, fear of rate cut, lax discipline, lack of interest. (13) Severity of discipline, natural dishonesty, low wage. (14) Laxity, lack of knowledge, lack of interest.	(1) Indifference, desire to turn out more work, device improperly designed. (2) Investigate, remove cause, personal talk, (3) Create interest in job, help obtain transportation. (4) Better instructions, check supervision, transfer to other work, (5) Personal talk, safety hazard explained, (6) Check supervisor's tolerance, allow clean-up time. (7) Investigate cause, give square deal, set up objective merit rating. Transfer, investigate wages inequity, check to see if work has been recognised. Investigate and recommend social outlets, redefine task, make employee realise that talking bothers others. Investigate reason, transfer, if personal issue try to settle or transfer, buildup interest in job. Better communication, give facts in understandable terms, buildup purpose of his job. Show safety movie, talk on personal danger, check time standards, check safety-aid design, penalty. Show safety hazard, get group action against, check task assignment,some social-play needed on job, allow break time. Show importance of job to final product, proper motion instruction, emphasise need for quality, penalty for poor work-rework; Investigate, recognition of work, add responsibility if merited, personal talk. Insist on quality of work, provide adequate washroom for all, check quitting time and bus schedule, allow employee to go to library so as to not interrupt work if task is done. Check time standards, maintain time rates once set, be firm, show importance of good job. (15) Cut opportunities for theft, lie-detector tests are sure but serve discipline, send to psychiatrist, check home and money needs. Place on waste committee, show importance of waste reduction to him, apply penalty.

Fig. 10.7. ***Examples of Techniques Useful in Solving Human Relations Problems.***
Source : John F. Mee, *Personnel Handbook*, pp. 936-37.

WAL-MART : A MODEL IN MOTIVATION

Sam [Walton, CEO of Wal-Mart] whips out his primary tool of empowerment his tape recorder. "I'm here in Memphis at store 950, and George has done a real fine thing with this endcap display Equate Baby Oil. I'd like to try this everywhere." Georgie blushes with pride.

A manager rushes up with an associate in tow.

"Mr. Walton, I want you to meet Renee. She runs one of the top ten pet departments in the country."

'Well, Renee, bless your heart. What percentage of store (sales) are you doing?"

"Last year it was 3.1 per cent," Renee says, "but this year I'm trying for 3.3 per cent."

This situation, as recalled by *Fortune* reporter, John Huey, typifies the management style of Sam Walton, founder of and inspiration behind Wal-Mart. For many years, such situations were commonplace as Walton and his tape recorder visited stores around the country. Until the organisation became too big, he visited every Wal-Mart store at least once a year.

"Right now there are probably about 30 stores I've never been to and a bunch of others I haven't seen in more than a little while," said Walton in the fall of 1991. "I've got to get to 'em soon." From one store in 1962, he developed his organisation into an $40 billion enterprise by the time of his death 30 years later. Walton never lost the personal touch. He was adored by his employees and took every step necessary, including buying airplanes for the Wal-Mart "air force," to remain close with the people he claimed were responsible for his company's success.

Visiting stores was as important to Walton as it was to the workers who received a personal connection to management. "This is still the most important thing I do, going around to the stores, and I'd rather do it than anything I know of. I know I'm helping our folks when I get out to the stores. I learn a lot about who's doing good things in the office, and I also see things that need fixing, and I help fix them. Any good management person in retail has got to do what I do in order to keep his finger on what's going on. You've got to have the right chemistry and the right attitude on the part of the folks who deal with the customers."

Walton's tape recorder — his "tool of empowerment"— was a constant reminder that Walton and Wal-Mart cared and listened. His taping of impromptu conversations with people at various stores not only served to refresh Walton's recollection later and remind him of things that needed to be done but also immediately demonstrated that he was listening to what his colleagues had to say. Perhaps most important about these taped conversations, however is that he later acted upon what he found out. If employees expressed dissatisfaction with their supervisors, Walton would often good-naturedly assure them, "Don't worry, I'll kick his butt." In addition, Walton treated people with respect. To start with, workers are called "associates", not employees. This indicates that these men and women have a substantial stake in the company.

"What sets us apart is that we train people to be merchants," said Walton. "We let them see all the numbers so they know exactly how they're doing within the store and within the company; they know their costs, their mark-up, their overheads and their profits. It's a big responsibility and a big opportunity. You give a department to someone like Renee and she gets at it. She learns that what's important is buying staff four gross at a time and then selling four gross. Nobody gets anything out of just standing there going through the motions."

Walton realised that all the cheerleading in the world could not feed an associate's family; therefore, he included financial incentives to keep associates happy. Profit-sharing, incentive bonus, and stock purchase plans linked associates to Wal-mart's financial success. "I know your backs are sore, and your feet hurt, but this is one of the very best Wal-Mart stores in the U.S. and no other stores have this much fun. Has sharing the profit with you made the difference? [A deafening YES! here]. A lot of companies would have shared them with the stockholders, but as you know, we don't pay much dividend."

Walton will always be remembered for the level of motivation he achieved from his Wal-Mart workforce. Indeed. Wal-Mart stands as a model that many strive to emulate. "Because of what he has done, virtually every consumer in this country is better off," said retail analyst, Kurt Barnard. "Giant corporations in the world of industry send their key executives to Bentonville, Arkansas, to learn how it is done."

Glass Takes Over Where "Mr. Sam" Left Off

Sam Walton had charisma. His people loved "Mr. Sam," as he was known throughout the organisation. Wal-Mart's associates were motivated not only by the company's treatment of employees, but by Mr. Sam himself. When Walton died, the Wal-Mart style could have faltered. But it did not.

In 1988, four years before Walton's death, David D. Glass was named CEO of Wal-Mart. At Fall, 1992, *Fortune Survey* named him the most admired CEO. After picking up the reins at Wal-Mart, he has demonstrated that the culture instilled by Walton can be carried on without its creator.

Like Walton, Glass recognises the value of the front line associates — those who interact with the customers daily. A shopper recognising Glass as the CEO, walked up to him and said, "So you're the big man." Without missing a beat Glass responded, "Nah,...I just front this deal."

Carrying a notebook in lieu of Mr. Sam's tape-recorder, Glass continues the practice of visiting stores. On one occasion, when an employee complained that the store was not using environmentally responsible trash bags, Glass responded," No? Well, the buyer's up here today. Just go and hang him."

Glass's interaction with associates entails more than seeking them out in the stores. He is available to his associates at all hours, wherever he is. He has even been known to receive phone calls at motels where he was staying while out-of -town. One warehouse worker in Texas, who felt he was unjustly fired, tracked Glass down at 11:00 p.m. at his motel-room. The worker had called Glass's home in Bentonville, Arkansas, where Mrs. Glass freely gave the worker the number where her husband would be reached.

The result is that Wal-Mart associates aim high. "Our people are relentless," said Glass. And a large part of their drive stems from the goals and expectations Glass sets. "There's no question that his expectation is 110 per cent" noted one senior executive I mean, he never has to tell you. You know what it is before you ever talk to him."

MOTIVATION EFFORTS BY ALL MANAGERS

At Wal-Mart, it's not just the CEO who takes responsibility for motivating associates. Regional Vice presidents such as Andy Wilson, also pitch in. Just before the opening of store no. 1,784 in Salem, Oregon, Wilson offered words of encouragement:

I'm really fired up...This is going to be a great store, and I just want you to know how much we appreciate the job you're doing. Give yourselves a hand." His words echoed the often-repeated words of Walton and Glass. "My job isn't important.... You're the people who make it happen." And, after rounds of applause, the group engaged in the Wal-Mart cheer: "Give me a W! Give me an A!"

During their visits, the regional vice-presidents interact with associates on the floor to ensure that adequate service is being offered. For example, when visiting an outlet in Susanville, California, Wilson did not hesitate to point out areas of weakness. In calling attention to areas that needed work, he said to district manager Rick Crawford, "You have a great opportunity here." According to Wal-Mart standards, such comments constituted a reprimand. But he gave Crawford the authority to make and implement the necessary decisions: he told Crawford, "Whatever you need to do, do it."

The Regional Vice presidents are the executives who spend typically 200 days a year travelling and visiting the stores within their regions. Now that the organisation is too big for a single CEO to visit every store annually, it is the vice presidents' responsibility to provide the personal link between the associates on the floor and top management.

The result? A Wal-Mart family, successful as individuals and as an organisation. According to one buyer, "The biggest thing I appreciate is that we're one big family." Another buyer added, "Wal-Mart's sure has been good to me." In years to come, one of the more interesting management stories will be how well Wal-Mart managers and associates can sustain the way of doing business that Sam Walton began back in Arkansas and across rural America.

THE ADRIAN STORY

"Mr. Herman W. Stein Kraus, Chairman, Bridgeprl. Brass Company, narrates one of his memorable experiences in motivation." One of my most dramatic experiences in motivating people to work towards a common goal occurred in 1954. "We leased a United States Air Force plant in Adrian, Michigan, that had been built to make aluminum forgings and extrusions for military aircraft during World War II. It had a poor post-war performance. Five companies operated it at various times, each without success. Several strikes of long duration had created bitterness in the community. The plant stood idle much of the time and finally became known as the "white elephant." It was a bleak example of failure on a big scale, and no one in the community was proud of it.

This was a special-purpose plant which was designed and built solely to sustain the defense air-frame business. It produced large parts needed for manned military aircraft. Consequently, it was one of the earliest casualties of the new missile age—but that's a different story.

We were just beginning to get into the aluminum business, and the plant had a lot of fine equipment which we knew how to operate. So we decided to take the risk of a long-term lease on the property. We felt we could motivate the union as well as the citizens of the community to co-operate with us in turning this plant into a successful operation.

The motivation for accomplishing this could not be financial, for the union contract which had existed was one under which no company could operate successfully because of its high-cost provisions and its many crippling restrictions on operations. As for the community, there was no financial incentive big enough to encourage the people to share in the responsibility of making this plant a success. Yet, there had to be a motivation strong enough to accomplish what had not been accomplished over a period of years. It had to be broad enough so that it would weld the officials and members of the community, the union members and their leaders, and the management of the company into a team which would turn this failure into a success.

The first requisite was to build the machinery to set this powerful effort in motion. Before much progress had been made to accomplish this, however, the union leadership threatened to strike the plant unless we assumed the terms of the existing contract—a contract which had been so damaging to the operations of our predecessors they were forced to quit.

The Approach

We decided that we had to create an opportunity to explain clearly the reasons for this project in terms of the interests of each of the three groups and of each individual in those groups. It was therefore decided to invite all employees and their union leaders to a meeting where the management would state its problems through its president and the union would be invited to state its position through its international president. Public officials and leaders of the community were also invited to the meeting and offered the opportunity to ask questions of either the president of the union or the president of the company, so that the entire community would know the facts.

The motivating forces in this situation were different for each group. In the case of the union, the motivating force would have to be recognised as at least partly financial. In the case of the community, the motivating force would have to be largely pride in the community and perhaps long-range benefits from job opportunities for their people and taxes for the town. Management, of course, wanted a successful operation in the aluminum field, thereby adding to the growth of the company.

Through the help of the mayor of the city a mass meeting was organised. The international president of the union stated that no one would be authorised to speak for the union. The responsibility for motivating constructive action, therefore, rested upon the president of the company.

An overflow crowd came to the local armory where the meeting was held. The rector of the Episcopal Church had agreed to preside. He announced that there would be no one speaking for labour, but that I, as president of the company, would speak for management. I could feel the pressure of the approaching crisis. The success or failure of the enterprise rested largely upon motivating these people to join in a constructive programme of operation of the plant.

I directed my first remarks to the officials and members of the community. I indicated to them that having the largest plant in their city known as a "white elephant" and being known as a failure throughout the whole state of Michigan was in effect declaring to all their sons and daughters that they could not expect to find work in their own home town and would have to seek their careers elsewhere. This was true, because with the largest plant in town such a complete failure, no company would look with favour upon selecting Adrian as a town in which to expand its operations. The white elephant failure spoke too loudly against the future growth of the community.

It was obvious that this approach was a powerful challenge to the pride of the community and to the long-range personal interests of the fathers and mothers as well as the young people. I could sense that this argument was making a deep impression upon them. I felt certain that it would motivate them to join in any reasonable and fair programme to remove this blemish from the town and help to make the operation, a success.

About half of the audience of 1,100 consisted of men who had been employed at the plant for longer or shorter periods up to twelve years. All of them belonged to the United Automobile Workers Union. There was evidence that this group was particularly bitter toward previous managements of the plant and was determined to carry out its bitterness against the newcomer by using every obstructive tactic it knew.

I asked the union members if it made sense for a successful company like our own to come to Adrian to take over the operation of a large plant and to risk millions of dollars in the hope of making that operation successful in the face of the statement of the union leadership that they would do everything in their power to make us fail in our attempt.

I indicated to them that we did not have to come to Adrian since we were a successful company without the Adrian operation and that we were undertaking a great risk even under favourable circumstances. But we were willing to undertake this risk if we had the co-operation of the people and the members of the union. Without that, however, we would surely fail, as others had failed.

I painted a picture of what it would mean if the union members, their leaders, the town fathers, the citizens, and the management of our company decided that together we would tackle this problem and do everything in our power to make a success of the enterprise. I emphasised that seniority in a successful plant is worth something, whereas seniority in a failing plant is worthless because there is no employment.

I stressed the characteristics of sportsmanship and fair play, which are inherent characteristics of the American people. I played all the stops I could. I tried to show them what success in this venture would bring, not only in financial rewards to all three of the major parties, but also in bringing prestige to the community and to the union for helping us instead of hindering us.

A question-and-answer period followed, which lasted about an hour. Many questions were asked by members of the union, and they were answered frankly and fairly without accepting responsibility for past failures, but giving assurance of our ability to operate the plant successfully if we could count on their help.

A Major Breakthrough

The first sign of success in creating powerful motives became evident when a tall, white-haired Abraham Lincoln type of man came walking up the centre aisle to the platform and took the microphone. Here is approximately what he said:

At first I wasn't coming to this meeting tonight because I felt nothing could be accomplished, but in listening to the radio and reading the local and Detroit papers, which were full of stories about our controversy here, I changed my mind.

I needn't tell you who I am. You know me. I was born in this town seventy-five years ago, and I have lived here all my life. I can remember when Adrian was just as important to the state of Michigan as Pontiac and Flint.

However, we didn't seem to care whether industry came to our community or not, and today we find ourselves way behind in the creation of opportunities for our children and our grandchildren, while Pontiac and Flint have become large, important cities in Michigan.

In 1937, when the CIO was organised, I became the counsel for your union, and I have given you advice from that time until now. I have listened to this man, and I am sure that the citizens of this community must take a greater interest in its future if we are going to be fair to our children. This means we have to solve the problem of this great white elephant plant, and we must help this management do so.

Now I want to give you union men the best advice I can. At my age I have no axe to grind. Forget the disappointments of the past. Put your shoulder to the wheel to help this fine company and its management operate this plant successfully to give you steady employment and a chance for advancement. Help wipe out the blot of failure which this plant carries. This can be done only by a successful firm coming in and operating it with the full and wholehearted support of the community and the union.

When that meeting was adjourned the union leadership and the management came to a fair written agreement, and all steps for starting the operation were taken.

Results

All the members of the plant were made charter members of an organisation promptly formed and called the White Elephant Club. Its purpose was to bring the plant to a successful operation, and it was understood that in the first month the plant operated in the black would be marked by a celebration dinner in Detroit at the expense of the company.

It wasn't long before the governor of the state, the senators and congressmen, and the local town officials all became honorary members of the White Elephant Club.

A huge celebration was held 14 months later, attended by the governor and many other dignitaries, at which time a huge, white papier-mache elephant'was painted a rosy pink by the 700 workers in attendance. The same powers of motivation with which this effort was started are still forceful and showing results. The National Public Relations Association selected the Adrian story for a special award. Instead of only the company accepting this award, we insisted that it must be a three-way award and that it should be given jointly to the mayor of Adrian, the president of the local union, and the industrial-relations manager of the plant as representatives of the three forces that had united to make the undertaking a success.

OGAWA'S PHILOSOPHY AND PRACTICE OF MOTIVATING PEOPLE

Mr. Morimasa Ogawa, Managing Director of Matsushita, Oriyorises shares how he motivates his people :

Keep the Company Vital

Twice in my career I lost my job when the company I worked for went bankrupt. The second failure was particularly hard, because as president of the labour union I had to help workers get their severance pay and help them find new jobs. So dismal was the situation that several union members and relatives of workers attempted suicide. It was a tragedy I will never forget as long as I live. It made me realise the magnitude of a manager's responsibility. He cannot allow corporate failure to occur, for the loss of jobs can cause severe hardship to the employees who put their faith in the company; it can even cause them to give up on life itself.

When a crisis looms, the entire company, managers and employees alike, must shift gears and press on. Once, after I became a division manager at Matsushita Electric, my division went into the red. One way we met the challenge was by tossing out the aggressive slogans we had been using, such as "Increase market share by five per cent" and adopting more sober ones, like; "Make enough to pay the wages." We posted these slogans in the offices, on the factory floor, and at the entrance to the building. I got into some trouble for this because at the time the company had launched a campaign to encourage public tours of our facilities, and the signs were obviously not what they wanted the visitors to see. But the signs stayed up for a year and a half until we got out of the red. We developed a strong sense of solidarity, and the crisis fostered a cost-consciousness that helped lay a solid foundation for the division's subsequent growth.

Everyone Is Responsible

"When I joined Matsushita Electric—after the company where I had worked for eight years went bankrupt —all I wanted to do was work hard, keep out of trouble (as a labour leader, I had been branded a "troublemaker"), and quietly draw my pay for the 20 years until retirement. I'm ashamed to admit its. but that is exactly how I felt. I soon found, however, that my career was not to be so uneventful.

"My involvement in the research and development (R&D) of Matsushita's first microwave oven led to my being put in charge of the division. The first microwaves were so expensive that the sales outlets avoided them; our stocks were piling up and our capital resources were rapidly declining. There was nothing to do but stop production and send everyone in the division—at that time there were about 40 employees —out as salesmen to try to get rid of our stock. I was perplexed by the situation because I had been under the impression that the sales outlets (the National/Panasonic shops) would automatically sell anything with the National/Panasonic trademark. Obviously they wouldn't. We didn't even have enough money to pay our salaries, so we had to get out and sell the microwaves ourselves, door to door if necessary. Going out to sell what they had made created a sense of responsibility among the employees and made them realise that the success of the microwave division was up to them. They had to succeed; their livelihoods depended on it. We continued the practice of taking turns at sales until it became a tradition, and even when the division had 500 employees, more than half of them had direct sales experience. The microwave oven division was proud of the willingness of everyone, from manager to lineworker, to drop everything and work "door to door" if sales dropped off. Every employee felt responsible for the success of the business.

Excess Inventory is the Root of All Evil

After the microwave oven division's domestic sales passed the ¥10 billion mark, a new type of oven—one with a convection heater built into a microwave oven —burst on the market and caused a sharp drop in the sales of older models. The outlets were filled with perfectly good merchandise that wouldn't sell. We finally came to the only feasible decision: we recalled all the old models from the shops. This reactivated the market and got sales moving briskly, but it also filled our warehouses with returned goods. Since these were good products in inventory, they generated in accounting terms neither profit nor loss. But these older models were fast becoming obsolete. We considered selling them at a cut rate, but that would have disrupted the market and created customer distrust of sales outlets that had been selling the product at list price. Neither the function nor the quality of the products were defective, but, stymied by warehouses full of them, I began to think of them as "the root of all evil."

I decided to exorcize this evil. First, I apologised to all the employees for the problems that had been caused by my failure as division manager. Then I ordered the destruction of all of the microwave ovens in the warehouse, over the equivalent of one month of production volume. Besides seeing the large amounts of red ink generated by the destruction, I watched as trucks hauled off the excess inventory, produced by the sweat of the people working under me, to be rendered into scrap. It was heart-breaking, and it taught me what would become a basic principle of my management philosophy: good products should not be allowed to pile up in the warehouse.

About 10 years after leaving the microwave oven division, I returned for a visit. Sales were fairly strong, but I noticed that part of the factory was shut down. When I asked why, I was told that the division was planning to put a new product or the market soon, so production was being reduced to cut inventory to zero. I was delighted to see that my management philosophy had been implemented and had become part of the regular management procedure.

A Company is not a Product

A corporate philosophy can be developed and become a vigorous motivating force for a company only if its management and employees have a sincere commitment to the future of the firm. I realised this when I met the president of an American company that we had contracted to supply us with a product.

The item was already being manufactured in Japan, so we supplied the blueprints and standards, as well as existing press tools and dies, to the American manufacturer. A test run was made, and the quality was declared acceptable. We were guaranteed the large volume we needed and the manufacturer was extremely happy, but the price of the item was too high. When I questioned this, he showed me his books. We checked the accounts and I was astonished to see he was making a profit close to twenty per cent. I asked him, "How can you expect such high returns when we've provided you with the base? This is excessive!" He replied, "I have to make this much profit in order to be in a good bargaining position when I try to sell the company."

Hanging on the wall of his office were portraits of his grandfather, the founder of the company, and his father, the second president. "You're the third-generation owner and president of this company. How can you sell a company that your grandfather worked so hard to make into such a profitable business?" Non-plussed, he said, "Isn't that the natural thing to do when you get a good offer? Would you like to buy it?" His attitude shocked me. He was treating his company like a product.

Sears Roebuck's Fair Deal

When I was the manager of the Matsushita Housing Products Corporation, the manager of the household heating products division at Sears Roebuck visited us. He said they wanted to sell kerosene space heaters, and asked if we would like to make a bid to supply them. Sears was then the world's largest department store chain, with 800 stores throughout the United States.

We had never done business with them before, and didn't even think there was a market for kerosene heaters in North America. Since the manager had taken the time to visit us, and to ensure that relations between our two companies remained friendly, I took him on a guided tour of our factory and research lab. I told him about our product concepts for the next several years and about the guidelines that we gave to our Matsushita retail stores. I also informed him that we required the store employees to learn the proper operation of the products so that they could instruct the customer on the proper operation of the heaters and provide good follow-up service. After the tour we gave him an estimate that was by no means low, and we hardly expected to get an order. We were surprised when a large order did in fact come in. At the end of the season. I was invited to visit Sears' Chicago headquarters where we were given a merit award and I was honored at a special dinner.

At that banquet, Sears Vice-President pointed out that Matsushita's and Sears' policies and methods meshed nicely. Even though our prices were not the lowest, Sears had chosen us because:

- the price was reasonable
- the quality and design were good
- co-operation in training and after-sales service were provided
- our response to further orders was flexible
- planning for new products looked at least three years into the future
- our operations were stable

Sears' basic philosophy is that it takes full responsibility for any product it sells, and all products sold in its stores are Sears products. For Sears to operate on that kind of philosophy, it needs suppliers who can meet its requirements.

Sears' philosophy and policies are what give people confidence and provide the basis for its dealings with more than 20,000 product suppliers from around the world. It happened that Matsushita was in total accord with those policies. Sears is a successful operation because it takes responsibility for the products its sells and gives everybody, suppliers and customers alike, a fair deal.

11 Developing Future Management

• Introduction • The Need and problem of Executive Development • A Set of Objectives • Growth • Some Attitudinal Blocks • Executive Development Policy• Executive Resources Planning • Executive Performance Appraisal• Inter-Industry Out-Company Programmes • Utilisation of Trained Executives• Executive Development Research• Executive Development Organisation• Communicating Executive Development Effort

INTRODUCTION

The chapter discusses the following areas of executive development drawn heavily from my publications, research, experiments and experiences of Global Companies where I had the pleasure of visiting top Institutions, Companies and Universities around the world and learning from the vast and varied experiences.

THE NEED AND PROBLEM OF EXECUTIVE DEVELOPMENT

The outlook for the years ahead suggests that the development of business and industrial executives will require substantial effort. Several conditions point to this :[1]

(a) The competition for talent capable of development.

(b) The continued growth and development of business.

(c) Increasing complexity and sophistication of business.

(d) Probable continued unsettled social, political and economic conditions (both domestic and world-wide) that add to the demands on executives.

(e) The need to press for continually improving performance despite these complicating factors.

(f) The need to compress the time taken for an executive to become fully competent.

A SET OF OBJECTIVES

Executive development is a process of growing leadership. It refers to all of the actions or influences — whether generated by the executive being developed, his boss, his associates or his company — that affect what he knows and can do, how he thinks, how he works, and how he grows as an executive. Some of the major objectives of executive development are :

(a) To assure executives in required numbers and with the required skills to meet the anticipated future needs of the business.

(b) To encourage executives to grow as persons and in their capacity to handle greater responsibility.

(c) To improve the performance of executives at all levels in the jobs they now hold.

(d) To sustain good performance of executives throughout their careers.

Some Basic Questions

The first real step towards "right thinking" is asking the right questions. When one has asked the right questions he has cleared the air somewhat about his problem and he has placed himself open to the discussion of these questions, out

1. M.N. Rudrabasavaraj, Executive Development, A Model and A Point of View, (Kolkata, Indian Institute of Personnel Management 2000 (revised) pp. 1 - 32, see also M.N. Rudrabasavaraj, Executive Development in India (Mumbai, Himalaya Publishing House, 1977). M.N. Rudrabasavaraj, Executive Development in the Public Sector, New Delhi, Orient Longman, 1974 for a very detailed treatment of the problems and techniques.

of which may emerge a higher level of certainty about action to be taken. This may sound like an overly-philosophical approach. But let us not forget that we are dealing with an important aspect of human development; and thoughtful men have been preoccupied about this matter since the beginning of recorded history. Yet, there is very little dependable codified knowledge available about it.

The following are a few questions of the kind that need to be asked and a brief comment about each :

1. Is my business getting the people it needs and wants?

What the individual brings with him in the form of intelligence, knowledge, integrity, drives, attitudes, emotional stability and health have a determining influence on subsequent development.

The access which any company has to those high in development potential rests on two questions. We need to ask :

(a) How is the company viewed by people it would like to hire? Do they see the business as offering challenge and opportunity to men of high potential? Is this business seen as attractive to the kind of people it needs?

(b) Is the selection process, discriminating enough to bring in those best suited and to reject the others? And are those who clearly will not prosper in your company separated early in their careers, both for their own good and for the good of your business?

2. Are the early formative years of promising young people being used effectively?

3. Do individuals assume responsibility for their own growth?

4. Are we realistic about what teaching the knowledge and skills of management requires?

5. Is the search for new knowledge (an indispensable condition of a sound organisation) being used effectively in the development of executives? Participation in a formal study of some aspect of the business, done at the right time in a man's career and with the right "mission", is one of the surest ways to help a man grow in management stature, particularly if it gives him a broad look at his business.

6. What is the attitude of the senior executives towards growth and change in people? In the long run, the effectiveness of an organisation in developing people will depend largely upon, what the senior executives, believe about growth and change in people. If they do not have a sound point of view about growth, some development opportunities will be wasted on unpromising people.

7. Are the bosses of managers using work experience effectively for development? People learn most about management by managing and by the way they are managed. A man may learn much from working for several bosses early in his career and studying the contrasts and similarities in their ways of managing. The boss of a new manager should have a programme of things for his subordinates to learn and do. Regardless of the amount of formal executive training that is offered, both boss and subordinate should feel that the real learning of how to manage is done on the job, with real situations in which mistakes are made and where there is accountability for mistakes.

8. Are the available incentives supporting the best possible executive development? Incentives are the influence that spur the desire to perform well.

9. Is performance in management judged adequately? One of the problems that limits the effective use of the available incentives is the difficulty of accurately judging executive performance. There is little question but that executive development hangs in the balance in this one.

10. Is there "breathing space" to take the time and do the things that develop people? To develop managers an organisation must have enough people, enough resources and enough flexibility to do the right things with the right people at the right time.

11. When a manager wants to talk to some one, is there someone available to talk to? Almost everybody needs somebody to talk to occasionally. People who are growing in management competence may need more of this than others, and the person who listens needs to understand although he may not give advice.

Ideally, the boss is the man to talk to. But the boss may not be a good listener, and may be it's the boss that the man wants to talk about.

Any effort to organise formally to provide the opportunity for this will probably be futile. But a company can develop the climate in which the importance of a person talking out his problems is recognised. And it can accept, as a natural development, that some people in management will be especially sought because they are good listeners.

12. Are opportunities outside the business being used effectively in developing executives? Part of the opportunity to develop a man lies outside a company in interbusiness groups, community affairs and courses aimed directly at broadening. The boss can create some of these opportunities.

13. Is the work organised so as to aid development? The primary consideration in organising work is to get the work done. But a long run view suggests that the way the work is organised also influences the development of people.

14. Are we making work sufficiently challenging? Men tend to grow as they experience challenge and opportunity for creative achievement in what they are doing. One man may find enough challenge and opportunity in a single job so that he will be viewed as a constructive, growing man for a whole career. Another man may lose the feeling of challenge in a particular job after a while and need a fresh start. For many, at the right stage in their development, they need a tough "crisis" assignment.

The growth of the capacity to carry important responsibility is learned by carrying responsibility. The knowledge needed for a particular job may be learned by holding subordinate positions, but it is not feasible to learn all one needs to know that way. Much must be learned by observation, reading, conversation with informed persons, or by just being aware. One of the ways a boss can keep a man challenged is to encourage his search for knowledge outside the range of his immediate job. If every boss has — and communicates — a strong feeling of total responsibility for his business, valuable executive development will take place from this alone. Beyond this, the important thing is that the challenge to growth is continuous and that, of all people, the man with potential for development in management sees himself as helping to run a business and not just tending an isolated corner of it. The feeling of personal significance is very important. The issue has never been more clearly stated than in the old story of the two stonemasons when asked about their work, one replied, "I am setting stone", the other, "I am building a cathedral".

15. Are the goals of the company adequate? Do they encourage executives to grow? The growth of a man is largely the product of effort and purpose coupled with a developing spontaneity. He is more likely to emerge in his mature years as an executive capable of carrying heavy responsibility, if his own purposes are formulated early within the framework of company goals which encourage the best in him to develop, and which recognise that he in turn will influence the future goals of the company.

The substance of the company's current goals must carry impact. The man must see and hear these goals expressed often enough, clearly enough, forcefully enough, and early enough so that he can understand and believe them. Nothing much happens without a dream. Somebody looks into the future and sees some accomplishment that is impossible according to present standards; and then he persuades people that it is a goal worth striving for. Only in this way do people seem to get their eyes off the ground and build up a feeling of faith in what they are trying to do. This is the way all human institutions get started; and the revitalisation process that keeps an institution alive appears to be the same kind of thing.

GROWTH

The beliefs, of senior executives about growth and change in their subordinates will probably determine, in the long run, how well the next generation of managers comes along.

This poses a difficult problem because very little is known about growth of mature people anywhere. We can only speculate from such fragments of information as are available. This speculation suggests the following as a definition of mature growth : "Mature growth is seen as a continuous process towards the fulfilment of what a person is uniquely capable of becoming".

Therefore, the executive who helps people to grow is one who can accept the idea of each individual becoming himself and who makes an effective team out of such people.

Growth is a risk-taking process. This is one of the first things a young person needs to learn in moving from academic to business life. Throughout his schooling the life of a youngster is largely risk-free, perhaps properly so. A big business may also look like this kind of life to a man just entering it. But quickly he must learn that the rewards and satisfactions no longer come wholly from doing well what others lay out for him to do. Even in the lowest management positions, he must learn to venture and 'decide' when there is not enough data to make a risk-free decision. One must use all the data one can get, and use reason as far as it will take him. But there is seldom enough data and it rarely fits together to support a certain judgment. The opportunity for success is always coupled with the risk of failure.

The growing person is likely to be a many-sided person with vital interests in family, job, religion, community, hobbies and recreation. He is probably making progress towards finding a unity and an inter-relation between all of these facets of his life. His job becomes less and less his occupation from eight to five, Monday to Friday, and his recreation becomes less and less the fun he has on week-ends.

The responsibility for personal growth of an individual is shared by all who have some influence upon him. Particularly, of course, it belongs to the individual himself. The role of the company and his boss is also of primary importance in helping a man to arrive at an understanding of what the company means by growth, what this growth might mean to the man, and in persuading him to accept the major responsibility for seeing that growth takes place within him. He should be encouraged to use all of the resources of the company wisely, which can contribute to his own growth. The company should keep the picture of his contribution to the organisation constantly before him as a stimulating, challenging and even an exciting prospect.

The view of personal growth, admittedly sketchy and built upon scattered fragments of data, has been stated deliberately in somewhat idealistic terms. It is suggested as a possible concept to move toward — never to achieve fully — because the chances are as one starts to move toward such a concept, the concept itself will have developed and improved.

PROGRESS FROM WHERE WE ARE

For a business that sees its future achievement partly in terms of developing more and better managers in a shorter period of time, five major areas of action are suggested :

1. *A clear understanding by the senior executive.* This Broadsheet has been undertaken to summarise a statement of the problem, a set of aims, some basic questions to guide our thinking, and a point of view about the question of growth after maturity. The senior executive who is going to do better in bringing along his subordinates should have a clear idea of his own, consistent with the basic company policy on all these points. It is his understanding of what he is doing that will be a determining factor.

2. *Adequate staff support.* There are two major staff fields: (a) to assist the bosses of young potential managers to watch closely the development of their subordinates, and (b) to research, to advise and teach the senior executives in order to support the best possible performance by them in developing their subordinates. The executive development staff should be concerned with the whole range of questions outlined above under *"Some Basic Questions"*. Perhaps this is only a part-time job in a small company, but nevertheless it is definitely a staff role.

3. *Effective formal classroom training where needed.* In an ideal situation, there will be little need for formal classroom training of executives. But we will never reach the ideal; so we will probably continue to do a substantial amount of formal executive training. In proceeding on this assumption there are four danger signs: (a) the pressure to do the pleasant and the popular, (b) the tendency for all things to crystallise and become static, (c) the illusion, on the part of either the trainee or his boss, that his development needs are fully taken care of by formal training, and (d) the failure of the boss to make clear what he expects to result from the training.

4. *Learning to operate less by tradition or routine and more by theory and experiment.* This means simply that in the area of how our business is managed we must, to a greater extent, extract and formulate principles from experience and research, explicitly test these principles in action, carefully examine how the principles work in practice, refine or modify the principles as the testing indicates, put them into practice again, and keep this process going as long as there is a strong urge in the management of a company to maintain a dynamic and growing business.

5. *Compelling company goals.* We live in a business-dominated society. This is something new in the world. The cumulative effect of the decisions of businessmen and business managers probably has more to do with shaping the character of our society than any other force.

The problems of size, new forms of competition, competition for capital, continued social, political and economic change, the continued urge to improve performance, all combine to suggest that the executive of tomorrow will face more exacting demands than those faced by executives today. And there will be considerable incentive to shorten the time taken for executives to become effective in their jobs.

The basic question we should be asking is not : "What does the future as we foresee it require of us?" though we should follow this inquiry as far as it will take us.

Rather, for those who have some share in bringing along the next generation of executives, the really fundamental question is : "What should we like that future to be?" For the future is not some inevitable pattern demanding that we conform to it. The future is being made now by people like us; by the faith which our choices demonstrate and what this communicates, especially to young people in business.

SOME ATTITUDINAL BLOCKS

Having said all that, it may be fair to admit there will be some who would find that all this effort is not worth it. There are some attitudinal blocks on the part of some executives. Briefly they are :

1. Executives are born, not made.
2. Why develop and train? Just buy.
3. Appoint a training man and leave it to him.
4. Personnel man should take care of the people and their development.
5. Executives are too busy to be developed.
6. Let us do the 'done thing'.

It is needless to over-emphasise the fact that such attitudinal blocks need to be overcome, if the organisation wishes to play a positive role in executive development effort.

SOME ESSENTIAL PREREQUISITES

The organisation (1) should be totally committed to the concept of the development of individuals, (2) must evolve and implement an effective programme with competent staff support and assistance, and (3) must provide an organisational climate and environment where individuals want to reach their maximum capabilities. Executive Development Programme is a system; with inter-related and inter-dependent phases of activities and it is essential to use a system approach where every critical input performs a prescribed task in a chronological sequence. Some of the essentials are :

1. Top management support and commitment.
2. Responsibility of the executive to develop his subordinates.
3. Executive Resources Planning and Career Development Plans.
4. Perception of development needs.
5. Effective Executive Development policy, programme and practice by competent specialists.
6. Evaluation of Executive Development Programme.
7. Organisational climate.

EXECUTIVE DEVELOPMENT POLICY

In order to achieve Executive Development objectives there is a need to formulate policies that would provide guidelines to thinking and action.

We suggest that the company's policy should be to organise an Executive Development Committee membered by the top executives of the company. The objective of this Committee is to review the executive resources, their performance and potential and plan their development.

There is a need to evolve Executive Development policies on :

1. the strategy of executive development — in-company or out-company programmes;
2. instructional methods in in-company programmes;

3. developmental approaches to be used in executive development process;
4. identification of individual developmental needs;
5. evaluation of out-company programmes;
6. utilisation of training personnel;
7. executive development budget; and
8. executive development, as an integral part of general personnel processes.

All the executives should be exposed to training and development and it should be the responsibility of every manager to develop his subordinates. Here, the companies must take a policy decision that every manager will be appraised on the basis of the above-criterion.

EXECUTIVE RESOURCES PLANNING

Executive resources planning is perhaps the crucial element in an effective and successful executive development system and without this critical input everything else done in Executive Development effort proves fruitless.

Dovetailing Executive Resources Planning with Business Plans :

It is essential that efforts to develop executives are put into effect with thorough consideration of the probable growth and changes in various functions of the companies. There are two major problems that crop up if Executive Development is not dovetailed with the total plans of the future of the company. First, the effort that is dictated by whim or fad may well be useless. Secondly, and more seriously, the problems can arise when business plans do not guide Executive Development and executive personnel implications are taken up only as an after-thought. For example, many Banking companies have committed themselves to Executive Development Programmes and equipment for rural banking with scant attention to the knowledge and skills which are required to operate such facilities. When it is determined that branches in urban, semi-urban and rural areas should attempt to be total banking-centres for their communities, it is apparent that major efforts to reducate present managers and to find additional people with different knowledge, skills and habits would be required.

There are four major elements in the process of executive resources planning that should claim the attention of the companies :

1. Executive resources inventory.
2. Executive resources forecasting.
3. Career development plans.
4. Management succession systems.

Executive resources planning is concerned with the implementation of the basic human resources objective of having the right people in the right place at the right time. Viewed in this light, the activities necessary to implement executive resources planning become as much an integral part of the human resources function as any other activity in the human resources development.

The need for a practical approach to executive resource planning is based on the obvious requirements of the organisational situation. As many companies are aware, the situation calls for advance planning and preparation with respect to executive manpower in much the same way it does with respect to buying and selling.

(a) Executive Resources Inventory

As a starting point, for executive resource planning in a going concern, information about future requirements would be just worthless unless accompanied by adequate information about present executive resources. In addition to knowing how many executives there are in the companies, in various categories and levels, we must find out in detail many other relevant aspects. In planning future utilisation of manpower, particularly at the managerial level, it is not enough to know that the present executive calibre is made up of so many executives in this and that kind of position. It is essential to have certain information about each executive's individuality. What kind of training and experience has he had? How old is he?

Is his health an asset or liability to his qualifications? What kind of ability has he demonstrated? Is he reliable, dependable? Is he capable of assuming greater responsibilities?

The importance of having information which will answer these and other similar questions is quite obvious. Effective planning to utilise present executive resources on future requirements simply cannot take place without it.

Each company should design an Executive Resources Inventory file containing basic information regarding the individual, his education, training and development, experience for executive resources requirements. This must be constantly updated so that the information is adequate and is in readily usable form. Three simple tests are suggested for determining whether executive resources inventory is adequate and put up in readily usable form :

1. Is it portable?
2. Is it in constant readiness to be taken into a meeting at short notice?
3. Will it quickly provide the pertinent information needed to make personnel decisions objectively with respect to filling vacancies, recruitment needs, development programmes, etc.?

Development of Executive Resources Inventory : The approach consists of:

1. Establishing and maintaining an inventory of present executive resources.
2. Setting up and maintaining a separate record of employees considered immediately qualified for promotion.

(b) Executive Resources Forecasting

Once we know "what we do have" the next step is "what we do need" taking into consideration our future growth plans. Forecasting executive resources requirements is the means of gaining the "necessary time to meet future requirements in the most effective manner possible". The dependence of advance planning and preparation on forecast information raises two issues : What kind of information is needed? How can it be developed?

The kinds of information needed : Forecasting executive resource requirements is essentially nothing more than trying to determine in advance what kind of executive employment requisitions to expect in the future. How many can be expected from the various parts of the organisation? In what lines of work? When? If the problem is visualised in this manner, the specific type of information which should go into the forecast for each part of the organisation can be readily determined.

How can it be developed : Forecasting, if it is to be done satisfactorily, must be approached in an objective manner. The problem of developing forecast information is primarily one of seeking out and systematically utilising information which will most reliably indicate future needs.

Future executive resource needs can be expected to reflect :

1. Loss of present executive resources.
2. Expansion or contraction in business.
3. Growing or declining needs for certain types of executives.

In the first instance, the resulting need will be for replacements. In the latter two, the resulting need will be for more or fewer executives, depending on the nature of the development or the direction of the trend. What kind of information is available in each of these areas which can be used in forecasting, what future executive resource requirements will be ?

For the purpose of forecasting replacement needs :

— An analysis of future separations under the retirement programme will provide one source of definite and reliable information.

— Early retirements, disability or otherwise, can frequently be determined in advance with reasonable accuracy. These can be reflected in the forecast.

— An analysis of past experience will provide a basis for projecting future loss through other types of separations such as resignations, involuntary quits, dismissals, etc.

To summarise :

1. Determine the number of replacements.
2. Adjust this figure up and down in light of:
   (a) expansion or contraction requirements;
   (b) growing or declining requirements for certain types of executives;
   (c) any long-term trends which should be reflected.

Project executive requirements sufficiently ahead to allow the necessary time to get ready to meet them. In actual practice this may mean anywhere from two to five or more years, depending on the nature of the requirements.

The Use of Forecast and Inventory Information :

Forecast and inventory information is one of the top management's most useful of human resources management tools. It is especially useful in such fundamental areas as :

(a) Planning and making personnel moves — promotions, transfers, demotions, lay-offs, etc.

(b) Determining recruitment needs.

(c) Determining training and development needs.

(d) Ensuring management the services of the best qualified executive and potential executives available.

(e) Ensuring consideration to all qualified candidates on an equitable basis.

(f) Planning changes in organisational structure.

Besides these obvious applications and uses, there are other very substantial benefits to be derived from its development, and use. For example, it will stimulate more effective personnel communications. It will serve to get attention focused in the right direction, by getting executives thinking in terms of performance, abilities, capacities, potential, etc. It will cause executives up and down the line to get better acquainted with their immediate subordinates and other employees. These benefits should not only make for a more constructive approach to dealing with the problems directly involved in meeting future executive requirements, but they should also have definite carry-over value in dealing with executive resources problems in general.

(c) Career Development Plans :

The next basic phase in executive resource planning is to get down to the specific from general executive resource planning — to individual career development plan, which would be essential for effective Executive Development effort. It will be necessary to determine career paths or development plans for every individual executive, because an individual executive when he joins a company expects a certain career within the company and it follows that the company should develop a career plan for the next immediate period of a year or two, then extend it to long-term of 4 or 5 or even 10 years as some organisations do. Individual development plan is designed to provide a record of current job assignments and performance, a projection of near and long-term potential and the development needs of the individual. It will be reviewed and revised periodically and shall be available for review by the management. The steps suggested are :

1. What is the current position responsibilities, along with the month and year assigned to the current position?
2. What is overall current performance appraisal?
3. What is his promotability? e specific. List positions to which you feel that the individual is promotable either now or within two/three years.
4. What is his possible ultimate potential?
5. Why do you say so and on what basis?
6. What are his development needs?
7. What is your development plan?
8. The development plan must be prepared and reviewed by the principal line and staff executives and dated.

(d) Management Succession Systems :

Management Succession System is the next important phase in the executive resource planning relevant and significant in Executive Development Management. Succession System should be worked out in the case of every executive position on an executive resource replacement table or a Management Succession Chart :

1. Identify the current executive position and incumbent.
2. Ascertain the age and date of appointment on the current appointment.
3. Establish the date due for replacement.
4. Determine the next appointment to which the incumbent could be promoted (unless he is retiring or quitting the company).
5. Is the incumbent ready for promotion? If not, what further training or development or experience is required ?
6. Identify the possible successors or replacements? Immediate and long-term.
7. Determine the successor's or replacement's current position, responsibilities and capacities.
8. Determine what further training or development or education or experience is required to fit successor for promotion.
9. Determine the date when the successor should be ready for promotion or succession and match this date with the date due for replacement of the incumbent.

Strategy of Executive Development

Talking about the strategy, it is essential to bear in mind that 90 per cent of the development occurs as a result of on-the-job experience — the way he manages, the way he is allowed to manage, the way his superior manages and the impact of his style on the subordinate, and the general environment created by the management system in vogue. Formal training and development programmes affect only 10 per cent of his development. Hence, the best of formal development programmes cannot help the individual much if he is unable to use new learning, knowledge, skills and techniques.

We suggest a combined unified strategy of Executive Development as depicted in the chart.

11.1 UNIFIED STRATEGY OF EXECUTIVE DEVELOPMENT

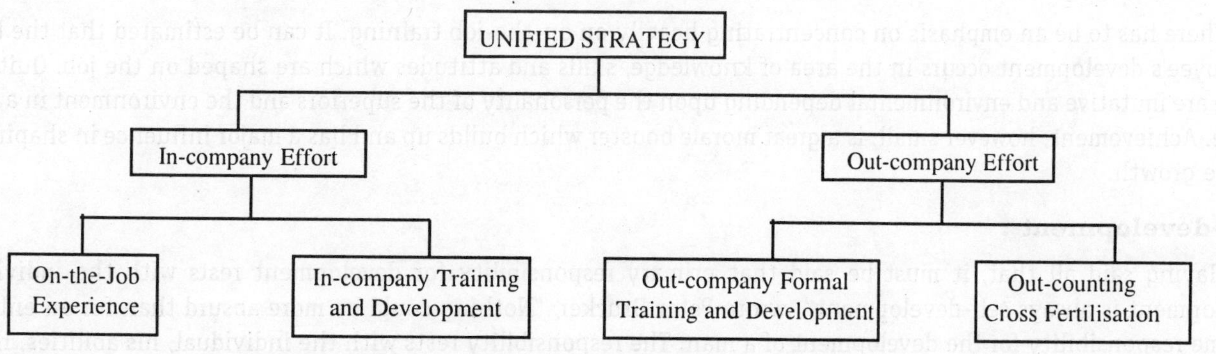

In our scheme, the in-company on-the-job experience plays critical role in the strategy of Executive Development. It is fair to concede that the executive or manager " *manages* " and uses the process of management.

Definition of Management :

Management is the total executive process of planning, organising, motivating, co-ordinating and controlling with a view to achieving predetermined ends with economy and effectiveness.

Management is not learnt by textbooks or formal training programmes but by managing, *i.e.*, by planning, organising, motivating, directing, co-ordinating and controlling. So he must manage and be allowed to manage.

Decentralisation and Delegation :

Decentralisation and delegation of authority commensurate with responsibility would set an organisational pattern that encourages and gives the freedom to the executive to manage and, by managing, he gains more insight into the process of management and acquires the skill and art of management.

Management Style of the Superior :

In the process of managing, he is to a great extent guided by the style of management of his superior and he tends to observe and imitate him quite unconsciously. Management used in the company also has a powerful influence on the way he would act.

Responsibility of Every Executive :

Every executive must be made responsible for the development of his subordinates. He must guide, counsel and coach the subordinate and he must encourage the individual to show initiative and to come with new ideas and must be prepared to allow him to experiment and test his ideas. Without it, there cannot be much growth.

Everybody Must and Can be Developed :

Often senior executives believe they need no development because they feel they are "fully developed". There is no such thing and everybody must and can be developed and there is a lot of room at the top for improvement. It is a wise man who perceives his needs, strengths, weaknesses and aspirations. If you do not know what you do not know, you had it! Knowing what you know and what you do not know is the hallmark of true wisdom.

Leadership :

It is best to remember that formal training is but a supporting function and cannot take care of the whole range of development of staff at all levels and at all stages. In an organisation, if the training responsibilities are but indifferently appreciated, the achievements can never be up to expectations.

Executive development cannot be limited in range to starting a college or sending an executive on a course. For instance, clearly spelt out organisational objective, a diligently implemented system of recruitment, delegation and accountability, pre-planned proper utilisation of human resources, managers who know their job and have leadership qualities, are all essential ingredients of the total atmosphere in which to build up people.

Even in the US., where there is much emphasis on training, only about 5 per cent of a member's entire career is spent on formal training.

There has to be an emphasis on concentrating heavily on on-the-job training. It can be estimated that the bulk of an employee's development occurs in the area of knowledge, skills and attitudes which are shaped on the job. Quite a few of these are imitative and environmental depending upon the personality of the superiors and the environment in a particular office. Achievement, however small, is a great morale booster which builds up and has a major influence in shaping a man's future growth.

Self-development :

Having said all that, it must be said that primary responsibility for development rests with the individual "For development is always self-development", wrote Peter Drucker, "Nothing could be more absurd than for an enterprise to assume responsibility for the development of a man. The responsibility rests with the individual, his abilities, his efforts. No business enterprise is competent,. let alone obligated, to substitute its efforts for the self-development efforts of the individual. To do this would not only be unwarranted paternalism, it would be foolish pretension".

The Role of the Individual — Some Essentials :

The whole of Individual Development Scheme is for the benefit and growth of individual executive, with the firm belief that in the growth of the individual lies the corporate growth. Hence the individual has a key role to play. The individual executive has to meet certain essential conditions.

1. The individual is committed to his self-development.
2. He perceives his developmental needs.
3. He goes along with the strategy of development of the company, preferably having a say in it.
4. He is committed to the concept of self-actualisation[1].
5. He is committed to the concept of self-renewal and self-innovation.
6. He associates his interests with organisational interests.
7. He co-operates with the company in Individual Development Scheme.

   Here also, these conditions are easier stated than realised. In the actual business world, the individual has his own inhibitions.

What are some of his problems?

1. The individual does not take responsibility for his own development.
2. He takes the attitude : "Well, let the company develop me. Why should I bother?"
3. He does not see any needs for development or training.
4. He feels that he is at the top; hence, no more of the training routine for him.
5. He feels that he is at his best; so, no more development necessary.
6. He takes this fatalistic attitude : "Either I have got it or I don't; why sweat about it?"[2]

We might well agree that no development can take place when the individual, has these attitudes. These problems have to be surmounted by the individual and he can do so himself; also with the help of the company.

The individual must show initiative, ingenuity and inventiveness. He must play a positive role and be an active partner in the schemes for Executive Development.

It is extremely important to integrate the organisational needs with individual needs and here one may adopt what late Professor McGregor called the "agricultural approach" to executive development, where the fundamental idea is that the individual will grow into what he is uniquely capable of becoming, provided we can create the proper conditions for the growth. " Such an approach involves less emphasis on manufacturing techniques and more on controlling the climate, fertility of the soil and methods of cultivation."

PERCEPTION OF INDIVIDUAL NEEDS

Companies must take a policy decision that they will always depute or put an executive on development programme only after identifying his needs of development. Perception of individual development needs can be accomplished through:

1. Recommendations of the superior/need of the department.
2. Analysis of job requirements.
3. Executive performance appraisal.
4. Suggestions by individual executives.
5. Report of the management consultant.
6. Peer suggestion.
7. Chairman's suggestion.

---

1. Prof. A. H. Maslow has identified self-actualisers to possess some attitudes such as: (1) commitment to work; (2) self-acceptance; (3) tolerance to uncertainty; (4) realism; and (5) appreciation.
2. Prof. Peter, author of *"Peter Principle"* says that some individuals just do not want development and as a consequence further promotion, because they are afraid that they might find their level of incompetence. His ' Principle' states: "In an hierarchy, every employee tends to rise to his level of incompetence".

Methods of Determining Training Needs are :

1. Analysis of an activity
2. Analysis of problems
3. Analysis of behaviour
4. Analysis of an organisation
5. Appraisal of performance
6. Brainstorming
7. Buzzing
8. Card sort
9. Checklist
10. Committee
11. Comparison
12. Conference
13. Consultants
14. Counselling
15. In basket
16. Incident pattern
17. Informal talks
18. Interviews
19. Observation
20. Problem clinic
21. Research
22. Role playing
23. Self-analysis
24. Simulation
25. Skills inventory
26. Slip writing
27. Studies
28. Surveys
29. Tests
30. Task force
31. Questionnaire
32. Workshop

EXECUTIVE PERFORMANCE APPRAISAL

We suggest a continuous appraisal system, instead of annual ritual and emphasis is on two aspects : (1) How well is he doing? (2) How can we improve his performance through development? There are various types of appraisals that are available to managements and they are :

1. Point system with weights for each factor.
2. Non-point system with a chart or form describing the factors to be appraised.
3. The rank-order - or forced-distribution method, in which each supervisor ranks his employees on overall performance of each employee or divides them into groups such as top 10 per cent, the next 20 per cent etc.
4. The field-review method in which the performance of each employee is reviewed in detail by the supervisor with the help of the personnel department.
5. The critical incident method.
6. Management by objectives method.
7. Self-appraisal.

The last three methods may be useful in respect of management staff. The management by objectives method would of course require adequate management information systems and reporting systems to be used effectively. Management by objectives would mainly comprise

(a) Position description,

(b) Definition of objectives, key tasks and targets, and

(c) Appraisal.

Typical Stages of a Good Performance Appraisal

1. An appraisal of the subordinate's job performance is written by his superior.
2. The superior submits the written appraisals to a committee which reviews and approves it.
3. The superior discusses the appraisal with the subordinate in a private interview.
4. The superior and the subordinate together prepare an individual development programme for the subordinate.

A Continuous Custom-made Performance Appraisal — An Alternate Proposal :

We suggest that the companies should adopt a continuous appraisal, where the appraiser watches and keeps a dossier on the subordinate, where he notes the highlights of the subordinate's performance during the course of the year as well as his short-comings in performance. With such a dossier the appraiser is on surer ground at the time of confrontation with the subordinate at the end of the year. Here the appraiser is on his toes through-out, not come alive only at the time of the annual ritual and then go back to sleep over the appraisals.

The Custom-made Appraisal is narrative or open-end type of appraisal, where ready-made answers are provided and you just check somewhat safely in the middle. We recommend a simple appraisal form that requires the appraiser to write answers to the following :

1. What are the employee's strengths?
2. What are the employee's weaknesses or areas that need development?
3. What is the employee's overall job performance?

This appraisal is custom-made to the individual being appraised by comparing his actual job performance with the performance expected of him (through a concept like management by objectives) by the superior. Conspicuous by its absence in this type of form is a list of traits or characteristics that might be checked off in varying degrees, ranging from poor to superior. Many times, degrees of such items as 'leadership', 'enthusiasm', and 'loyalty' have led to bickering between the author of the appraisal and the man being appraised and have thus diverted all concerned from the true purpose of appraisal. They also soon lead to a discussion of personality.

The Foundation for Research on Human Behaviour at Ann Arbor, Michigan, in a recent report entitled : "Performance Appraisal and Review" makes this statement :

"Personality ratings are notoriously unreliable, for the same man will be rated differently by different people. Appraisal of performance is more reliable and consistent. People can be more objective about their jobs, for they generally know how to improve results, while they seldom know how to change their personalities."

Review and Check

The written appraisal must be checked and reviewed by several people, preferably in a committee, so that it may be based on more objective considerations and deliberation and it may have the complete support of management. Often there are complaints that the superior was prejudiced or there was a snap judgment.

Appraisal Interview

The next important step is the appraisal interview where the employee finds out where he stands and what they think of his performance. This also gives the appraiser an opportunity to fully explain the details of the appraisal so that the employee is fully aware of his strengths and weaknesses. The interview provides the appraiser an opportunity to find out what the employee thinks of the facilities and job conditions provided by the management and what improvement management could make in them.

Personal Development Programme

A successful appraisal interview will provide time for a *joint determination* by the appraised employee and his superior of just what steps the employee should take to capitalise on his strengths and overcome his weaknesses. We would like to emphasise the joint aspect of this determination, for in the final analysis only the employee himself can bring about the desired changes in his job behaviour and attitude.

Training for Appraisers

There is a need for training the appraiser in the appraisal concepts, tools and techniques. The training programme accomplishes the following ends :

1. Instructs in techniques of writing appraisals.
2. Points out the pitfalls to be avoided in writing appraisals, *e.g.*, the halo effect, the constant error, the error of recent events and personal prejudices.
3. Gives each participant in the training programme an opportunity to write a sample appraisal.
4. Offers each participant training in the fundamentals of conducting an appraisal interview, with an opportunity to role-play a part in a mock appraisal interview.

5. Points out the steps to take in creating an effective personal development programme with an employee.

In-company Programme

To maintain a down-to-earth approach, a development programme should meet the following criteria :

1. It should be based on a real need.
2. It should be targeted at the areas where the need is great.
3. It should stress the development of an individual's ability to think effectively and his skill in human relations.
4. In so far as possible, it should be integrated into regular operations.
5. Since we learn best by "doing", the methods employed should be as close to "doing" as possible.
6. Methods should be appropriate to the status of the personnel involved. Development methods will work and achieve best results when individuals realise the benefits to themselves and want the programme.

Broadly, two types of developmental processes can be identified with In-company Programmes— (1) on-the-job experience, (2) formal training and development programmes. Let us first turn to a discussion of various on-the-job experiences that would assist in the Executive Development effort.

1. On-the-job training.
2. Planned progression.
3. Rotational assignments.
   (a) Trainee rotation in non-supervisory work situation (as is done during probation).
   (b) Rotation on observation assignment.
   (c) Rotation among managerial training position.
   (d) Middle level in "assistant" position.
   (e) Creation of 'assistant to' positions.
4. Understudy.
5. Temporary promotions.
6. Committee and Junior Boards.
7. Conference programmes.
8. Management Workshop programmes.
9. Coaching.
10. Special assignments.
11. Staff assignments.
12. Planned reading programme.
13. Inter-departmental meeting.
14. Management periodicals.
15. Executive position enlargement.
16. "Ring" system.
17. Problem solving conferences.

Planned Progression : The technique of planned progression is concerned with blue-printing the path of promotion that lies before the manager who occupies a given position. The path may be traced through the successive levels of the organisation structure within one department. But this may lead to narrow excessive specialisation without diversified experience. However, the path may be traced through three or four departments providing broad experience and wide opportunities.

Job Rotation : This is a plan geared to provide diversified training. There are varieties of job rotation.

(a) Trainee Rotation in Non-supervisory Work situations : The selected candidates for training are assigned to predetermined jobs within a list of departments for a given period of time. The purpose is to acquaint trainees with the range of activities undertaken by the firm. But the problem is that employees may resent the trainees and their preferred position and also the fact that trainees may take away the jobs from the permanent help. The trainee also may be discouraged during this type of training.

(b) Trainee Rotation in Observation Assignments : This concept envisages the creation of opportunities for trainees to observe a group of department managers on a rotating basis. The purpose is to acquaint the trainee with the various managerial problems and their solutions. This gives an opportunity for the trainee to "sell" himself and to learn the type of work he would like to do. But observing and doing are two different things and it does not provide any practical-experience. Many executives also feel that candidates do not know what to observe and how.

(c) Rotation among Managerial Training Positions : This involves the designation of certain managerial positions on the same level in the organisation structure as training stations to be successively occupied by trainees. The purpose is to give actual supervisory experience in a variety of positions in several departments. But when suitable placement is not forthcoming after training, disillusion grows greater on the part of the trainee.

(d) Middle-level Rotation in 'Assistant' Position : This involves shuffling trainees as assistant managers in several departments. The purpose is to broaden their experience at high level in each department. This creates a pool of trainees for later appointment to department managerships.

(e) Unspecified Rotation among Managerial Positions : This is an unplanned and unspecified rotation of managers from one department to another. The purpose is to give managers responsible experience in a variety of positions.

In-company Formal Training and Development Programmes :

Well-designed and administered in-company formal training and development programmes with specific objectives, course content, teaching methodology, utilisation and evaluation should be organised from time-to-time within the Company. A top executive must be in charge of this programme assisted by the Department dealing with Executive Development. They may take the form of short courses, conferences, panel discussions, seminar, symposium, meetings, workshops, etc; depending on the content of the programme, designed to impart:

The in-company effort may be designed to impart:

1. Information-based programmes.
2. Technique-centred programmes.
3. Function-oriented programmes.
4. Skills-centred programmes.
5. Orientation programmes.
6. Management biased programmes.
7. Refresher courses.

Specially this in-company formal programmes must strive to develop the following skills:[3]

1. Leadership skills.
2. Management skills.
3. Conceptual skills.
4. Analytical skills.
5. Human relations skills.
6. Communication skills.
7. Technical skills.

We must gear these programmes to the needs of all the executives including top executives. It is a sheer torture to train lower executives and not higher level executives and the resulting break-down in communications will have positively deleterious effects on not only the executives but also on the performance of the Company in the long-run.

One of the learning principles is that learning is facilitated when a variety of teaching methodologies is used instead of a single method.

3. Harwood Merrill and Elizabeth Marting, Developing Executive Skills (New York, American Management Association, 1967) General Electric Company, Harold F. Siniddy. p. 261 - 2.

In-company Facilities

In-company formal programmes must be supported adequately by the following facilities :

1. A good Library and Reading Room. (books and journals on Management, Economics of Planning, Growth, Development, etc., Sociology, Psychology, Co-operation, Public Administrations etc.).

2. Films, slides, projectors, movies, stills, graphs, charts, flash cards, flannel, boards, pamphlets, brochures, note-books, manuals, exhibits, posters and displays notice boards, bulletin boards and enlarged drawings. cartoons, comic books, books, stationerys etc.

INTER-INDUSTRY OUT-COMPANY PROGRAMMES

We suggest that companies should use the opportunities provided by the following institutions in developing various skills through inter-industry out-company programmes.

1. American Management Association
2. Conference Board
3. Harvard School of Business
4. Stanford University
5. British Institute of Management
6. International Management Association of Japan
7. Administration Staff College
8. European School of Magagement
9. Professional Associations.
10. Chambers of Commerce.
11. Management Consultants and etc.,

Inter-industry programmes expose executives to the executives of other industries such as steels engineering, chemicals, computers, airlines, etc. and sharing and exchanging experiences, ideas and views help the company executives enormously, particularly in the area of management of human relations, marketing, public relations, etc. This helps in the cross-fertilization of ideas and views.

Co-operative Area Programme

We also suggest, in view of the enormous training needs that companies adopt the Co-operative Area Programmes and organise training and development programmes area-wise for the executives in the area. This would cut down some of the development expenses of individual companies and proximity also would be a help, particularly for smaller companies.

Education Refund Plan

It is suggested that the companies, who can institute an Education Refund Plan, where the companies encourage employees to further their education or gain more knowledge and specific skills in their spare time and the companies reimburse the executive 100 per cent of the total cost of tuition and 50 per cent of the total cost of books and other equipment. We also suggest to those companies who have the capacity, to provide book allowance so that executives develop their own personal libraries while developing their minds.

Membership in Professional Associations

The companies who can, must also encourage and support the executives joining professional associations and societies and facilitate their active participation. They benefit from keeping up-to-date with developments in their profession through association with others outside their companies and, pass on their own knowledge and experience to others who wish to learn from them.

Writing and Speaking Engagements

It is also suggested that companies must encourage their executives to think, speak and write and share their knowledge and experiences with others. There is a great need for this. The companies, but for a few, are completely left out of the mainstream of public life. They must accept speaking engagements and cultivate the art and skill of speaking and communication.

More important, they owe it to themselves, to their profession and the country to make a solid contribution to the literature on Company Management. It is a pity that this effort is completely and singularly lacking. Perhaps this is largely because of the very conservative, traditional and archaic policies of the companies and they must sweep these anachronistic policies completely overboard into the Arabian Sea. Thinking, reading, speaking and writing are good habits for the development of any individual which must be cultivated, developed and nurtured.

OUT-COUNTRY EXECUTIVE DEVELOPMENT PROGRAMMES

The companies must strive to utilise the programmes offered by out-country agencies in U.S.A., West Germany, U.K., Japan, etc. Some of our leading companies do send their key executives to out-country programmes. The only suggestion is that this must be streamlined and planned on a systematic basis, so that the company as well as the executive both benefit from this experience. It means that before sending an executive on an out-country programme, the company must determine what his need is considering his present and potential assignments and how you plan to use his experience. There is no point in sending him on a foreign jaunt without aim or purpose and it will be a wasted effort. We suggest also that executives, apart from getting training from the agencies there, must also be exposed ,to an inter-industry programme as well as study visits to some of the leading business and industrial organisations. This would be a very worthwhile experience. Even that is not enough. He must be provided opportunities to use some of the ideas he has got from the out-country programme. I remember one top Executive complaining bitterly : " Yes, I learnt a lot from my trip abroad. I wanted to introduce so many things. But they wouldn't let me. It is a very frustrating experience."

The Pedagogical Methods, that may be used are :

(1) Case Method, (2) Syndicate Method, (3) Lecture Method, (4) Sensitivity Training and T-Groups or D-Groups, (5) Business Games, (6) Conferences (7) Seminars, (8) Workshops, (9) Symposia, (10) Executive Listening, (11) Executive Speaking, (12) Role Play, (13) Executive Writing, (14) Incident Process, (15) Executive Exercises, (16) Management Grid, (17) Brain Storming Sessions, (18) Book Reviews, (19) Simulation, (20) Quantitative Methods, (21) Computerisation, (22) Observation Tours, (23) Counselling and Guidance, (24) Correspondence Course, (25) Visits Abroad, (26) Research.

UTILISATION OF TRAINED EXECUTIVES

This must be pre-planned. It may be said that what happens *before* and *after* training and development is as important as training and development itself. Haphazard selection of executives for programmes also lead to hapazard or no utilisation. Development must be dovetailed with development needs, career plans and management succession and utilisation.

A cardinal principle of learning is that learning is reinforced when it is applied almost immediately. Otherwise people tend to forget what they have learnt.

The companies should take a policy decision to give all opportunities to the trained executives and to create an environment where his new knowledge, skills or techniques are used for the benefit of the company's as well as the individual's growth. For example, a bank executive trained in financing agriculture must be utilised there and when he is exposed to training in financing small industry, his services and knowledge must be utilised there. After exposing him to a programme in financing agriculture, you send him to the foreign exchange department and this is obviously a wasted effort. Or sending one person to all programmes, regardless of his needs, is another example of wasted effort. This requires better planning and utilisation.

Evaluation Process of the Impact of Executive Development Programme

Companies must make an effort to evaluate the impact of Executive Development Programmes. The evaluative process will largely depend on the objectives with which we set out to organise training and development programmes.

Broadly speaking, the objectives of training and development are:[4]

1. Knowledge change.
2. Attitude change.
3. Skills change.
4. Behaviour change.
5. Performance change.

---

4. Earl Brooks, "Developing Tomorrow's Leaders", *ibid.*, p. 413.

As a result of changes in the first four, changes in performance occur. One type of evaluative process would be at four levels :

Step I — Reaction : How well did the participants like the programme ? (Tools : questionnaire — observation — interview)

Step II — Learning : What principles, facts and techniques were learnt ? (Tools : tests — examinations — quiz — projects).

Step III — Behaviour : What changes in job behaviour resulted from the programme ?

(Tools :

1. Systematic appraisal of on-the-job performance before and after the programme.
2. Appraisal of performance by —
   (a) self-appraisal
   (b) by his superior(s)
   (c) by his subordinates
   (d) by his peers
3. Post-training appraisal (3 months, 6 months, 1 year).
4. Statistical analysis to compare performance before and after and related changes to programme.
5. A control group not receiving training could be used).

Step IV — Results : What were the tangible results of the programme in terms of reduced cost, improved quality, improved productivity, etc.?

(Tools : tests — checklists — attitude surveys—learning curves—cost accounting — employee appraisals — depth interviews — mailing questionnaires — follow up).

EXECUTIVE DEVELOPMENT RESEARCH

Companies should conduct research on Executive Development effort and identify various problem areas and develop solutions. Research can be done in any number of areas such as managerial effectiveness, organisational effectiveness, decentralisation and delegation, problems in development, utilisation of trained executives, correlations between development and performance, executive appraisal, executive morale, executive communications, effectiveness of teaching methodologies, management succession plans and practices, superior responsibility for developing subordinates, top executive profile, history and development of the organisation, history of management systems, executive health, training and developments and their effectiveness, executive resources planning, identifying sound sources of recruitment, developing research tools for evaluation of development, leadership patterns and so the list could go on. In addition, the companies must encourage research in all the other areas so that decisions are based on sound data and information. Research provides a good base for sound decision-making.

PURSUIT OF EXCELLENCE — CHALLENGE AND RESPONSE

Earlier we said that Executive Development is the process of growing leadership and it is not easy even with the best of company interests. Imagine how it is when no serious efforts are made. Much depends upon the kind of leadership that the top management would provide to this growth process, because this is one of the most crucial aspects of Executive Development effort. Apathy towards it percolates all the way down setting a bad trend. Mr. Michael Haider, former Chairman of one of the largest industrial enterprises in the world, Standard Oil, New Jersey, looking at the problem of executive development, said :

"In the life of a corporation, today's success is largely a product of three types of executive actions taken yesterday: Selecting the right people; placing them in the right jobs; and seeing to it that they were able to grow to meet both their own needs and those of the organisation. This activity is not a programme in the usual sense, any more than selling or making profits are programmes. It has no fixed dimensions, no time-table, no cut-off point."

How seriously he regards this activity, is indicated by the fact that Mr. Haider assumed the executive development function as his personal responsibility. He, the President and four Executive Vice-Presidents of the company, acting as a committee met 37 times in 1964, to review the company's human resources. This committee is " involved in a continuing examination of management throughout the Jersey organisation... Once a year the chief executive officer of each of the larger affiliates meets the committee and reviews in depth his company's development activities and its replacement situation and appraises the performance and potential of all his key management personnel. He goes over his replacement tables, his plans for job rotation assignments and the specific steps being taken to increase the effectiveness of his organisation".

Yes, the top executives and all executives must consciously develop this habit of looking closely at their subordinates and their potential and make a generous contribution of their time and effort to make them bloom into flowers.

Top management commitment and interest may manifest itself in several ways and some of them are :

(a) Participation of the top management in courses (inauguration, valediction, etc.).

(b) Participation on the faculty in training programmes.

(c) Participation in the committee on Executive Development.

(d) Participation in designing Executive Development Programmes.

(e) Participation in the Development of Executive Development Policies.

(f) Participation in the selection of faculty and trainers.

(g) Review of Executive Performance.

(h) Identification of individual development needs.

(i) Selection of executives for training and development.

(j) Management and control of Executive Development Programmes.

(k) Preparation of career development plans.

(l) Evaluation of training and development.

(m) Utilisation of trained personnel.

(n) Follow-up of trained personnel.

(o) General guidance and support to Executive Development Programmes.

Top management must also attend and take development programmes. Apart from developing them it serves as a symbolic gesture of commitment and support and others will follow the lead and fall in line.

EXECUTIVE DEVELOPMENT ORGANISATION

Top management must have assistance of competent specialists. In the large organisations there should be a few specialists, working primarily in the Executive Development function, which may be headed by a Chief Adviser, Management Development. He may be assisted by Executive Resource Planning and Research Officer, Training and Development Officer and the Evaluation of Training and Development Officer. The Chief Adviser may report to the Personnel Director.

There is a great deal of work involved — very specialised know-how and this cannot be accomplished by tentative gestures of having an officer here and there, but by providing for a full-blown competent and expert division of executive development.

COMMUNICATING EXECUTIVE DEVELOPMENT EFFORT

Every effort should be made to communicate Executive Development effort, principles, policies, programmes, practices and procedures involved and every one employed in the organisation should know that there is an effort to build a continuingly effective executive cadre. The "Crown Prince" concept should be avoided to the extent it implies that only a chosen few will move ahead. Communication on this point is accomplished less by words than by deeds.

Particular attention should be given to those persons who were not hired as officer-trainees but who demonstrate the capacity for assuming more difficult and important positions. Their upward movement can be the most important way of telling all employees that *achievement* is not determined by college degrees, personal friendships, kith and kin relationships or blood ties or caste affiliations or other extraneous considerations irrelevant to the attainment of results.

The second group with whom effective communication is necessary includes those whose development is at issue.

The managers who are responsible for carrying out developmental experiences of others should be aware of and in agreement with the goals of such activities.

The most important point to remember about Executive Development is that emphasis should be on process rather than programmes. Focus should be on accomplishment of end-results rather than on routines and procedures.

But by far the single greatest challenge facing the executive is closer home and right under his nose — his subordinate. Providing him opportunities to develop and an environment in which he can reach his maximum potentialities is indeed a creative process. What we are attempting is not merely to make him a good and efficient executive, but we must strive to make him a better manager, a better leader and most important, a better human being with humanistic values where the concern in our country is for the fulfilment of the individual human being, resulting in the commitment to the concept of self-actualisation and self-renewal.

The essence of Executive Development effort ought to be towards developing better human beings who would single mindedly pursue the path of excellence in order to build a better world around them.

12 Managing Diverse People and Culture

We shall discuss the above challenging chapter under the following sub-headings
• The challenging issues of diverse people and cultures • Defining multiculturalism • Managing multicultural organisations • 3 principles of global human growth in multicultural Management

THE CHALLENGING ISSUES OF DIVERSE PEOPLE AND CULTURES

The contemporary workforce in a global company is diverse, meaning they come from different countries, it may be drawn from 10 to 50 different countries, Kuwait Air employs pilots, air hostesses, ground staff drawn from 40 different nationalities. They have different cultural values. They are also from different races, white, black, brown, yellow, etc., there are Christians, Hindus, Muslims, Jews, and many other sects and denominations. At one time, the work force was mainly male, today, there are both men and women and some in between with gay and lesbian orientations. In some countries like Seychelles or Singapore nearly 52 per cent of working population is female, bringing its own challenges to the management. I remember a consumer survey we were doing for a client in Singapore. Some female customers complained, how come there are mostly salesmen, why not have some sales women. One said that the salesman keeps on staring at me and it is quite intimidating. Another Malaysian customer complained why there were only Indian staff working in the store. Another Chinese customer demanded that there was a need to employ some Chinese staff and also some Chinese women. He said that he will find it more attractive to come and buy some stuff. The management started recruiting women sales staff, Chinese, Malaysian, Philippinos and Indians so that it was reassuring to the other ethnic communities of Singapore. My client philosophy was to listen to the customer and it has paid handsome dividends to the company.

From the manager's point of view, when a professional manager from a Global company is transferred to Indonesia, he will have to learn how to deal with the Indonesian Government System, legal controls of enterprise, workforce with their own cultural values, social aspirations, lifestyles, social mores, so many Indonesian languages and what makes them tick. He must learn to understand the competition, markets and external environmental influences . Eg, understanding and following the English spoken by an Indian will pose a problem initially because the Tamilian speaks English with a strong Tamil accent, similarly a Keralite with a strong Malayalam accent, Andhraite with a Telugu accent; Gujarathi with a Gujarathi accent; so much so an American CEO said to me half in jest "my God, it is too complicated. I give up".

The problem is compounded when the same manager a moved to another country like India and he has to learn all about Indian workforce, business markets, legal tax systems. Generally, in the manager's life, he may be asked to work in several countries even as much as 10 countries in the course of his career. It can be tough but the successful ones learn fast and adopt fast to the situation and succeed not only with their career but also help their company grow fast.

Stoner, Freeman and Gillent Jr point out the dilemma is a multicultural workforce.[1]

Today's workforce is multicultural : a mix of people from different cultures, ethnicities and lifestyles; if organisations are to adapt to this reality they must better understand multiculturalism and its impacts. An exercise in multicultural understanding is presented in Exhibit 12.1

1. *Management,* pp. 190-191.

Exhibit 12.1. An Exercise in Multicultural Understanding

1. Imagine that Jack a young white, male graduate from your college, is entering a management training programme with a large manufacturing firm or a large bank. Can you list some barriers that may prevent jack from reaching the very top position in the organisation? For starters, consider that there is a relatively large number of people like Jack competing for a very few spots at the top of any organisation.
2. Suppose that Jack is an African American competing or Hispanic American or Asian American. What traditional barriers does he face? How do these barriers impact Jack's chances of making it to the top?
3. Suppose that the new management trainee isn't Jack, but Tara, a young, white woman who has graduated from your school. What are the barriers to the top for Tara? What are the differences between Tara and either version of Jack?
4. Suppose that Tara is an African American, or Hispanic American, or Asian American. What additional barriers does she face?
5. What would be the barriers if Tara or of Jack came from France? Haiti? Japan? Brazil?
6. Suppose that Tara or Jack is gay; What are the additional barriers?
7. Suppose that Tara or Jack has a physical disability and must use a wheelchair.
8. Suppose that Tara or Jack is older than 50?

DEFINING MULTICULTURALISM

Stoner et.al. define multiculturalism thus : Multiculturalism can be defined as the view that there are many different cultural backgrounds and factors that are important in organisations, and that people from backgrounds can co exist and flourish within an organisation. Usually multiculturalism refers to cultural factors such as ethnicity, race, gender, physical ability, sexual orientation, age and other factors.

The Workforce 2000 Report

The above report of the Hudson Institute in 1987, generated a great deal of renewed concern and interest in multiculturalism.

The report identified four key trends.

THE WORKFORCE 2000 REPORT

While many of the issues surrounding multiculturalism and diversity have been around for a long time, many organisations adopted a renewed concern with the publication of the Hudson Institute's 1987 report, entitled *Workforce 2000*. The report identified four key trends expected to become more important as the 20th century draws to a close. First, the report predicted that renewed productivity growth will lead to a healthier U.S. economy. Second, manufacturing will become a smaller part of that economy as service jobs become a bigger factor in creating wealth and new jobs. Third, these new service industry jobs will require a high level of skill, leading to employment for the educated and unemployment for the uneducated. Finally, the demographic composition of the workforce in the U. S. will become older, more female, and more disadvantaged. The percentage of white males in the workforce was 47 per cent in 1987 when the report was issued, but the report predicted the percentage of new white males entering the workforce will be greatly reduced. Estimates have varied from 15 to 30 per cent.

The Hudson Institute suggested six policy initiatives to cope with these changes:

1. Stimulate balanced world economic growth.
2. Increase efforts to stimulate productivity in service industries.
3. Maintain the adaptability and flexibility of the aging workforce.
4. Help resolve the often conflicting needs of women in relation to work and family.
5. Work to integrate African American and Hispanic American workers more fully into the economy.
6. Improve the education of all workers.

Concurrent with the release of the "Workplace 2000" report, many organisations began to worry more than ever about how to manage such a diverse workforce. How could women, Hispanic Americans, African Americans, and others with cultural heritages different from white males be integrated into the workforce? Many organisations began to have "diversity programmes" or "multiculturalism programmes."

In a more recent study, William Johnston concluded that the labour supply is becoming more global. This will ensure that any particular company has an even more diverse labour pool from which to draw its workers. Most of the population growth is occurring in "developing economies," where the workforce is relatively young and the educational level is rapidly improving. Over 570 million of the 600 million new workers entering the workforce will come from these developing economies such as Mexico, Indonesia, the Philippines, etc. Although the statistics on women in the workforce vary widely by country, many more women will enter the workforce all over the world. Organisations will have more choices about where to locate their facilities to take advantage of particular labour markets, and will thus be forced to learn to accommodate many different cultural factors into their individual organisational cultures.

Gender Issues in Multiculturalism

The report points out that the workforce is rapidly moving from being male dominated to one of equality in numbers between men and women. Nevertheless there remain many barriers for women seeking equal treatment.

Glass Ceiling: Women in top executive positions are scarce. Although more and more have managerial positions, invisible barriers are still prevent most while climbing to the highest corporate levels.

Glass Ceiling Syndrome : The view that even though women and minorities can get hired into organizations, they have difficulty getting promoted, particularly to senior levels; it is as if there is an invisible barrier; they can see opportunities above, but they cannot reach them.

Studies estimate that men hold 97 per cent of the top positions, and women comprise fewer than 0.5 per cent of the highest paid officers and directors positions in the top 1000 US companies.

Sexual Harassment: Many women face sexual harassment in the workplace and it consists of any unwanted sexual behaviour that can involve words, gestures, sounds, actions or physical touching. Sexual favours are demanded. I.L.O reported on surveys in 23 countries that 15 per cent to 30 per cent of the women polled had experienced sexual harassment by supervisors and colleagues. A 1991, British survey revealed that 47 per cent of the women and 14.5 of the men said that they had been sexually harassed. In Spain, a 1986, survey indicated that sexual remarks or jokes were made on the job towards 84 per cent of the women workers polled, sexual looks or gestures were made towards 55 per cent and strong verbal advances or touching towards 27 per cent. The Spanish government subsequently adopted a provision against workplace harassment in 1989.

Stereotyping: Women may be stereotyped as HR managers or PR managers rather then manufacturing and marketing Vice Presidents.

Racial and Ethnic Minority Issues

Although 30 per cent of the US population consists of racial minorities, very few minority members have made it to the top. John Fernandez reports that of the 15 typical large corporations, only 8 per cent of middle managers and 2 per cent senior Managers were people of colour. He says "In professional sports, an area where African Americans have supposedly excelled, African Americans represent 72 per cent of the basketball players, but only 11 per cent of head coaches, in football they are 60 per cent of the players, but only 7 per cent of the head coaches, in baseball they represent 18 per cent of the players and 8 per cent of the managers."

EARNINGS GAP : The Statistics reveal earnings gap, which are discrepancies between the earning power of workers of similar educational background but different races. For example, a white worker with BS degree earns an average annual salary of $44,426. A similarly qualified Afro – merican earns $ 34,290; Hispanic Americans earn $ 33,817. The gap actually widens among the more educated.

MANAGING MULTICULTURAL ORGANISATIONS

Taylor Cox's Six Arguments

TAYLOR COX'S SIX ARGUMENTS

Managing the issues of diversity and multiculturalism is crucial to organisational success. Professor Taylor Cox of the University of Michigan has suggested six arguments, summarised in Table 12.1 to support his belief that managing cultural diversity can improve organisational performance.

The *cost argument* says that if organisations do a poor job in managing multicultural issues they will have higher costs. The revolving door syndrome is expensive. When women and minorities leave, the organisation gets no return on the investment it has made in them. In addition, if multicultural issues aren't managed well, then people are not as comfortable as they could be in the work environment and they spend time and energy worrying about discrimination, harassment, and other issues rather than their jobs.

Table 12.1
Six Arguments for Managing Cultural Diversity

1. Cost Argument	As organizations become more diverse, the cost of a poor job in integrating workers will increase. Those who handle this well, will thus create cost advantages over those who don't.
2. Resource Acquisition Argument	Companies develop reputations on favourability as prospective employers for women and ethnick minorities. Those with the best reputations for managing diversity will win the competition for the best personnel. As the labour pool shrinks and changes composition, this edge will become increasingly important.
3. Marketing Argument	For multinational organisations, the insight and cultural sensitivity that members with roots in other countries bring to the marketing effort should improve these efforts in important ways. The same rationale applies to marketing to subpopulations within domestic operations.
4. Creativity Argument	Diversity of perspectives and less emphasis on conformity to norms of the past (which characterise the modern approach of management of diversity) should improve the level of creativity.
5. Problem-solving	Heterogeneity in decision and problem solving groups potentially produces better decisions Argument through a wider range of perspectives and more thorough critical analysis of issues.
6. System Flexibility	An implication of the multicultural model for managing diversity is that the system will Argument become less determinant, less standardised, and therefore more fluid. The increased fluidity should create greater flexibility to react to environmental changes (*i.e.,* reactions should be faster and at less cost).

Source: Taylor H. Cox, Jr., and Y. Blake, "Managing Cultural Diversity Implications for Organizational Competitiveness" *Academy of Management Executive.* Vol. 5, Issue 3, August 1991. p. 47.

The *resource acquisition argument* says that companies that handle multiculturalism well will have an advantage over other companies in hiring multicultural workers—an increasingly important advantage in an era of Workforce 2000 demographics. For example, a recent book discussed the best places to work for women and African Americans. The impact has been positive for companies listed, including Merck, Xerox, Syntex, Hoffman LaRoche, and Hewlett Packard.

The *marketing argument* says that organisations that manage multicultural issues well have an insight into markets consisting of minority group members and women. Markets, too, are diverse, and cultural issues have some effect on the buying decisions of customers. Nancy Woodhull, President of Gannett News Media, claims that USA today is successful precisely because it has a variety of people from different cultural backgrounds involved in daily news meetings.

The *creativity and problem-solving arguments* hold that groups of people from diverse backgrounds can be more creative than groups with homogeneous backgrounds, and are better at solving problems. However, steps must be taken to realize these benefits; in particular, team members must become aware of possible attitude differences in others. And there must be a core of shared beliefs or shared values around which people can express their differences.

Finally, the *system flexibility* argument says that the ability to manage diversity increases the adaptability and flexibility of an organisation. External and internal issues can be responded to more quickly. In addition, to manage diversity successfully, an organisation must question outdated policies and procedures that emerged in days when multiculturalism was not a large concern for the organisation.

MANAGING DIVERSITY

To reap the benefits just listed, managers must take positive steps to manage the issue of diversity. Figure 7.4 outlines seven spheres of activity that together provide a comprehensive approach to managing diversity issues.

But a higher CEP comes with greater expectations and if the person does not perform as expected, his CEO grade is lowered. The underlying principle in Shell is meritocracy. People who shine find themselves basking in the rarefied atmosphere that top executives enjoy, said Mr. Saravanamuthu.

Someone who has found that system in Shell has opened many doors for her to challenge herself is Mrs. Slyvia Lee, 37, a lead technologist at Pulau Bukom refinery. In her 11 years in Shell, the British-trained chemical engineer has worked in four jobs that have developed her abilities. She said: "The Shell system is demanding because you always have higher targets to meet. But that is only fair and gives you the chance to prove yourself."

Critics of the CEP concept say it is a self-fulfilling prophecy, as individuals who have been identified as high-flyers are always given a leg up. But said Mr. Saravanamuthu: "It is always possible to poke holes in any system. Like it or not, any company of our size needs a system to develop people and we found this is one that works. We're not prescribing an answer to the whole world.

Mr. Steven Morris, managing director of Hay Management Consultants, agrees the Shell system does not suit every organization. "Shell's is not The system. Organizations should look at their own needs and borrow from other systems.

"And different organizations need different qualities in their leaders. The qualities that a successful entrepreneur, businessman and a political leader have are all different."

Many developing countries can learn from the experience of Singapore and adapt Shell system to suit their particular circumstances and needs.

Singapore Transformation

Singapore has transformed itself from a poor developing country into a modern metropolis, the envy of not only developing countries and even the developed countries in a short time of 25 years under the dynamic leadership of Mr. Lee Kuan Yew. In the face of heavy odds, he has created a unique multi-ethnic, clean and green city-state, that, in itself, has become an object of study by the developing countries and even the developed. What Mr. Lee has achieved will go down in history. Not only did he develop a strong, stable, efficient and clean government dedicated to meeting needs of Singaporeans, by eliminating poverty and unemployment but also a crop of young, brilliant and clean leaders to lead the people in the future to become a developed country by the end of this century. He is their role model.

What is even more unique, he planned to give up power by carefully picking and developing young successors and that is, perhaps, one of the rarest acts of leadership in modern history. Mr. Lee is widely sought today in many parts of the world including China, India, Pakistan, Kazakhastan, Ukraine, Brunei, Taiwan, etc. for guidance and advice.

On July 29, 1994, Mr. Lee Kuan Yew spoke to the undergraduates of the two universities in Singapore on the subject. What if I were a young undergraduate again?" and laid out a blueprint of how he would plan to develop his career to realise his maximum potential. In the process, he was telling the world how Singapore develops its leaders for Government and business and it is a grand design or blueprint that the developing and even the developed countries could draw lessons from and emulate the Singapore-Confucian Model of developing people and countries.

SM Lee Addresses Hopes of the Young

Mr. Lee Kuan Yew addressed the hopes and concerns of young Singaporeans in a novel way — by telling the story of how he would relive his life all over again, if he were a young undergraduate today.

Speaking to students from the two universities, he related the choices he would make in education, career, marriage, and service to the nation, if he had been born in 1973 instead of 1923. The Senior Minister's speech was filled with personal anecdotes as he related both his past real-life experience and his hypothetical future to illustrate how times had changed, and so too the values and realities of the world.

Underlying this was a message to young people: Plan long-term, maximise your natural endowments and seize the many economic opportunities that East Asia offers. As he put it: "My chances were different. A whole world was in a stage of revolution. Empires were being dismantled, empires that crashed in the Japanese occupation."

"You can't start a revolution now. People would think you are mad. So you can't travel my path. But the whole of East Asia is opening up. This is one enormous big world which is going to be integrated. There are enormous opportunities. And if I were a young man. I would seize them."

Speaking on the topic, 'What if I were a young undergraduate again?' at the National University of Singapore, he said he would choose a career which would give him options.

He would aim for an overseas Singapore Armed Forces or overseas merit scholarship, as that would give him a 'passport' he could flash and dash through the door. "Once you are through the door, you are then tested on your merits. But you must get through the door first," he said at the talk organised by the NUS Political Association and Democratic Socialist Club, and the Nanyang Technological University's Current Affairs Society.

The scholarship would also give him a network of friends who would one day be in key places. He would opt to study engineering, architecture or hard sciences in a top American university, rather than in Britain, followed by an MBA.

He would choose America over Britain as the former would have a big role in Asia. If he failed to get an overseas scholarship, he would do law or engineering at NUS, followed by an MBA in America.

He would also keep up with his language skills in English, Mandarin, Malay and Japanese. After serving his Government bond, he would move a statutory board or a Government-linked Company with regional projects.

At 28 to 30, he would marry "an equal or somebody better than I am," as she would then be able to carry the load as much as he could. She must also be able to imbue the right values into their children.

As to housing, he would start off with a five-room or executive flat, before upgrading five to seven years later. Owning a car, he acknowledged, was harder today. However well-educated a person was, only the top 270,000 people would own one.

But he gave the undergraduates some reassurance about the prospects of owning a private house and car. On housing, for example, however high prices were, it would not matter so long as the young became high wage-earners.

"Because that is what decides who gets there," he said. "If you can get into the top 20 per cent of wage-earners, you will get a house." By the time he was about 40, he would set up a partnership in business or start his own company.

He would also join the People's Action Party, and be ready to be a minister and contribute to the society in his mid-forties because, without a good government, everything would go down the drain. He would stay at least two terms to leave his mark. If he went back to his business, he would remain an MP.

Mr. Lee reassured the students that even if he was not in the top 2 or 3 per cent of his generation, he would not lose heart. "I won't be discouraged because many of the more successful men in the world never were at the top 2 or 3 per cent of their generation, at least not the scholarship route," he said, adding that Singapore entrepreneur, Sim Wong Hoo did not have an MBA.

Rounding up, he exhorted his young audience to "maximise your natural endowments, your gifts, the things you do well, and then seize your chances in a given society at a given stage of development."

A 'passport' that you can flash.

I would want a career which would give me options because you cannot foretell what openings the future will have. So I would go for an SAF overseas scholarship or overseas merit scholarship as the first step.

My journalist friends and academic friends tell me — no, that's not what the present generation would go for. They would say the eight-year bond restricted career. They would go for an SIA scholarship or DBS scholarship — more openings.

"I thought about that. No, I think that's short-sighted because what you want in life is a passport you can flash. And I dash through, the door. Once you are through the door, you are then tested on your merits. But you must get through the door first.

"And if you have taken an SAF scholarship, an overseas merit scholarship, there are one of about 50 each year. Any minister, any civil servant, any judge, looks through your CV and say: Ah, one of 50 for that year.

"And the other thing you must have in life is a network of friends, of being part of an old boy network. You have friends in key places and they will rise. Twenty years later, they are in key, strategic positions. All you do is pick up the phone, your name and you'll have them.

Engineering for a good grounding, then on to an MBA.

What would I do if I got the scholarship? I think if I were good with my hands I would do Engineering: Not to spend my life on it, but to have a good grounding.

And the Japanese have always believed that a good CEO, Chief Executive Officer, must have a real good grounding and understand the factory floor. And Mr. Morita, the man who founded Sony, tells me that's the weakness of the American corporations.

They all rise through business schools and they're shuffling papers. But they don't understand how the productive part of the business can be improved. Of course, after that I would want to take an MBA, because you don't want to be an engineer or a researcher in the lab all your life.

Going to America: Because the US Has a Big Role in Asia

Where would I go? Oxbridge? Bom in '73, I would say: no, I would go to America because the Americans would have a big role in Asia, and I have to understand the Americans.

So, it's not just learning data, it's networking. And if I go for my undergraduate or my first degree there, I would go for an MBA later in Europe. Then I'd understand also the Europeans. Or if I'm good in my Chinese and I pick up some Japanese, I'd spend a year with the Japanese.

It's the hard facts of life: Who will be relevant in this part of the world in the next 10, 20, 30, 40 years. There's cultural lag we suffer from. The PSC suffers from it. Parents suffer from it. Many of our students are still being sent to Oxbridge and top British universities.

Club Membership, Holidays Abroad

"I'd probably want to be a member of a golf club, to have a swimming pool, a health club. I'd want to have school holidays with my children abroad now. Not just go up to Fraser's Hill or Cameron Highlands.

People take children to Disney World or Disneyland or whatever, New Zealand, Australia, exotic places in China, in Europe and so on. But in your lifetime you're going to see world-class concerts and plays in Singapore because we're going to put up the facilities for it, and we're on the main trunk route.

And whether you're Pavarotti or Placido Domingo or whoever, they have to travel, because Europe has heard enough of them and everybody's watched them on television. So, we are no longer isolated.

Medishield Plus, Blue-chip Stocks

I would go in for either comprehensive co-payment or subsidised outpatient scheme, but I would buy myself Medishield Plus. And for my CPF, I will put as much as I can because it's tax-free. I will reach the maximum and put it by and use it to invest wisely and safely in blue-chip stocks.

Every time I watch SBC financial reports, all those shares that go up and down every day, you should stay away from. If you think you are smart, you want to gamble. God bless you. But I buy what I know will go up with the economy of Singapore. If you buy a bank, good sound, well-run bank, it is in every business, it's financing every business, if Singapore's economy prospers, it must prosper. Or, you buy a property company, if the economy prospers, the infrastructure improves, property must go up.

Opportunities Would Still Abound

Now, what if I were not in the top 2 or 3 per cent of my generation? I will tell you that I would not lose heart, I won't be discouraged because many of the more successful men in the world never were at the top 2 or 3 per cent of their generation, at least not the scholarship route.

Henry Ford didn't get an MBA with distinction. Neither did Rockefeller. And Sim Wong Hoo of Creative Technology. He only made polytechnic and he's got a good brain and he's made it. So what it really means is, can you get advice from your parents, from your uncles, from teachers, from friends, how to maximise your natural endowments, your gifts, the things you do well, and then seize your chances in a given society at a given stage of development.

My chances were different. A whole world was in a stage of revolution. Empires were being dismantled, empires that crashed in the Japanese Occupation. You can't start a revolution now. People would think you're mad.

So you can't travel my path. But the whole of East Asia is opening up. This is one enormous big world which is going to be integrated. There are enormous opportunities. And if I were a young man, I would seize them.

English First, Then Chinese and Malay

I think it's important that you know the English language because it is the International language. And you speak it in the standard form. Do not speak Singlish! If you do, you are the loser. Your interlocutors, when they hear you, their ears go askew.

You detract from the message that you're sending them. I don't have to speak with an English upper-class accent. But I speak in a way which makes it easy for them to understand me and therefore, they are not distracted by my background.

I would learn Chinese. It's a life-long facility which should be of enormous value, economic value. Then I would learn Malay, perhaps the Indonesian pronunciation. We live in this region, therefore, I think it's a value to have it.

And HDB flat, for Starters

My children were fortunate: they had a mother who worked and when they started life they had a home. Not very posh, but comfortable. If I didn't have a father or a mother to give me that, I would start off with a five-room or an HDB executive.

Quickly! Before my income ceiling takes me beyond that. You buy a flat in Bishan for $ 160,000, it's going today for half a million. So I would get there first, stay five years, seven years, and then move out. I'll give you some reassurance about the prospects.

Take your time. Don't get too anxious. Whatever asset inflation or scarcity value there is, remember that the private homes in Singapore belong to about the top 12% of wage earners. National Development's plan is: today, we have 15% or 120,000 (private) units; by the year 2000, 20% or 208,000 units; and by year 2010, some 23% or 290,000.

So let me put it this way: However high they go, it does not matter. Can you get to the top 15%? Or the top 20%. Or the top 20%? That is what decides who gets there. Because a rich man's son gets house; he hasn't got the earning capabilities; after he lives well, then he has to sell the house, you buy it.

It's been like that from times immemorial.

Cars are Scarcer Than Graduates

In 1959, I was wealthy enough, successful enough to buy a Mercedes 220S. But you'll remember, at the time I came back, I was one out of 150 practising lawyers. Today, there are 2,600 plus lawyers.

The number of cars in 1951, was 22,000. The number of cars today has gone up to 300,000 — 13 times. But lawyers have gone up to 20 times. Now, I think I would wait three to five years after graduation, then I'll buy a Japanese car, maybe 1,300-1,500 cc — that would be not bad.

In 1974, my son Hsien Loong came back, graduate. He had to use my old Mercedes-Benz. In 1980, he bought himself a Honda Civic, 1,300 cc. Then in 1985, he changed to a Toyota Cressida 2,000 cc.

My younger son, Hsien Yang, graduated in '79. He used his grandfather's Honda Civic because the brother was using my car. He got married in '81 and he bought himself a Ford Laser, 1,300 cc. So with each passing year, cars became smaller and more expensive. That was before COE's!

I put it in a objective way in this manner: However well-educated you are, remember that only the top 260,000 to 270,000 people own cars — 31% of all households (this was from the 1992/93 household expenditure survey).

Houses and cars, which require land, have what it known as 'scarcity value' and what the young now call "asset inflation".

When I came out from university I was one out of the top 1% — that's all that made it to university in my generation. When my son, Loong, came back in '74, he was one out of 3.8%. And when my son, Yang, came back in '79 he was one out of 4.5%.

Now you are part of 19%. By the time you graduate, you may be part of 21%. So you see, the scarcity value of graduates goes downs the scarcity value of land goes up.

A Minister, Because the Price is Well Worth Paying

So, what would I do? I think I will catch the eye of some minister. And if I have the right credentials — SAF scholarship, overseas merit scholarship, preferably a first at a top university, an MBA with distinction — they cannot miss me; they have been looking for me.

But that only gets you an interview, a tea session. Then we to know whether you inter-relate well, have you got the right social intelligence, have you got the right commitments.

Now, born in 1973, without that hardship, the idealism, I think, will still be latent if you've got it. Otherwise you can't explain why people go to Rwanda. You see them on television. They go to Somalia, they go to Bosnia.

You know: Medecins San Frontieres, Oxfam, and so on. They are able to find highly intelligent people, well-qualified, driving lorries, catering for the miserable. SIF Singapore International Foundation gets people willing to go to Botswana, Nepal, Philippines, do things for other people.

We are also tapping that same wellspring of idealism. It is a powerful force for good. Now in, say, 2010, 2015, I think I will be ready to be a minister. And probably I would stay a minimum two terms, preferably three terms, to leave my mark. But even if I go back to my own business, I would want to stay on as an MP.

This is something which the younger generation does not understand. There are 80 MPs, and in a crisis, everyone counts. But of course, it also means, as the phrase goes, "your Sundays are burnt" because that's the time when the constituents want to see you and they are free.

But that's life — you pay a price, and I would think it's a price worth paying.

MANAGEMENT : THE PERSONAL TOUCH

Anita Roddick, founder and managing director of the Body Shop International demonstrates how much a manager's personality and values can actually define the manager's role and help to shape an organisation. The Body shop sells products that leaves and polish the skin" and while it may appear to be a "boutique, cosmetics company", it is really quite different.

The Body Shop was founded in 1976, by Roddick and her husband Gordon. At that time, the couple formed the business so Anita would have a means of supporting herself and their two children while her husband Gordon fulfilled his dream of riding on horseback from Buenos Aires to New York City. When Gordon left, Anita was operating a single shop in England; when he returned ten months later there were two shops, with another one soon to follow.

By the eariy 1990s, the Body Shop had blossomed into a financial success. In 1992, The Body Shop boasted earnings of $265 million worldwide and enjoyed a 23 per cent growth rate for the first half of 1993. As of November 1993, nearly 1000 Body Shop stores were located around the world in 43 countries.

Many of Roddick's personal values have influenced The Body Shop's corporate culture. Indeed, the company is driven by her intense commitment—what she calls "electricity and passion"—that can't help but engender enthusiasm and boost employee, customer, and community morale. At the same time, Roddick also focuses on her specific managerial responsibilities, primarily (though not exclusively) product development and marketing.

Roddick's use of marketing tends to distinguish The Body Shop not only from direct competitors but also from most other companies. The Body Shop does not spend money on consumer advertising. The organisation is premised upon the belief that consumers are underwhelmed by the commercial hype already clouding the marketplace. The Body Shop therefore allocates promotional money to social activism instead of consumer advertising. "In the old days we couldn't afford [to advertise]," recalled Roddick. "Now we would be deeply embarrassed to." In a way, the organisation's refusal to advertise has become an element of the corporate culture.

Roddick does not market the company in a traditional way. Instead, she aggressively pursues avenues through which the company can enjoy media coverage for free. In this way, the marketing of The Body Shop resembles a political campaign. "I'm always available to the press," noted Roddick. "I fervently believe that passion persuades, and I emit a lot of enthusiasm." Clearly, Roddick recognises the value of media coverage of the Body Shop. "(I) put our poster for Colourings [a line of makeup] in the shop windows, that creates sales and profits," asserted Roddick. "A poster to stop the burning of the rain forest doesn't. It creates a banner of values, it links us to the community, but it will not increase sales. What increases sales is boring *Glamour* magazine saying Princess Diana uses Body Shop products. Then We'll get 7,000 bloody phone calls asking for our catalog. You can measure the effect."

Roddick has also found that she must market herself as well as the company, and that the image she conveys is one that falls in line with the values she articulates. "The staff doesn't want me in fur coats or in big cars or acting like I've got the million dollars that I have," said Roddick. "They want me to be as I am. Other people, the City [London's Wall Street], want me to be respectable. So you are dealing with multitudes of different people. There are so many planks in the platform of running a business."

It is Roddick who controls the press coverage, though, not the other way around. She demonstrated her ability to create favourable coverage early on when The Body Shop first opened. Roddick opened the first store next door to a funeral home. When she received a formal letter of complaint from the neighbouring undertakers, she leaked it to the press that they were ganging up on her—a struggling female shopkeeper. The day the story ran, Roddick rang up $ 200 in sales.

Attention to communication has played a major role in Roddick's management of The Body Shop's success. In the early days, Roddick felt it necessary to hide her true financial woes. "I used to have friends call me when a potential franchisee was arriving so I could have an absolutely ridiculous conversation. Ring, Ring. Oh, yes, this is where you'd like the franchisee, Barry Street, Edmonds? No, I don't think it's the right town for that. Besides, we've already had 14 other applications.' That went on all the time." This image of success that she fabricated soon turned into reality.

EDUCATION AT THE HEART

"There's no scientific answer for success," said Roddick. "You can't define it.... You've simply got to live it and do it." And that is what she has done. Roddick has treated The Body Shop as an extension of herself. She has built upon her own background and taken an approach that builds upon her strengths. "I've just taken what every good teacher knows." said Roddick, a former teacher herself, "You try to make your classroom an enthralling place. When I taught history, I would put brilliant graphics all around the room and play music of the period we were studying. Kids could just get up, walk around, and make notes from the presentation. It took me months to get it right, but it was stunning. Now I'm doing the same thing. There is education in the shops. There are anecdotes right on the products, and anecdotes adhere. So I've really gone back to what I know how to do well."

Roddick places great emphasis on employee empowerment. In as much as training is a prerequisite for empowerment. The Body Shop opened a training school in 1985. It features courses on employee relations, employment law, and time management. It was important to Roddick that the staff know more about The Body Shop products than the customers, and that they be able to answer all the questions "they hoped they would never be asked."

Unlike similar schools sponsored by other companies, The Body Shop's schools accept anyone offiliated with the company—including franchisees and their employees—and students attend for free. However, people must be admitted, and currently the school is not able to meet the demand for its courses.

Roddick considers such an educational investment in the community to be integral. "If you think enducation is expensive, try ignorance," she asserted." Education is at the very heart of The Body Shop. We encourage the development of the human spirit as well as the mind." Whereas some companies "train for sale," at The Body Shop, according to Roddick, "We train for knowledge."

This education and information serve to motivate The Body Shop employees. According to Roddick, "They're much more motivated and they actually enjoy their jobs....We find that people who are not trained are less motivated in their jobs, which is why we place such a heavy emphasis on training." In addition, Roddick said,"We did not want our staff...to stop learning just because they had started working."

Together, the company's education and social activism have enabled Roddick to motivate employees beyond their own expectations. "I'd never get that kind of motivation if we were just selling shampoo and body lotion," said Roddick. "I'd never get that sort of staying late, talking at McDonald's after work, bonding to customers. It's a way for people to bond to the company. They're doing what I'm doing. They're learning. Three years ago I didn't know anything about the rain forest. Five years ago I didn't know anything about the ozone layer. It's a process of learning to be a global citizen. And what it produces is a sense of passion you simply won't find in a Bloomingdale's department store."

Most important to Roddick is that she encourages employees to put their best foot forward. "I want them to understand that this is no dress rehearsal," said Roddick. "You've got one life, so just lead it. And try to be remarkable."

Now let us proceed to the Part Four in which Chapter 13 discusses how Global Companies can promote the application of Global Human Growth Model. The development of every human being to realise his maximum potential particularly those who are employed in the global companies. The last chapter touches upon the Dynamics of Global Management where the essential purpose is to create a New world order of peace, prosperity, happiness and compassion.

Now shall we tackle the promotion of Global Human growth through dynamic global management.

13 Global Human Growth Model

• The Human Condition • Unemployment • Definition of Human Growth • Philosophy of Global Human Growth • Global Commitment • GHM I: Education for All • GHM II: Employment for All • GHM III : Energising All to Self-Actualisation • Empowerment of People • Global Co-operative Advantage • Global Human Vision and Future

THE HUMAN CONDITION

The International Labour Organisation (ILO) in a new report on the global economy entitled "Defending Values, Promoting Change" paints a bleak picture of the contemporary human condition[1]. 30 per cent of the labour force in the world is out of work or underemployed. A global job crisis is gripping both rich and poor nations. It is a crisis that in some countries could really explode and undermine the social fabric very badly", proclaimed by Mr. Ali Taqi, Chief of Staff, ILO.[1]

UNEMPLOYMENT

ILO estimates that more than 820 million people worldwide are either unemployed or working at a job that does not pay even a subsistence wage. Releasing the report, the Director-General of ILO, Mr. Michael Hansenne points out: "Industrialised market-economy countries, most of which had achieved and they thought they could sustain, virtually full employment two decades ago, now faced an unemployment rate of 8.5 per cent. But it is in the poor countries, where the crisis is most acute, that the dangers are the greatest. The situation in Africa was troublesome, with most countries there experienced major decline in the living standards. Sub-Saharan Africa is a general disaster."[2]

"The global jobs crisis was not just the result of the recession that has plagued the world economy in recent years. It is something more ... and longer lasting than that and reflects the rapid pace of technological change and increasingly fierce global competition. Close to half of those people out of work in the European Community, for example, have been without a job for over a year. The ILO found it particularly worrisome for Europe that the unemployment rates were going up from the depth of one business cycle to the next; 6 per cent in 1980; above 8 per cent in 1989. The trend in the US, though, has been in the other direction."

According to ILO, unemployment is the highest among unskilled workers and immigrants in most countries. Poor countries are the hardest hit. Long-term unemployment is up. In Europe, nearly half of all unemployed are long-term cases, compared with fewer than one in five in Japan and one in 15 in the United States. Youth unemployment is worsening. In many countries, notably the US and Britain, the gap has been growing between high and low wages. The difference has been less pronounced in countries where wages are set nationally or by industry.

In mid-March 1994, the G-7 nations-USA, Britain, Canada, France, Germany, Italy, Japan-held G-7 Jobs Summit in Detroit to address the problems posed by the 35 million out of work in the industrial world at the invitation of formen President Clinton, who maintained that the job crisis was the most important problem facing the rich nations and needing an urgent solution. While the central focus was on unemployment for the first time in the G-7 Summit, it became clear for the first time that there was a methodological problem of defining unemployment and identifying the rate of unemployment.

A report from Detroit stated: "Every country at the two-day G-7 Job Conference agrees that people need work, but no one agrees on how many of these people there are or how to compare one country with another. Each of the Group of seven nations has more idle people than its unemployment rate shows. For example, people, who are out of work but do not bother to look for it – they may be discouraged or not know how — will not be counted unemployed in many countries."

---

1. International Labour Organisation, "Defending Values, Promoting Change", 1994, ILO, Geneva.
2. World Bank, *Poverty: World Development Report* 1990, Oxford University Press, New York, pp. 1-6.

A better indicator of the prevailing conditions would be a statistic that showed the number of people who wanted a job but could not find one. That number would be astonishingly high.

Mr Keith Brooks, Director of New York Unemployed Committee, made the essential point. "Does not government recognise the depth of the jobs crisis in this country? I think not." If this is the state of affairs in the richest country, with one of the highest jobs producing record, one might shudder to think of the situation in the large number of developing countries with some of the highest rates of population in Asia, Africa and South America!

Former President Clinton, the only Head of the State attending the Jobs Summit, stated that "the G-7 nations must co-operate in facing their common problem-unemployment—in the same way they have co-operated for the last 50 years to defeat Communism, to stand-up against Iraqi aggression and to expand the global trading system. In effect, he called on the Group to transform itself from the exclusive club of statesmen, who gather annually to talk about issues of high finance or high diplomacy into a global employment agency focused on "the challenge of creating a high wage, high-growth society in the mature industrial countries". And the same focus be extended to the developing countries also, without which a solution to global unemployment crisis shall be illusory.

Illiteracy

Illiteracy is the mother of unemployment. More than half of the world's population live in nine developing countries—Bangladesh, Brazil, China, Egypt, India, Indonesia, Mexico, Nigeria and Pakistan - which account for more than 70 per cent of the world's adult illiterates and which are also among the world's poorest, according to a United Nations Education Scientific and Cultural Organisation (UNESCO) Report in December 1993.

The countries have a combined population of 2.7 billion people, more than half of the world's population. A total of 638 million adults cannot read or write. 78 million or more than half of its children, between the ages of 6 and 11, who should be in school, are not. The report noted that illiteracy and poverty (unemployment, I might add,) appeared to go hand in hand. It was in recognition of these facts that representatives of nine countries met in New Delhi, India in December 1993 for the first Education for all Summit. There may not be conclusive proof that education leads to rich and less populous societies. But enough evidence suggests that these countries with the highest enrolment and literacy rates are also those with highest GNP, according to the report.

Said Sylvian Lourie, former Director of UNESCO's International Institute of Educational Planning: "It is not difficult to see that the map of World Illiteracy coincides with that of world poverty." Nor is it difficult to see that this same map corresponds to regions of the world with the highest population. In almost every country educated mothers have been found to have fewer children than their less-educated sisters."

Delhi Declaration

The Delhi Declaration adopted by the nine delegations at the end of the conference wowed a place in primary schools or alternative teaching for every child by the year 2000 or sooner. It pledged to expand adult education programmes, especially literacy programmes, erase educational inequalities of sex, income, or other factors and make teaching more relevant to everyday needs like basic numeracy or improving living conditions. The Declaration pledged to improve quality of education, reduce drop outs, improve effectiveness of education system and resource use. It asked donors for more aid to achieve its goals and urged international financial institutions not to impose tough loan conditions, which the then Prime Minister of India, Mr. P .V. Narasimha Rao said, closing the Summit: "What is required now is action, not only by governments but also by non-governmental organisations and the community at large. It is not a question of lighting a candle. The whole world must be lit with the glow of literacy."

Poverty

The World Bank, in its World Development Report 1990 on Poverty, presents grim figures on world poverty. 1115 million people or one-fifth of the World's population are poor, living on a dollar (US) a day. One-third of the population of the developing countries are poor.

630 million or 18 per cent of the world population are extremely poor, living on less than 75 cents a day. 47 per cent of Sub-Saharan Africa or 180 millionn are poor and 30 per cent of those are extremely poor. 520 million or 51 per cent of South Asia are poor and 20 per cent of those are extremely poor.

60 million or 31 per cent of population of Middle East and North Africa are poor and 21 per cent of those, extremely poor.

More than 70 per cent of the world's poor are women, followed by the elderly.

In the US and 12 countries of the European Union, nearly 15 per cent of the population live below the poverty line.

Africa has 16 per cent of the world's poor, but nearly half of all Africans are impoverished.

The World Bank observes that, inspite of considerable achievements, "it is all the more staggering — and all the more shameful — that more than one billion people in the developing world are living in poverty, struggling to survive on less than a dollar a day."

The UN World Summit for Social Development at Copenhagen, where more than 130 Heads of Governments from 184 countries assembed in March, 1995, to discuss the eradication of poverty, unemployment and social disintegration, declared war on poverty with a noble and ringing call that "poverty is morally and politically intolerable for the first time in history."[3]

Poverty reduces humankind to sub-human levels of existence and leads to wastage of human talent—and potential.

Human Migration

More than 100 millions live out of their countries of origin due to political strife and civil wars. 37 per cent of these are political refugees. One in every 115 people in the world is a migrant or refugee. Illegal immigrants are increasing. The situation in Africa, particularly sub-Saharan Africa, is the worst. In China and India, millions of people are migrating from rural to urban areas looking for a living and a job. Their living conditions are deplorable.

Human Insecurity

The 1994, Human Development Report of the UN, which ranks all the countries of the world on a Human Development Index said that 17 countries including Mexico, Nigeria and Algeria, could face collapse. 13 countries, were in various stages of collapse and they were Afghanistan, Angola, Haiti, Iraq, Mozambique, Myanmar, Sudan, Zaire, Ruanda, Burundi, Georgia, Liberia and Pakistan, The report said Algeria was experiencing severe internal tensions and Egypt, Mexico and Nigeria had large regional disparities in income and life expectancy, which were strong indicators of disintegration.

The report identified six indicators of human insecurity that could help pinpoint trouble spots and they are:

(1) Food scarcity. (2) High unemployment and declining wages, (3) Human rights violations, (4) Widening regional disparities, (5) Ethnic violence and (6) An overemphasis on military spending. Countries like Iraq, Somalia and Nicaragua, spending 3½ to 5 times more on military expenditure than on education and health care, have collapsed.[4]

While countries around the globe were spending billions on arms for territorial security, personal security within the borders was getting worse and the US was no exception. The US spends $ 290 billion a year to defend its borders, while crime within the borders cost an estimated $ 425 billion in 1992. That year, the report said, 14 million crimes were reported to the police; more than 2 million workers were attacked physically, nearly 6.5 million others were threatened with violence and 20 children a day died of gunshot wounds. There were more than 150,000 rapes in the US last year. Consumer spending on narcotics in the US is thought to exceed the combined incomes of more than 80 developing countries.

During the 80s, real earnings of Americans fell by 3 per cent and nearly 15 per cent of the population - 36 million - now live below the poverty line. Between 1987 and 1990, real benefit spending per old age pensioner declined by 40 per cent.

"What is bad for white America is much worse for African America: One-third of the whites live in areas polluted by Carbon monoxide but the figure for blacks is nearly 50 per cent. The unemployment rate for blacks is twice that for whites. But the report said that the disparity between blacks and whites in south was four times larger than the disparity in South Africa.

3. *Ibid*, p. 1.
4. UN, *Human Development Report*, 1994, United Nations Organisation, New York.

The ILO, in its 1994, World labour Report, highlights the following world labour trends:

1. World unemployment is increasing and wages falling
2. Russia: Unemployment low but wages falling
3. Globalisation will intensify
4. Informal employment increasing
5. Feminisation of the workforce
6. Line between home and workforce blurred
7. Greater emphasis on employers organisation
8. Health care still low in developing countries
9. More Asian workers covered by social health insurance
10. Health threat from chemicals accelerated

The report estimates that 43 million people are being added to the global labour force very year. Agriculture is still the largest employer and two-thirds of the global workforce are still employed in agriculture.

Conclusion

It is clear from the above discussion of contemporary human condition that we are being challenged by one of the worst social, political and economic crises of human kind. "Employment, with all its resulting evils, has become the most widely feared phenomenon of our times," observes OECD report after a two-year study.

The ILO stated: "The employment crisis has brought in its train despair, insecurity and worsening problems of social exclusion and poverty worldwide...solving the global employment crisis is thus the key to restoring hope, social justice and rising living standards."

The World leaders are congregating in the World Social Summit under the aegis of UN, celebrating its 50th anniversary, in March (6-12) 1995 to tackle the human crisis brought about by poverty, unemployment and social alienation. Mr. Ali Taqi, Chief of Staff, releasing the ILO report observed: "Nobody has the answer or a set of answers that could end the crisis."

Our contention is that there is a solution — albeit not a quick fix one, but a longer term, strategic and dynamic one — through the global human growth model, which aims to provide three fundamental Es — (1) Education for all; (2) Employment for all; and (3) Energising all people of the world to realise their maximum potential through global approach, global leadership and global co-operation, which we shall elaborate in the following pages.

We need a new approach, a new concept and a new philosophy to the development of people and development of nations. The new approach must emphasise the centrality of human growth as the greatest resource and asset for the development of nations. That means every nation must accord first priority to this vital aspect in nation-building.

Concept of Human Growth

The central thesis of this treatise is that people are the key not only to the development of organisations but also to the development of nations and the world. So far we have placed great deal of emphasis on agricultural development, industrial development, economic development, security and defence development, and of late on environmental development, technological development, information and communications development, hoping somehow that this will, in the final analysis, contribute to the common-weal and human development. The World Bank in its World Development Report 1991, on the thesis, The Challenge of Development, maintained: "Few policies promote development as powerfully as effective investment in human resources. An estimated 80 per cent of the world's population lives in developing countries — a proportion that is rising. Crucial issues in many of these countries include expanding primary education, alleviating poverty, and controlling population growth through better education, healthcare, and family planning..."

Global Challenge

"In the time it takes to read this paragraph, roughly a hundred children will be born — six in industrial countries and ninety-four in the developing countries. Here lies the global challenge. No matter what the outlook in the industrial economies, the world's long-term prosperity and security by sheer force of numbers - depend on development."

Human Growth

Unlike classical economic growth, where the concern is for the production of goods and services and economic wealth, in the new and contemporary concept of human growth, the centrepiece is the human being and his/her growth.

Three Stages

In the life of the human being there are three stages of growth as shown below:

Three Stages

S/No.	Age	Stage	Development
I	1 — 25 years	Education	Learning, knowledge, skills, specialisation and expertise
II	26 — 50 years	Employment	Training and development, cross fertilisation, career development and experience
III	51 — 75 years	Energising for Self-actualisation	On-the-job development, top of career, career goals, professional goals, life goals, organisational goals, national goals, global goals, personal fulfilment

The first stage of growth is between 1 to 25 years from childhood going onto young adulthood, which is concerned with education and learning — the most crucial stage of development of human personality, that is unique, fundamental and individualistic. This is the stage of enlightenment and discovery. This is perhaps the most wonderful stage of life, full of dreams, fun, joy of living and growing, full of love, happiness and innocence. I remember my son, when he was eight years old in the second grade in the Jakarta International School in Indonesia and when he was asked by his teacher to write what he wanted to be, when he grew up, wrote; "When I grow up, I want to be God. I want to bless and protect people. I want to be strong, and I will eat egg to do that. Please God, let me be God." The Principal of the School put it upon the notice board for all the parents to read. He said in all his years of experience he had never heard of anything like that. At the age of eight, anything is possible! Isn't that absolutely fantastic!

The second stage of human growth is that of employment and work, through which we express our personality through work, innovation and creativity. We build careers by building institutions, organisations, businesses, nations and the world through new ideas, concepts, materials with the help of other people. We generate wealth for the society and world through the application of our knowledge science, technology and management. This is also the wonderful stage' of commitment, responsibility and sharing through love and marriage, family, community, nation and humanity. More important, we help build people to become a great resource and asset in the organisations, nations and the world.

The third stage of growth is the stage of self-realisation and self-actualisation – the highest stage of life – where we use all our energies, motivation and challenge to realise our maximum potential. This is the stage of fulfilment of the ultimate potential of the individual. This is the key to human growth, happiness, prosperity, peace and decency.

Each of the three stages of human life is very important in the achievement of human growth. In the first stage of 25, you are laying the foundation of growth by acquiring knowledge, education, skills, habits, attitudes, character, expertise, specialisation and professionalism. In the second stage, you are building the superstructure of your career and development by utilising your expertise and professionalism and putting into practice your ideas, concepts and philosophy to generate wealth for the organisation, society, through your work in industry, business, trade. In the third stage, you try to achieve the pinnacle of success by realising your maximum and ultimate potential, your ideas and dreams in building institutions, nation and the world. Your happiness knows no bounds when you realise your dreams and ultimate potential and the pursuit of the achievement of ultimate potential is a process that keeps you challenged,motivated and offers you great joy and happiness.

The Concept

The concept of human growth is that every human being, regardless of his race, religion, age, sex, colour or nationality, etc, is given the opportunity to grow to realise his maximum and unique potential. Self-actualisation is the core of the concept of human growth.

The concept of human growth goes beyond the concept of full employment, which in itself seems like a mirage, almost unattainable, in most parts of the world. In our new concept, not only do we provide a job to every able-bodied and willing person but also we provide an equal and full opportunity to grow and develop his unique personality and potential. Every human being is provided full and equal opportunity to realise his maximum potential. In the growth and development of individual lies the growth and development of companies, organisations and nations. It was Adam Curie who said very aptly: 'Countries are underdeveloped largely because most of the people are undeveloped, having had no opportunity of expanding their potential capacities in the service of society." Underdevelopment of nations is the function of underdevelopment of their people. Lack of opportunity is the crux of the problem of human growth. Given the opportunity, the fundamental assumption of human growth is that people strive to grow and realise whatever is their unique individual potential.

Years ago, when I went to Indonesia as a management consultant, some of my Chinese clients used to tell me that Indonesians are basically lazy; they do not want to work hard; they believe in 'jam karet' or rubbertime; they can never be depended upon; and they can never be trained to work hard and smart. But systematic training, guidance, supervision and management could completely transform them to become excellent workers, managers and directors. Soon my clients were convinced that it is not in their nature to be lazy, to be late and undependable.

One of my Japanese clients is proud to claim that the productivity of the Indonesian workers is as high as the productivity of the Japanese worker in Osaka. It is so because the system of management, training, supervision and development or, in short, utilising the potential of the worker, is the same.

Without the opportunity, people remain uneducated, unemployed, untrained, unutilised and unfulfilled. This is perhaps the fate of 70 per cent of the 5.5 billion of the world, particularly in Asia, Africa, South America. But even in advanced countries like USA, Europe, Japan, etc, while a majority are exposed to education, employment, training and development, research in some of the organisations indicates that only 5 to 10 per cent are able to realise their maximum potential.

Basic Premise

The first basic premise of human growth model is that every human being has potential, that is unique to the individual. In other words, there is no human being without potential.

The second premise is that given the right environment and opportunity, every person is capable of realising his unique potential. The limiting factors are the environment and the lack of opportunity, not the human being.

The third premise is that every individual has the basic urge to fulfil himself and to realise his potential.

The fourth premise of human growth is that it is dynamic, not static. You can never know what a person can achieve in the future.

The fifth basic premise is that the promotion of human growth results in the promotion of human peace, prosperity and happiness.

The sixth is that human growth is achieved through global effort, co-operation, research and management. In modern times, you cannot realise yourself, if you do not go global. If we plan to promote the growth of all the 5.5 billion people of the world, we need global effort, co-operation, expertise and management. Long ago, Mr. Lee Kuan Yew, the dynamic leader of Singapore observed wisely: "The development of Singapore cannot be left in the hands of Singaporeans only. We need everybody in the world, who can make a contribution to the development of Singapore and we welcome them with open arms."

DEFINITION OF HUMAN GROWTH

We may define human growth as the dynamic process of systematically identifying the potential and the ultimate potential of the individual, through a human resources inventory, developing the potential through education, training and development, providing the right employment opportunities at the right time through the right career pathing and progression and energising the individual through the right motivation for the greatest possible realisation of one's intrinsic abilities, ideas, and dreams, contributing to the success of the organisation, nation and world and thus, human progress, prosperity, happiness and peace.

The above definition of human growth focuses on the major facets of management of human growth:

1. Systematically and scientifically identifying the potential of an individual on a continuous basis through a global human resource inventory;
2. Developing the potential through education, training and development;
3. Providing the right employment opportunity at the right time through career pathing and progression, on-the-job rotational assignments and evaluating performance and realisation of the potential at every level;
4. Energising through right motivation to realise one's maximum, ultimate and unique potential;
5. Encouraging individuals for the greatest realisation of their intrinsic abilities, ideals, goals and dreams; and
6. Enabling the individuals to contribute to the success of the organisations and nations and thus to human prosperity, peace, progress and happiness.

It is clear that the management of human growth is extremely complex, dynamic and sophisticated and appears almost herculean. For example, the very first phase of systematically and scientifically identifying the potential and ultimate potential of every individual of a human population of 5 billion around the globe is indeed an Olympian task, not to speak of developing, utilising and realising the potentialities of the people. What we need is a system — a global management system or model of global human growth.

PHILOSOPHY OF GLOBAL HUMAN GROWTH

For the formulation, development and implementation of global human qua growth model, the first essential prerequisite is a management philosophy, which stipulates the values, principles, vision and goals of human growth management system. There are eight-fold tenets of the philosophy and they are as follows:

1. *Respect for human kind*. We must respect every human being, regardless of one's race, colour, sex, religion and nationality.

2. *Respect for cultural differences of humanity*. We must respect and enjoy the cultures, social mores and beliefs of different people of the world.

3. *Promotion of human growth*. Every human being has one's own unique set of ideas, skills, concepts, motives, goals and dreams and it is essential to spot and nurture his individual potential.

4. *Plan human development*. Each and every human being of 5½ billion population needs individual human development plan - long-term, mid-term and short-term, based on individual potential.

5. *Strive for human fulfilment*. Find the right job for the right man at the right time, taking into consideration individual interests and organisational interests, since work is the vehicle through which we give expression to the full range of our personality.

6. *Achieve human prosperity*. Through human growth, we pursue the achievement of human prosperity, not just the elimination of poverty, illiteracy and unemployment, where the per capita income of every individual is a minimum of US $5000 and per capita contribution to GNP is 20 times one's per capita, *i.e.*, $ 100,000.

7. *Establish human peace*. Establishment of peace on Earth is a *sine qua non* for the development, implementation and achievement of human growth model, since every individual is busy pursuing and striving hard and smart to realise his maximum potential in the service of society, nation and the world. There is no time for hate, strife, violence, crime, destruction and war.

8. *Utilise global co-operative advantage*. Through promotion of global co-operation, the developed and developing countries assist each other in the development and implementation of global human growth, instead of mere financial aid. For example, the developing countries would need the help of developed countries in developing national human resources inventories and updating them annually. A consortium of developed countries can help India and China or some other

countries in the areas of providing education for all or employment for all and energising all to self-actualisation. This is the concept of utilising global co-operative advantage, instead of pursuing competitive advantage. We must harness what Mr. Konosuke Matsushita calls Shuchi - collective wisdom of people—to tackle the problems of poverty, illiteracy, unemployment and social disintegration.

The philosophy provides guidance and sense of direction for the implementation of global human growth model.

GLOBAL COMMITMENT

It is necessary for every nation to make a policy decision and national commitment, to human growth, to provide the fundamental 3Es — education for all, employment for all and energising all to reach their maximum potential and convert every human being into a great asset. All the nations join together in according top priority to human growth and make a global commitment to assist each other in the development, implementation and achievement of global human growth. This is the first step towards the management of global human growth model.

GLOBAL HUMAN RESOURCES INVENTORY (GHRI)

The first-phase of the model is to develop a global human resources inventory —the opening stock of global human resources which represents the human capital of the world, the wealth of the world. The first step in developing the global human resources inventory (GHRI) is to develop national human resource inventories in all the nations of the world, which is a daunting task to most countries of the world and which will need expert and professional assistance to draw up national inventories. The diagram next page shows the process of formulating GHRI.

Utilising the latest information technology, GHRI is drawn up annually covering every citizen beginning from the ages 6 to 60, paying particular attention to people between the ages of 9 to 35. In addition to all the demographic, economic, psychographic, socio-cultural details, the core of the inventory is: "What is the potential of the individual? What is the ultimate potential of the individual? What are the dreams of the individual? What are the strengths and weaknesses of the individual?"

In order to develop the right data on potential, we have to utilise assessment tools in the form of a battery of psychological and tests, personal interviews to identify the potential and ultimate potential of each child and citizen.

GLOBAL HUMAN RESOURCES INVENTORY & EXCHANGE 13-1

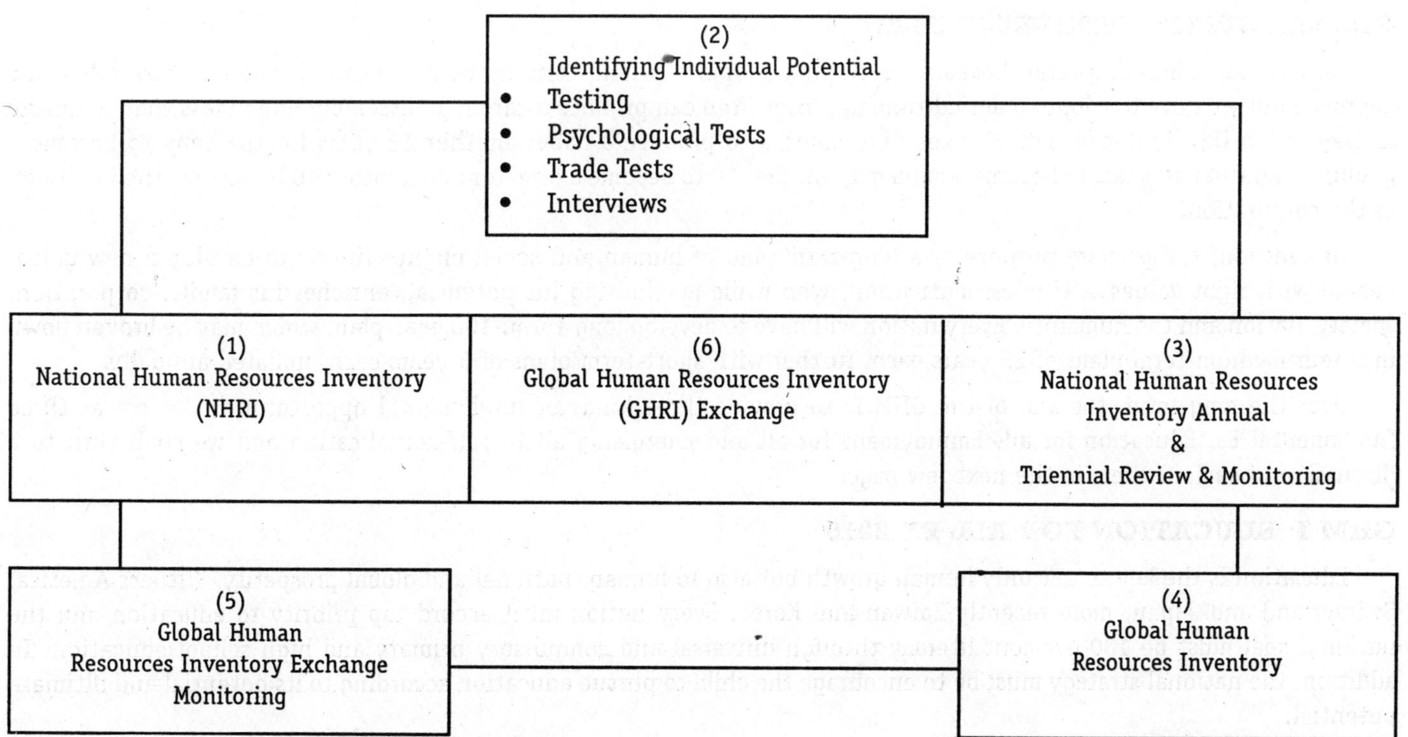

Once we have this data, we have to assist the individual to develop, nurture, maximise and reach the ultimate potential by providing opportunities of education suited to one's potential, employment suited to his potential and education and energise the individual through motivation to realise the maximum and ultimate potential and we have to monitor and evaluate the progress at every stage of the career of the individual, as he/she makes progress through the three stages of life.

Potential Dynamic

The reason we have the annual and triennial reviews is because human potential is dynamic, not static. They keep changing or "growing" new goals, new aspirations, new dreams, new vistas, new horizons.

Pyramid of Human Growth

Energising : Self-actualisation

Employment : Career Pathing and Progression

Education : High School, Vocational and University

Human Resource Planning

Identification of Individual Potential

Why Global?

If we leave this exercise to national initiative, it might be feasible for a few nations to undertake this gigantic exercise unheard of in human history but the majority of the nations may not be able, in view of lack of expertise, funds or priorities or leadership. That's why the global approach and leadership is necessary. We want every child and person – 5.5 billion of the world — to benefit from the human growth process. We want every child to go to school and pursue education suited to its potential. Next, every person is provided with employment based on one's education and training and potential. Next, every person is energised to self-actualisation, reaching one's potential. If the individual has potential to become a driver, he becomes a good driver. He has potential to become a president of a company or MNC or a country, he becomes that, through the model.

The global inventory offers global human resources information and exchange so that it can be used like global stock exchange in human resources.

GLOBAL HUMAN RESOURCES PLAN

We have to think long term, because developing people is a long-term process. We cannot adopt an assembly line approach but we have to adopt an agricultural approach. You can produce a car on an assembly line in less than a minute as they do in USA or Japan; but it takes nine months to produce a baby; another 22 years for the baby to become a graduate; another 10 years to become a manager; another 10 to become a director and another 10 to become the Chairman of the corporation!

In addition, the primary purpose of a long-term plan of human and social engineering is to develop a new global person with right values, attitudes, motivation, who while maximising his potential, enriches his family, corporation, society, nation and the humanity. Every nation will have to develop long-term -100 year-plan, which may be broken down into four medium-term plans of 25 years each, further with short-term plans of 5 years each, updated annually.

Over the long-term, the aim of the GHM is to provide three kinds of fundamental opportunities, known as three fundamental Es: Education for all, Employment for all and Energising all to self-actualisation and we shall turn to a discussion of each of them in the next few pages.

GHM I: EDUCATION FOR ALL BY 2010

Education is the key to not only human growth but also to human, national and global prosperity. Witness America, Switzerland and Japan, more recently Taiwan and Korea. Every nation must accord top priority to education and the national goal must be 100 per cent literacy through universal and compulsory primary and high school education. In addition, the national strategy must be to encourage the child to pursue education according to its potential and ultimate potential.

Child Development and Home Environment

Childhood is perhaps the most vital part of human life, one of the most memorable and enjoyable periods in many cases. The family is the first school of learning for a child and the child learns the most basic building blocks of personality and character — love, respect, honour, caring, service and ten commandments - and love of father and mother must be the elixir of life, providing the happiness and emotional security to the child. A good family and good home environment have the most decisive impact on the child's development and personality for the rest of its life and the ability to learn and grow into a fine upright responsible human being. Every nation must nurture family values and human values, so that children of the world are loved and well taken care of and have a bright future.

Identification of Potential

By the age of 6, every child is given series of psychological and trade tests and interviews to determine the potential of the child and we must nurture, develop and maximise through 12 years of school education. In addition to 3 Rs and languages we must instill and develop in very child power of analysis, creativity leadership and capacity to change the world for better. We must give special attention to the children and people who want to change the world through their creativity. Children must be provided opportunities to play games and sports and develop leadership and sportsmanship qualities which stand in good stead in life. They learn to win and lose gracefully and give and take, team spirit and school spirit, national spirit.

Career guidance and counselling and part-time work and weekend working and recreational placement experiences prepare children and young people to learn to work and enjoy the joy of working and learn self-discipline.

35 per cent Vocational Education

Depending on the potential, every nation should plan to achieve a target of 35 per cent of students going into vocational and trade schools to provide an abundant supply of technicians and skilled employees for nation's industrial, business and economic development. We need all kinds of technicians like programmers, systems analysts, medical and health technologists, IT specialists, lab technicians of all kinds, textile, chemical, petrochemical, oil, energy, machine tool, space, computer, etc and every nation adds value to its human power pool by giving access to polytechnic and vocational and trade schools.

35 Per cent University Education

Nations, particularly developing, must aim to reach 30 per cent to 35 per cent university education for their people and thus add great value to their human resources. The university is a place where young minds come together to study and to research with a view to not only acquiring knowledge but also to create new knowledge, discover new theories, principles and concepts in science, technology, education, management that help humankind to make progress and help change the world for better. Developing countries must send some of their best and brightest students to top universities in America, Britain, Germany, etc. and bring them back to develop wealth through the application of techniques of applied sciences, technology and management in industry, agriculture, business and trade, government. The Asian dragons – Hong Kong, Taiwan, South Korea and Singapore are good examples who have benefitted by giving access to their best students to foreign universities and later to apply their knowledge to develop their nations.

The developing countries would do well to study the NIEs and learn to emulate in providing opportunities to 30 per cent to 35 per cent of young to go to universities and acquire knowledge to fulfil themselves and to develop their nations. We believe that the universities of the world can play a vital and significant role in developing people, nations and the world.

To achieve the above targets of 100 per cent school education, 35 per cent vocational and 35 per cent university education, every nation will have to give top priority in the national budgets to develop thousands of schools, hundreds of polytechnic and hundreds of universities in each nation and they will have to seek help of advanced countries to build schools, labs, playgrounds, polytechnic and vocational centres and universities and this is the most productive investment, the rate of return is the highest, because their products of the educational institutions will produce wealth for nations beyond one's imagination.

Thailand, with a population of about half of Japan's has only about 50 universities, while Japan has more than 520. Even though 20 per cent of Thailand's 18-year-old students want to enter universities each year, only a small per centage are able to do so. The figure in Japan is more than 32 per cent. Thailand will need at least two universities in each of the 76 provinces. The cost of investment is huge but not all that unrealistic. The government has to provide its people with opportunities for the best possible education. How well Thailand can develop its human resources and its potential will affect its development and its capability to survive in what will assuredly be a very competitive 21st century. The most important factor impeding the development of nations is the lack of skilled human power pool. China, to educate its millions, has 713,000 primary schools, 5.5 million teachers and 122 million pupils under its compulsory nine-year education programme. The 71,000 junior high schools are staffed by 3 million educating 41.2 million students. About 70 per cent of the schools are in rural areas. By the end of the century, elementary school enrolment is expected to reach 145 million, an increase of 23 million and junior high schools aim to enrol 60 million students. The basic education expenditure is quadrupling from 44 billion Yuan in 1991, a mere 270 Yuan ($31) per student to 160 billion Yuan by 2000, which represents 65 per cent of national education fund then, an average annual increase of more than 11 per cent.

It is necessary for the developing nations to use the global co-operative advantage by inviting the developed nations, with their experience and expertise in education, to participate in the development of millions of primary, secondary and higher secondary schools, polytechnic and vocational schools and universities, campuses, playgrounds, and sports facilities, labs and libraries, computers and international super-highways, millions and millions of teachers, professors, readers, lecturers, curriculum development, teaching techniques and methodologies, dormitory facilities, audiovisuals, interactive multimedia learning, etc. for mutual benefit and advantage. The nations can provide opportunities to their people through scholarships to study in various parts of the world. The developing countries invite experts and specialists and professors to help develop appropriate educational systems so that no child or person is deprived of education at any level either in the country or outside in some other country. The fundamental principle is that if there is an Einstein in a child in Bangarpet, in India, we must help that child to become an Einstein! If we leave this matter only to individual nations, they may not be able to fulfil the aspirations of their people and we need global co-operation, co-ordination and leadership. The resources are there and we need to reorder our national and global priorities. It is a matter of creativity and coming up with ideas to reach the goal of education for all and leading every child from darkness to light. Aid is not the only answer.

The super highway to riches is education at the primary, secondary, higher secondary, polytechnic and vocational and university levels. The nations of the world will have to come together and help each other to achieve universal basic education (100 per cent), 35 per cent vocational and polytechnic education and 35 per cent university education to acquire knowledge and professional skills to create the wealth of nations. The nations will have to give top priority to education in their national budgets and invest in their people to create intellect. They need professional and technical assistance from the developed nations, who can use their expertise, knowledge, technology, management and resources and thus create employment opportunities in human development, infrastructure development, economic development and social development around the world.

A good school leaves indelible impact on students. Mr. Lee Buechler, '78, President of Phamis, a technology company in Seattle told me, "The School (Harvard Business School) changed my personal expectations about what I achieve in my career, about what I do with my life. It put a monkey on my back that probably I will never shake the idea that I can achieve a whole lot more than I have so far. I attribute the awakening: of that belief to my experience at the school[5]

GHM II: EMPLOYMENT FOR ALL

The second phase of GHM - Employment for all — is even more daunting and challenging not only for the developing nations but also for the developed nations, all of whom are reeling under the burden of unemployment anywhere from 11 per cent to 60 per cent in some of the developed and in some of the developing nations respectively. The great potential of the people created by achieving the target of education for all will be completely dissipated and amount to nothing, if we do not create opportunity for every knowledgeable and skilled individual to put his/her knowledge and skills to great use for his/her benefit, career and growth as well as for the benefit and growth of one's organisation and nation.

5. David Ewing, Inside the Harvard Business School 1990, Random House, New York, pp. 10-11.

That brings us to the second major policy commitment and decision to give top priority, after education, to employment for all its citizens based on their education, potential and ultimate potential, either within the country or without, in cooperation with other nations. While this target — employment, for all - looks like a mirage to most nations of the world, it is possible, like in the case of 6 dragons in East Asia — Hong Kong, Taiwan, South Korea, Singapore, Malaysia and Thailand — to achieve the target by engaging the world to participate in development through free markets and free trade. The developing countries can provide opportunities to the developed nations, particularly the MNCs, to start industries, joint ventures and subsidiaries to create employment opportunities for the people and in addition the MNCs will provide advanced human resource development, capital, technology, management, R&D, science and export products and services, which means the quality, costs, prices become competitive.

Human Resources Development

The nations of the world must give great attention to training, development and education — human resources development — in the employment stage, the second important stage of human life, which will last most of the best part of human life — 25 to 75 years.

At the start of employment career, every organisation must identify the potential and ultimate potential and provide a career suited to his potential, education qualifications. Konosuke Matsushita's human resources philosophy was: "We make men, before we make products". The individual starts with induction/orientation and job skills training to learn the job, skills, techniques, attitudes, habits in order to do the job effectively. Good companies develop human resource planning to forecast the needs of the people at various levels of the organisation and to supply the people over a period. The individual is developed for higher assignments depending on one's potential and organisational needs since the ideal is to promote individual interests and organisational interests together.

The organisations must conduct an annual training needs survey to determine the organisation, division and department and individual needs of training and development and formulate a human resources development plan and organise training and development programmes to meet the needs of all employees, workers, supervisors, managers, directors — every year so that not only do they implement company philosophy, objectives, policies, systems, and procedures but also achieve organisational objectives, high profits, high productivity and high quality. The human resource development strategy is to use in-company off-the-job classroom theoretical training and on-the-job practical training and out-company formal training courses and out-country foreign training and development programmes, seminars and conferences. Most of the individual training and development takes place on the job, although people can learn all the time, anywhere and everywhere, if they keep their eyes, and more important, mind open from anybody and everybody, from their superiors, peers and subordinates, if only the individual and the organisations cultivate a learning culture, as learning is the key to the development of individual, organisations and nations. A simple idea can transform the universe, just as human action, proclaimed the Vedas, the great scriptures of Hinduism in India, can transform the nature of the universe.

I must have, through our MNR Associates, international management consultancy firm, trained, developed and educated more than a million people from sales girls to chairmen of corporations in various parts of the world, and it is always amazing to see the transformation of the personality of people after systematic, training, guidance and supervision. I remember a Chairman of a large corporation in Indonesia exclaiming "Professor, how can you ask me to smile when I am speaking?" during a coaching session for a video programme. But within a year, he not only learned to smile but also to charm an international audience of top executives in a world conference. Plain Janes are converted into Singapore girls, delivering great customer service and high profits to Singapore Airlines. The potential of people always amazes me in my work around the world regardless of whether they are Indians, Americans, Japanese, Nigerians, Egyptians, Bolivians, Indonesians, Chinese, Singaporeans, British, Fijians, Australians, Seychellois, etc.

Continuous life-long training, development and education — human resources development — at every stage of the career and employment is necessary to develop, nurture, maximise and realise the potential of people and to update their skills, knowledge and concepts and to keep up with the new developments in their fields of specialisation, business, markets, customers, technologies, applied and fundamental sciences, research and development, design and management. You stop learning, you stop growing.

Every nation must ask organisations to allocate 4 to 5 per cent of labour costs like in Singapore and Indonesia respectively, to human resources development budgets. It may be necessary for nations to organise National Industry

Training Boards to provide training and development to people working in different industries, particularly medium and small-scale industries and businesses.

Strategies of Employment for all

Employment for all is a very simple goal, but like all simple propositions, the hardest to achieve, unless there is a global co-ordinated and systematic effort and mechanism put in place to achieve the goal by the end of 2020. So far there is no global effort, although there are plenty of piecemeal measures in USA, France, Germany, Italy, India, China, Indonesia, Thailand, Mexico, Brazil, etc.

America at G-7 Jobs Summit unveiled $ 13 billion job training to provide centralised assistance, school-to-world assistance programme and retrain retrenched workers with a view to boosting employment. France and Germany are considering work sharing programme, where a radical 4-day 33-hour week idea is supposed to generate new jobs.

In Denmark, the government gives workers paid one year leave to stay home, so that other people are given employment opportunities. McKinsey Global Institute in its study states that the main challenge for Europe is to expand the workforce and increase its productivity to provide for the imminent wave of retirees.

OECD, after a 2-year in-depth study of unemployment crises urged the world's richest democracies to reduce minimum wage protection employment security and unemployment benefits and to overhaul economic, labour and social policies, flexibility in working time, encourage more entrepreneurship, new technologies to create more high-tech jobs, better job-training, improved education programmes, such as on-the-job training apprenticeships, US style head-start programmes, which encourage early entry into education systems for young children.

China is trying to liberalise with market reforms to promote growth to absorb its millions in urban cities and start village enterprises to keep rural people from migrating to urban coastal cities and creating congestion and jobs crisis. It has worked out a strategy to develop labour-intensive enterprises in cities to absorb surplus labour, incentives like loans, tax exempting reduction to employ more people. Various training centres to train people and provide skills, project of reemployment for retrenched and unemployed for six months or more, to provide career introduction, new skills training, job seeking instruction and self-relief production.

India has opened the country with liberalised market reforms and foreign investment to create employment opportunities for the millions, particularly educated unemployed.

Singapore has no unemployment problem but a labour shortage problem. However, many high-tech industries are laying off old and unskilled people almost 100,000 of them, creating a big worry to the government. The government plans to retrain them, so that they become employable.

Indonesia is planning to provide 11 million jobs during the current five-year plan through further liberalisation and market reforms, attracting foreign investment to open up employment opportunities. It is also trying to provide more emphasis on human resource development and quality of people to attract MNCs to start enterprises in Indonesia.

Some Strategies for Employment for all

1. Policy Commitment. National policy and commitment to accord top priority to provide employment to all citizens from the age of 18 through national schemes and global co-operation;

2. Global Co-operation. Accurate unemployment data. Every nation has to gather accurate data on unemployment, so that they are aware of the extent of the problem, through global study and methodology. China just revised its methodology of counting the unemployed.

3. Adopting Countries. The G7 and OECD, NIES, China, India, Indonesia, etc. could come together and design a global plan of adoption of some countries to develop the people, infrastructure and economy.

4. World Security. The national, regional, global security Corps of 10 million people under the auspices of UN may be organised not only to provide employment but to also provide personal and national security in cases of ethnic, civil, political, religious strife and conflicts.

5. Regional Co-operation. ASEAN, EU, APEC, SAARC, NAFTA and more such blocks may get involved to promote trade, development and peace and create employment opportunities.

6. Keep them in school. Every nation must promote compulsory high school education of 12 years, instead of allowing child labour and depriving children of education. Keep the best and brightest in polytechnic and universities for another 5 years or so and thus enhance their potential.

7. Government employment strategy. Provide employment through Government, public sector, private and cooperative sectors, Civil Service, Military Service, National Development Corp, Peace Corps, Trusteeship, Small Business Authority, Rapid Emergency Force, Entrepreneurship, National Sector or Joint Sector between Government and private sector or Corporate sector, etc., (Build-operate and transfer) BOT ventures, joint ventures; Education Corps, Social Service Corps, Research and Development Corps, National Employment Exchange, National Human Resources Information and Exchange, foreign investments and subsidiaries, National Apprenticeship Scheme, Industry Training Boards.

8. Retailing System. A modern retailing and distribution system can generate a lot of self-employment, entrepreneurship and employment, contribute to the development of economy and industries.

9. Co-operation. Co-operatives are self-help and employment-generating enterprises and they can be organised in any sector of the economy, banking, manufacturing, education, retailing, marketing, services, transportation, etc.

10. Handicrafts. There is a rich heritage of arts and crafts around the world, which can be preserved, promoted, marketed and exported, generating a lot of employment.

11. Tourism. Global travel and tourism provides great opportunities to developing countries and that last year world's people spent $350 billion on travel alone.

12. Sports and Games. Every nation must encourage every kid in school to play games and sports as a part of its personality development. There is a fantastic opportunity in this business to generate employment. Building good sports infrastructure will provide employment to teachers, coaches, doctors, nurses, masseurs, groundsmen, utilities people, security staff.

If the world — the developed and developing — were to concentrate on human development, infrastructure development and economic development, we believe that we can achieve the global goal of employment for all, the able and willing people to work. What we need now, in the beginning of this new millennium, is a global solidarity, co-operation and leadership to single mindedly pursue and achieve the goal by 2020.

GHM III : ENERGISING ALL TO SELF-ACTUALISATION

Once the fundamental Es are achieved, the next equally important but more challenging task - Energising - of the global model is to assist people to realise their maximum potentialities and to grow to their fullest stature and to reach self-actualisation or self-realisation. It calls for a carefully orchestrated individual career development plan based on one's potential and performance on the job.

There are four important characters influencing the process of energising and they are shown below:

People Potential and Ultimate Potential			
(1) Government	(2) Education	(3) Organisation/Company	(4) Individual
Human Resources inventory Human Resources Plan Monitoring Human Resources Plan and GH Model	1. High School 2. Polytechnic/Vocational 3. University 4. Professional 5. Higher/Refresher	1. Training—Basic Skills 2. Career Development 3. Management Succession 4. Motivation 5. Continuous Learning 6. Job Enrichment	1. Potential Dreams, Goals 2. Educational 3. Career Development 4. Achievement 5. Learning Commitment 6. Self-actualisation 7. Contribution to Profession, Community Nation and World

The government plays a vital role in establishing national policy, commitment to human growth, formulates Human Resources Inventory and identifying the potential and ultimate potential of the people, and Human Resources plan—long, middle and short-term - and establishes macro-economic environment and global co-operative advantage to achieve the 3Es and targets of $ 5000 per capita income, 100 per cent high school, 35 per cent vocational and 35 per cent university education, and every person achieving self-actualisation.

The education system develops the personality and potential of all people by providing 100 per cent high school education; 35 per cent vocational education and 35 per cent university education based on their potential and career choices.

The organisation or the company provides employment to all the citizens, trains and develops them, according to their potential to reach their ultimate potential over a period of 25 to 35 years through individual career development plans, management succession systems, right motivation, compensation and benefit plans.

Fourthly and ultimately, the individual must play the pivotal role of assuming responsibility for his own growth by utilising all the opportunities provided by other three characters and strive hard and smart to realise his maximum and ultimate potential in order to enrich his professional career, family, organisation, society, the nation and finally the humanity.

EMPOWERMENT OF PEOPLE

Exxon Example

Mr. Michael Haider, former Chairman of Exxon, the largest oil company and the second largest industrial company in the world, observed the key to the success of Exxon:

"In the life of a corporation, today's success is largely the product of three types of executive actions taken yesterday: selecting the right people; placing them in the right jobs; and seeing to it that they were able to grow to meet their own needs and those of the organisation. This activity is not a programme in the usual sense, any more than selling or making profits are programmes. It has no fixed dimensions, no timetable, no cut-off point."

He and four top executives in a Committee would meet every Tuesday to review the potential and performance of their executives throughout Exxon. "Once a year, the chief executive officer of the larger affiliates meets with the Committee and reviews in-depth his company's development activities and its replacement situation and appraises the performance and potential of all his key management personnel. He goes over his replacement tables, his plans for rotational assignments, and specific steps being taken to increase the effectiveness of the organisation." Yes top executives and indeed all executives must consciously develop the habit of looking closely at their people and their potential and make a generous contribution of their time and effort to make of the budding flowers really bloom.

Shell Study

The Shell Oil is the second largest oil company and first largest non-American company in the world and one of the few companies in the world which has done considerable amount of research to evolve a methodology to spot the potential and ultimate potential of people working in Shell companies around the world. More than of a quarter of a century ago, Shell wanted to find out who, among the hundreds of thousands of people employed in more than 80 countries are likely to become the top executives and Directors of the Main Board. They organised a global project, a top Shell Executive at Shell Centre in London explained to me, to formulate a methodology, to identify the potential and ultimate potential of their people. Prof. Van Lennep of Utrecht University and Dr. Mueller, a senior executive, the Project Team, conducted a 3-year study first, studying leaders in all walks of life, second the performance appraisals of Shell executives for 10 years to identify the qualities that made them leaders and top executives respectively and then, third, conducted personal interviews with the top executives, asking them to look back on their careers in order to identify the qualities that helped them to become top executives and the qualities that their superiors looked for when they promoted them. After considerable research, and discussions and rationalisation, the team came up with five qualities that help spot potential and ultimate potential in Shell:

5 Qualities

1. Helicopter Quality
2. Power of Imagination
3. Sense of Realism
4. Power of Analysis
5. Power of Anticipation.

Shell, introduced these qualities in the appraisal system, which contains two parts, Performance Report, which evaluates the performance of the individual in the past year and Potential Report, which looks at the potential and ultimate potential using the five qualities to which are added a few more qualities as shown below:

1. Helicopter Quality,
2. Power of Analysis,
3. Power of Imagination,
4. Sense of Realism,
5. Achievement motivation,
6. Business Sense,
7. Decisiveness,
8. Capacity to Motivate,
9. Delegation, and
10. Communication.

Shell prepares individual career development plans and promotion routes, which are broadly classified into two categories — one takes you to the top of management through your area of specialisation, Marketing, Production, Research and Development, Human Resources, etc., and the other is that of generalisation where you reach the top through general management. It requires considerable orchestration of career development. First as a trainee you are strengthened in your area of marketing or production through training and challenging assignments for 2 to 3 years. Then you are rotated in various related departments and through quality control, human resources, production, marketing for 5 to 8 years and through further training and your performance is evaluated every year. Then you become the General Manager of a factory for 3 to 5 years and tested and evaluated. Then for another 3 years or so, you are deputed to be Managing Director in a foreign country to give foreign experience. Then you are brought to the headquarters to give you overall corporate experience and tested. Then you go back to become the Chairman of your country company. If you do very well for 5 to 10 years, you go to the top as a Director of the Main Board of Directors, then Vice Chairman and ultimately Chairman of Shell. This may take 25 to 35 years of very careful career planning, management succession, excellent performance and lots of training and development off the job and on the job. Your potential is constantly evaluated against your performance.

Senior Minister, Mr. Lee Kuan Yew said recently in Parliament that after having spent 40 years selecting men for big jobs - ministers, civil servants, Chairmen and CEOs, and having asked many CEOs on how they selected top executives, he found that Shell had the best system. He sent top ministers and civil servants to London to study the Shell system and implement it in Singapore.

Singapore Transformation

In an address to the undergraduates from two universities in Singapore on "what if I were a young undergraduate again?" Mr. Lee sketched the blueprint of selection and development of leaders in Singapore which is something very unique in the world. Mr. Lee, being himself top of the top 1 per cent of his class, believes in meritocracy, looked for the best and brightest in the school. They win SAF or Overseas Merit Scholarship and they study abroad in the best universities in America and the scholars are obligated to serve the government for 6-8 years. They are given challenging assignments and tests. They get married to a wife, either equal or better than them, because the wife has to bring up the children with the right values. Their careers are followed by the ministers. They are encouraged to participate in community, professional, social activities and evaluated. They are picked to serve as Members of Parliament and the very best are selected to serve as Ministers.

Global Human Growth Wheel

After a couple of terms, they can become a deputy Prime Minister and if they do very well, they can become Prime Minister. If they wish to go to Private sector after a term or a couple of terms as MP or Minister they can become CEOs and Chairmen of Statutory Boards, Private Sector Companies, Government listed companies or MNCs. Mr. Lee and the Prime Minister spend considerable time and effort to spot potential in people, develop them to achieve their maximum stature.

What happens to others, the non-high flyers? There is no need to despair because a country needs all kinds of skills and talents at all levels. We need salesmen, welders, machinists, cashiers, tellers, typists, programmers and people find careers suited to their talent, potential and qualifications. Mr. Matsushita dropped out of school at the age of nine but went on to build one of the biggest business corporations in the world, Matshushita Electrical Industries, employing 260,000 in 78 countries with a turnover of $ 24 billion and for many years he was the highest taxpayer in Japan!

There is the story of a Jewish billionaire, who signed with a cross mark. Once his banker got the nerve to ask the businessman: "Sir, why do you sign with just a cross mark? It is very easy to forge". The billionaire retorted: "If I knew how to sign, I would have been still the bellringer in the synagogue in my home town. They fired me because I couldn't sign, and they said that synagogue couldn't employ a person, who could not read or write!" There is always hope for everybody.

Every human being has potential and we must enhance the potential through the fundamental 3Es. We must raise the per capita income to US $ 5000 and every person contributes US $ 100,000 to the GNP of the nation. We would like to assist every nation to achieve this kind of income targets for the people of the world.

Global Human Growth Research

Global human growth has a fantastic field full of opportunities for fundamental and applied and empirical research, experimentation and experiences. Nations singly or together, or region wise or worldwide must conduct research on human growth, human resources inventory, human resources planning - long-term, mid-term and short-term, how to educate people in the rural areas, how to use multi-media information technology and interactive learning in the villages and urban areas, how to spot people for polytechnic and universities and for different disciplines, how to improve methodology to spot potential and how to monitor potential, how to dovetail human resource planning with national development planning and corporate planning, how to improve learning effectiveness, how to improve training and development of people, how to develop career development plans, management succession systems and implement them, how to develop methodology to identify the number of unemployed, how to develop human resources accounting, how to put people on the balance sheet, and financial statements, how to calculate the rate of return on investment on people, how to enrich jobs and enlarge jobs, how to develop global co-operative advantage and global consortiums to tackle poverty, unemployment, illiteracy and social alienation, how to improve human growth index - national and global, how to motivate people, how to improve morale of the people, how to develop global funding for various projects, how to develop global human resources Directory, Exchange and Information.

We need to undertake many global research projects on the experiences, experiments and research on human growth to develop and improve the theory and practice of global human growth in the new millennium.

GLOBAL HUMAN GROWTH INDEX

It is necessary to establish global standards to measure the progress of nations in achieving human growth on the basis of certain factors. The United Nations has a Human Development Index based on three factors.

1 *Life expectancy*, dealing with the life span of people in a country.

2. *Education level*, dealing with levels of education attained by the individuals in a country.

3. *Basic Purchasing Power*, dealing with income and its purchasing power in the country.

The latest report studied human development in 173 countries and ranked them all in order of achievement. Canada stood first, followed by Switzerland in the second spot and Japan in the third place. The World Bank issues a World Development Report, giving the World Development Indicator, covering the basic indicators like population, area, GNP and per capita, rate of inflation, life expectancy and adult illiteracy, and several other indicators.

We propose a comprehensive Global Human Growth Index based on 10 factors, which indicate and measure the state of human growth in all countries of the world on a ten-point rating scale, with the help of which we can rank the nations of the world every year. We must aim to achieve certain standards of human growth, if we want to enhance not only the quality of life but also human prosperity, happiness, progress and peace.

Education

1. 100 per cent education and literacy in all the nations
2. 35 per cent vocational education
3. 35 per cent university education
4. 100 per cent development of total human personality
5. 35 per cent leadership - political, business, education, economic, social, cultural, technological.

Employment

1. 100 per cent employment in the nation, region and world
2. Individual career development plans based on potential
3. 100 per cent training, development and education
4. Per capita income of US $ 5000 minimum and US $ 100,000 maximum (Average)
5. Global Human Resources Inventory
6. Global Human Resources Information and Exchange

Energising Potential

1. 100 per cent self-actualisation
2. Equal opportunities of employment and energising all people
3. No retirement age - people can work as long as they are fit, able and willing

The 10 Factors

The 10 factors in the Global Human Growth Index (GHI) are as follows:

1. Life Expectancy
2. Education level
3. Employment
4. Energising potential
5. Income
6. Population growth
7. Health and Fitness
8. Prosperity
9. Happiness

10 Achievement

The inter-country comparison will stimulate countries to shoot for higher standards and to learn from each other and annual report would motivate countries to excel and highlight the strengths and weaknesses of nations and how to capitalise on strengths and overcome the weaknesses.

GLOBAL CO-OPERATIVE ADVANTAGE

Inaugurating the World Summit for Social Development in Copenhagen, Mr. Boutros Boutros-Ghali, Secretary General of United Nations, called for a new social contract: "A new social contract at the global level, is required to bring hope to states and nations and to men and women around the world... In making social issues a universal priority, our intention is to take responsibility for the collective future of international society and to pledge ourselves anew to the idea of global solidarity... Today's global economy affects everyone. We also know that its effects are not at all positive. It erodes traditional ties of solidarity among individuals.

It has marginalised entire countries and regions, The gap between the rich and poor is getting wider poor is getting wider."

Prof. Paul Kennedy, the Yale Historian and author of *"Preparing For the 21st Century"* warns us of the great divide that if nothing is done about the imbalances in global population growth and wealth distribution, the survival of the planet earth will be threatened in the 21st century.

It is imperative that we move away from global divide, traditional concepts of national competitive advantage, beggar thy neighbour policy, neo-imperial economic and political colonialism, zero sum game to a new mindset and a new concept of co-operation, that is highly creative, constructive and co-operative — where the developed and developing nations come together in order to work together sharing knowledge, expertise, technology, science, information, research and management in order to develop every nation in the world to reach certain minimum standards of human growth, economic development and infrastructure development. Thus, we operate on the principle of global co-operative advantage, collecting the wisdom of the people of the world to solve problems of poverty, illiteracy, unemployment and social disintegration and to provide for education for all, to liberate humankind from the scourge of darkness; employment for all, to break the shackles of poverty and idleness; and energise all to create a new world human order of prosperity, peace, progress and happiness.

We have to look for a new set of middle axioms to work the global co-operative advantage to the benefit of all humankind, using the Model. Some of it is already happening in a haphazard and unsystematic way in bilateral, regional and multi-lateral co-operation but the systematic way in global co-operative advantage is yet to take place in the world.

There are already growth triangles like Indonesia-Singapore-Malaysia, Malaysia-Indonesia and Thailand, regional groups like ASEAN, SAARC, APEC, NAFTA, trying to help others.

We need, like the Marshal Plan, a very comprehensive plan and global compact between G-7 and nine countries in the Delhi meet (India, China, Brazil, Indonesia, Egypt, Pakistan, Mexico, Bangladesh) to tackle illiteracy and provide education for all. Another consortium of developed countries can work with some African countries. OECD countries can combine for example, their resources to promote economic development and infrastructure development of several countries in Asia and Africa. Japan, Germany, USA, Switzerland can work with China, India, and Indonesia on human resources development, using their superior technological, scientific, financial and managerial acumen, using MNCs, joint ventures, free flow of people from the developed to the developing and *vice-versa.* A developed China, India, Indonesia, Africa and Latin America would provide great markets and profits for the developed. Rich neighbours make rich markets; poor neighbours, poor markets. Free markets, trade and flow of people would generate mutual benefits and advantages for the developed and developing countries. To begin with, we must start with a few pilot projects around the world in the next year and gradually involve the whole world by the end of the decade.

GLOBAL HUMAN VISION AND FUTURE

World population has risen from about 1 billion in 1825, to 2 billion in 1925, to 4 billion in 1976 and to 5.3 billion in 1990. Estimates for 2025, range between 7.6 billion and 9.4 billion. 95 per cent of the world's population growth will take place in the developing nations.

In 1950, the population of Africa was half of Europe's. By 1985, it had drawn level and in 2025, it will be three times Europe's. China's population may rise from today's 1.3 billion to about 1.5 billion by 2025. India's population may rise from 853 million to 1.5 billion, too. India may have the largest population in the world by 2025, eventually reaching 2 billion. While the world must try to control the burgeoning billions, in view of limited natural resources, there is no time to lose for the global and national leadership to come together, as they have done in Copenhagen and regularly and periodically bi-annually in the future and develop a global vision of World Human Order that is global in perspective, national in operations and individual in approach.

The historic World Summit issued a declaration and a Global Action Plan approved by 193 countries of which 121 were heads of Governments in Copenhagen, ushering in a new era, where the focus is on human beings. The main points of the Declaration and Action Plan are as follows:

World Summit for Social Development Commitment and Action

DECLARATION	THE SITUATION	THE COMMITMENT	THE ACTION
	(1) ERADICATING POVERTY		
"For the first time in history, we gather as heads of state and government to recognise the significance of social development and human well being for all and to give these goals the highest priority both now and into the 21st century."	More than a billion people living in abject poverty, most in the developing countries. 70 per cent of the people are women.	Eradicating poverty in the world through decisive national actions and international co-operation, especially in Africa and the least developed nations.	• Urgent action preferably by 1996, to set national target dates and pursue comprehensive strategies for the eradication of absolute poverty, especially among women and children.
	(2) CREATING EMPLOYMENT		
	120 million people worldwide unemployed, many more under-employed.	Promote the goal of full employment as a basic priority of economic and social policies.	• Concerted efforts to meet established targets for improving access to adequate food, water, shelter, health care and education. • Urgent action to relieve debt burden of the countries that are in greates difficulty. • Expand and improve land ownership through land reform to tackle rural poverty. • Re-commitment to achieving full employment through emphasis on small and micro-enterprises and to explore new forms of work opportunities. • Ensure that World Bank and IMF policies give much higher priority to reducing poverty, unemployment, and hardship. • Provide education and training so that workers and entrepreneurs can adopt to changing technologies and economic conditions.
	(3) PROMOTING SOCIAL INTEGRATION		

The Indian Prime Minister, Mr. P.V. Narasimha Rao, observed in his statement to the Plenary Session: "It is only now, at the end of the century, that the leaders of the world have begun to think how to live, rather than how to kill or escape killing... Our vision for the summit should go beyond the summit itself so as to translate the vision into action. Commitments must be backed by the will to act."

The Vision

The vision is to convert every human being into a human asset through the provision of the fundamental 3Es, education to all, employment for all and energising all — men and women and young and old to realise all their maximum potentialities to rebuild and reinvent New World Human Order of great human prosperity, progress, peace, happiness and compassion. In order to achieve this, we need leaders of a very high order, who can think in global terms, mobilise national resources to promote human growth through the utilisation of human resources inventory, human resources planning, long, medium-and short terms —human resources development. We need leaders with a vision, dedication and commitment, who understand the aspirations of people, who motivate and lead the people to achieve their own goals and aspirations while contributing to the national objectives and global goals; who are good at combining individualism with nationalism and globalisation through the concept of global co-operative advantage; who are clean, honest and selfless; who have the capacity to inspire ordinary people to do extraordinary things in the interests of the people, society, nation and world, and convert people into the greatest asset of the nation; who can eliminate illiteracy, unemployment, poverty, crime, violence, war, disease and destruction; who are compassionate, decent, caring and loving; who have the capacity to create a New World human order and motivate everybody to contribute to the New Order, using the global human growth model. We are ready, willing and able to assist the leaders of the world to bring about such a great transformation, hitherto unheard of in human history.

Dynamics of Global Management

We shall discuss the chapter under the following sub-heading :
• Challanges in the Future • Matsushita talks how industrlalisation brings out prosperity
• The Information Superhighway under Construction • Conclusion

We shall look at the crystal ball, what kind of dynamics the future holds for global companies. How better can the global management have a substantial say in creating the future with their vision and mission and prepare their organisations to meet the challenging future known and unknown. We shall discuss the dynamics under the following headings :

CHALLENGES IN THE FUTURE

1. Managing growth and expansion
2. Creating Wealth for the Society
3. Nurturing Executive Talent
4. Learning life long to meet and create the future
5. Building a New World Order
6. Conclusion.

1. Managing Growth and Expansion of Global Companies

The Global companies in view of globalisation ethic, and resources available are able to face the challenges of expanding their companies and the operations in several more countries. Today India, China and South-East Asia, Middle-East, Brazil, Argentina, Chile in South America, Canada and of course USA, UK, Europe, etc., provide great opportunities for global companies to start and expand their business.

Lym Townsend, former Chairman and CEO of Chrysler Corporation, speaks about four fields of action for business growth.[1]

On the basis of my own experience with an automobile company which has operations in 18 countries in six continents, and which has tripled its world-wide sales in the past 10 years, I believe that modern business management to meet the challenge of growth must be concerned with four broad fields of action. Let me list these four fields of action; and then make a few comments about each.

Here they are:

First, business management should try to see the operations of the whole company in perspective and to keep all of its operations in balance and moving in phase with one another.

Second, management should take the greatest care in setting sound and realistic objectives, and must develop current information feedbacks to keep the company on course toward those objectives.

Third, it should structure the organisation of the company so as to make the best use of its human talents.

And. . .

Lynn Townsend, (Chairman and CEO, Chrysler Corporation) Management for Growth, A talk delivered to the management club, School of Business Administration, University of Michigan, Ann Arbor, Michigan, USA, February 19, 1969.

Fourth, it should make every effort to keep informed about, and related to the many social changes in contemporary life so as to discharge the responsibilities of the company as a good citizen.

Now let's consider the first point. Nothing is more characteristic of a man with first-class management talent than his ability to see a company's operations in the round, with balanced and appropriate attention being given to each of its component parts. Most of us have the natural human tendency to concentrate our attention on that part of a complex business operation that interests us the most. Engineers like to concentrate on engineering. Marketing men like to go on working at marketing. Production men feel most comfortable with production. And, accountants like to stay with accounting.

It would be a mistake to criticise this tendency too severely, because every company needs specialists who stay with their specialties. But it is also true that every company needs men who know how to look at the operation in true perspective. A company needs men who keep their eyes open to the long-range demands for the company's products, and who give adequate time and attention to making sure the company's programme of investment in productive capacity is adequate to estimated future demands. And a company is fortunate if the same man or men who plan capacity for the future are also giving thought to ways and means of maintaining the company's competitive firepower on the marketing front in the current period.

This is only one of the many problems of balance facing management in this period of growth. The needs of the present – including the needs of a company's shareholders for an adequate return on their investment – must be balanced against the needs of the future. Improving the known products upon which a company currently places its main reliance must be balanced against exploring the unknown to discover new products and services for future exploitation. And good performance in the domestic markets must be balanced by good performance in the markets outside our borders.

When a company begins to forget the need for balance, and especially when a company begins to be content with old formulas and spends too little time searching out new approaches and new opportunities, trouble is never far away. And that trouble usually shows up in the form of unsatisfactory numbers. Those numbers can apply to almost any part of a company's operations. But normally they show up first in relation to sales and earnings. This brings us to the second point.

If there is any one characteristic that makes modern management different from the kind of management that was common forty or fifty years ago, it is the emphasis today on what many people have called management by objective. Not too many years ago it was possible to manage a company by personal contact. Under this arrangement, the management picked men to manage the key areas of a company's operations and held them personally responsible for getting results. If the results were not forthcoming, the key men were discharged or transferred to positions of lesser responsibility. In other words, the pressures were personal and solutions were attempted almost entirely in terms of new personalities.

Under modern conditions, this arrangement is no longer feasible. A company cannot operate through personal pressure alone. It has to work as a company towards generally agreed-upon objectives that are understood by everyone in the organisation. Consequently, although there is still plenty of pressure for meeting those objectives, it is pressure of a fa[r] different and far *less* personal kind.

Today, a company must have plans that include sales objectives, investments to provide productive and marketing capacity to meet those objectives, and a realistic profit plan. What this boils down to is financial planning, without which no modern management can hope to succeed. With a good financial plan, management has a criterion always at hand to set up against current performance. If performance fails to measure up to the planned objectives, action can and must be taken immediately to change operating strategies so as to improve performance and bring it in line with plans.

Fortunately, for those of us who are responsible for measuring performance against objectives and for seeing to it that appropriate action is taken immediately when performance falls below planned levels, a new and wonderful battery of informational techniques has been placed in our hands. The electronic computer — in all its varied applications – has had a revolutionary impact on the practice of management. In the past 10 years, this new management tool has completely changed the nature, the amount, and the timeliness of the information available to the executive. This in turn is having its effect upon the speed and the quality of central decision-making, and the agility with which a company can change course of action when the information feedback indicates the need for change. It is also freeing some of the manager's time and energy for the increasingly demanding task of planning for the future.

The increased use of computers in the automobile industry over the past 10 years has astounded all of us. In 1958, for example, we had only 12 computers in operation at Chrysler — and these were used chiefly for accounting purposes and for processing the payroll.

Today, we have 155 computers. They are being used by virtually every department, division, and subsidiary of the company in all parts of the world, and for a constantly increasing number of applications. We use computers to give us an immediate feedback on the sales of our cars — market by market, model by model, and dealer by dealer. We use them to trace the progress of every car order through every stage of assembly and shipping until the completed car is in the dealer's hands ready for delivery to the customer.

We use them to consolidate the cost and profit plans of all the divisions into an overall profit plan for the corporation. We use them to prepare and send out engineering specifications and timing requirements to suppliers inside and outside the company on each of the 16,000 parts that must be combined to build an automobile. We use them to control machine tools, which automatically cut complicated dies for use in our plants.

Modern management can make use of computers to sort out the advantages of a wide range of options, technical and otherwise, having to do with decisions about the future course of the company. It can use computers to link together communications systems for worldwide operations. But above all, management uses computers to improve the quantity and quality of information about current operations. This information makes it possible to manage by objective in a way that was not even dreamed of twenty or thirty years ago.

When I arrive at my office in the morning, a three-by-five card is on my desk. On this card are four numbers - the objective for the number of units to be shipped during the current month - the number actually shipped the previous day from all our United States and Canadian assembly plants - the cumulative total of shipments for the month - and the number to be shipped during the rest of the month.

In the course of every working day I get additional information. This includes a daily domestic sales report, a vehicle-production summary of each plant's output, a report on new orders, a cash report, and a "tracking" report comparing orders, production, and retail deliveries. All of these reports come to me with comparisons of performance in previous periods.

Timely and complete information of this kind would not be possible without computers. And it is this kind of information, this current feedback, that makes sound and prompt decision-making possible. I think we should mention, however, that in addition to helping us check on progress toward objectives, computers have also made it possible for modern management to establish its sales and profit objectives with more precision than would be possible without them. At Chrysler, for example, computers enable us to project trend lines for sales for some years in advance. And they also enable us to estimate upper and lower limits of deviations from that trend for any given year. These three lines — the trend line and the upper and lower limits of deviation from the trend —form the basis of our planning. We try to be ready with enough capacity, if it is worked overtime, to meet the highest foreseeable demand. We use the middle trend line to establish sales goals for our dealers. And we use the lower line as the basis for budgeting. We can change our plans for capital investment or current operating expenditures quickly in response to changes in the demands of the market.

A few minutes ago I mentioned that the modern emphasis on management by objective has superseded to some extent the older method of management by personal pressure. But this of course is a matter of emphasis. No matter how good or how fast the flow of information may be, it can never replace the human element. And this brings me to my third point, concerning the importance of structuring the organisation of a company so as to make the most effective use of its human talents.

A very substantial part of any management's time must be devoted to structuring and restructuring its organisation to make sure that functions and responsibilities are properly grouped so people can work together most effectively. I'm sure, for example, that all of you have read lengthy discussions in your text-books on management about the respective merits of centralisation and decentralisation. This is an interesting debate with a long history. And decisions by managements to centralise or decentralise have affected the lives of many management people. But the fact is that the modern information revolution we have been talking about has given us an entirely new approach to this familiar old problem.

Now that the current operating results of divisions and subsidiaries can be made almost immediately visible to central management by the help of electronic equipment, it is possible to reach a much more effective balance than ever before between centralised planning and policymaking and decentralised execution of those plans and policies. So, we can now enjoy the merits of both decentralisation and centralisation without being hurt by the weaknesses of either.

The enormously expanded volume of information made available through the new techniques has also helped to bring about a closer co-ordination between the staff and line executives. Many of us can remember the days — not too long ago —when there existed what amounted almost to a cold war between staff and line in many organisations. But in recent years we have seen something of a detente in this traditional animosity. This is all to the good.

It is the staff executives who help a company map its course, study alternatives, set and monitor standards of quality, direct research and development, and so on. Under the increasingly complex conditions of contemporary business, this kind of help has become more and more valuable to the line executives, who have the direct operating responsibility for getting the product built and sold.

A prime objective in designing a structure of organisation in this period of incessant change is to maximise the opportunities for co-operation among staff and line executives and to minimise the chances for friction. One way to accomplish this result is to form what some people have been calling the "team at the top. " This team is composed of the company chairman and president and of key executives from both staff and line. It usually numbers not more than a dozen and preferably not more than eight or ten. Together these men carry the prime responsibility for a company's success. It is the job of such a group to review major plans and programmes, approve or reject project appropriations, appraise current performance, and recommend new courses of action.

At Chrysler it is standard operating procedure to make sure that staff men and line men consult one another not only at meetings of the top decision making group, but at every stage in the development of important new proposals.

We think this arrangement helps to create a healthy atmosphere of orderly give and take. It also helps us to adapt flexibly and quickly to change. And it provides the best possible insurance against wrong and costly decisions being made by dominating individuals who are beyond the reach of being challenged or checked by others. Checks and balances are just as important in a corporate structure as in government.

Beyond all these considerations of organisational structure, management for the growth of a company must also be deeply concerned with the growth of its men. This is a big subject, and it certainly cannot be covered in a brief talk. Let me only say that the growth of men with executive talent is chiefly a matter of increasing their responsibility and broadening their experience.

A few minutes ago I suggested that a management could be properly geared for growth only if its executives could see the whole operation in the round, so to speak, with due attention being given to all the component activities and their interrelations. This kind of perspective is possible, of course, only if management gives rounded experience to its promising executive talent.

By the time an executive moves into the higher levels of responsibility, he should be able to think like the chief executive officer. In other words, he should be able to think not just like a sales executive, but like an accountant, an engineer, a production man, and a public relations officer. At the higher levels of responsibility there is no place for the near-sighted specialist. And for this reason, every modern management moves promising young executives around the company systematically to give them an understanding of the whole organisational system.

I might say that a management does well to put its men where their peculiar individual talents and strengths show to the best advantage. And over and beyond the benefits that it brings to the efficiency of the company, this practice also brings personal rewards, satisfaction, and happiness to the individual executive.

Of all the challenges to management in this time of change and growth, none is more important than the challenge to keep itself closely related to the many revolutionary social developments taking place in all parts of the world. In our own country, private business is still relied on more heavily than in any other country to provide the goods and services needed to maintain a civilised way of life — and to improve life through innovations made possible by science and technology. In the process of doing so, business itself creates social change. And it cannot stand aloof from that change. Now as never before a business organisation must be a good citizen.

The greatest social responsibility of business management is to keep the national economy growing. From the growth of private business come the tax revenues that make possible the adequate support of the civilizing institutions —like schools, courts, libraries, hospitals, and all the rest. And I believe that a well-managed and well-structured business organisation — disciplined by the need to show a satisfactory return on invested capital — and energised by the anticipation of personal reward and fulfilment —is the most efficient engine of progress the world has yet evolved.

Entirely apart from this basic responsibility of business, there is the added responsibility for becoming involved in the social problems of every community where a company has its operations. This means doing what it can to provide jobs for those who are the victims of social and technological change. It means providing counsel and support to communities that have difficulties in conducting their educational and welfare programmes. It means encouraging executives to become involved in community activities and in politics at every level. Above all, it means taking a constructive rather than an obstructionist attitude toward government. Whether we like it or not, government is here to stay, and the best option open to the businessman is to try to make government as good as possible through his own counsel and participation.

We are living in a time of unlimited promise and unlimited trouble. The challenge to management is to make as big a contribution as possible to fulfilling the promise of our century — and in so doing to help countries and communities to deal more effectively with their many troubles. This is the broadest dimension of business management. And it is this dimension that makes management a truly important profession — possibly the most important profession of all.

2. Creating Wealth for The Society

While developing Singapore into a global city — the Government envisaged that there are three roles played by three institutions of the society, state, business and society. The role of business is to create wealth in the country; the role of the state is to distribute the wealth of the country; and the role of the society is to promote welfare of the people. The global companies generate the wealth of the country by utilising the resources — human, material, natural, financial, etc., generating employment, income, profits, goods and services, energy, transportation, infrastructure, etc., and also developing the economy. That's why the mantraindustrialise or perish — for the developing economies. Why the underdeveloped countries are remaining underdeveloped, because their people are underdeveloped, having had no opportunity to develop themselves.[2]

Enriching Lives

After many years of working by his own commons sense, Mr. Matsushita came to realize the higher goal for manufacturing. He thought man can be happy only when he has both spiritual and material wealth. Neither one by itself brings happiness to man religion aims at the spiritual enrichment of man, but what about business.

Even though business strives to create the material goods and wealth indispensable to human life, it is not accorded as much respect as religious activity. Yet this is scanning for while religion promotes the happiness of man. It is business that provides the material goods that maintain human life and as such it too is indispensable for human happiness doesn't that make it a noble activity also.

Business is in fact a very noble activity because it brings pleasure and happiness to people. And it business people would think about their profession in this light, it would give new meaning to their work and strengthen their sense of worth. Thus Konosuke Matsushita came to the conclusion that the mission of an industrialist is to remove poverty from this world my manufacturing as many quality products as possible to make everyone's life prosperous.

2. M.N. Rudrabasavaraj, *Global Human Growth Model*, pp. 374-5.

Since that time, Mr. Matsushita had made this mission the basic policy of his company's management and has constantly emphasized its importance to his employees. His employees were influenced by this philosophy and in turn found a sense of mission and meaning in their jobs.

In other words, you might say that a soul had been put into the company's management, giving it renewed strength and leading to vigorous development. Mr. Matsushita not only established a clear overall management philosophy and proclaimed other concept that entrprise management is noble work on the oerational level he also established specific goals for the corporation at regular intervals or when the business clients made this necessary. This attention to specific goals is one of the indispensable lies to success in management.

Setting goals

He carefully but boldly presented concrete goals to all his employees, covering such diverse areas as individual work objectives for the next month, specific company objectives for the next one-five and 10-year periods, sales volume goals and so on.

In 1956, Mr. Matsushita made an announcement to his employees that he would like his company's sales to reach 80 billon yen in five years. This announcement surpised not only the public, but also the employees of Matsushita Electric, because its sales at that time were only a little more than 20 billion yen and it seemed almost impossible to quaduple that figure in five years. Yet the goal was achieved, in four years the sales amounted to more than 80 billion yen, and they climbed to more than 100 billion by the end of the fifth year.

3. Nurturing Executive Talent

Mr. Micheal Haider, former Chairman of Exxon, talks about the increasing need for good managers :[3]

If a company is to continue to prosper, its current mangers must devote a major share of their thought to the selection and development of their successors. As business becomes more complex, the demand for well-qualified corporate executives is becoming increasingly difficult to satisfy. One reason is the rapid growth of economy in USA and abroad in recent years with an attendant increase in the number of business enterprises. Expansion by existing companies of their international commitments has also enlarged the need of managers. American business interests abroad have increased tremendously, with a noticeable acceleration in recent years.

Still another reason for the dearth of able executives is the shortening of industrial careers. Insistence upon higher educational attainment means employment at more advanced ages than heretofore. At the other end of the scale is the trend towards earlier retirement, quickened by both absolescence sole sense of executives, who have been unable to adjust to the increasing complexities of business and industry, and by the affluence of industrialised societies which permit many men, desirous of leisure, to get out of harness earlier than in the past. Further, more the opportunity to develop and utilise executives within their shortened career spans has been curtailed due to reduction in working hours and shrinking work year as vacations get longer and the number of holidays increases.

The Exxon Mobil, the No.1 company in Fortune 500 in 2006 and one of the largest and oldest of the multinational corporations is naturally very much concerned with the whole problem of early identification and development of management at home and abroad. As a holding company with worldwide family of affiliates engaged in all phases of the oil business, exploration, producing, refining, transportation, petrochemical manufacturing, research marketing, it provides a good case study of the continuing task of supplying management needs. Its affiliated companies do business of supplying management needs. Its affiliated companies do business in the United States and over a hundred foreign countries. Exxon job is to co-ordinate their activities, review their investment plans, give them guidance and counsel, and ensure that each affiliate has sound management.

Many years ago, Exxon Board adopted several principles such as "Continuity of Management" with the belief that highly qualified management is essential to both profit and survival in business; the second principle of "Decentralisation"

3. Micheal L. Haider, "Tomorrow's Executive : A Man for All Countries", Exxon Publication. pp. 109-113.

meaning that broad authority is given to the affiliates, with its own officers and board of directors drawn from the nationals of the country where the affiliate is located. By pinpointing responsibility, decentralisation provides the best opportunity possible for the exercise of judgement and for the development of resourcefulness and leadership among employees of the affiliates.

This refers to the process of "isation" i.e., the process of nationalization of the top executives of affiliates or the process of Indianisation or Brazialisation or Indonesianisation of the top management. In other words, an Indian is developed to head the Indian affiliate, A Brazilian of the Brazil affiliate, etc., this more is also because of the demand of the local aspirants and local governments and national community to hand over the reins of running the company to a national of the country, instead of importing American executives to head the Board, as was the earlier custom. Now Mr. Haider talks about how they develop management talent for Exxon and its affiliates.

Design for Growth

We start with the conviction that a man grows fastest in managerial ability by holding a succession of exacting positions. In the past, possibly we over-estimated the desirability of having promising managers become familiar with specialised functions of the company through short-term rotation with little or no managerial responsibility. We feel now that it is much more useful for them to be given responsibility for some element of the company's business for a reasonably long period of time—to have the opportunity to make and live with their mistakes, and show that they can learn from them.

Accordingly, management at all levels is requested to view every key position in the main-stream of operations as an opportunity to further the development of a high-potential man. We ask that when such a position becomes vacant it be given not to the "logical" or "convenient" candidate necessarily, but to the man who is expected to be able to profit most from the job and advance through it—even if this means asking that he be transferred from another member of the Jersey family of companies. We ask that management not to block key positions by expedient promotion of men who, no matter how well they may do the job, can be expected to go no further. Adhering strictly to these concepts can obviously cause inconvenience and create morale problems in affiliated companies. We believe, however, that failure to observe them is short-sighted. We simply cannot afford to misuse any developmental opportunity that arises.

Four Steps at Affiliate Level

Executive development efforts are reduced to a fairly strict procedure only at the affiliate level. It consists of four steps. The first is identification of executive potential. Affiliate managements are encouraged to search aggressively through their organisations for people who appear to have promise. Second, managements are requested to predict—or, more accurately, guess at—the highest position that an individual so identified can aspire to. This position then becomes the target toward which he is directed. Long-range predictions with respect to anything are likely to be in error, of course. In a matter as subjective as human potential, this is even truer. Thus, our managements are not held accountable for accuracy, although we do look to them for responsible judgments.

The third step is an enumeration of development needs. An analysis is made of the training, work, and other experiences each high-potential person may need to equip him best for his target position. And fourth is preparation and implementation by affiliate managements of development plans covering four-to-five-year periods. This doesn't mean that men are expected to become well-rounded managers in that short space of time. It is simply a convenient period for planning. A man's progress is reviewed through-out, and at the end further development plans will normally be made for him in the light of his performance. Actually, of course, the process of becoming an effective manager never stops. The target is always moving, and one always has more to learn.

While these procedures have proved practical by and large, they still leave a good deal to be desired. We must, for example, learn to distinguish between performance on a given job and potential for advancement to positions of considerably greater responsibility. The two are quite different. While a man's performance on his present and previous assignments is an indication of his potential, it is only one of several factors. People doing an outstanding job in their current assignments frequently have little or no potential for higher positions. Their particular characteristics suit them peculiarly for the jobs they are in, but not necessarily for other types of positions.

Above all, though, we need to find more precise ways of identifying men with potential early in their careers. For the last 10 years we have conducted a research programme which we hope will in time be of significant help. Experiments have been made with a series of measurements in the hope of finding reliable gauges of such qualities as judgment, sensitivity, initiative, and stability. Enthusiasm about these efforts is tempered with a certain skepticism. This is a result, doubtless, of the respect most of us acquire for the complexity of the human being. Perhaps a man's potential managerial worth will never lend itself completely to accurate measurement. At the very least, however, our research makes it less likely that we will overlook promising managerial candidates.

No Manager's Exempt

Perhaps the most important aspect of Jersey's executive development effort is the fact that it is an important dimension of every manager's job. Managements of affiliates throughout the world are held accountable for executive development, just as they are held accountable for profits. Just as we try to make cost reduction a state of mind throughout the organization by constant reminders of its need, by making clear what each management must do to meet that *need* and by stressing accountability to assure the job is done, so have we sought to impress on affiliates the importance of management development.

Accountability for executive development is made to a committee composed of the chairman, president, and the four executive vice presidents of Jersey. This committee is involved in a continuing examination of management throughout the Jersey organisation. All promotions to senior executive positions are subject to its review. In 1964, it reviewed 109 such promotions—an average of a little more than two a week. It met 37 times in that year to consider these and other executive development matters.

The positions that the committee reviewed were with both the parent company and the worldwide affiliates. Quite apart from managerial ability and understanding of petroleum operations, many of the jobs require special talent in dealing with a difficult political or sociological situation. As always, the committee reviewed not only the particular move a man was making, but the next move, or several moves tentatively planned for him. And again, as always, it tried in each case to see that three needs were satisfied: those of Jersey as a whole, those of the organization the man would be working for, and those of the man himself.

The Annual Review

Once a year the chief executive officer of each of the larger affiliates is expected to meet with the committee and review in depth his company's development activities and its replacement situation. For example, the president of Jersey's affiliate, International Petroleum Company, comes annually from the company's headquarters in Coral Gables, Florida, armed with appraisals and evaluations of personnel made to him there by the company's managers in Peru and Colombia, two centres of International Petroleum's operations. These men have given him information received from management reviews in Lima and Bogota, at which the head of producing operations in Talara, Peru, say, and the head of the company's refinery at Cartagena, Colombia, have given their reports. In turn, these reports are based on reviews conducted by the functional managers in Talara and Cartagena at which department heads have made an accounting of their personnel. While this whole process is subject to the dangers of any routinised activity, we do our best to convince management at all levels of its vital importance. It is the only way, it seems to us, that we can avoid over-looking men with good potential, and it is in our interest as well as theirs that they be recognised.

At these reviews with Jersey's top management committee, the chief executive officer of the affiliate is asked to appraise the performance and potential of all his key management personnel. He will also go over with the committee his replacement tables, plans for job rotation assignments, and the specific steps being taken to increase the effectiveness of his organisation.

"How *Far Will He Go?*"

Since each affiliate is expected to supply executive talent to the parent company and, as needed, to other affiliates, each chief executive is asked to alert the committee to those promising young executives in his organisation who he thinks may be used elsewhere, or who may have potential that cannot be fulfilled by the affiliate. In doing so, he is also expected to present the individual four-or-five-year development plans that he and his staff have projected for these men. We expect him to be as specific as possible about a man's potential.

Potential for what is always the question. Merely to say a man has high or unlimited potential is not very definitive or enlightening. As I have said, we want the executive always to indicate specifically the maximum position the man might ultimately attain— not limiting himself to jobs in the particular affiliate. Incidentally, when it comes to appraising the chief executive himself, we take into account the kind of job he is doing in the area of management development.

As young men emerge as potential corporate executives through an affiliate's four-step development procedures, they become the special concern of Jersey's executive development coordinator—and of Jersey's highest level of management—to assure that their talent is properly developed. A great deal of individual and joint effort goes into planning work assignments and educational experiences that will accelerate, their advancement. They will perhaps be moved from job to job—and often from country to country— to develop their inherent abilities, expose them to new backgrounds, and help them learn by actual participation in a variety of activities. Emphasis is always on giving them jobs of increasing responsibility. A young chemical engineer, for example, who has shown managerial promise after six or eight years in a variety of increasingly important jobs with one of our domestic affiliates would be taken out of the affiliate's programme and put on the roster of Jersey's executive development coordinator. The chief executive of the affiliate would long since have made his prediction to Jersey's committee as to the ultimate job he believes the man will be capable of filling—board member, let us say, of Jersey's largest domestic affiliate.

On the Way to the Top

With the sanction of the top management committee, he would perhaps be asked to take an assignment in Europe or Latin America for a few years to assist in the operation of an affiliate's refinery. After rising to a management position in some area of that company's activities, he might be sent to one of our new operations—an ammonia or fertilizer plant, for example. Here he would have an opportunity to acquire experience in an area outside the oil industry perse, and would profit from association with men whose chief interests would be in fields other than petroleum.

In time our man might be brought back to the parent company for on-the-job training in employee relations, marketing, production, or some other phase of the business that would help fill out his background. Possibly he would be asked to attend an advanced management course at one of the many colleges and universities to which companies send men to give them a wider perspective on their business and cultural world.

Where this man would go from there would depend largely on how well he had profited from all this experience. The chances are good that he would eventually arrive in the higher echelons of management, either with Jersey or with an affiliated company in the United States or abroad. The same sort of opportunities for career development would be available to a man with promise entering sales, transportation, production, or any other branch of our business.

Interchangeable Jobs

Obviously, all our efforts at developing corporate and functional managers are conditioned by the fact that Jersey Standard is a company with both domestic and widespread foreign interests. Since we are an American company, our headquarters personnel are mainly United States citizens. Most on the upper managerial levels, however, have served with one or more affiliates overseas earlier in their careers. Our future managers, if they are to measure up to the requirements of their jobs, will also have to spend a part of their careers living and working abroad. They will need opportunities for such experience. Similarly, national employees of our foreign affiliates who show managerial promise need opportunities to work in the United States and elsewhere.

Changes that have taken place in recent years in the complexion of the management ranks of many of our foreign affiliates have helped open a wide range of such opportunities. In the developing countries our affiliates once depended heavily on expatriates to fill executive positions. Indeed, men often went directly from college in the United States to one of our foreign affiliates and made a career with that one company. Gradually, however, national employees have acquired the skills of our business in sufficient numbers to move into the management staff and thus release a large body of expatriate personnel. This trend has been encouraged by the practice of employing national personnel to the greatest extent possible.

Over the years Jersey affiliates have offered a wide variety of training opportunities to local personnel, developing managers as well as technicians. It has sent experienced people abroad to aid in this work. It has provided scholarships to promising young nationals, and given extensive aid to local educational institutions.

In response to the changing character of its overseas employment needs, Jersey a few years ago made a basic change in its staffing policy. Henceforward its domestic companies would supply experienced manpower and managerial personnel to overseas affiliates for loan as well as regular assignments. "The job abroad" would be merely part of an executive's career with Jersey Standard. International and domestic jobs would be thought of as virtually interchangeable.

This policy has worked to the advantage of our management development activities in a number of ways. It has helped meet our need for finding appropriate training posts for the potential corporate manager. By their very nature these jobs test a man's general managerial ability rather than merely his skill at a specialty. It also permits us to make greater use of our worldwide management resources by providing opportunities for our European, Latin American, and Middle and Far Eastern personnel to develop and demonstrate their potential for management posts outside their own countries.

Looking to the future, we see our foreign affiliates manned largely by local citizens and a small cadre of highly qualified expatriates, from other countries as well as the United States. Increasingly, careers with Jersey will consist of extensive overseas and domestic assignments characterised by frequency of movement. We hope that our management development efforts will provide us with the globally trained executives we shall need-men who are able to attune themselves to the rapid changes going on throughout the world and reconcile Jersey's interests with those of the countries in which they are working.

It should be remembered that the multinational company is not only an employer, a taxpayer, and a provider of goods and services in countries round the world. It is also a representative of the system of enterprise and incentive in many areas where the benefits of this system are unfamiliar and subject to discrediting propaganda.

Accordingly, choosing men who give promise of assuring success to such enterprise and giving them sound preparation early in their careers is vital not only to the company but to our whole society. Nothing the executives of a company can do is more important than devoting their most careful consideration and their most imaginative thought to the selection and the development of the men who will succeed them.

4. Learning Life Long to Meet the Future

"I am a good learner" says Jeffrey Immelt, Chairman and CEO of GE and one of world's most admired business leaders, a worth successor to Jack Welch. He has transformed GE into a $ 165 billion power house. Kumar Mangalam Birla quizzes him on learning people, profit and plenty more.[4]

MATSUSHITA TALKS HOW INDUSTRIALISATION BRINGS OUT PROSPERITY

New Horizons

In October 1968, a joint convention of local businessmen and industrial leaders from throughout the Kansai region was held in the city of Kochi on the island of Shikoku. At a party held after the meeting, I overheard a local businessman say, "We feel isolated and left out." He was referring to the prosperity that prevailed in central areas of the country. I learned that the population of Kochi prefecture alone was decreasing by about 7,000 each year as a result of the manpower drain.

'Ten years ago, Kochi had a population of 900,000; today, it is only 800,000 and decreasing with added momentum each year," the man explained. 'The young people who are the promise of our future are leaving in droves for the big cities on the mainland. In some cases, whole villages were abandoned and have literally ceased to exist. This population drain fills those of us who remain behind with a sense of unutterable desolation. What can the future bring —both for us and for the prefecture—if the outflow goes on? There must be some way of stemming the tide and promoting prefectural development, but we simply do not know what to do."

4. Jell Immelt, "I am a good learner", Straight Talk, *The Economic Times*, April 6, 2008, p. 6.

After hearing the man out, I began to ponder the situation back in Osaka. By the end of the sixties, the population had greatly increased, and many new problems were occurring as a result. Intense overcrowding could create a real crisis. It was hard for us city folks to imagine that some loss of population could be anything but good. All the same, I could not put the words of the man from Kochi out of my mind. Were I to put myself in his position no doubt I, too, would feel desolated by the shrinking of my community. Even Osaka would become a lonely place if its residents were to desert it by the thousands.

It came to me then that corporations ought to make a special effort to build plants in outlying regions so that young people could find good jobs without moving away from their hometowns. Talented young people were leaving home because the attractive jobs were in the big cities. Building plants outside the mammoth urban areas would help to solve the problems of depopulation and over-crowding. Here, I was convinced, was an idea worthy of promotion.

It had been standard practice among modern industries when building factories to think first of efficiency, choosing sites that were convenient for transport and communication. This is quite natural given a corporation's social obligations and its duty to supply consumers with ever better, cheaper products. The problem was—and it has by no means been overcome today—businesses often take too narrow a view of economic rationality. I realised that there was an urgent need to build plants in the prefectures where population losses were conspicuous. Efficiency might suffer to some extent, but other advantages were surely to be found—better living conditions for workers, cheaper land and more space for factory facilities—not to mention the invigorating effect a large plant would have on a local economy. After all, part of our corporate mission was promoting a better society. Depopulated, lonely communities in one part of the country and overcrowded, unhealthy cities in other parts could only result in a weak economy. What industry needed was a vigorous, growing economy. It was very much in our own interest and in the interest of society as a whole to make factories built in distant locations an integral part of our system of management.

A bit of research revealed that the prefecture with the highest rate of population loss was Shimane, located on the Japan Sea side of the main island of Honshu; the greatest loss in absolute numbers had been suffered by Kagoshima, the southernmost prefecture of Kyushu. In the latter case, over 10,000 people left each year to work elsewhere. I decided forthwith that we would build our next plant in Kagoshima and mentioned my plan at a certain meeting. The news made the papers the next day, and I received several telegrams from Kagoshima. Among them were polite invitations from the governor and local Chamber of Commerce and Industry. "By all means, do come to Kagoshima. The whole prefecture welcomes you," these messages read. This immediate response to my plan went to show just how acutely Kagoshima felt the population drain.

After setting up a plant in Ijuincho, a town in Kagoshima, we built many other factories in sparsely populated areas throughout the country. These factories have helped stem the outflow of population in places from Hokkaido to Kyushu. Of the 47 prefectures in Japan, only 5 are still without Matsushita plants. Building plants in areas where they were most welcome helped us to secure the understanding and co-operation of local residents. All of the local factories have proved very successful in business terms.

Overcrowding and depopulation are twin problems that continue to plague our country, even in the 1980s. Unless some drastic measures are taken to counter these trends, the whole nation will suffer, not only economically but in the social and political realms as well. The tendency for all the functions of society—political, economic, cultural, and so forth—to concentrate in Tokyo alone has become even more prominent in recent years than it was in the sixties and seventies. Much has been done to disperse industries and bring jobs to remote parts of the country, but a much stronger national consensus is needed in order to achieve a decentralised economy.

In our management development activities we take advantage of a second Jersey principle, "decentralisation," which means that broad authority for running their individual companies is given to the affiliates. Each has its own officers and board of directors, many of them nationals of the country where the affiliate is located. The extent to which authority can be delegated depends, of course, upon the particular operation and the capabilities of the management involved. By pinpointing responsibility, decentralsation provides the best opportunity possible for the exercise of judgment and for the development of resourcefulness and leadership among employees of affiliates.

Over the years Jersey has experienced a steadily mounting need not only for specialists, but for executives of breadth, adaptability, and imagination. The broad-gauged executive becomes constantly more important to our operations. In the future we shall doubtless place an even greater premium on imagination and resourcefulness in executives as against a high degree of specialisation.

The emphasis on "generalists" has necessitated changes in Jersey's development activities. Previously our development work had been largely geared to producing the functional executive—for example, the marketer and refiner. This was a logical outgrowth of leaving development work pretty much up to department managers. Being human, they tended to develop people for their own functions and guard their particularly promising individuals from inter-functional exposure and raiding.

Apprentice Programmes Won't Do

As a consequence, some of our executive development efforts had fallen into the pattern of trade-type apprentice programmes, where employees made step-by-step progress through jobs within a function, with the less competent leveling out en route to the top and the more competent emerging as functional executives. Jersey has had the good fortune of finding, among this group, men who also had corporate abilities of a high order. This process, however, does not produce enough such men to meet the greater needs of today, and it produces them at a relatively late age.

What has been developed in the years since World War II is not a programme in the usual sense, any more than selling or making profits are programmes. It has no fixed dimensions, no timetable, no cutoff point. It has few of the stratifying lines that delight the organisational chartist. The whole undertaking is subject to constant experimentation and change. It can best be described as a commitment by management to develop executive talent, using whatever means seem best, and it perhaps may be discussed most profitably from four aspects: as a special responsibility of top management; as a set of procedures; as a research effort; and as a part of every manager's job.

The seriousness with which this activity is taken is indicated by the fact that the chief executive officer assumes the executive development function as his personal responsibility. The involvement of the whole management team is strongly urged in both the search for executive potential among young employees and in providing promising men with opportunities for growth.

THE INFORMATION SUPERHIGHWAY UNDER CONSTRUCTION

In the 1960s and 1970s, the words "Road Under Construction" were familiar and frustrating to any American who traveled across states, much less across the nation, by car. No, it was not an epidemic of potholes. Rather, the United States Federal Government, together with private contractors, embarked on a massive capital project to build America's interstate highway system. The interstate highways brought Americans in general, and American consumers and producers in particular, together like never before. Most of us probably take for granted these highways that parallel the old U.S. route system (*e.g.*, Interstate 80 traces the route of US 6) while providing an unparalleled opportunity to go new places and see new faces (and distant cousins, aunts, and uncles). It is no wonder then that what many see as the next major change in America's infrastructure is being referred to as "the information superhighway."

Just as the interstate highway system paralleled the old US highways, the information superhighway is designed to parallel the nationwide telephone network that we have long taken for granted. Whereas we travel the interstate system by car or van or motorcycle, entry to the information superhighway will be available at home or at work. Our access will be the telephone, the personal computer, the television set, and new hybrids of these familiar devices.

The term "information superhighway" refers to a number of changes in the way Americans can communicate with each other and with people around the world. The superhighway is *increased capacity* in the nation's telecommunications networks. The superhighway is also multiple available *means of communication,* from traditional wired telephones to cellular telephones to satellite delivery to an antenna on your windowsill. The superhighway is also multiple forms of messages sent and received over the *same* network, even simultaneously. Cellular telephone users can send and receive voice and FAX messages. Some homeowners can receive movies over their telephone lines. Some television viewers can receive telephone calls over their cable TV lines. And voice and data messages can be sent together over a single line from one personal computer user to another. All of these possibilities, and more, rely significantly on *fibreoptic cable,* a high-volume, versatile, low-distortion, glass replacement for the copper wiring network that has connected people in the United States over the past century.

The information superhighway is developing into a dizzying array of business relationships between the Federal Government and all sorts of businesses, as well as among telephone companies, movie producers, computer makers, telephone manufacturers, satellite operators, and cable TV franchisees. If this superhighway is to be "paved" across the nation, these suppliers must co-operate on technical matters—such as communications compatibility among their, products—and on economic matters/such as who pays for the highway construction. Perhaps the ultimate question yet unanswered is: Will Americans use this "road," or not?

The information superhighway has significant implications for the design, scope, and uses of information systems at any one organisation. First, managers must decide—to a greater extent than ever before—what information is and is not necessary for running the organisation. The prospects for "information overload" are enormous as[1] managers confront situations equivalent to a homeowner receiving 500 channels on a cable TV system! Ultimately, strategic planning is crucial in,this 'decision. Knowing "who you are" sets limits on what you need to know.

Second, following from the first issue, managers face new decisions about investments in equipment and services with which they and their employees can "travel" the information superhighway. For example, must all salespersons have a laptop computer and cellular telephone? Are so-called "voice mail" systems more cost effective than having answering machines or extra secretarial staff? These kinds of questions, once again, can be framed by the results of strategic planning. Otherwise, new technologies can become "playthings" rather than tools for running an organization efficiently and effectively.

Third, managers and their employees can feel a loss of control over information that is key to their business, now that it becomes more and more publicly available over the information superhighway. Information about competitors' products, market growth trends, impending regulations, and global prospects can be a source of competitive advantage if your organisation has it and others do not. So, possession of information becomes less important than using that information in ways that serve customers distinctively (see "Management 2000 and Beyond" in Chapter 21), in the new information superhighway era.

Fourth, and on the heels of the preceding point, the information superhighway continues the trend *within* organizations of decentralisation of information systems management. If end-user computing began to change the role of MIS professionals from remote experts working behind closed doors to advisors and teachers, the information superhighway portends continuation of that shift. With groupware, picturephones, and fiber optic cables, a buyer at one retail organisation can simultaneously talk and compare sketches and send data to a supplier of children's clothing, for example. In traveling the information super-highway, such buyers, more and more, become MIS professionals in the regular course of their job. Job redesign for MIS becomes a real possibility.

Fifth, ownership of information becomes more complicated than it already is under copyright laws. If more and more people are acquiring and transforming information on the information superhighway, protection for those who created the information becomes a heightened concern for all. More extensive negotiations and new kinds of property protection will likely emerge.

Sixth, the spread of the information superhighway raises ethical concerns about who knows what about whom. In particular, more information about consumers will become diffused around the nation's network and databases. And those consumers might be testy, if not militant, about how that information is used. Managers must keep in mind that new terms of relationships with customers will probably become necessary. That requires sensitivity to consumers' concerns, not merely assuming that more information makes everyone better off.

The so-called Caller ID (or Automatic Line Identification) is a prime case in point. Available now in many states, Caller ID is a software feature of the telephone network that displays on an inexpensive device or special phone the telephone number of the person making the call to the person receiving the call. Along the information superhighway, in other words, the caller's voice and telephone number are transmitted simultaneously.

To some users, Caller ID can be a big help. People running a "911" centre want to know where a call originates in a life-or-death crisis. Some people might want to ignore calls from unfamiliar numbers. Still others might want advance notice of who is calling, even if for only a moment before picking up the receiver, so they can prepare a greeting or other response.

But some people complain that Caller ID can also enable the receiver to act too familiarly. If you call a mail-order organisation equipped with, say, Caller ID and state-of-the-art end-user computing capabilities, your call might be answered by a stranger who says, "Hello, (your name). I hope that the shoes you ordered last month are satisfactory" before you can open your mouth. The old distance between caller and receiver has faded. For managers, this can usher in the need to rethink how employees interact with customers.

All in all, the information superhighway will require new kinds of co-operation among the many participants traveling on that "road." The information highway is one more example of a point that has permeated this book: Management is a process of arranging *and* re-arranging relationships among different parties who hold dear their own interests and whose interests are always subject to change.

Globalism

In the era of globalism, to achieve human growth, economic development and global development, we need greater global co-operation, commitment and leadership through global exchange and sharing of information, science, technology, management and expertise. We need global leadership in solving global problems of illiteracy, poverty, infrastructure, crime, violence, ethnic conflict and ethnic cleansing, national conflicts and wars. The World Social Summit in March 1995 was the first step in tackling social ills facing the world.

The global leaders need to realise that in the development of the individual lies the development of nations and in the development of nations lies the development of the world. The individual is the key to the prosperity, peace and progress of the organisations, societies, nations and world. We rebuild the world through the concept of human growth using the global co-operative advantage through education for all, employment for all and energising all to achieve the maximum potential. We must realise that, in the era of globalism, an individual — a leader, scientist, hybrid developer, a manager, bio-technologist, information-technologist, industrialist, etc. can change the world with his creativity, innovation and concept. One individual — Lee Kuan Yew, Suharto, Mahathir, Deng Xioping, and Rao, etc. can build nations.

But we have a world, in spite of all the progress, in which a one-fourth are illiterates, one-fifth poor, and hungry, one-third unemployed, underemployed. We must change this world and take the long hard difficult road, almost an impossible task and pull ourselves up by our bootstraps in order to tackle the problems of poverty, unemployment and illiteracy by understanding, accepting and implementing concept and philosophy of human growth and rebuild a new world human order by educating every individual to realise his maximum potential and re-engineer a new individual — educated, employed and energised — who is capable of contributing to the development of his family, organisation, society, culture, nation and the world.

This is the greatest challenge facing the people of the world and leaders of the world in the 21st century. We have the middle axioms through the global human growth and we have goals and standards of human prosperity, peace, happiness, progress and compassion.

Now we must bring the leaders of the world together to think, to co-operate, to create and share ideas as to how to improve the global co-operative advantage to educate, employ and energise 5.5 billion people (and 8.5 billion people by 2050) of the world to realise their maximum potential in order to create a world unmatched in prosperity, peace, happiness, co-operation and compassion to evolve and implement the global human model.

The leaders of the 21st century have a great challenge ahead of them in improving the human condition, social cohesion, global peace and prosperity, happiness and compassion, and ensuring respect for human decency. We are at the service of the leaders of the world, ready, willing and able to assist them in rebuilding a new world human order hitherto undreamt of through human and social engineering beginning at the level of the individual moving on to the level of nations and finally, the world.

CONCLUSION

We believe that global companies and management have a great opportunity to usher in a new era of prosperity, happiness, peace and compassion through their expertise in management, science, technology, information technology in generating societal, national and global wealth, productivity and an abundance of goods and services as well as solutions to climate change, poverty, unemployment, illiteracy and human insecurity. This needs a new global philosophy, vision, mission of service, excellence, synergy and life-long learning to build a new world human order of not only love thy neighbor but also respect thy neighbor and the promotion of global human growth, where every human being is educated, employed and energized to realise his maximum potential as well as the potential of all nations of the world.

This generation of global management and the coming future ones have a great challenge and opportunity to change the world and human condition for the better. I am sure that this little treatise, will inspire successful effective action to build a new and better world that we have been dreaming about. May you, the wise reader, have a great time in this pursuit of adventure! Now I wish you all the very best!!